Soft Computing in Case Based Reasoning

Springer

London
Berlin
Heidelberg
New York
Barcelona
Hong Kong
Milan
Paris
Singapore
Tokyo

Sankar K. Pal, Tharam S. Dillon and
Daniel S. Yeung (Eds)

Soft Computing in Case Based Reasoning

Springer

Sankar K. Pal, MTech, PhD, DIC, Fellow IEEE
Distinguished Scientist and Head, Machine Intelligence Unit,
Indian Statistical Institute, 203 Barrackpore Trunk Road, Calcutta 700 035, India

Tharam S. Dillon, BE, PhD, FSaRS, FIE, SMIEEE
Department of Computer Science and Computer Engineering,
La Trobe University, Bundoora, Melbourne, Victoria 3083, Australia

Daniel S. Yeung, BA, MA, MSc, MBA, PhD, FHKIE
Department of Computing, The Hong Kong Polytechnic University,
Hunghom, Kowloon, Hong Kong

ISBN 1-85233-262-X Springer-Verlag London Berlin Heidelberg

British Library Cataloguing in Publication Data
Soft computing in case based reasoning
 1. Soft computing. 2. Case-based reasoning
 I. Pal, Sankar K. II. Dillon, Tharam S. III. Yeung, Daniel S.
 006.3'33
ISBN 185233262X

Library of Congress Cataloging-in-Publication Data
Soft computing in case based reasoning / Sankar K. Pal, Tharam S. Dillon and Daniel S.
Yeung (eds.),
       p. cm.
    Includes bibliographical references.
    ISBN 1-85233-262-X (alk. paper)
      1. Soft computing. 2. Case-based reasoning. I. Pal, Sankar K. II. Dillon, Tharam S.,
    1943- III. Yeung, Daniel S., 1946-

    QA76.9.S63 S625 2000
    006.3—dc21
                                                           00-032973

Typesetting: Camera ready by editors
Printed and bound at the Athenæum Press Ltd., Gateshead, Tyne & Wear
34/3830-543210 Printed on acid-free paper SPIN 10755259

To the co-authors of all my
research publications
- Sankar

To my parents
Gurdial Singh and Kartar Kaur Dillon
for their constant support,
tolerance and unselfish love
- Tharam

To Jesus Christ, my Lord and God and
Foo Lau, my wife and best friend
- Daniel

Foreword

When, at the beginning of the 90s, the three areas of fuzzy set theory, artificial neural nets and genetic algorithms joined forces under the roof of soft computing or computational intelligence, people considered as their common feature the origin of the three areas; namely, the observation of biological systems and the mimesis of certain features which were promising to improve human reasoning, problem solving, diagnosis or decision making. The three areas were considered to be complementary and synergies were expected. These hopes have turned out to be justified. It was, however, not sufficiently realised that another of the common features is that all three paradigms require for their efficient application to varying degrees the support by modern computer equipment and that in all three cases one of the most serious bottlenecks is to input data, information, or knowledge into the computer system before it can be processed efficiently. Hence some important areas, e.g. machine learning, were neglected at the beginning. In recent years this negligence has partly been recognized and cured. In Europe, for instance, two years ago a European Network of Excellence was started with the name COIL (Computational Intelligence and Learning) which includes, apart from the above mentioned three areas, also machine learning. The positive effects of this expansion are already becoming obvious and it is to be expected that other areas, for instance, from artificial intelligence will follow.

The most recent step in this direction is the inclusion of case based reasoning (CBR). This is certainly a well established area in AI, but so far it has not been a focus of soft computing. It deserves, therefore, high appreciation that a book is published that focuses on the interrelationship between CBR and the methods of what has so far been known as soft computing or computational intelligence. The publication of such a book is certainly a formidable task, which could at least at the present time only be solved by convincing the leading experts in the relevant areas to contribute to this volume. The editors of the book have to be congratulated that they have achieved exactly this!

In addition they have created a book that, even though very much at the forefront of scientific progress, is structured and written almost like a textbook. After a tutorial introduction into CBR, three chapters are dedicated to the application of fuzzy sets, neural nets and genetic algorithms to CBR, followed by a chapter that merges three areas (fuzzy sets, neural nets and CBR) and finally the book is concluded by three chapters which show the application of hybrid approaches to interesting and important real problems. This is certainly a book that will be of high interest to scientists as well as to practitioners and that presumably will become a classic and an often cited source in future publications in this area. I can only hope that very many readers will take advantage of this unique opportunity and I can again congratulate the editors of this book and the authors of the contributions in it for their excellent and professional work.

Aachen, March 2000   H.-J. Zimmermann

Preface

There has recently been a spurt of activity to integrate different computing paradigms such as fuzzy set theory, neural networks, genetic algorithms, and rough set theory, for generating more efficient hybrid systems that can be classified as soft computing methodologies. Here the individual tool acts synergetically, not competitively, for enhancing the application domain of each other. The purpose is to provide flexible information processing systems that can exploit the tolerance for imprecision, uncertainty, approximate reasoning, and partial truth in order to achieve tractability, robustness, low solution cost and close resemblance with human like decision making.

Neuro-fuzzy computing, capturing the merits of fuzzy set theory and artificial neural networks, constitutes one of the best-known visible hybridizations encompassed in soft computing. This integration promises to provide, to a great extent, more intelligent systems (in terms of parallelism, fault tolerance, adaptivity, and uncertainty management) to handle real life ambiguous recognition/decision-making problems.

Case based reasoning (CBR) may be defined as a model of reasoning that incorporates problem solving, understanding and learning, and integrates all of them with memory processes. It involves adapting old solutions to meet new demands, using old cases to explain new situations or to justify new solutions, and reasoning from precedents to interpret a new situation. Cases are nothing but some typical situations, already experienced by the system. A case may be defined as a contextualized piece of knowledge representing an experience that teaches a lesson fundamental to achieving the goals of the system. The system learns as a by-product of its reasoning activity. It becomes more efficient and more competent as a result of storing the experience of the system and referring to them in later reasoning.

The case based system, in contrast to the traditional knowledge-based system, operates through a process of remembering one or a small set of concrete instances or cases and basing decisions on comparisons between the new situation and the old ones. Systems based on this concept are finding widespread applications in problems like medical diagnosis and law interpretation where the knowledge available is incomplete and/or evidence is sparse.

Research articles integrating CBR with a soft computing framework for developing efficient methodologies and algorithms for various real life decision-making applications have started to appear. Design of efficient knowledge based networks in the said paradigm is also being attempted. Here soft computing tools become effective in tasks like extracting cases from ambiguous situations and handling uncertainties, adapting new cases, retrieving old cases, discarding faulty cases, finding similarity between cases, maintaining an optimal size of case bases, and in approximate reasoning for justifying a decision. This makes the system robust and flexible in its activity.

The present volume is aimed at providing a collection of fifteen articles, including a tutorial one, containing new material describing, in a unified way, the basic concepts and characteristic features of these theories and integrations, with recent developments and significant applications. These articles, written by different experts over the world, demonstrate the various ways this integration can be made for designing methodologies, algorithms and knowledge based networks for handling real life ambiguous situations efficiently. The first chapter by J. Main, T.S. Dillon and S.C.K. Shiu provides a tutorial introduction to CBR along with its basic features and an evaluation of its strengths and weaknesses in its current symbolic form, followed by the relevance of soft computing. Various application domains are also reviewed. This chapter is included for the convenience of understanding the theory of CBR and hence the remaining chapters of the book.

Chapters 2 and 3 focus on the role of fuzzy set theory, alone, in enhancing the capabilities of CBR systems. One may note that fuzzy logic, which is mainly concerned with providing algorithms for dealing with imprecision, uncertainty and approximate reasoning, is the one primarily responsible for the emergence of the theory of soft computing. In Chapter 2, the authors H.-D. Burkhard and M.M. Richter have described the notions of similarity in the discipline of CBR and fuzzy set theory. Both local and global measures of similarity are discussed. It is shown how the concepts of CBR can be interpreted in terms of fuzzy set technology. A comparison of the reasoning processes in CBR and fuzzy control is provided. E. Hüllermeier, D. Dubois and H. Prade have proposed, in Chapter 3, case based inferencing methodologies using fuzzy rules within the framework of approximate reasoning. Gradual inference rules and certainty rules are described, in this regard, as the basic model of inferencing, using the notion of fuzzy sets. Cases are viewed as individual information sources and case based inferencing is considered as a parallel combination of such information sources. A technique for rating the cases with respect to their contributions to the prediction of outcomes is provided.

The next two chapters deal with the hybridization of artificial neural networks which are reputed, as a soft computing tool, to provide the machinery for learning and curve fitting through its generic characteristics like adaptivity, massive parallelism, robustness and optimality. M. Malek has presented in Chapter 4 several hybrid approaches for integrating neural networks and CBR. Various modes of integration with two degrees, namely, loose and tight coupling, are discussed. These are followed by a detailed description of a tightly coupled hybrid neuro CBR model, called ProBIS, for case retrieval adaptation and memory organization. Its effectiveness is demonstrated for medical diagnosis, control and classification problems. The task of classification is also addressed in Chapter 5 where C.-K. Shin and S.C. Park have described a hybrid system of neural networks and memory based reasoning for regression and classification. It incorporates a feature weighting mechanism which plays an important role in the underlying principle. This hybrid approach has synergetic advantages other than giving example based explanations together with prediction values of neural networks. Extensive experimental results are provided. The system is applicable to various research fields such as hybrid learning strategy, feature selection, feature weighting in CBR and rule extraction.

Chapters 6–8 concern the integration of CBR with another biologically inspired tool, namely genetic algorithms (GAs), along with some important illustrations. GAs are randomized search and optimization techniques guided by the principles of evolution and natural genetics. They are efficient, adaptive and robust search processes, producing near optimal solutions and having a large amount of implicit parallelism. W. Dubitzky and F.J. Azuaje have presented in Chapter 6 two approaches to (introspective) learning case retrieval knowledge structures, namely learning of global and local feature weights using an evolutionary computing approach, and learning of useful case groupings using a growing cell structure neural model. The former method uses feedback of systems performance during the learning process, while the latter does not. The authors also provide a brief description of four general case retrieval models, namely computational, representational, partitioning and model based, and the basic features of GAs for the convenience of readers. The effectiveness of the methodologies is demonstrated on medical data for predicting coronary heart disease. In Chapter 7, a computational hybrid architecture for creative reasoning is described by A. Cardoso, E. Costa, P. Machado, F.C. Pereira and P. Gomes. Here, CBR explores the previous knowledge and provides a long term memory, while the evolutionary computation complements with its adaptive ability. The cross-contribution, therefore, benefits creative reasoning. An example is shown demonstrating how a case library of images and a retrieval metric can be coupled with an evolutionary system in this regard. Chapter 8 describes a system called Teacher (Technique for the Automated Creation of Heuristics) for learning and generating heuristics used in problem solving. Here B. W. Wah and A. Ieumwananonthachai employ a genetics based machine learning approach. The design process is divided into four phases, namely classification, learning, performance verification and performance generalization. The objective is to determine, under resource constraints, improved heuristics methods as compared to existing ones. Experimental results on heuristics learned for problems related to circuit testing are demonstrated.

So far we have discussed the role of fuzzy sets, artificial neural networks and genetic algorithms, as an individual soft computing tool, in case based systems. The next four chapters highlight the importance of integration of two of these tools, namely fuzzy sets and neural networks, in a similar context. One may note that neural fuzzy integration or neuro-fuzzy computing is proved to be the most visible hybrid soft computing tool with generic and application specific merits available so far. The literature in this area is also considerably rich compared to other integrated soft computing paradigms. Of the four articles considered here, Chapter 9 discusses the role of fuzzy neurons in handling uncertainties in input data, while Chapters 10, 11 and 12, which are from the groups of the editors, deal with the problems of case selection/deletion and case retrieval.

A case based decision support system is designed in Chapter 9 by Z.-Q. Liu. Here, the network model uses two types of fuzzy neurons, namely fuzzy AND neuron and fuzzy OR neuron. The system is capable of handling uncertainties in linguistic inputs and contractory data. Its effectiveness is demonstrated rigorously in many domains including telecommunications. The case selection method described by R.K. De and S.K. Pal (Chapter 10) includes a design procedure for a layered network for selection of ambiguous cases through growing and pruning of nodes. The notion of fuzzy similarity between cases is used. The effectiveness of the network is demonstrated on speech recognition and medical diagnosis problems. The performance is validated by a 1-NN classifier with the selected cases as input. The authors have also described, in brief, a few existing case based systems for ready reference. Chapter 11 by S.C.K. Shiu, X.Z. Wang and D.S. Yeung provides a method of selecting the representative cases for maintaining the size of a case base without losing much of its competence.

The algorithm involves computation of feature importance, enhancement of classification in the transformed feature space, and computation of case density. The features are demonstrated with a real life glass classification example. In Chapter 12, J. Main and T.S. Dillon mainly focus on showing how to use fuzzy feature vectors and neural networks for improving the indexing and retrieval steps in a case based system. The feasibility of such a system is illustrated on the problem of fashion footwear design.

The remaining three chapters deal with some more real life significant applications under the aforesaid different modes of integration. In Chapter 13, J.M. Corchado and B. Lees have presented a connectionist approach for oceanographic forecasting using the notion of CBR. The system combines the ability of a CBR system for selecting previous similar situations and the generalizing ability of artificial neural networks to guide its adaptation stage. The system is able to forecast the thermal structure of water ahead of an ongoing vessel. Here the CBR method is used to select a number of cases (from a large case base), and the neural network produces final forecasts in real time based on these selected cases. The system has been successfully tested in the Atlantic Ocean. G. Stahl in Chapter 14 has dealt with an interesting application in space mission by designing a fuzzy case based system (called CREW) which can predict the key psychological factors, e.g., stress, morale, teamwork, of the crew members in an astronaut team over time. The work was carried out at NASA in order to select crew members for the international space station. Here the notion of CBR is used over a rule based approach as the latter would need to acquire a large number of formal rules capable of computing predictive results for all the combinations of 12 psychological factors and eight event types. The theory of fuzzy sets helps in encoding various conditions of adapting rules in terms of linguistic variables, e.g., low, medium and high, for matching similar old cases to a new one.

Chapter 15 demonstrates how the principle of CBR and fuzzy sets together can be applied to the areas of medical equipment diagnosis, plastics color matching, residential property valuation and aircraft engine monitoring, for the purpose of selecting cases. Here B. Cheetham, P. Cuddihy and K. Goebel use the theory of fuzzy sets to find similarity between cases. For medical equipment diagnosis and residential property valuation, membership functions characterizing fuzzy sets provide greater selection accuracy through their noise tolerance. In the case of a plastic color matching system, the use of multiple selections allows detection of potential problems during the case selection phase. Incorporation of adaptive fuzzy clustering technique for fault classification in aircraft engines enhances the ability to deal with extremely noisy sensors and to adjust to unpredictable slow drift.

This comprehensive collection provides a cross-sectional view of the research work that is currently being carried out over different parts of the world applying CBR in a soft computing framework. The book, which is unique in its character, will be useful to graduate students and researchers in computer science, electrical engineering, system science, and information technology not only as a reference book, but also a textbook for some parts of the curriculum. Researchers and practitioners in industry and R&D laboratories working in the fields of system design, control, pattern recognition, data mining and vision will also benefit.

We take this opportunity to thank all the contributors for agreeing to write for the book. We owe a vote of thanks to Ms. Karen Barker of Springer-Verlag London for her initiative and encouragement. The technical/software assistance provided by Dr. Rajat K. De, Mr. Pabitra Mitra, Mr. Suman K. Mitra and Dr. Simon Shiu, and the secretarial help by Mr. I. Dutta and Mr. S. Das during the preparation of the book, are gratefully acknowledged. Particular mention must be made of Pabitra for his sincerity, enthusiasm and dedicated effort, without which it would have been difficult to complete the project in time. The work was initiated when Prof. S.K. Pal was working as a visiting professor in the Department of Computing, Hong Kong Polytechnic, Hong Kong, during April–June 1999.

February 2000   S.K. Pal
                                                                                                                    T.S. Dillon
                                                                                                                    D.S. Yeung

Contents

Applications

List of Contributors

- Francisco Azuaje
  Department of Computer Science
  Trinity College, University of Dublin
  Dublin 2
  Ireland.
  E-mail: francisco.azuaje@cs.tcd.ie

- Hans-Dieter Burkhard
  Institut fur Informatik
  Humboldt Universitat Zu Berlin
  Unter den Linden 6
  10099 Berlin
  Germany
  E-mail: hdb@informatik.hu-berlin.de

- Amílcar Cardoso
  Centro de Informaticae Sistemas da
  Universidade de Coimbra (CISUC)
  Pinhal de Marrocos
  3030 Coimbra
  Portugal
  E-mail: amilcar@dei.uc.pt

- Bill Chcctham
  GE Research and
  Developement Center
  Building K-1 Room 5C21A
  1 Research Circle
  Niskayuna, NY 12309
  USA
  E-mail: cheetham@crd.ge.com

- Juan M. Corchado
  Artificial Intelligence Research Group
  Escuela Superior de
  Ingenieria Informatica
  University of Vigo
  Campus Universitario As Lagoas
  Edificio Politecnico
  Ourense 32004
  Spain
  E-mail: corchado@ei.uvigo.es

- Ernesto Costa
  Centro de Informaticae Sistemas da
  Universidade de Coimbra (CISUC)
  Pinhal de Marrocos
  3030 Coimbra
  Portugal
  E-mail: ernesto@dei.uc.pt

- Paul Cuddihy
  GE Research and Developement
  Center
  Building K-1 Room 5C21A
  1 Research Circle
  Niskayuna, NY 12309
  USA
  E-mail: cuddihy@crd.ge.com

- Rajat K. De
  Machine Intelligence Unit
  Indian Statistical Institute
  203 B. T. Road
  Calcutta 700 035
  India
  E-mail: rajat@isical.ac.in

- Tharam S. Dillon
  Department of Computer Science
  and Computer Engineering
  La Trobe University
  Bundoora, Victoria 3083
  Australia
  E-mail: tharam@cs.latrobe.edu.au

- Werner Dubitzky
  German Cancer Research Centre
  Intelligent Bioinformatics Systems
  Im Neuenheimer Feld 280
  69120 Heidelberg
  Germany
  E-mail: W.Dubitzky@dkfz-heidelberg.de

- Didier Dubois
  Institut de Recherche en
  Informatique de Toulouse
  Universit Paul Sabatier
  118, route de Narbonne
  31062 Toulouse
  France
  E-mail: dubois@irit.fr

- Kai Goebel
  GE Research and
  Developement Center
  Building K-1 Room 5C21A
  1 Research Circle
  Niskayuna, NY 12309
  USA
  E-mail: goebel@crd.ge.com

- Paulo Gomes
  Centro de Informaticae Sistemas da
  Universidade de Coimbra (CISUC)
  Pinhal de Marrocos
  3030 Coimbra
  Portugal
  E-mail: pgomes@dei.uc.pt

- Eyke Hüllermeier
  Institut de Recherche en
  Informatique de Toulouse
  Universit Paul Sabatier
  118, route de Narbonne
  31062 Toulouse
  France
  E-mail: eyke@irit.fr

- Arthur Ieumwananonthachai
  NonStop Networking Division
  Tandem Computers Inc. 10501 N.
  Tantau Avenue, LOC201-02
  Cupertino, CA 95014-0728
  USA
  E-mail: ieumwananonthachai
  _arthur@tandem.com

- Brian Lees
  Applied Computational
  Intelligence Research Unit
  Department of Computing
  and Information Systems,
  University of Paisley
  Paisley PA1 2BE
  UK
  E-mail: lees-ci@paisley.ac.uk

- Zhi-Qiang Liu
  Computer Vision and Machine
  Intelligence Lab (CVMIL)
  Department of Computer Science
  University of Melbourne
  221 Bouverie Street, Carlton
  Victoria 3053
  Australia
  E-mail: zliu@cs.mu.oz.au

- Penousal Machado
  Centro de Informaticae Sistemas da
  Universidade de Coimbra (CISUC)
  Pinhal de Marrocos
  3030 Coimbra
  Portugal
  E-mail: machado@dei.uc.pt

- Julie Main
  Department of Computer Science and
  Computer Engineering
  La Trobe University
  Bundoora, Victoria 3083
  Australia
  E-mail:main@cs.latrobe.edu.au

- Maria Malek
  EISTI-Computer Science Department
  Ave du Parc, 95011 Cergy
  France
  E-mail:maria.malek@wanadoo.fr

- Sankar K. Pal
  Machine Intelligence Unit
  Indian Statistical Institute
  203 B. T. Road
  Calcutta 700 035
  India
  E-mail: sankar@isical.ac.in

- Sang Chan Park
  Department of Industrial Engineering
  Korea Advanced Institute of Science
  and Technology
  Yusong, Taejŏn 305-701
  South Korea
  E-mail: sangpark@major.kaist.ac.kr

- Francisco C. Pereira
  Centro de Informaticae Sistemas da
  Universidade de Coimbra (CISUC)
  Pinhal de Marrocos
  3030 Coimbra
  Portugal
  E-mail: camara@dei.uc.pt

- Henri Prade
  Institut de Recherche en
  Informatique de Toulouse
  Universit Paul Sabatier
  118, route de Narbonne
  31062 Toulouse
  France
  E-mail: prade@irit.fr

- Michael M. Richter
  Institut fur Informatik
  Humboldt Universitat Zu Berlin
  Unter den Linden 6
  10099 Berlin
  Germany
  E-mail: richter@informatik.uni-kl.de

- Chung-Kwan Shin
  Department of Industrial Engineering
  Korea Advanced Institute of Science
  and Technology
  Yusong, Taejŏn 305-701
  South Korea
  E-mail: ckshin@major.kaist.ac.kr

- Simon C.K. Shiu
  Department of Computing
  Hong Kong Polytechnic University
  Hung Hom, Kowloon
  Hong Kong
  E-mail: cskshiu@comp.polyu.edu.hk

- Gerry Stahl
  Center for Life Long Learning
  and Design
  Department of Computer Science and
  Institute of Cognitive Science
  University of Colorado, Boulder
  CO 80309-0430
  USA
  E-mail: gerry.stahl@colorado.edu

- Benjamin W. Wah
  Electrical and Computer Engineering
  Coordinated Science Laboratory
  446 Computer and Systems Research
  Laboratory, MC-228
  1308 West Main Street
  Urbana, IL 61801
  USA
  E-mail: b-wah@uiuc.edu

- X.Z. Wang
  Department of Computing
  Hong Kong Polytechnic University
  Hung Hom, Kowloon
  Hong Kong
  E-mail: csxzwang@comp.polyu.edu.hk

- Daniel S. Yeung
  Department of Computing
  Hong Kong Polytechnic University
  Hung Hom, Kowloon
  Hong Kong
  E-mail: csdaniel@comp.polyu.edu.hk

1. A Tutorial on Case Based Reasoning

Julie Main, Tharam S. Dillon and Simon C.K. Shiu

Abstract. This tutorial chapter introduces the concepts and applications of case based reasoning (CBR) systems. The first Section briefly describes what CBR is, and when and how to use it. The second Section looks at the description and indexing of cases in CBR systems. The retrieval and adaptation processes for finding solutions are outlined in Section 1.3. Learning and maintenance of CBR, owing to the changes in domain knowledge and task environments over time, are discussed in Section 1.4. The role of soft computing in CBR is briefly described in Section 1.5. The final Section gives some examples of successful CBR applications in different areas.

1.1 What is Case Based Reasoning?

1.1.1 Introduction

A short definition of case based reasoning (CBR)is that it is a methodology for solving problems by utilizing previous experience. It involves retaining a memory of previous problems and their solutions and, by referencing these, solving new problems. Generally,[1] a case based reasoner will be presented with a problem. It may be presented by either a user or another program or system. The case based reasoner then searches its memory of past cases (the case base) and attempts to find a case that has the same problem specification as the current case. If the reasoner cannot find an identical case in its case base, it will attempt to find the case or cases in the case base that most closely match the current query case.

In the situation where a previous identical case is retrieved, assuming its solution was successful, it can be returned as the current problem's solution. In the more likely case that the retrieved case is not identical to the current case, an adaptation phase occurs. In adaptation, the differences between the current case and the retrieved case must first be identified and then the solution associated with the retrieved case modified, taking into account these differences. The solution returned in response to the current problem specification may then be tried in the appropriate domain setting.

The structure of a CBR system therefore is usually devised in a manner that reflects these separate stages. At the highest level a CBR system can be thought of as a black box (see Fig. 1.1) that incorporates the reasoning mechanism and the following external facets:

- The input specification, (or problem case)
- The output suggested solution

---

[1] This tutorial describes an average case based reasoning system. There have been many variations used in implementations, which we do not discuss

• The memory of past cases that are referenced by the reasoning mechanism

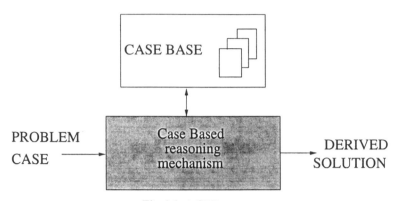

Fig. 1.1. A CBR system.

In most CBR systems, the CBR mechanism, alternatively referred to as the problem solver or reasoner, has an internal structure divided into two major parts: the case retriever and the case reasoner, as shown in Fig. 1.2.

The case retriever's task is to find the appropriate cases in the case base, while the case reasoner uses the retrieved cases to find a solution to the given problem description. This reasoning generally involves both determining the differences between the retrieved cases and the current query case; and modifying the retrieved solution appropriately, reflecting these differences. This reasoning part itself may or may not retrieve further cases or portions of cases from the case base.

Thus, we begin to see the internal structure of the CBR system. This approach in CBR can be contrasted with that used in other knowledge based systems such as rule based systems or combined frame–rule based systems. In rule based systems, one has a rule base consisting of a set of production rules of the form IF A THEN B where A is a condition and B an action. If the condition A holds, then action B is carried out. 'A' can be a composite condition consisting, say, of a conjunction of premises $A_1, A_2, ..., A_n$. In addition, the rule based system has an inference engine, which compares the data it holds in working memory with the condition parts of rules to determine which rules fire. Combined frame–rule based systems also utilize frames in addition to rule to capture stereotypical knowledge. These frames consist of Slots, which can have default values, actual values or attached daemons which when triggered use a procedure or a rule set to determine the required values. These rule based and combined frame–rule based systems require one to acquire the symbolic knowledge represented in these rules or frames by knowledge acquisition using manual knowledge engineering or automated knowledge acquisition tools. Sometimes one utilizes a model of the problem, as a basis of reasoning to a situation; such models can be qualitative or quantitative. Such systems are referred to as model based systems.

CBR systems are an alternative in many situations to rule based systems. In many domains and processes, referring to cases as a means of reasoning can be an advantage owing to the nature of this type of problem solving. One of the most time consuming

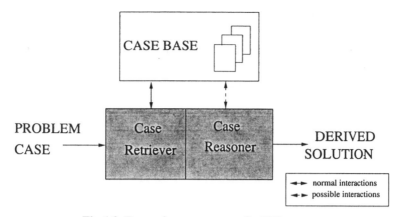

Fig. 1.2. Two major components of a CBR system.

aspects when developing a rule based system is the knowledge acquisition task. Acquiring domain specific information and converting it into some formal representation can be a huge task and, in some situations, especially in less understood domains the formalization of the knowledge cannot be done at all. Case based systems usually require significantly less knowledge acquisition as it involves collecting a set of past experiences without the added necessity of extracting a formal domain model from these cases. In many domains, there are insufficient cases to extract a domain model. There is another benefit to CBR, which is that a system can be created with a small, or limited, amount of experience and incrementally developed, adding more cases to the case base as they become available.

The processes that make up CBR can be seen as a reflection of a particular type of human reasoning. In many situations, the problems humans encounter are solved with a human equivalent of CBR. When a person encounters a previously unexperienced situation or problem, they often refer to a past experience of a similar problem. This similar, previous experience may be one they have had or one another person has experienced. In case the experience was obtained by another human, the case will have been added to the (human) reasoner's memory via either an oral or written account of that experience.

In general, we have referred to CBR being applied to the solving of problems. CBR can also be used in other ways, most notably in arguing a point of view. For example, many students will come to their teacher or lecturer with various requests. These requests might be for an extension to a deadline or perhaps additional materials. It is a common experience of the teacher on refusal of one of these requests to have the student argue the point. One of the common techniques a student will use is to present evidence that in another course, or with another lecturer or teacher, their request was granted in a similar situation, with similar underlying rules.

This sort of reasoning is another way CBR systems may be implemented and is very common in law domains. Just as a barrister argues a point in court by reference to previous cases and the precedents they set, CBR systems can refer to a case base of court cases and find cases that have similar characteristics to the current one. The similarities may be in the whole case or only on certain points that led to a portion of the ruling.

Cases can be discovered therefore that may both support some portions of the current case but oppose other parts. Case based systems that perform this sort of argument are generally referred to as interpretive reasoners.

1.1.2   What is a Case?

A case can be said to be the record of a previous experience or problem. The information recorded about this past experience will, by necessity, depend on the domain of the reasoner and the purpose to which the case will be put. In the instance of a problem solving CBR system, the details will usually include the specification of the problem and the relevant attributes of the environment that are the circumstances of the problem. The other vital part of the case is the solution that was applied in the previous situation. Depending on how the CBR system reasons with cases, this solution may include only the facts of the solution or, additionally, the steps or processes involved in obtaining the solution. It is also important to include the achieved measure of success in the case description if the cases in the case base have achieved different degrees of success or failure.

When a comparison is made between the knowledge stored in a model/rule based system and that stored in a case base, it is apparent that the information in the case base is of a more specific nature than that of the model/rule based system. While the knowledge in a model/rule based system has been abstracted so that it is applicable in the widest variety of situations possible, the knowledge contained in a case base remains specific to the case in which it is stored [1]. Because of the specific knowledge of a case base, we find that related knowledge and knowledge applicable in a specific circumstance is stored in close proximity. Thus, rather than drawing knowledge from a wide net, the knowledge needed to solve a specific problem case can be found grouped together in a few, or even one, location.

The case base in the CBR system is the memory of all previous stored cases. There are three general areas that have to be considered when creating a case base:

- The structure and representation of the cases themselves
- The memory model used for organizing the entire case base
- The selection of indices which are used to identify each case

1.1.3   When to Use Case Based Reasoning?

While CBR is useful for many types of problems and in may different domains, there are times when it is not the most appropriate methodology to employ. There are a number of characteristics of problems and their domains that can be used to determine whether CBR is applicable [1–3].

Does the domain have an underlying model?
If a process is random, or if the factors leading to the success or failure of a solution cannot be captured in the case description, any reasoning from past cases may be futile.

Are there exceptions and novel cases?
Domains without novel or exceptional cases may be better modeled with rules, which
could be inductively determined from the cases.

Do cases recur?
If a case is not likely to be used in a subsequent problem because of a lack of similarity
then there is little, if any, value in storing the case. In these domains, when cases are
not similar enough to be adapted then perhaps it would be better to build a model of
the process for developing the solution, rather than a model of the solution domain.

Is there significant benefit in adapting past solutions?
One must consider whether there is a significant difference in the resources expended
(time, processing, etc.) between creating a solution to a problem from scratch and creating a solution through modifying a similar solution.

Are relevant previous cases obtainable?
Is it possible to obtain the data that records the necessary characteristics of past cases?
Do the recorded cases contain the features of the problem and its context that influenced the outcome of the solution? Is the solution recorded in the detail necessary for
it to be adapted in future?

If the answer to the majority of the above questions is positive, then it is likely that a
CBR may be applicable and relevant.

1.1.4   Why Use Case Based Reasoning?

As many authors have discussed previously, when used in the appropriate situations
CBR offers many advantages [2–4]. In this Section we summarize many of them.
Some points have appeared in more detail in some of the above references, and often
from varying points of view. The order in which they appear here is not indicative of
their level of importance.

Reduction of the knowledge acquisition task
By eliminating the extraction of a model or a set of rules as is necessary in model/rule
based systems, the knowledge acquisition tasks consists mainly of the collection of
the relevant existing experiences/cases and their representation and storage.

Avoid repeating mistakes made in the past
In systems that record failures as well as successes, and perhaps the reason for those
failures, the system can use the information about what caused failures in the past to
predict any failures in future. An example of such a system could be one which stores
successful or failed lessons.

Graceful degradation of performance
Some model based systems cannot even attempt to solve a problem on the boundaries
of its knowledge or scope, or when there is missing or incomplete data. In contrast

case based systems can often have a reasonably successful attempt at solving these types of problem.

Able to reason in domains that have not been fully understood, defined or modeled
While insufficient knowledge may exist about a domain to build a causal model of it or derive a set of heuristics for it, a case based reasoner can function with only a set of cases from the domain. The underlying theory does not have to be quantified.

May be able to make predictions as to the probable success of a proffered solution
Where information is stored regarding the level of success of past solutions, the reasoner may be able to predict the success of the suggested solution to a current problem. This may be done by referring both to the stored solutions and to the differences between the previous and current contexts of the solution.

Learn over time
As CBR systems are used, they encounter more situations and create more solutions. If cases are tested in the real world and a level of success determined, these cases can be added into the case base to reason with in future. As we add cases, a CBR system should be able to reason in a wider variety of situations, and with a higher degree of refinement/success.

Reason in a domain with a small body of knowledge
While a domain in which there is little known underlying knowledge and few cases from which to start limits the type of reasoning that can be done in it, a case based reasoner can start with the few known cases and incrementally increase its knowledge as cases are added to it. The addition of these cases will also cause the system to grow in the directions encountered by the system in its problem solving endeavors.

Reason with incomplete or imprecise data and concepts
As cases are retrieved not just when identical to the current query case but also when they are within some measure of similarity, incompleteness and imprecision can be dealt with. While these factors may cause a slight degradation in performance due to the current and retrieved having increased disparity, reasoning can still continue.

Avoid repeating all the steps that need to be taken to arrive at a solution
In problem domains that require significant processes to carry out the creation of a solution from scratch, the modifying of a previous solution can significantly reduce this processing. By reusing a previous solution, the steps taken to reach the retrieved solution can be reused themselves.

Provide a means of explanation
CBR can supply a previous case and its (successful) solution to convince a user, or justify to a user, a solution it is providing to their current problem. In most domains, there will be times when a user wishes to be reassured about the quality of the solution they are being given. By explaining how a previous case was successful in a situation, using the similarities between the cases and the reasoning involved in adap-

tation a CBR system can explain its solution to a user. Even in a hybrid system that may use multiple methods to find a solution, this explanation mechanism can augment the causal (or other) explanation given to the user.

Can be used in different ways
The number of ways a CBR system can be implemented is almost unlimited. It can be used for many purposes as has been seen: for creating a plan, making a diagnosis, arguing a point of view, etc. As the data dealt with is likewise able to take many forms, so are the retrieval and adaptation methods. As long as stored past cases are being retrieved and adapted, CBR is taking place.

Can be applied to a broad range of domains
As will be discussed in the Section on application areas, CBR has many areas of application. Because of the seemingly limitless number of ways of representing, indexing, retrieving and adapting cases, CBR can be applied to extremely diverse application domains.

Reflects human reasoning
As there are many situations where we, as humans, use a form of CBR, it is not difficult to convince implementers, users and managers of the validity of the paradigm. Likewise, humans can understand a CBR system's reasoning and explanations and are able to be convinced of the validity of the solutions they are receiving. If the human user is wary of the validity of the received solution, they are less likely to use the solution given to them by the reasoner. The more critical the domain, the lower the chances of use, and the higher the level of the user's understanding and credulity will need to be.

1.2   Case Representation and Indexing

1.2.1   Case Representation

Cases in a case base can represent many different types of knowledge and store it in many different representational formats. The objective of a system will greatly influence what is stored. A CBR system may be aimed at the creation of a new design or plan, the diagnosis of a new problem, or the argument of a point of view with precedents. In each type of system, a case may represent something different. The cases could be people, things or objects, situations, diagnoses, designs, plans or rulings, among others. In many practical CBR applications, cases are usually represented as two unstructured sets of attribute value pairs, i.e. the problem and solution features [5]. However, the decision of what to represent can be one of the difficult decisions to make.

Example: In some sort of medical CBR system that diagnoses a patient, a case could represent an individual's entire case history or be limited to a single visit to a doctor. In this situation the case may be a set of symptoms along with the diagnosis. It may also include a prognosis or treatment. If a case is a person then a more complete model is being used as this could incorporate the change of symptoms from one visit to the next. It is, however, harder to find and use cases in this format to search for a particular set of symptoms in a current problem and obtain a diagnosis/treatment. Alternatively, if a case is simply a single visit to the doctor involving the symptoms at the time of that visit and the diagnosis of those symptoms, the changes in symptoms that might be a useful key in solving a problem may be missed.

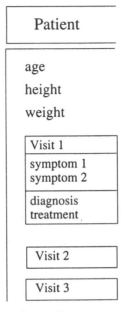

Fig. 1.3. A patient case record.

In a situation such as the above, cases may need to be broken down into sub-cases. For example, a case could be a person's medical history and could include all visits made by them to the doctor as sub-cases. In an object-oriented representation this may be as shown in Fig. 1.3.

No matter what the case actually represents as a whole, its features have to be represented in some format. One of the advantages of CBR is the flexibility it has in this regard. Depending on what types of features have to be represented, an appropriate implementation platform can be chosen. Ranging from simple Boolean, numeric and textual data to binary files, time dependent data, and relationships between data, CBR can be made to reason with all of them.

No matter what is stored, or the format it is represented in, a case must store that information that is relevant to the purpose of the system and which will ensure that the most appropriate case is retrieved in each new situation. Thus the cases have to include those features that will ensure that case will be retrieved in the most appropriate contexts.

In many CBR systems, not all existing cases need to be stored. In these systems criteria are needed to decide which cases will be stored and which will be discarded. In the situation where two or more cases are very similar, only one case may need to be stored. Alternatively, it may be possible to create an artificial case that is a generalization of two or more actual incidents or problems. By creating generalized cases the most important aspects of a case need only be stored once.

When choosing a representation format for a case, there are many choices and many factors to consider. Some examples of representation formats that may be used include database formats, frames, objects, and semantic networks. There are a number of factors that should to be considered when choosing a representation format for a case:

- The cases may have segments within them that form natural sub-cases or components. The forms this internal structure of a case may take need to be capable of representation in the chosen format.
- The content or features that describe a case have associated types and structures. These types have to be available or able to be created in the cases representation.
- The language or shell chosen in which to implement the CBR system. The choice of a shell may limit the formats that could be used for representation. It should also be noted that the choice of language or shell is going to be influenced by a number of factors. The availability of those shells or languages and the knowledge of the implementer of the possible choices are the primary influences here.
- The indexing and search mechanism planned. Cases have to be in a format which the case retrieval mechanism can deal with.
- The form in which cases are available or obtained. If the case base is to be formed from an existing collection of past experiences, ease of translation into another appropriate form could be important.

Whatever format the cases are represented in, the collection of cases itself has to be structured in some way to facilitate the retrieval of the appropriate case when queried. Numerous approaches have been used for this. A flat case base is a common structure; in this method indices are chosen to represent the important aspects of the case and retrieval involves comparing the current case's features to each case in the case base. Another common case base structure is a hierarchical structure that stores the cases by grouping them to reduce the number of cases that have to be searched. The memory model in the form of case representation chosen will depend on a number of factors:

- The representation used in the case base.
- The purpose to which the system is being put. For example, a hierarchical structure is a natural choice for a classification problem.
- The number and complexity of cases being stored. As the number of cases grows in the case base a structure such as a flat case base that is sequentially searched becomes more time consuming.
- The number of features that are used for matching cases during searches.
- Whether some cases are similar enough to group together. Where cases fall into groupings, some structuring facility may be useful.
- The amount of knowledge that is known about the domain will influence the ability to determine how similar cases are. If there is little domain knowledge then structuring cases is apt to be wrong.

1.2.2 Case Indexing

Case indexing refers to assigning indices to cases for future retrieval and comparisons. This choice of indices is important in being able to retrieve the right case at the right time. This is because the indices of a case will determine in which context it will be retrieved in future. These are some suggestions for choosing indices [1,6,7].

Indices must be both predictive and also useful. This means that they should reflect the important aspects of the case, the attributes that influenced the outcome of the case and also those which will describe the circumstances in which it is expected that they should be retrieved in the future.

Indices should be abstract enough to allow for that case's retrieval in all the circumstances in which the case will be useful, but not too abstract. When a case's indices are too abstract that case may be retrieved in too many situations, or too much processing would be required to match cases.

Although assigning indexes is still largely a manual process that relies on human experts, various attempts to use automated methods have been proposed in the literature. For example, Bonzano [8] uses inductive techniques for learning local weights of features by comparing similar cases in a case base. The method can determine which features are more important in predicting outcomes and improve retrieval. Bruninghaus [9] employs a factor hierarchy (a multi-level hierarchical knowledge that relates factors to normative concerns) in guiding machine learning programs to classify texts according to the factors and issues that apply. This method acts as an automatic filter of irrelevant information and structures the indexes into a factor hierarchy which represents the kinds of circumstances which are important to the users. Other methods include indexing cases by features and dimensions that are predictive across the entire problem domain [10], by computing the differences between cases, adaptation guided indexing and retrieval [11] and explanation-based techniques.

1.3 Case Retrieval and Adaptation

1.3.1 Case Retrieval

Case retrieval is the process of finding within the case base those cases that are the closest to the current case. To carry out case retrieval there must be criteria that determine how a case is judged to be appropriate for retrieval and a mechanism to control how the case base is searched. The selection criterion is necessary in deciding which case is the best one to retrieve, that is, to determine how close the current and stored cases are.

This criterion depends in part on what the case retriever is searching for. Most often the case retriever is searching for an entire case, the features of which will be compared to the current query case. There are, however, times when a portion of a case is required. This may be because no full case exists and a solution is being built by selecting portions of multiple cases, or because a retrieved case is being modified by adapting a portion of another case in the case base.

The actual processes involved in retrieving a case from the case base depend very much on the memory model and indexing procedures used. Retrieval methods employed by researchers and implementers are extremely diverse, ranging from a simple nearest neighbor search to the use of intelligent agents. We discuss here the most common, traditional methods.

1.3.1.1   Nearest Neighbor Retrieval

In nearest neighbor retrieval, the case retrieved is chosen when the weighted sum of its features that match that query case is greater than the other cases in the case base. In simple terms, a case that matches the query case on n number of features will be retrieved rather than a case which matches on k number of features where $k <$ n. Some features that are considered more important in a problem solving situation may have their importance denoted by weighting these features more heavily in the matching.

1.3.1.2   Inductive Approaches

When inductive approaches are used to determine the case base structure, that is, to determine the relative importance of features for discriminating between similar cases, the resulting hierarchical structure of the case base provides a reduced search space for the case retriever. This may in turn reduce the search time for queries.

1.3.1.3   Knowledge Guided Approaches

Knowledge guided approaches to retrieval use domain knowledge to determine the features of a case which are important for that case in particular to be retrieved in future. In some situations different features of each case will have been important for the success level of that case.

As with the inductive approaches to retrieval, knowledge guided indexing may result in a hierarchical structure, effective for searching.

1.3.1.4   Validated Retrieval

There have been numerous attempts at improving these forms of retrieval. Validated retrieval proposed by Simoudis is one of these [12].

Validated retrieval consists of two phases, firstly the retrieval of all cases that appear to be relevant to a problem, based on the main features of the query case. The second phase involves deriving more discriminating features from the group of retrieved cases to determine whether they (the cases) are valid in the current situation. The advantage of this method is that inexpensive methods can be used to make the initial retrieval from the case base, while more expensive methods can be used in the second phase as they are applied to only a subset of the case base.

This is just one of many possible alternatives for retrieval. There are a number of factors to consider therefore when determining the method of retrieval. They are:

- The number of cases to be searched.
- The amount of domain knowledge available.
- The ease of determining weightings for individual features.
- Whether cases should be indexed by the same features or whether each case may have varying important features.

Once a case has been retrieved there is usually a phase to determine whether a case is close enough to the problem case or whether the search parameters need to be modified and the search conducted again. There can be a significant time saving if the right choice is made. The adaptation time for a distant case could be significantly greater than searching again. When considering an analysis method for this determination, the following points should be considered:

- The time and resources required for adaptation.
- The number of cases in the case base, i.e. how likely it is that there is a closer case.
- The time and resources required for search.
- How much of the case base has already been searched in previous pass(es).

If we now look at the processes involved in CBR thus far we can represent these succinctly as shown in Fig. 1.4:

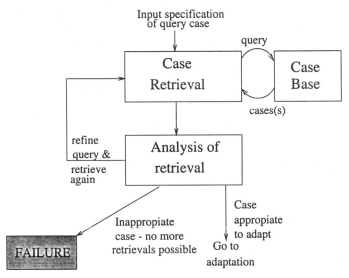

Fig. 1.4. Process involved in CBR.

1.3.2   Case Adaptation

Case adaptation is the process of translating the retrieved solution into the solution appropriate for the current problem. It has been argued that adaptation may be the most important step of CBR as it adds intelligence to what would otherwise be simple pattern matchers [13].

There are a number of approaches that can be taken to carry out case adaptation:

- The solution returned could be used as a solution to the current problem, without modification, or with modifications where the stored solution is not entirely appropriate for the current situation.

- The steps or processes that were followed to obtain the previous solution could be re-run, without modifications, or with modifications where the steps taken in the past solution are not fully satisfactory in the current situation.
- Where more than one case has been retrieved a solution could be derived from multiple cases, or alternatively several alternative solutions could be presented.

Adaptation can use various techniques, including rules or further CBR on the finer grained aspects of the case. When choosing a strategy for case adaptation it can be helpful to consider the following :

- On average how close will the retrieved case be to the query case?
- How many characteristics will differ between the cases in the usual situation?
- Are there common-sense or otherwise known rules that can be applied to do the adaptation?

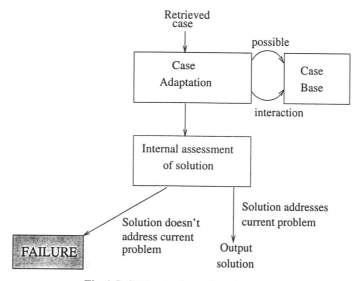

Fig. 1.5. CBR enter into a learning state.

After adaptation has been carried out it is desirable to check that the adapted solution takes into account the differences between the retrieved case and the current problem, that is, that adaptation has addressed the differences between them. There is a need to consider here what action is to be taken in the event that this check determines that the proposed solution is unlikely to be successful.

At this stage the developed solution is ready for testing/use in the applicable domain. This stage concludes the necessary steps for all CBR systems; however, many systems will now enter a learning phase as shown in Fig. 1.5.

1.4   Learning and Maintenance

1.4.1   Learning in CBR Systems

Once an appropriate solution has been generated and output, there is some expectation that the solution will be tested in reality. To test a solution we have to consider both the way it may be tested but also how the outcome of the test will be classified as a success or a failure. In other words some criteria need to be defined for the performance rating of the proffered solution.

Using this real world assessment the CBR system can be updated to take into account any new information uncovered in the processing of the new solution. This information can be added to the system for two purposes. Firstly the more information that is stored in the case base, the closer the match found in the case base is likely to be. The second purpose of adding information to the case base is to improve the solution the CBR is able to create.

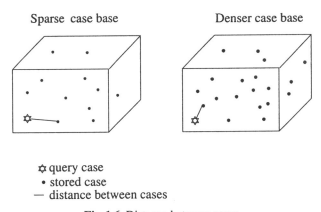

Sparse case base   Denser case base

✿ query case
• stored case
— distance between cases

Fig. 1.6. Distance between cases.

Learning may occur in a number of ways. The addition of the new problem, solution and outcome to the case base is a common method. The addition of cases to the case base will increase the range of situations covered by the cases and reduce the average distance between an input vector and the closest stored vector as shown in Fig. 1.6.

A second method of learning in the CBR system (see Fig. 1.7) is using the solution's assessment to modify the indices of the stored cases or to modify the criteria for case retrieval. If a case has indices that are not relevant to the contexts they should be retrieved in, adjusting these indices may increase the correlation between the times a case is retrieved and the times a case ought to be retrieved.

Likewise, the assessment of the solution's performance may lead to an improved understanding of the underlying causal model of the domain which can be used to the improved adaptation processing. If better ways to modify the cases with respect to the distance between the query and retrieved cases can be found, the output solution will be likely to be improved.

In the event that learning is occurring by way of the addition of new cases to the case base there are a number of considerations:

In which situations should a case be added to the case base and in which situations should it be discarded?

To determine this we have to consider the level of success of the solution, how similar it is to other cases in the case base and whether there are important lessons to be learned from the case.

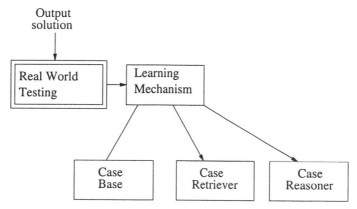

Fig. 1.7. Learning mechanism in CBR.

If the case is to be added to the case base, both the indices of the new case must be determined and how that case is to be added to the case base?

If the case base's structure and retrieval method are highly structured, for example an inductively determined hierarchical structure or a set of neural networks, the incorporation of a new case may require significant planning and restructuring of the case base.

1.4.2   CBR Maintenance

When applying CBR systems for problem solving, there is always a trade-off between the number of cases to be stored in the case library and the retrieval efficiency. The larger the case library, the more the problem space covered; however, it would also downgrade the system performance if the number of cases grows to an unacceptably high level. Therefore, removing the redundant cases or less useful cases under an acceptable error level is one of the most important tasks to maintain CBR systems. Leake and Wilson [14] defined case base maintenance as the implementation of policies for revising the organization or contents (representation, domain content, accounting information, or implementation) of the case base in order to facilitate future reasoning for a particular set of performance objectives.

The central idea for CBR maintenance is to develop some measures for case competence, that is, the range of problems the CBR can solve. There are various properties that may be useful, such as the size, distribution and density of cases; the coverage of individual cases; and the similarity and adaptation knowledge of a given system [15]. Coverage refers to the set of problems that each case could solve, while reachability refers to the set of cases that could provide solutions to the current problem [16]. The higher the density of cases, the more the chance of having redundant cases increases. By expressing the density as a function of case similarity, deletion policy could be formulated for removing cases which are highly reachable by others.

Another need for CBR maintenance is the possible existence of conflicting cases in the case library due to changes of domain knowledge or task environments. An example is when more powerful cases exist which may contain inconsistent information either with other parts of the same case or with other more primitive original cases. Furthermore, if two cases are considered equivalent (with identical feature values) or one case subsumes another by having more feature criteria, then a maintenance process may be required to remove these redundant cases.

1.5   The Role of Soft Computing in CBR

Increasingly, CBR is now being recognized as an effective problem solving methodology that constitutes a number of phases, i.e. case representation, indexing, similarity comparison, retrieval and adaptation. For complicated real world applications, some degree of fuzziness and uncertainty is always encountered; soft computing techniques, such as fuzzy logic, neural networks and genetic algorithms, will be very useful in areas where uncertainty, learning or knowledge inference are part of the system's requirement. In order for us to gain an understanding of these techniques so as to identify approaches for their use in CBR, we briefly summarize them in the sections below.

1.5.1   Fuzzy Logic

Fuzzy set theory has been successfully applied to computing with words or matching of linguistic terms for reasoning. In the context of CBR, when quantitative features are used to create indexes, it involves the conversion of the numerical features into qualitative terms for indexing and retrieval. These terms are always fuzzy terms. Moreover, one of the major issues in fuzzy theory is about measuring similarities for designing robust systems. The notion of similarity measurement in CBR is also fuzzy in nature. For example, Euclidean distances of features are always used to represent the similarity among cases; however, the use of fuzzy theory for indexing and retrieval has many advantages [17] over crisp measurements such as the following:

- Numerical features could be converted to fuzzy terms to simplify comparison.
- Fuzzy sets allow multiple indexing of a case on a single feature with different degrees of membership.
- Fuzzy sets make it easier to transfer knowledge across domains.
- Fuzzy sets allow term modifiers to be used to increase the flexibility in case retrieval.

Other applications of fuzzy logic to CBR include the use of fuzzy production rules to guide case adaptations. For example, fuzzy production rules may be discovered from a case library to associate the similarity between problem features and solution features of cases.

1.5.2   Neural Networks

Artificial neural networks (ANNs) are usually used for learning and generalization of knowledge and patterns. They are not appropriate for expert reasoning and their explanation abilities are extremely weak. Therefore, many applications of ANNs in CBR systems tend to employ a loosely integrated approach where the separate ANN components have some specific objectives such as classification and pattern matching. The benefits of using neural networks for retrieving cases include the following: essentially case retrieval is the matching of patterns, a current input pattern (case) with one or more stored patterns or cases. Neural networks are very good at matching patterns. They cope very well with incomplete data and the imprecision of inputs, which is of benefit in the many domains, as sometimes some portion is important for a new case while some other part is of little relevance. Domains that use the CBR technique are usually complex. This means that the classification of cases at each level is normally non-linear and hence for each classification a single-layer network is not sufficient and a multi-layered network is required.

Hybrid CBR and ANNs are very common architectures for complicated applications. Knowledge may first be extracted from the ANNs and represented by symbolic structures for later use by other CBR components. On the other hand, ANNs could be used for retrieval of cases where each output neuron represents one case.

1.5.3   Genetic Algorithms

Genetic algorithms (GA) are adaptive techniques that are used to solve search and optimization problems inspired by the biological principles of natural selection and genetics. In GA, each individual is represented as a string of binary values; populations of competing individuals evolve over many generations according to some fitness function. A new generation is produced by selecting the best individuals and mating them to produce a new set of offspring. After many generations, the offspring will bear all the most promising characteristics, and will be adopted as the potential solution for the search problem. Learning local and global weights of case features is one of the most popular applications of GA to CBR. The discovery or learning of these weights will indicate how important the features within a case are with respect to the solution features. This weight information can improve the design of retrieval accuracy of CBR systems.

1.6   Application Areas for CBR

CBR has been applied in many different areas, as the systems mentioned here will testify. A look at what they have done shows the versatility of the paradigm and also provides an insight into the directions artificial intelligence research can take. The domains seem limitless and the following systems are just a fraction of the research and commercial systems in existence.

1.6.1 Law

Hypo is an adversarial case based reasoning system that deals with trade secrets law [18]. Probably the best known and most documented of all CBR systems, Hypo was developed by Kevin Ashley and Edwina Rissland at the University of Massachusetts. Hypo analyses problem situations in the trade law area, retrieves relevant cases from its case base, and forms them into legal arguments.

Kowalski's system, the Malicious Prosecution Consultant (MPC) [19], is a CBR system that operates in the domain of malicious prosecution.

HELIC-II [20] (Hypothetical Explanation constructor by Legal Inference with Cases by two inference engines) is a hybrid legal system for the penal code, using legal rules (the law) and cases (precedents).

William Bain, in his PhD dissertation [21], discusses the system JUDGE. JUDGE is a CBR system that attempts to model the sentencing of criminals carried out by real-life judges by comparing current cases to what judges have done in the past. He used interviews with judges, asking them to describe what they would do in certain hypothetical cases, to determine the factors involved.

Zeleznikow et al. [22] have developed a system called IKBALS operating in the field of workers compensation law. This is implemented as a hybrid rule based and case based system.

Another system is OPINE [23], a generic case based reasoner for use in legal domains. OPINE is different from the previously described CBR systems as it has only a single function and that is to provide evaluation of likely case outcome.

An earlier system by Lambert and Grunewald [24] is LESTER (Legal Expert System for Termination of Employment Review), a CBR program in the area of unjust discharge from employment under collective bargaining agreements.

A fuzzy CBR system for legal inference was developed by Hirota et al. [25]. This implemented fuzzy features and case rules for contract legal cases.

Another system which used ANNs for knowledge extraction is HILDA [26], which uses the knowledge extracted from an ANN to guide the rule inferences and case retrieval.

Hollatz [27] also developed a neuro-fuzzy approach in legal reasoning which tried to find structure in precedent decisions as well as identifying legal precedents.

1.6.2 Medicine

CASEY [28,29] is a program designed by Koton at MIT for her PhD dissertation. It analyses descriptions of patients with heart disease and produces a diagnostic explanation of the symptoms of the patient's condition. CASEY integrates CBR and causal reasoning with a model based expert system.

Protos [30] is an exemplar based learning apprentice. It is not domain specific but it has been applied in the field of clinical audiology. It is used to classify cases into categories and to find an exemplar that closely matches the current input case.

BOLERO [31,32], designed by Lopez and Plaza, diagnoses the cause of pneumonia in patients so they can be treated. It learns not only from its successes but also from its failures.

Kolodner and Kolodner [33] discuss the role of experience in diagnosing psychological problems and mention their system, SHRINK, which models a small part of this problem.

Hsu [34] developed a hybrid case based system to help physicians. It uses a distributed fuzzy neural network for case retrieval, and other decision support techniques for selecting and adapting relevant cases from the case library for assisting medical consultation.

1.6.3   Engineering

Archie [35] is a case based design support tool, for use in the architectural design of office buildings. It gives architects a case base of architectural designs created by other architects, and aids in determining factors that solved problems in past designs. It is used in the high-level conceptual design of buildings, rather than at the drafting or engineering stage.

CADSYN, developed by Maher and Zhang [36], is a hybrid case base designer in the field of structural design. CBR is combined with decomposition, that is, a design is composed of a number of parts. To adapt a design it can be broken down into smaller adaptation problems, so that part of a design is transformed at one time.

On a different tangent is GENCAD [37], applied to the layout of residential buildings so that they conform to the principles of feng shui.

1.6.4   Computing: Help-Desk Support

Cascade [12] is a case based system that uses validated retrieval. Its purpose is to aid help-desk engineers find solutions to resolve device driver failures affecting Digital Equipment Corporation's VMS operating system. Device driver failure causes 60% of VMS crashes.

Kriegsman and Barletta [38] have built a system using ReMind, Cognitive System's CBR building tool for creating a case based reasoner to utilise the logs at General Electric's help-desk to provide solutions to the constant stream of problems their help-desk operators attempt to solve.

1.6.5   Communication Networks

CRITTER [39–41] is a CBR trouble ticketing system for managing and resolving network faults in computer/telecommunication systems. In trouble ticketing systems, when a problem is detected a ticket is created which is kept until the problem is resolved. The ticket includes information describing the ticket's problem and its resolution when solved. Therefore in this system tickets are used as the past cases in the case base and from these new solutions are created.

Schenker [42] combines fuzzy logic and CBR to determine fault-prone modules in a communication network.

1.6.6 Manufacturing Design

Clavier [43] is a case based planning system that aims to help autoclave loaders design successful autoclave loadings. An autoclave is a large pressurized convection oven that is used to cure graphite threaded composite materials. Autoclave operators work with a list of prioritized parts and try to create a loading configuration that includes the greatest possible number of high-priority parts. It is more difficult than it seems as all the parts must heat up at approximately the same rate, and this is affected by a number of factors.

Main and Dillon [44–46] developed a system for fashion foot design, using a fuzzy approach to case representation and neural networks for retrieval.

Klinger et al. [47] developed a system, Bidder's Associate, which assists in the preparation of bids for manufactured parts.

1.6.7 Finance

Morris describes a system in this area called SCAN [48]. It is a CBR system in the field of information systems auditing and is designed to help the inexperienced auditor in evaluating controls and proposing audit recommendations. Cases in SCAN are traces of past audit cases, and they are indexed and retrieved in a traditional CBR fashion.

Jo [49] has integrated CBR, ANNs and discriminant analysis for bankruptcy prediction. The prediction ability of the integrated model is superior to the three independent predication techniques.

1.6.8 Job Shop Scheduling

Miyashita and Sycara [50] use CBR in their system CABINS, a system which uses a case based learning method for acquiring context-dependent user optimization preferences and trade-offs and using them to incrementally improve schedule quality in predictive scheduling and reactive schedule management in response to unexpected execution events. Cases in this system are used in three ways: for repair action selection; evaluation of the intermediate repair results; and in recovery from revision failures.

Kettler et al. [51] are using their CAPER (parallel retrieval) system in the car assembly domain. Kettler et al. use the parallelism of the connection machine to retrieve cases and plans from a large unindexed memory. Their system can retrieve cases and plans based on any feature of the target problem, including abstractions of target features.

1.6.9 Scheduling

Koton's SMARTplan [52] is used to schedule the tasks involved in and allocate resources for large scale airlift operations which involve thousands of individual tasks. The requirements for a plan involve requests to move personnel and cargo from one location to another within a specified time window. The resulting plan consists of aircraft allocations, routing networks and airfield assignments.

Miyashita [53] proposed an integrated architecture for distributed planning and scheduling that exploits constraints for problem decomposition, coordination and CBR.

1.6.10 Language

The problem MBRTALK [54] solves is the pronunciation of novel words and the cases it contains in its case base are words with their phonetic pronunciation (defined in combination of structures). MBRTALK first calculates the dissimilarity between the current letter of the word to be pronounced and those letters in the case base. It retrieves n of the most closely matching cases and if the pronunciations of the target letter is the same for all n cases, then a pronunciation is predicted; otherwise, the possible pronunciations are ordered in terms of which is the most likely to be correct.

There is also another system called PRO [55,56]. PRO differs from MBRTALK in the environment it runs in and hence in the memory structure it uses. PRO also differs a little in how it solves the problem of word pronunciation. It first looks up a hypothesis base to find hypotheses for the pronunciation of a certain word and then uses its case base and statistical base to decide which of these hypotheses is most likely. Thus both systems for word pronunciation, MBRTALK and PRO, fall into the statistically based paradigm, and both use large case bases to find the most likely pronunciations of letters and combinations of letters within a case base.

1.6.11 Explanation and Understanding of Stories

Kass's ABE [57,58] (Adaptation-Based Explanation) project develops explanations for events in stories.

Kass and Leake [59] describe SWALE, which had to understand a story – that of Swale, a three-year-old racehorse who died suddenly. TWEAKER follows on from the SWALE system and focuses on the tasks of explanation application and adaptation. TWEAKER is designed to explain deaths and disasters.

1.6.12 Food

Chef [60] is a case based planner in the domain of Szechwan cooking and its purpose is to create new recipes on the basis of the user's request(s). It builds plans out of its memory of old ones and the approach it takes is to anticipate problems and avoid them.

Kolodner's JULIA program [61–64] is used in meal planning: how to plan a meal based on the guests' preferences, to cater for people who are vegetarians or don't like fish etc. There is another system, JULIANA, by Hong Shinn, one of Kolodner's students. JULIANA plans meals for institutions such as schools and nursing homes [64].

1.6.13 Route Finding

Liu et al. [65,66] developed a system for finding routes in Singapore called R-Finder. This system combines Dijkstra's algorithm to search for shortest routes, knowledge approaches to reduce the area to be searched, and CBR to remember whether it has a route stored in memory the same as that required or one to very close places that can be adapted.

Goel et al. [67] have also implemented a number of systems for route planning: ROUTER1, ROUTER2, and ROUTER3. ROUTER2 uses CBR while ROUTER3 uses CBR in combination with model based reasoning. These systems are involved in route planning around the Georgia Tech Campus.

Kettler et al. [51] are using their CAPER (parallel retrieval system) in the transportation logistics domain.

1.6.14   Materials Handling

Li and Dahan [68] developed a system, COESDOES (Case-Oriented Expert System for the Design of Orienting Systems), which designs orienting systems that are used to feed components for automatic assembly. These can be systems such as automatic vibratory and centrifugal feeders, and their design is time consuming.

1.6.15   Telephone Demand

Lee et al. [69] created an expert system using CBR for forecasting irregular telephone demand which will occur in specific areas by region development.

Kopeikina et al. [70] describe a system for continuous management of traffic in the standard public switched telephone network which involves allocating a changing set of network resources to satisfy demands from a fluctuating pattern of calls.

1.6.16   The Environment

AIRQUAP [71] is a system that is used to predict the level of a particular air pollutant in Athens, Greece. The pollutant it predicts the level of is NO_2 , a secondary photochemical pollutant which is one of the hardest to predict and has high concentration levels in Athens and other cities with similar climates. It uses data collected over previous years to predict by 9 a.m. what the level of NO_2 will be that day.

Krovvidy and Wee [72] developed a system for wastewater treatment using CBR. The task in such a system is to determine a treatment train of processes to be performed on wastewater to lower the impurity levels to acceptable ranges.

1.6.17   Fault Diagnosis

Karamouzis and Feycock [73] have developed a system called EPAION which combines CBR with MBR and is being tested in the domain of in-flight fault diagnosis and prognosis of aviation subsystems, particularly jet engines.

Liu and Yan [74] have developed a CBR system using fuzzy logic type neural networks for diagnosing electronic systems.

1.7   Recapitulation

In this tutorial, we have given a brief explanation of CBR, its main components, advantages and situations in which it is most useful. We next briefly outlined some of the most common soft computing techniques and their relevance to CBR. Lastly we provided a bird's-eye view of some of the most important applications. There are many important books and monographs the interested reader should follow up and these include but are not limited to the following:

- *Case Based Reasoning Research and Development, Proceedings of the Third International Conference on Case-Based Reasoning*, (Eds) Klaus-Dieter Althoff, Ralph Bergmann and L. Karl Branting, ICCBR-99, Seeon Monastery, Germany, July 1999.
- *Applying Case-Based Reasoning: Techniques for Enterprise Systems*, by Ian Watson, Morgan Kaufmann, San Mateo, CA, 1997.
- *Case-Based Reasoning Experiences, Lessons and Future Directions*, (Ed.) David B. Leake, AAAI Press/MIT Press, 1996.
- *Case Based Reasoning*, by Janet Kolodner, Morgan Kaufmann, San Mateo, CA, 1993.

The following two web sites provide many useful information and links to other CBR resources:

- Ian Watson at the University of Salford maintains a site with URL http://www.ai-cbr.org.
- Ralph Bergmann, Ivo Vollrath and Sascha Schmitt at the University of Kaiserslautern maintain a site with URL http://www.cbr-web.org.

References

1. J.L. Kolodner, *Case-Based Reasoning*. Morgan Kaufmann, San Mateo, CA, 1993.
2. J.L. Kolodner, An introduction to case-based reasoning. *Artificial Intelligence Review*, 6(1):3–34, 1992.
3. J.L. Kolodner and W. Mark, Case-based reasoning. *IEEE Expert*, 7(5):5–6, 1992.
4. K.D. Ashley, Case-based reasoning and its implications for legal expert systems. *Artificial Intelligence and Law: An International Journal*, 1(2–3):113–208, 1992.
5. F. Gebhardt, A. Vob, W. Grather and B. Schmidt-Beltz, *Reasoning with Complex Cases*, Kluwer Academic Publishers, Norwell, MA, 1997.
6. L. Birnbaum and G. Collings, Remindings and engineering design themes: a case study in indexing vocabulary, in *Proceedings of Second Workshop on Case-Based Reasoning*. Pensacola Beach, FL, 1989.
7. K.J. Hammond, On functionally motivated vocabularies: an apologia, in *Proceedings of Second Workshop on Case-Based Reasoning*, Pensacola Beach, FL, 1989.
8. A. Bonzano, P. Cunningham and B. Smyth, Using introspective learning to improve retrieval in CBR: a case study in air traffic control, in *Proceedings of Second International Conference on Case-Based Reasoning*, RI, USA, 1997, pp. 291–302.
9. S. Bruninghaus and K.D. Ashley, Using machine learning for assigning indices to textual cases, in *Proceedings of Second International Conference on Case-Based Reasoning*, RI, USA, 1997, pp. 303–314.

10. T. Acorn and S. Walden, SMART: support management cultivated reasoning technology: Compaq customer service, in *Proceedings of AAAI-92*, AAAI Press/MIT Press, 1992.

11. B. Smyth and M.T. Keane, Adaptation–guided retrieval: questioning the similarity assumption in reasoning. *Artificial Intelligence*, 102: 249–293, 1998.

12. E. Simoudis, Using case-based retrieval for customer technical support. *IEEE Expert*, 7(5):7–12, 1992.

13. M. Adalier and C. Tsatsoulis, Redesigning for manufacturability using REINRED. *Applied Artificial Intelligence*, 6(3):285–302, 1992.

14. D.B. Leake and D.C. Wilson, Categorizing case-base maintenance: dimensions and directions, in *Proceedings of Fourth European Workshop*, EWCBR–98, 1998, pp.197–207.

15. B. Smyth and E. McKenna, Modelling the competence of case-bases, in *Proceedings of Fourth European Workshop*, EWCBR-98, 1998, pp. 208–220.

16. K. Racine and Q. Yang, Maintaining unstructured case bases, in *Proceedings of Second International Conference on Case-Based Reasoning*, RI, USA, 1997, pp. 553–564.

17. B.C. Jeng and T.P. Liang, Fuzzy indexing and retrieval in case-based systems, *Expert Systems with Applications*, 8(1): 135–142, 1995.

18. K.D. Ashley, *Modeling Legal Argument: Reasoning with Cases and Hypotheticals*. MIT Press, Cambridge, MA, 1990.

19. A. Kowalski, Case-based reasoning and the deep structure approach to knowledge representation, in *Proceedings of the Third International Conference on Artificial Intelligence and Law*, Oxford, UK, 25–28 June, 1991, pp. 21–30.

20. K. Nitta, Y. Ohtake, S. Maeda, M. Ono, H. Ohsaki and K. Sakane, HELIC– II: a legal reasoning system on the parallel inference machine, in FGCS '92: *Proceedings of the International Conference on Fifth Generation Computer Systems*, Tokyo, Japan, 1–5 June 1992, Vol. 2, pp. 1115–1124. ICOT, IOS Press, Burke, VA, 1992.

21. W.M. Bain, *Case-Based Reasoning: A Computer Model of Subjective Assessment*. PhD thesis, Department of Computer Science, Yale University, 1986.

22. J. Zeleznikow, G. Vossos and D. Hunter, The IKBALS project: multi-modal reasoning in legal knowledge based systems. *Artificial Intelligence and Law*, 2:169–203, 1994.

23. K.A. Lambert and M.H. Grunewald, Legal theory and case-based reasoners: the importance of context and the process of focusing, in *Proceedings of the Third International Conference on Artificial Intelligence and Law*, Oxford, UK, 25–28 June, 1991, pp. 191–195.

24. K.A. Lambert and M.H. Grunewald, LESTER: using paradigm cases in a quasi–precedential legal domain. in *Proceedings of the Second International Conference on Artificial Intelligence and Law*, Vancouver, BC, Canada, 1989, pp. 87–92. ACM Press, New York, 1989.

25. K. Hirota, H. Yoshino, M.Q. Xu, Y. Zhu and D. Horie, A fuzzy case based reasoning system for the legal inference, in *Proceedings of Fuzzy Systems*, 1998, World Congress on Computational Intelligence, pp. 1350–1354.

26. P.A. Egri and P.F. Underwood, HILDA: knowledge extraction from neural networks in legal rule based and case-based reasoning, in *Proceedings of IEEE International Conference on Neural Networks*, 1995, Vol. 4. pp. 1800–1805.
27. J. Hollatz, Neuro–fuzzy in legal reasoning, in *Proceedings in Fuzzy Systems, International Joint Conference of the Fourth IEEE International Conference on Fuzzy Systems and the Second International Fuzzy Engineering Symposium*, 1994, Yokohama, Japan, pp. 655–662.
28. P. Koton, Reasoning about evidence in causal explanation, in *AAAI–88: Proceedings of the Seventh National Conference on Artificial Intelligence*, Saint Paul, MN, 1988, Vol. 1, pp. 256–261. American Association for Artificial Intelligence, Morgan Kaufmann, Palo Alto, CA, 1988.
29. P. Koton, A medical reasoning program that improves with experience. *Computer Methods and Programs in Biomedicine*, 30(2–3):177–184, 1989.
30. R. Bareiss, *Exemplar-Based Knowledge Acquisition: A Unified Approach to Concept Representation, Classification and Learning*. Academic Press, Boston, MA, 1989.
31. B. Lopez and E. Plaza, Case-based learning of strategic knowledge. in Y. Kodratoff (ed.), *Machine Learning–EWSL-91: European Working Session on Learning Proceedings*, Porto, Portugal, 6–8 March, 1991, pp. 398–411. Springer, Berlin, 1991.
32. B. Lopez and E. Plaza, Case-based planning for medical diagnosis, in J. Komorowski and Z.W. Ras (eds), *ISMIS'93: Methodologies for Intelligent Systems. Proceedings of the Seventh International Symposium*, Trondheim, Norway, 15-18 June, 1993, pp. 96–105. Springer, Berlin, 1993.
33. J.L. Kolodner and R.M. Kolodner, Using experience in clinical problem solving: introduction and framework. *IEEE Transactions on Systems, Man and Cybernetics*, 17(3):420–431, 1987.
34. C.C. Hsu and C.S. Ho, A hybrid case-based medical diagnosis system, in *Tools with Artificial Intelligence, Proceedings of the Tenth IEEE International Conference*, 1998, pp. 359–366.
35. A.K. Goel, J.L. Kolodner, M. Pearce, R. Billington and C. Zimring, Towards a case-based tool for aiding conceptual design problem, in E.R. Bareiss (ed.), *Proceedings of a DARPA Workshop on Case-Based Reasoning*, Washington, DC, 1991, pp. 109–120. DARPA, Morgan Kaufmann, San Mateo, CA, 1991.
36. M.L. Maher and D.M. Zhang, Cadsyn: a case-based design process model. *AI EDAM: Artificial Intelligence in Engineering Design, Analysis and Manufacturing*, 7(2):97–110, 1993.
37. A.G. de Silva Garza and M.L. Maher, An evolutionary approach to case adaptation. in Althoff et al. [75], pp. 162–172.
38. M. Kriegsman and R. Barletta, Building a case-based help desk application. *IEEE Expert*, 8(6):18–26, 1993.
39. L. Lewis, A case-based reasoning approach to the management of faults in communications networks, in *IEEE INFOCOM '93: Proceedings of the Conference on Computer Communications. Twelfth Annual Joint Conference of the IEEE Computer and Communications Societies. Networking: Foundation for the Future*, San Francisco, CA, 28 March–1 April, 1993, Vol. 3, pp. 1422–1429. IEEE Computer and Communications Societies, IEEE Computer Society Press, 1993.

40. L. Lewis, A case-based reasoning approach to the management of faults in com-
    munications networks. in *Proceedings of the Ninth IEEE Conference on Artificial
    Intelligence for Applications*, Orlando, FL, 1–5 March, 1993, pp. 114–119. IEEE
    Computer Society Press, Los Alamitos, CA, 1993.
41. L. Lewis, A case-based reasoning approach to the resolution of faults in commu-
    nications networks. *IFIP Transactions C [Communication Systems]*, C–12, Inte-
    grated Network Management, III:671–682, 1993.
42. D.F. Schenker and T.M. Khoshgoftaar, The application of fuzzy enhanced case-
    based reasoning for identifying fault–prone modules, in *Proceedings of Third
    IEEE International Conference on High-Assurance Systems Engineering Sympo-
    sium*, Washington DC, USA, 1998, pp. 90–97. IEEE Computer Society Press,
    1998.
43. W.S. Mark, Case-based reasoning for autoclave management, in *Proceedings of
    a DARPA Workshop on Case-Based Reasoning*, Pensacola Beach, FL, 1989 [79],
    pp. 176–180.
44. J. Main, T.S. Dillon, and R. Khosla, Use of neural networks for case– retrieval in
    a system for fashion shoe design, in G.F. Forsyth and M. Ali, (eds), *IEA/AIE 95:
    Industrial and Engineering Applications of Artificial Intelligence and Expert Sys-
    tems: Proceedings of the Eighth International Conference*, Melbourne, Australia,
    June 6-8, 1995, pp. 151–158. Gordon Breach, 1995.
45. J. Main, T.S. Dillon, and R. Khosla, Use of fuzzy feature vectors and neural net-
    works for case retrieval in case based systems, in M.H. Smith, M.A. Lee, J. Keller,
    and J. Yen (eds), *NAFIPS: 1996 Biennial Conference of the North American Fuzzy
    Information Processing Society*, Berkeley, CA, 19–22 June 1996, pp. 438–443.
    IEEE, New York, 1996.
46. J. Main and T.S. Dillon, A hybrid case-based reasoner for footwear design. in
    Althoff et al. [75], pp. 499–509.
47. D.W. Klinger, R. Stottler and S.R. LeClair, Manufacturing application of case-
    based reasoning, in *NAECON 1992: Proceedings of the IEEE 1992 National
    Aerospace and Electronics Conference*, Dayton, OH, 18–22 May 1992, Vol. 3,
    pp. 855–859. IEEE, New York, 1992.
48. B.W. Morris, SCAN: a case-based reasoning model for generating information
    system control recommendations. *International Journal of Intelligent Systems in
    Accounting, Finance and Management*, 3(1):47–63, 1994.
49. H. Jo and I. Han, Integration of case-based forecasting, neural network, and dis-
    criminant analysis for bankruptcy prediction, *Expert Systems with Applications*,
    11(4): 415–422, 1996.
50. K. Miyashita and K. Sycara, CABINS: a framework of knowledge acquisition and
    iterative revision for schedule improvement and reactive repair. *Artificial Intelli-
    gence*, 76(1–2):377–426, 1995.
51. B.P. Kettler, J.A. Hendler, W.A. Anderson and M.P. Evett, Massively parallel sup-
    port for case-based planning. *IEEE Expert*, 9(1):8–14, 1994.
52. P. Koton, SMARTplan: a case-based resource allocation and scheduling system. in
    Proceedings of a DARPA Workshop on Case-Based Reasoning, Pensacola Beach,
    FL, 1989 [79], pp. 285–289.
53. K. Miyashita and M. Hori, A distributed architecture for planning and scheduling
    that learns through negotiation cases, in *1996 Proceedings of IEEE Conference on*

Emerging Technologies and Factory Automation, Kauai Marriott, Kauai, Hawaii, pp. 136–142. IEEE Industrial Electronic Society, 1996.

54. C.W. Stanfill, Memory–based reasoning applied to English pronunciation. in *AAAI–87: Proceedings of the Sixth National Conference on Artificial Intelligence*, Seattle, WA, 1987 [76], pp. 577–581.

55. W.G. Lehnert, Case-based problem solving with a large knowledge base of learned cases, in *AAAI–87: Proceedings of the Sixth National Conference on Artificial Intelligence*, Seattle, WA, 1987 [76], pp. 301–306.

56. W.G. Lehnert, Word pronunciation as a problem in case-based reasoning. in *Program of the Ninth Annual Conference of the Cognitive Science Society*, Seattle, WA, 1987 [78], pp. 120–130.

57. A. Kass, Adaptation–based explanation: explanation as cases, in *Sixth International Workshop on Machine Learning*, Ithaca, NY, 1989, pp. 49–51. Morgan Kaufmann, San Mateo, CA, 1989.

58. A. Kass, Adaptation–based explanation: extending script/frame theory to handle novel input, in *IJCAI 89: Proceedings of the Eleventh International Joint Conference on Artificial Intelligence*, Detroit, MI, 20–25 August 1989, Vol. 1, pp. 141–147. Morgan Kaufmann, San Mateo, CA, 1989.

59. A.M. Kass and D.B. Leake, Case-Based reasoning applied to constructing explanations, in Kolodner [80], pp. 190–208.

60. K.J. Hammond, *Case-Based Planning: Viewing Planning as a Memory Task*. Academic Press, Boston, MA, 1989.

61. J.L. Kolodner, Capitalizing on failure through case-based inference. in *Program of the Ninth Annual Conference of the Cognitive Science Society*, Seattle, WA, 1987 [78], pp. 715–726.

62. J.L. Kolodner, Extending problem solver capabilities through case-based inference. in *Fourth International Workshop on Machine Learning*, Irvine, 1987, pp. 167–178. Morgan Kaufmann, San Mateo, CA, 1987.

63. J.L. Kolodner, Extending problem solver capabilities through case-based inference, in Kolodner [80], pp. 21–30.

64. J.L. Kolodner, Understanding creativity: a case-based approach, in S. Wess, K.-D. Althoff, and M.M. Richter, (eds), *EWCBR–93: Topics in Case-Based Reasoning. First European Workshop, Selected Papers*, Kaiserslautern, Germany, November 1993, pp. 3–20. Springer, Berlin, 1993.

65. B. Liu, S.H. Choo, S.L. Lok, S.M. Leong, S.C. Lee, F.P. Poon and H.H. Tan, Finding the shortest route using cases, knowledge, and Dijkstra's algorithm. *IEEE Expert*, 9(5):7–11, 1994.

66. B. Liu, S.H. Choo, S.L. Lok, S.M. Leong, S.C. Lee, F.P. Poon and H.H. Tan, Integrating case-based reasoning, knowledge–based approach and Dijkstra algorithm for route finding, in *Proceedings of the Tenth IEEE Conference on Artificial Intelligence for Applications*, San Antonio, TX, 1–4 March 1994, pp. 149–155. IEEE Computer Society Press, Los Alamitos, CA, 1994.

67. A.K. Goel, T.J. Callantine, M. Shankar and B. Chandrasekaran, Representation, organization, and use of topographic models of physical spaces for route planning, in *Proceedings of the Seventh IEEE Conference on Artificial Intelligence Applications*, Miami Beach, FL, 24–28 February 1991, pp. 308–314. IEEE Computer Society Press, Los Alamitos, CA, 1991.

68. H. Li and M. Dahan, A case–oriented expert system for materials handling, in A. Croisier, M. Israel, and F. Chavand (eds), 1993 *CompEuro Proceedings. Computers in Design, Manufacturing and Production, Pris–Evry, France*, 24–27 May 1993, pp. 523–530. IEEE Computer Society Press, Los Alamitos, CA, 1993.

69. K. Lee, S. Hwang, K. Um and S. Park, An extraction method of analogical information for efficient knowledge processing, in Y. Baozang (ed.), *TENCON '93. Proceedings of the 1993 IEEE Region 10 Conference on 'Computer, Communication, Control and Power Engineering'*, Beijing, China, 19–21 October 1993, Vol. 2, pp. 644–647. IEEE, New York, 1993.

70. L. Kopeikina, R. Brandau and A. Lemmon, Case based reasoning for continuous control. in Kolodner [80], pp. 250–259.

71. G.P. Lekkas, N.M. Avouris and L.G. Viras, Case-Based reasoning in environmental monitoring applications. *Applied Artificial Intelligence*, 8(3):359–376, 1994.

72. S. Krovvidy and W.G. Wee. Wastewater treatment systems from case-based reasoning. *Machine Learning*, 10(3):341–363, 1993.

73. S.T. Karamouzis and S. Feycock, An integration of case-based and model- based reasoning and its application to physical system faults, in F. Belli and F.J. Radermacher (eds), *IEA/AIE 92: Industrial and Engineering Applications of Artificial Intelligence and Expert Systems: Proceedings of the Fifth International Conference*, Paderborn, Germany, June 9–12 1992, pp. 100–108. Springer, Berlin, 1992.

74. Z.Q. Liu and F. Yan, Case-Based diagnostic system using fuzzy neural network, *Proceedings IEEE International Conference on Neural Networks*, Vol. 6, 1995, pp. 3107–3112.

75. K.D. Althoff, R. Bergmann and L.K. Branting (eds), *ICCBR–99: Case-Based Reasoning Research and Development: Proceedings of the Third Innational Conference on Case-Based Reasoning*, Seeon Monastery, Germany, July 27–30 1999, Vol. 1650 of Lecture Notes in Artificial Intelligence. Springer, Berlin, 1999.

76. American Association for Artificial Intelligence, *AAAI–87: Proceedings of the Sixth National Conference on Artificial Intelligence*, Seattle, WA, 1987. Morgan Kaufmann, San Mateo, CA, 1987.

77. Association for Computing Machinery, *Proceedings of the Third International Conference on Artificial Intelligence and Law*, Oxford, UK, 25–28 June 1991. ACM Press, New York, 1991.

78. Cognitive Science Society, *Program of the Ninth Annual Conference of the Cognitive Science Society*, Seattle, WA, 1987. Lawrence Erlbaum Associates, Hillsdale, NJ, 1987.

79. DARPA, *Proceedings of a DARPA Workshop on Case-Based Reasoning*, Pensacola Beach, FL, 1989. Morgan Kaufmann, San Mateo, CA, 1989.

80. J. Kolodner (ed.), *Proceedings of a DARPA Workshop on Case-Based Reasoning*, Clearwater Beach, FL, 1988. Morgan Kaufmann, San Mateo, CA, 1988.

2. On the Notion of Similarity in Case Based Reasoning and Fuzzy Theory

Hans-Dieter Burkhard and Michael M. Richter

Abstract. Notions of similarity and neighborhood play an important role in informatics. Different disciplines have developed their own treatment of related measures. We consider this problem under the viewpoint of case based reasoning and fuzzy theory. While distance and similarity can be considered to be formally equivalent, there exist some differences concerning their intuitive use which have impact on the composition of global measures from local ones.

2.1 Motivation

Notions of similarity and neighborhood play an important explicit or implicit role in many fields in informatics and other disciplines. We may think, for example, of statistics, classification, machine learning, data mining, information retrieval, or neural networks. Two such fields, namely case based reasoning (CBR) and fuzzy theory, are considered in this chapter.

Similarity itself is not a fixed notion, it depends on the aspects under consideration:

Any two things which are from one point of view similar may be dissimilar from another point of view. (POPPER)

Thus, two people may be similar because of similar faces, or they may be similar because of related characters, respectively. Moreover, it is possible to find similarities between very different things:

An essay is like a fish. (TVERSKY)
(Why: Both have head, body, tail etc.)

Similarity always depends on the underlying contexts, and it is often used as an attempt to handle deeper or hidden relationships between objects from a more shallow level. Such a deeper relationship is, for example, the usefulness of a case in CBR for solving a new problem. It is the acceptance of a document in information retrieval as an answer to a query. It is the customer's satisfaction with a product found in an electronics catalogue. It is present in the matching of linguistic terms in fuzzy theory.

When talking about similarity, people often consider similarity as a naturally given fixed property. They are not aware that there must have been some choice before as to which features are considered for similarity. Thereby, aspects of availability and tractability may play a major role, and aspects of intuitive feeling may play another major role.

For the design of systems which exploit some notion of similarity, there exists some freedom in the choice of similarity: when designing similarity based systems, it is useful to start with the underlying purposes. The features and relations establishing similarity should then be chosen corresponding to the relationships of actual interest. The interesting relationship in information retrieval is in fact not the similarity between a query and a document. Rather, the question of interest concerns *acceptance*: would the user accept a document as an answer to his question? It makes things much clearer when talking about the underlying relationships.

But the actually interesting relationships are often not directly accessible, for different reasons. They may be not tractable, or they may be more or less unpredictable (like the user's expectations about an acceptable document). Here similarity comes into play as a vehicle for the approximation of the really interesting things. Thus, we have two aspects for considering similarity: the obvious aspect concerns tractability, availability and intuitiveness. But the second aspect, namely the correspondence to the actually interesting relationships, is differently treated in different disciplines, and we will compare CBR and fuzzy theory for their uses of similarity related notions.

We assume that the reader is familiar with both CBR and fuzzy theory, and we will recall only the notions when needed in the text. Especially we will use the term 'query' for the description of a problem which is to be solved using former cases in CBR, or a set of fuzzy rules, respectively. A query is matched against the problem description parts of cases or against the preconditions of the rules. To solve the problem described by the query, the solution parts of best matching cases are adapted or the conclusions of the rules are combined according to their activations.

The chapter is organized as follows: we start with primary considerations of similarity and distance as related notions. Common axioms for both kinds of measures are discussed. In the following section we consider the composition of global measures from local ones. The relations between fuzzy notions and similarity are considered in Section 2.4. The reasoning processes in CBR and in fuzzy theory are then compared.

While distance and similarity can be considered to be formally equivalent, there exist some differences concerning their intuitive meaning in the use of composite measures. This is discussed in Section 2.6, and Section 2.7 provides a related viewpoint for fuzzy theory.

2.2 Similarity and Distance: Primary Considerations

There are many different intuitive and formal approaches to similarities and distances. In general, they may even cover analogies establishing relations between objects from different domains. They may consider very complex structural relationships, too.

In this chapter we will restrict ourselves to the consideration of similarity and distance measures between finite sets of feature (attribute) values. Moreover, all feature values are taken from real ones. Thus we consider real valued vectors u over the universe

$$U := \mathcal{R} \times \mathcal{R} \times ... \times \mathcal{R}. \tag{2.1}$$

2.2.1 Some Basic Notions

Similarity can be considered as

- Binary relation, R_{SIM} between objects from U (where $R_{SIM}(u, v)$ stands for 'u is similar to v'):

$$R_{SIM} \subseteq U \times U. \tag{2.2}$$

Example: Two things are called similar, if they coincide w.r.t. at least two of three features:

$$R_{SIM}([x_1, x_2, x_3], [y_1, y_2, y_3]) \Leftrightarrow \exists i, j : 1 \leq i < j \leq 3 : x_i = y_i \wedge x_j = y_j. \tag{2.3}$$

- Measurement of the degree of similarity by a similarity measure SIM (where $SIM(u, v)$ stands for the degree of similarity between u and v). The degree may range over some interval S:

$$SIM : U \times U \to S. \tag{2.4}$$

According to fuzzy theory, stochastics, certainty theory etc., the range S is often the real interval $[0, 1]$. Varying the example from above, we can consider the so-called *simple matching coefficient*:

$$SIM([x_1, x_2, x_3], [y_1, y_2, y_3]) := \frac{1}{3} \cdot card(\{ i \mid x_i = y_i \}). \tag{2.5}$$

More sophisticated measures rely on the differences $x_i - y_i$ between the feature values, e.g.:

$$SIM([x_1, x_2, x_3], [y_1, y_2, y_3]) := \frac{1}{3} \cdot \sum_{i=1,2,3} \frac{1}{1 + |x_i - y_i|}. \tag{2.6}$$

- Neighborhood according to a distance $DIST$ (where $DIST(u, v)$ stands for the distance between u and v):

$$DIST : U \times U \to S. \tag{2.7}$$

An often used distance measure with $S = [0, \infty)$ is the *Manhattan distance*:

$$DIST([x_1, x_2, x_3], [y_1, y_2, y_3]) := \sum_{i=1,2,3} |x_i - y_i|. \tag{2.8}$$

2.2.2 Relations Between the Different Notions

There are some relations between these approaches. At first, binary relations R_{SIM} are equivalent to special similarity measures SIM with only the two binary values 0 and 1.

Vice versa, similarity relations R_{SIM} can be defined by the 'most similar' objects according to a similarity measure SIM. The concept of a *nearest neighbor* is often used for such purposes. We consider a subset $C \subseteq U$ (e.g. a case base in CBR). Then

$c \in C$ is called a nearest neighbor of an arbitrary object $u \in U$ (a query in CBR) if it satisfies the following definition:

$$NN_C(u, c) :\Leftrightarrow \forall c' \in C : SIM(u, c) \geq SIM(u, c'). \tag{2.9}$$

Equivalently, for a distance measure we can define the nearest neighbor concept by

$$NN_C(u, c) :\Leftrightarrow \forall c' \in C : DIST(u, c) \leq DIST(u, c'). \tag{2.10}$$

In a related way, the concept of the '*k nearest neighbors*' is defined.

By another common concept, objects u, v are called similar if their degree of similarity exceeds a certain threshold value b:

$$R_{SIM}(u, v) := SIM(u, v) > b. \tag{2.11}$$

Equivalently, for a distance measure we would use $DIST(u, v) < b$.

Related concepts are basic in CBR: the most (hopefully) useful cases from a case base C are selected according to a query q by such concepts.

Extending the concept of a nearest neighbor, we can consider the ordering between the pairs of objects induced by a similarity/distance measure:

$$ORD_{SIM}(x, y, u, v) :\Leftrightarrow SIM(x, y) \geq SIM(u, v), \tag{2.12}$$
$$ORD_{DIST}(x, y, u, v) :\Leftrightarrow DIST(x, y) \leq DIST(u, v). \tag{2.13}$$

We call two (similarity or distance) measures m_1 and m_2 *relationally compatible* iff

$$\forall x, y, u, v \in U : ORD_{m_1}(x, y, u, v) \Leftrightarrow ORD_{m_2}(x, y, u, v). \tag{2.14}$$

If a subset S of the reals is given, any one–one order inverting mapping f of S to itself induces for a similarity measure with range S a relationally compatible distance measure and vice versa in a natural way. If $S = [0, 1]$ is the range of SIM then $f(1) = 0$, and $SIM(x, x) = 1$ would be translated to $DIST(x, x) = 0$ for the induced distance measure. In the same way any property of similarity measures can be expressed in terms of distance measures and vice versa. This new expression is, however, not always of a simple character. Nevertheless, in a principle sense both notions are mathematically equivalent.

Measures with different ranges can be mapped by related functions f, too.

2.2.3 First Look to Asymmetry and Missing Values

Similarity and distances are usually considered to be symmetrical. We will discuss this point later in detail, but one important fact should be mentioned here. It is due to the usage of similarity/distances. In CBR, a query q is matched against the cases c of the case base C. While q might be (in principle) arbitrarily chosen from U, the cases c are restricted to come from the (usually finite) set $C \subseteq U$. As a consequence, the nearest neighbor relation $NN_C(u, c)$ is not symmetrically defined. Moreover, even for $u, c \in C$ the relation $NN_C(u, c)$ is in general not symmetric.

Similarly in fuzzy rules, the linguistic terms can be considered as referring to special focal values, and the most queries will match the rules only to some extent.

In consequence, missing values appear in different meanings. A missing value in a case in CBR (as well as an attribute not mentioned in a fuzzy rule) means that the related attribute was not *relevant* for that case. On the other hand, an *unknown* value in a query makes it difficult to find the best matching case.

2.2.4 The Range of Measures

We assume that the range S of measures is always an interval of real numbers. Most of our considerations are related to $S = [0, 1]$ which has two major characteristics:

- There is a maximal value for the similarity, and a minimal value for the distance, respectively.
- There are no negative values.

A second possibility is an unbounded range, say $S = [0, \infty]$. The impact for similarity is some difficulty for defining reflexivity (see below), if there is no maximal similarity value. For the distances the consequence is less dramatic because it only means that there are no maximal distances.

A third possibility is the existence of negative values. For distances this is not intuitive, and it would raise difficulties with reflexivity when $DIST(x, x) = 0$ is not the minimal value. An unwanted consequence could be elements which are not the nearest neighbor of themselves. There are no direct consequences for similarity measures. But for combining global measures from local ones, negative similarity values could be of some interest (cf. Section 2.6).

2.2.5 Common Axioms for the Measures

There are various possible axioms for distance measures as well as for similarity measures in the literature. We discuss a few of them and assume that the range is $[0, 1]$.

Reflexivity

$$SIM(x, x) = 1 \quad \text{for distance} \quad DIST(x, x) = 0. \tag{2.15}$$

Symmetry

$$SIM(x, y) = SIM(y, x) \quad \text{and} \quad DIST(x, y) = DIST(y, x). \tag{2.16}$$

Triangle inequality

$$DIST(x, z) \le DIST(x, y) + DIST(y, z). \tag{2.17}$$

(For similarity, see the discussion below.)

Note that only reflexivity in the form (2.15) will be assumed in the later sections of our discussion.

2.2.6 Reflexivity

Reflexivity in the presented form is the only axiom which should necessarily hold; it guarantees that u is always the nearest neighbor of itself.

Sometimes the opposite direction is demanded, too, as in the case of a metric:

$$SIM(x, y) = 1 \rightarrow x = y \quad \text{and} \quad DIST(x, y) = 0 \rightarrow x = y. \tag{2.18}$$

We call this *strong reflexivity*.

2.2.7 Symmetry

We have already discussed the basic unsymmetry concerning queries and cases in the usage of similarity/distances. We furthermore mention that 'directed' comparisons in daily life may be unsymmetric, too:

- A daughter is similar to her mother, but not vice versa.
- A penguin is similar to a bird, but not vice versa.
- A query may be similar to a document, while the document might not be similar to the query.

On the other hand, symmetry is a usual property of distances (especially of metrics). While similarity/distance measures are equivalent from the formal point of view, there can be discovered differences in their daily usage.

Nevertheless, similarity is often considered as a symmetric measure.

2.2.8 Transitivity, Triangle Inequality

Similarity relations R_{SIM} are in general not transitive (as in daily life). In the example (2.3) we have $R_{SIM}([1, 1, 1], [1, 1, 0])$ and $R_{SIM}[1, 1, 0], [1, 0, 0])$, but not $R_{SIM}([1, 1, 1], [1, 0, 0])$.

As an extension of transitivity we might look for some kind of triangle inequality for similarity measures. The direct translation for a concrete inverting function f would mean

$$f(SIM(u, w)) \leq f(SIM(u, v)) + f(SIM(v, w)). \tag{2.19}$$

This shows that the triangle inequality is not easy to express if all inverting functions f have to be regarded. For the concrete function $f(x) = 1 - x$ we simply get $SIM(u, v) + SIM(v, w) \leq 1 + SIM(u, w)$. As another candidate we might consider the inverted triangle inequality of distances:

$$SIM(u, w) \geq SIM(u, v) + SIM(v, w). \tag{2.20}$$

Together with reflexivity and symmetry, we obtain

$$1 = SIM(u, u) \geq SIM(u, v) + SIM(v, u) = 2SIM(u, v) \tag{2.21}$$

and therewith $SIM(u, v) \leq 0.5$ for arbitrary u, v. On the other hand,

$$SIM(u, w) \leq SIM(u, v) + SIM(v, w) \qquad (2.22)$$

makes problems, too. It would lead to $SIM(u, v) \geq 0.5$ for arbitrary u, v.

As a concrete illustration we consider

$$SIM([x_1, x_2], [y_1, y_2]) := Min(\{ 1, card(\{ i \mid x_i = y_i \} \}. \qquad (2.23)$$

There we have

$$SIM([0, 0], [0, 1]) = SIM([0, 1], [1, 1]) = SIM([0, 0], [0, 0]) = 1$$

$$SIM([0, 0], [1, 1]) = SIM([1, 1], [0, 0]) = 0$$

and hence

$$SIM([0, 0], [0, 1]) + SIM([0, 1], [1, 1]) > SIM([0, 0], [1, 1])$$

$$SIM([0, 0], [1, 1]) + SIM([1, 1], [0, 0]) < SIM([0, 0], [0, 0]).$$

If we replace SIM by $DIST$ using an invertion function f with $f(0) = 1$ and $f(1) = 0$, then we have especially

$$DIST([0, 0], [0, 1]) + DIST([0, 1], [1, 1]) < DIST([0, 0], [1, 1]).$$

That means that there are intuitive distance measures where the triangle inequality does not hold. It turns out that metrics may be too restrictive and cannot be used for implementing nearest neighbor concepts in certain cases. (Remark: we could slightly modify the example such that it satisfies the 'strong' reflexivity as in Equation 2.18, but still misses the triangle inequality.)

We feel that this observation is important, since many distance based approaches do have in mind a metric. On the other hand, it is always possible to define a relationally compatible metric to a given similarity function $SIM : U \times U \rightarrow [0, 1]$ by

$$DIST(u, v) := \begin{cases} 0 & , \quad \text{if} \quad u = v \\ \frac{1}{2} \cdot (2 - SIM(u, v)) & , \quad \text{otherwise.} \end{cases} \qquad (2.24)$$

There we have always $\frac{1}{2} \leq DIST(u, v) \leq 1$, and hence the triangle inequality must be satisfied.

2.3   Composite Measures

2.3.1   The Local–Global Principle

We have restricted ourselves to the description of objects (problem descriptions) by real valued vectors $u \in U$. Thus we will consider only attribute-value representations (leaving, e.g., object oriented representations for future discussions). The attributes $A_1, ..., A_n$ constitute the components of our objects (queries: problem descriptions in the cases, preconditions in the fuzzy rules). This forces appropriate connections between the level of the attributes and the level of the objects.

The *local–global principle* for similarities (and distances) is formulated in the following way.

There are similarity measures sim_i on the domains of the attributes A_i (on the reals in our case) and some *composition function* $COMP : \mathcal{R} \times \cdots \times \mathcal{R} \to \mathcal{R}$ such that

$$SIM([q_1, ..., q_n], [u_1, ..., u_n]) = COMP(sim_1(q_1, u_1), ..., sim_n(q_n, u_n)). \quad (2.25)$$

The measures sim_i are called *local measures* and SIM is the *global measure*. A similarity measure SIM is called *composite* if it can be combined from some local similarity measures as in Equation 2.25.

Weighted Hamming measures, i.e. weighted linear functions $COMP$, are popular:

$$SIM([q_1, ..., q_n], [u_1, ..., u_n]) = \sum_{i=1,...,n} w_i \cdot sim_i(q_i, u_i). \quad (2.26)$$

2.3.2   The Global Monotonicity Axiom

The local–global principle connects the representation language for objects with measures. This gives rise to a new axiom for composite measures which we call the *global monotonicity axiom*:

$$SIM(u, v) > SIM(u, w) \to \exists i \in \{1, ..., n\} : sim_i(u_i, v_i) > sim_i(u_i, w_i). \quad (2.27)$$

The axiom states a necessary condition: a higher global similarity must be supported by at least one higher local similarity.

There are situations where the monotonicity axiom does not hold. As an example we adopt the XOR-problem known from neural nets: we consider two Boolean-valued attributes and therefore $U = \{[0, 0], [0, 1], [1, 0], [1, 1]\}$. The XOR-problem is represented by $SIM([u_1, u_2], [v_1, v_2]) = 1$ iff $XOR(u_1, u_2) = XOR(v_1, v_2)$, i.e.

$$SIM([0, 0], [1, 1]) = SIM([0, 1], [1, 0]) = 1$$
$$SIM([0, 0], [0, 1]) = SIM([0, 0], [1, 0])$$
$$= SIM([1, 1], [1, 0]) = SIM([1, 1], [0, 1]) = 0.$$

We have $SIM([0, 0], [1, 1]) > SIM([0, 0], [0, 1]$. The global monotonicity axiom is not satisfied since we have for the local similarity values: $sim_1(0, 1) \leq sim_1(0, 0) = 1$ (reflexivity) and $sim_2(0, 1) = sim_2(0, 1)$.

A new attribute (in this case XOR(u,v)) would be needed in order to represent the XOR-problem by monotonous global similarities, i.e. an extension of the language is necessary. It is an important issue to find attributes such that the monotonicity axiom holds. For practical reasons, such new attributes must be easy to compute, which limits the search for useful attributes. In particular, it is usually impossible to find an attribute which provides the solution directly. It is, however, fair to say that the representation is not good if the monotonicity axiom does not hold.

There is also a *local monotonicity axiom* which demands decreasing distances/ increasing similarities with decreasing absolute differences $|u_i - v_i|$. This axiom is intuitive in many cases, but we could also think of a similarity relation over the reals, especially where the natural numbers are similar to each other:

$$sim(x,y) := \begin{cases} 1, & \text{if} \quad x = y \quad or \quad x,y \in \mathcal{N} \\ 0, & \text{otherwise.} \end{cases} \tag{2.28}$$

2.3.3 Transformations for Composite Measures

Relationally equivalent transformations can be considered on the local level as well as on the global level.

We have already used the function $\frac{1}{1+x}$ for a transformation on the local level of single attributes in example (2.6). Thereby, $dist_i(x_i, y_i) = |x_i - y_i|$ are local distances, while $sim_i(x_i, y_i) = \frac{1}{1+|x_i-y_i|}$ are relationally equivalent local similarity measures. They are composed in Equation 2.6 to the global similarity measure SIM using a (normalized) sum. We obtain a completely different similarity measure SIM' using the transformation by the same function $\frac{1}{1+x}$ on the global level:

$$SIM'([x_1, x_2, x_3], [y_1, y_2, y_3]) := \frac{1}{1 + DIST([x_1, x_2, x_3], [y_1, y_2, y_3])} \tag{2.29}$$

i.e.,

$$SIM'([x_1, x_2, x_3], [y_1, y_2, y_3]) = \frac{1}{1 + \sum_{i=1,2,3} |x_i - y_i|}. \tag{2.30}$$

The example shows that composition and transformation in general do not commute.

2.4 Fuzzy Notions and Similarity

2.4.1 Fuzzy Sets

Fuzzy subsets A of U are denoted by $A \subseteq_f U$, and $\mu_A : U \to [0, 1]$ is the membership function of A. A fuzzy partition of U into n fuzzy subsets is given by membership functions $\mu_1(x), ..., \mu_n(x)$ such that

$$\forall x \in U : \sum_{i=1,...,n} \mu_i(x) = 1. \tag{2.31}$$

The classical Boolean operations are replaced by real-valued functions which compute the membership function of a Boolean combination of fuzzy sets from membership values of the arguments. It is common to assume some axiomatic properties of these functions. For our further discussion it is convenient to list two examples.

- *t -norms* $f(x, y)$ (intended to compute $\mu_{A \cap B}$):
  Axioms:
  (T1) $f(x, y) = f(y, x)$

(T2) $f(x, f(y, z)) = f(f(x, y), z)$

(T3) $x \leq x' \wedge y \leq y' \rightarrow f(x, y) \leq f(x', y')$

(T4) $f(x, 1) = x$

Typical t-norms are $f(x, y) = min(x, y)$ or $f(x, y) = x \cdot y$.

- *co-t-norms* $f(x, y)$ (intended to compute $\mu_{A \cup B}$):
  Axioms:
  (T1), (T2), (T3) and

  (T4*) $f(x, 0) = x$

  Typical co-t-norms are $f(x, y) = max(x, y)$ or $f(x, y) = x + y - x \cdot y$.

Consequences are $f(x, 0) = 0$ for t-norms, and $f(x, 1) = 1$ for co-t-norms, respectively. There are other fuzzy combination rules available which are fuzzy versions of general Boolean operators like different types of implication.

2.4.2 Similarities and Fuzzy Sets: First Observations

For any similarity measure SIM over U we define a fuzzy subset $SIM \subseteq_f V :=U \times U$ by

$$\mu_{SIM}(u, v) := SIM(u, v). \tag{2.32}$$

We can also associate to each $u \in U$ a fuzzy subset $F_u \subseteq_f U$ by

$$\mu_u(v) := \mu_{F_u}(v) := SIM(u, v) \tag{2.33}$$

where symmetry of SIM implies $\mu_u(v) = \mu_v(u)$. Starting with a fixed SIM, we obtain for each $u \in U$ some fuzzy subset F_u, which describes how U is structured by SIM from the viewpoint of u. This treatment of similarity was essentially introduced in [5], where similarity was treated as a fuzzy equivalence relation with the membership function μ_{SIM} from above.

The 'similarity class' of u (representing the fuzzy equivalence of u) was introduced as ([2])

$$\mu_{SIM, u}(v) = \mu_{SIM}(u, v). \tag{2.34}$$

Essentially the same is the treatment of fuzzy equality as a fuzzy equivalence relation

$$E(u, v) \subseteq_f V := U \times U. \tag{2.35}$$

If one argument, say $u = a$, is fixed then this leads to a fuzzy set

$$E_a(v) = E(a, v) \subseteq_f U. \tag{2.36}$$

Now we can use μ_u like a measure of usefulness in a case base C. For example, the nearest neighbor relation for $C \subseteq U$ reads as

$$NN_C(u, c) \Leftrightarrow \forall c' \in C : \mu_u(c) \geq \mu_u(c') \tag{2.37}$$

or equivalently

$$NN_C(u,c) \Leftrightarrow \forall c' \in C : \mu_{SIM}(u,c) \geq \mu_{SIM}(u,c'). \qquad (2.38)$$

These considerations show that we can interpret the basic CBR concepts in terms of fuzzy set terminology.

The other direction of an interpretation needs some addition. One aspect is easy. Suppose we have a fuzzy subset $S \subseteq_f V := U \times U$ with related properties of reflexivity ($\mu_S(u,u) = 1$), and symmetry ($\mu_S(u,v) = \mu_S(v,u)$) – as far as wanted. Then μ_S obviously defines a similarity measure.

But if we have simply a fuzzy set $K \subseteq_f U$ then we would need in addition a reference object in order to define a measure. Such a reference object a has to satisfy $\mu_K(a) = 1$ since we want to have reflexivity for the similarity measure. We call a a *focal value* for K.

We can then define a similarity measure by

$$SIM(u,a) = \mu_K(u). \qquad (2.39)$$

Suppose that there is a subset $C \subseteq U$ such that for each $c \in C$ we have some fuzzy subset $K_c \subseteq_f U$ with membership functions $\mu_c(u)$ satisfying $\mu_K(c) = 1$. We can then define a similarity measure on $U \times C$ by

$$SIM(u,c) := \mu_c(u) \text{ for } u \in U, c \in C. \qquad (2.40)$$

As an example we consider a partition of U into two (unknown) classes K and $U \setminus K$. We suppose that the classification of the elements of a case base $C \subseteq U$ is known. We may then regard the fuzzy subsets

$$K_c \subseteq_f U \text{ for } c \in K \quad \text{and} \quad \overline{K}_c \subseteq_f U \text{ for } c \in U \setminus K \qquad (2.41)$$

as 'fuzzy versions' of K and $U \setminus K$, respectively (i.e. again these are K and $U \setminus K$ from the viewpoint of c). $C \cap K$ and $C \cap U \setminus K$ can be regarded as prototypes of K and $U \setminus K$ respectively, presented by the case base C.

These considerations show that the basic notions of fuzzy theory and CBR can be mathematically interpreted in terms of each other. In principle, each problem and statement in one terminology can also be expressed in the other terminology. This does not mean that both approaches are equivalent in each respect because they have developed individual computational models and techniques.

As an example we mention the treatment of unknown values which ask either for completing the object description in an optimal way or working with incomplete descriptions. In CBR both aspects have been studied systematically. In the fuzzy approach this has not yet played a major role (except for the case of attributes which are not considered in a certain fuzzy rule; related attributes being redundant for that rule).

2.5 Comparing the Reasoning Processes in CBR and in Fuzzy Control

We give a rough comparison of the reasoning processes in both approaches. We assume that a new problem is presented by a query $q = [q_1, ..., q_n] \in U$. The solution

$s(q)$ has to be determined by solutions s from former similar cases c of the case base C, or by the conclusions s of activated fuzzy rules, respectively. We can identify three comparable steps:

1. Matching of a query q against the available knowledge.
   CBR: Retrieve the most similar cases $c^1, ..., c^k$ (k nearest neighbors according to q) from the case base C.
   Fuzzy Control: Fuzzify q and determine the resulting activations for the fuzzy rules $r^1, ..., r^l$.
2. Adaptation of proposed solutions to a solution $s(q)$.
   CBR: $s(q)$ is computed by combining the solutions s^j of the cases c^j. The s^j might be weighted according to the differences between c^j and q.
   Fuzzy Control: $s(q)$ is computed by combining the solutions s^j of the activated fuzzy rules r^j and by defuzzification. The impacts of the s^j are related to the activation of r^j, i.e. the strength of matching between r^j and q.
3. Learning after applying $s(q)$ to the problem q in reality.
   CBR: The result of applying $s(q)$ for solving q can be stored as a new case 'result of $s(q)$ for solving q' in C immediately.
   Fuzzy Control: The results can be used for adjusting the rules, but this is usually not done immediately.

As this comparison shows, the relevant steps of both reasoning processes are related to each other. In more detail, CBR uses different strategies for the steps, while there are well defined common procedures in fuzzy theory.

Since we are interested in similarity, we are going to have a closer look at the step of matching.

CBR: The problem description parts of the cases c from the case base have to be considered. They are of the form $[c_1, ..., c_n] \in C \subseteq U$. Matching to a query $q = [q_1, ..., q_n]$ consists of computing $SIM([q_1, ..., q_n], [c_1, ..., c_n])$. If SIM is a composite measure, then it is computed according to (2.25) by

$$SIM([q_1, ..., q_n], [c_1, ..., c_n]) = COMP(sim_1(q_1, c_1), ..., sim_n(q_n, c_n)).$$
(2.42)

Fuzzy Control: The preconditions of a fuzzy rule r^j are expressed using linguistic terms l_i^j for the attributes A_i. For simplicity we can assume that all n attributes are considered in a rule, which formally makes no problem.
Fuzzification is done using membership functions μ_i^j for the linguistic terms l_i^j, where $i \in \{1, ..., n\}$ is the index of attribute A_i, and $j \in \{1, ..., l\}$ is the index of the fuzzy rule r^j. Each linguistic term l corresponds to some $K_l \subseteq_f U$. We can then define a local similarity measure $sim(u, a)$ at the special point a by

$$sim(u, a) = \mu_{K_l}(u)$$
(2.43)

as in (2.39), where a has to satisfy $\mu_{K_l}(a) = 1$.
In such a way we have focal values a_i^j for each linguistic term l_i^j, which can now be interpreted as 'having a value of attribute A_i about a_i^j'.

For each attribute A_i we get a similarity measure sim_i which is defined over $\{a_i^1, ..., a_i^l\} \times U$ by (2.43). The values $\{a_1^j, ..., a_n^j\}$ for each fuzzy rule r^j are representatives of the linguistic terms l_i^j. They can be considered to as the 'standard case' $[a_1^j, ..., a_n^j]$ which is covered by the rule r^j.

We need to have a value a with $\mu_{K_i}(a) = 1$ for reasons of reflexivity of sim_i. But obviously sim_i is not symmetrical because of different ranges of the arguments. Strong reflexivity may also be missing since there may exist different values a with $\mu_{K_i}(a) = 1$.

Using the similarity measures from above, the activation of a fuzzy rule r^j is then computed by a composition function $COMP^j$ according to fuzzy operations in the form of a composite measure:

$$ACT^j([u_1, .., u_n], [a_1^j, .., a_n^j]) = COMP^j(sim_1(u_1, a_1^j), .., sim_n(u_n, a_n^j)).$$
(2.44)

Again we have a close relationship between both approaches. But in the computational details, there are also essential differences. We will discuss this matter in the following.

2.6 Implementing Intuitive Meanings by Composite Measures

It is a central problem in the design and maintenance of CBR systems to adopt a notion of similarity/distance such that the following assumptions are satisfied:

1. Similarity between a query and a case implies usefulness.
2. The similarity is based on a priori known facts.
3. As cases can be more or less useful for a query, similarity must provide a quantitative measurement.

It starts with the choice of appropriate attributes and ends up with a measure that (intuitively) corresponds to usefulness. Because there is much freedom in design, the choice of the measures often appears as a non-trivial task.

Related assumptions have to be met in fuzzy control, but there the design task is much more guided by the ideas of linguistic terms and by the fuzzy operators. Fuzzy rules can easily be related to intuitive meanings.

There are two basic choices when constructing similarities/distances:

1. Appropriate definitions of the local similarities/distances. Since they are directly connected to the attributes, they should have an intuitive impact on the intended usefulness. In the case of linguistic terms the relation is usually obvious.
2. Appropriate definition of intuitive composition functions. Fuzzy approaches are usually restricted to the use of t-norms and t-co-norms, while CBR allows more flexibility for composition functions.

Both global and local monotonicity appear as a good guidance for intuitiveness.

2.6.1 Local Measures

Local similarities/distances can be considered as preferences on the local level (in correspondence to global preferences by the global monotonicity axiom).

We have considered local measures ranging over $[0, 1]$, where 0 indicates minimal similarity/distance, and 1 indicates maximal similarity/distance. Minimal similarity corresponds to maximal distance and vice versa.

The intuitive meaning of maximal similarity is maximal preference (identity on the local level: strong reflexivity, or at least 'as good as identity': reflexivity). The intuitive meaning of minimal similarity is not so obvious. It could mean 'no impact to global similarity' (if weighted sums are used for composition), but it could also mean 'global similarity has to be minimal' (if t-norms are used).

The intuitive meaning of minimal distance is the same as for maximal similarity: maximal preference on the local level. The intuitive meaning of maximal distance is again not so obvious, but the interpretation differs from that for minimal similarity: it could mean a 'considerable impact to global distance' (if weighted sums are used for composition), and it could mean 'global distance has to be maximal' (if t-co-norms are used), respectively.

Using other ranges we might have different pictures. For example, the range $[0, \infty]$ for local distances together with weighted sum compositions intuitively implies a really big distance if only a single local distance has a big value. In terms of preferences, one such value counts enough to reject a candidate ('accumulation for rejection' in [1]; it is used in decision tree approaches for retrieval). It is interesting to note that the t-norm plays a comparable role in rejecting a candidate with only one 'bad' local value.

Negative local similarity values could be used to indicate that the related attribute actually decreases the global similarity (when, for example, using addition for composition). Large negative similarity values could count for rejection as well as large distances do. On the other hand, negative distance values would be in conflict with the nearest neighbor concept based on reflexivity for distances.

While distances and similarities are formally equivalent, it becomes obvious by our discussion that there exist basic differences concerning the underlying intuitions. This will be emphasized further when discussing the composition of local measures.

2.6.2 Composition Functions

Weighted sums have an intuitive meaning for composition: they *accumulate* local values to global ones. By their weights they may assign different (fixed!) importances to the attributes, and they may consider scaling problems, respectively. Nevertheless, it is often a non-trivial task to find appropriate weights. The global monotonicity axiom can be satisfied in an easy way. Nevertheless, there must exist some underlying 'inductive bias' (cf. [3]) which assumes that the intended usability can be approximated by a composition function, the local similarities, and the chosen attributes.

Similarity and distances are formally equivalent. Now it appears that different strategies can be realized (especially if addition is used for composition):

- Similarity measures positively accumulate arguments of preferences.
- Distance measures positively accumulate arguments of exclusion.

In consequence (including intuitive aspects of accumulation) the influence of single attributes becomes different:

Accumulation for rejection as nearest neighbor: Larger distances count for rejecting a candidate. Intuition says that a large distance in only one dimension (attribute) is enough to definitively reject a candidate. The other way round: a candidate may become a nearest neighbor only if it has 'good' values for *all* attributes.

Accumulation for acceptance as nearest neighbor: Larger similarities count for accepting a candidate. A candidate may become a nearest neighbor even if it is similar enough in *some but not necessarily all* attributes. This corresponds to the intuitive meaning of compromises when dealing with trade-offs (note that weights can only distinguish fixed priorities, while here we can differentiate individually).

In consequence we need different approaches for similarity based retrieval strategies (cf. [1]): accumulation for rejection allows for pruning strategies as it is used in (top-down) decision trees. Accumulation for acceptance permits (bottom-up) net-like procedures which collect local contributions for similarity.

2.7   Accumulation of Similarities in Fuzzy Theory

Suppose now we represent the local measure by fuzzy sets as indicated above. We remark that although a local measure is concerned with a single attribute it can still be regarded as a measure on all of U (usually not a very good one). Strictly speaking, the combination of local measures extends the local measures to the product space.

In the terminology of fuzzy sets then a combination function applied to membership functions is needed. Suppose we want to accumulate sim_1 and sim_2 where $SIM1 \subseteq_f V$ and $SIM2 \subseteq_f V$ are the corresponding fuzzy sets. At first glance the phrase 'look for the accumulation of sim_1 and sim_2' would ask for the fuzzy intersection of $SIM1$ and $SIM2$ and would therefore require the application of some t-norm. The situation is, however, somewhat more involved, due to the fact that it is not clear what we mean by the 'accumulation of similarities'. There are basically two ways to think of such an accumulation as discussed above: from the viewpoint of similarity and from the viewpoint of distances, respectively, which we will reformulate as two types concerning some 'equivalence'.

Type 1: Each measure contributes a non-negative evidence to the proposition that two elements a and b are equivalent. $sim(a, b) = 0$ contributes just nothing, and $sim(a, b) = 1$ guarantees for sure that a and b are equivalent.

Type 2: Each measure contributes also a negative evidence to the proposition that a and b are equivalent. $sim(a, b) = 0$ guarantees that a and b are not equivalent.

If we have several measures (e.g. several local measures) then some may be of type 1 and others of type 2. The standard similarity measures (e.g. weighted Hamming measures and their variations) assume all type 1 because otherwise negative weight factors occur, while Hamming distances favor type 2.

Difficulties arise if measures of type 1 and type 2 occur in the same context (see below).

In terms of fuzzy operations we can state the following:

Type 1:   For the accumulation of sim_1, sim_2 of type 1 some co-t-norm f is applied to $SIM1$ and $SIM2$.

Type 2:   For accumulating sim_1, sim_2 of type 2 some t-norm f is applied to $SIM1$ and $SIM2$.

It is easy to see that at least on the present level of discussion the axioms (T1) - (T3), (T4) and (T4*) are meaningful. They do not cover, however, all situations discussed so far. If we consider fuzzy sets SIM derived from weighted Hamming measures, then axiom (T1) fails, i.e. conjunction and disjunction are not commutative. This means that fuzzy sets coming from very common measures in CBR need to be treated in a more generalized manner.

Accumulating similarities of type 1 has the consequence that even small contributions can only add something in favor of the similarity; the missing part is regarded as ignorance and not automatically as a contribution to the opposite. This point of view interprets similarities of x and y as *evidences* about the event that x and y are equivalent in the sense of Dempster–Shafer. This is discussed in [4].

The viewpoint of measures of type 2 is basically that of *probability* (although this is for many situations too narrow a view): The similarity of x and y represents the probability that x and y are equivalent. A consequence is that independent contributions to a similarity are combined multiplicatively. Fuzzy t-norms are in this context more related to probabilities and co-t-norms are more related to evidences.

A problem arises when sim_1 is of type 1 and sim_2 is of type 2 . At first, a non-solvable conflict arises when $sim_1(a,b) = 1$ and $sim_2(a,b) = 0$, and in this case we have a contradiction. As a consequence, the accumulation of sim_1 and sim_2 should be undefined. In evidence theory an analogous contradiction occurs if one evidence says with certainty 1 that $a \subseteq_f U \setminus K$ and another evidence guarantees that $a \subseteq_f K$. Here again the accumulation of evidence is not defined. Our above considerations suggest that

- sim_1 should be treated from the additive point of view.
- sim_2 should be treated from the multiplicative point of view.

From the viewpoint of fuzzy sets

- sim_1 asks for the application of a co-t-norm.
- sim_2 asks for the application of a t-norm.

Here we have a related difficulty. One way is to apply one of the fuzzy versions of other Boolean operators (in particular employing negation or some of the various forms of implication).

2.8   Conclusions

There are different approaches to deal with 'problem solving by experience', i.e. by referring to past situations. Reasoning by experience is an alternative for situations where exact computations are not possible. Reasons may be a lack of exact knowledge (missing formulae etc.) as well as intractability of exact algorithms. Such approaches are established in different disciplines. The bases are collections of related cases, and most disciplines try to extract generalizations from such case collections (in the form of rules, clusters, decision trees etc. – note that even the retrieval structures in CBR provide such generalizations). Thereby, the knowledge is compiled to a more dense description using congregations of 'similar cases'. Afterwards in later applications, a new problem has to be matched against these descriptions using 'similarity' once again.

All these disciplines have developed their own treatment of similarity. Comparing these treatments may give deeper insights into the underlying problems. Two of them, namely fuzzy theory and case based reasoning, have been investigated in this chapter. Both are successful in science as well as in commercial applications. Further research may concern the comparison of related system architectures, and their application for working systems. Interesting application fields include picture processing and localization of robots, and synergies may arise from considering both disciplines. Comparisons with other disciplines may give more interesting results and may stimulate further research and system development.

Acknowledgements

The authors wish to thank their colleagues R. Kruse, R. Bergmann, M. Hannebauer, G. Lindemann-v.-Trzebiatowski, and K. Schröter for inspiration and helpful discussions.

References

1. Burkhard, H. D. (1998) Extending some Concepts of CBR – Foundations of Case Retrieval Nets. in *Case-Based Reasoning Technology: From Foundations to Applications.* (ed. M. Lenz, B. Bartsch-Spörl, H. D. Burkhard, S. Wess), LNAI 1400, Springer-Verlag, 17–50.
2. Klawohn, F., Gebhardt, J., Kruse, R. (1995) Fuzzy Control on the Basis of Equality Relations with an Example from Idle Speed Control. *IEEE Transactions on Fuzzy Systems* 3, 336–350.
3. Mitchell, T. M. (1997) *Machine Learning.* McGraw-Hill.
4. Richter, M. M. (1995) On the Notion of Similarity in Case-Based Reasoning. in *Mathematical and Statistical Methods in Artificial Intelligence* (ed. G. della Riccia, R. Kruse, R. Viertel), Springer-Verlag, 171–184.
5. Zadeh, L. (1971) Similarity Relations and Fuzzy Orderings. *Information Sciences* 3, 177–200.

3. Formalizing Case Based Inference Using Fuzzy Rules

Eyke Hüllermeier, Didier Dubois and Henri Prade

Abstract. Similarity based fuzzy rules are described as a basic tool for modeling and formalizing the inference part of the case based reasoning methodology within the framework of approximate reasoning. We discuss different types of rules for encoding the heuristic reasoning principle underlying case based problem solving, which leads to different approaches to case based inference. The use of modifiers in fuzzy rules is proposed for adapting basic similarity relations, and hence for expressing the case based reasoning hypothesis to be used in the inference process. Moreover, the idea of rating cases based on the quality of information they provide is touched upon.

3.1 Introduction

The guiding principle underlying most of the case based reasoning (CBR) systems is the 'CBR hypothesis' which, loosely speaking, assumes that 'similar problems have similar solutions'. More precisely, the idea of CBR is to exploit the experience from (attempts at) solving similar problems in the past and then adapt successful solutions to the current situation. CBR research has focused on issues such as the organization of case bases, the efficient retrieval of cases, the assessment of the similarity of cases, and the adaptation of past solutions to the current problem. Apparently, few attempts have been made, however, at formalizing the CBR hypothesis and the associated reasoning mechanism in a systematic way [9–11,21,28,31,40]. Moreover, little work has been done yet in combining CBR (or, more generally, analogical reasoning) and the theory of fuzzy sets, even though close relations between the modeling of fuzzy systems and CBR methodology can be observed [10,44]. Worth mentioning are some exceptions such as the use of fuzzy sets for supporting the computation of similarities of situations in analogical reasoning [23], the formalization of aspects of analogical reasoning by means of similarity relations between fuzzy sets [7], the use of fuzzy logic for handling fuzzy descriptions in the retrieval step [34], the case based learning of fuzzy concepts from fuzzy examples [39], the use of fuzzy predicates in the derivation of similarities [5], and the integration of case based and rule based reasoning [20].

Fuzzy rules are generally expressed in the form 'if X is A then Y is B', with X and Y being so-called linguistic variables, i.e., variables ranging on a set of symbolic (natural language) labels represented by fuzzy sets. In [32], it has been argued that fuzzy rules in conjunction with associated (approximate) inference procedures provide a convenient framework for modeling the CBR hypothesis and the inference part of CBR reasoning methodology. There are several aspects which motivate the use of fuzzy rules in connection with CBR. Firstly, the CBR hypothesis itself corresponds to an *if–then* rule since it can be formulated as 'if two problems are similar, then the associated solutions are similar as well'. Secondly, the notion of *similarity*, which lies at the heart of CBR, is also strongly related to the theory of fuzzy sets. Indeed, one of the main interpretations of the membership function of a fuzzy set is that of a similarity relation; i.e., membership values can be thought of as degrees of similarity [18]. Thirdly, linked with the framework of possibility theory, fuzzy sets provide a tool for the modeling and processing of *uncertainty*. In connection with CBR, this aspect seems to be of special importance if one realizes the *heuristic* character of this problem solving method. In fact, the CBR principle should not be understood as a deterministic rule, but rather in the sense that 'if two problems are similar, it is *likely* that the associated solutions are similar as well'. According to this formulation, the CBR hypothesis relates the similarity of problems to the (uncertain) *belief* concerning the (similarity of) solutions, not to the (similarity of) solutions directly.

Fuzzy rules can be modeled formally as possibility distributions constrained by some combination of the membership functions which define the condition and conclusion part of the rule (where the concrete form of the constraint depends on the interpretation of the rule [17].) This way, they relate the concepts of similarity and uncertainty, which is the main reason for their convenience as formal models of the CBR principle. Work on fuzzy *if–then* rules has mainly concentrated on algebraic properties of (generalized) logical operators. However, going into the semantics of such rules, it turns out that different interpretations lead to different types of fuzzy rules [13], which can be associated with corresponding classes of implication operators. As will be seen, different types of rules correspond to different (more or less permissive) interpretations of the CBR hypothesis.

The formalizations we shall propose are not related to the complete methodological framework of CBR, often illustrated by means of the so-called 'CBR cycle' [1]. Rather, we focus on the inference step within the overall process of CBR, which essentially corresponds to the REUSE process within the (informal) R^4 model of the CBR cycle. More precisely, we emphasize the idea of CBR as a *prediction* method [9,11,22], which is in line with the idea underlying *case based learning* algorithms [2], *exemplar based reasoning* [35] and *instance based reasoning* [3]. According to this point of view, the main task of CBR is to exploit past experience in the form of observed cases, against the background of the CBR hypothesis, in order to predict the *result* or *outcome* $r_0 \in \mathcal{R}$ associated with a new *situation* $s_0 \in \mathcal{S}$, where $\mathcal{S}$ and $\mathcal{R}$ denote sets of situations and results, respectively.[1]

A case is defined as a tuple $\langle s, r \rangle \in \mathcal{S} \times \mathcal{R}$ consisting of a situation and an associated result. We do not assume that a situation determines a unique outcome, which would be too restrictive for many applications. That is, we may well encounter cases $\langle s, r \rangle$ and $\langle s, r' \rangle$ such that $r \neq r'$. Let $\varphi \subset \mathcal{S} \times \mathcal{R}$ denote the set of potential observations. Thus, a case is always an element of the relation φ. In the following, we shall look upon φ also as a set-valued function $\varphi : \mathcal{S} \to 2^{\mathcal{R}}$, i.e., we denote by $\varphi(s)$ the set $\varphi \cap (\{s\} \times \mathcal{R})$ of possible outcomes in the situation s. We shall further abuse this notation and write $r = \varphi(s)$ instead of $(s, r) \in \varphi$ or $\{r\} = \varphi(s)$ if φ is an ordinary function.

---

[1] We prefer the slightly more general expressions 'situation' and 'result' to the commonly used terms 'problem' and 'solution'.

We assume data to be given in form of a (finite) memory

$$\mathcal{M} = \left\{ \langle s_1, r_1 \rangle, \langle s_2, r_2 \rangle, \ldots, \langle s_n, r_n \rangle \right\}$$

of precedent cases. Let $\mathcal{M}^*$ denote the class of all finite memories $\mathcal{M} \subset \varphi$. Moreover, we suppose the similarity of situations and results to be specified by means of (reflexive and symmetric) fuzzy relations[2]

$$S_{\mathcal{S}} : \mathcal{S} \times \mathcal{S} \to [0, 1], \qquad S_{\mathcal{R}} : \mathcal{R} \times \mathcal{R} \to [0, 1].$$

Let

$$D_{\mathcal{S}} = \{ S_{\mathcal{S}}(s, s') \mid s, s' \in \mathcal{S} \},$$
$$D_{\mathcal{R}} = \{ S_{\mathcal{R}}(r, r') \mid s, s' \in \mathcal{S}, r \in \varphi(s), r' \in \varphi(s') \}$$

denote the sets of actually attained similarity degrees.

The remaining part of the chapter is organized as follows: in Section 3.2 and Section 3.3, two basic models which make use of gradual fuzzy rules and certainty rules, respectively, are introduced. Section 3.4 considers case based inference in the context of information fusion, and provides a probabilistic interpretation which relates the gradual rule and the certainty rule model. The rating of cases based on the information they provide and the related idea of 'exceptionality' of cases is considered in Section 3.5. Section 3.6 generalizes the previously introduced models by applying the CBR hypothesis in a more local way. Section 3.7 concludes the chapter with a summary.

3.2 Gradual Inference Rules

3.2.1 The Basic Model

Gradual rules [41] depict relations between variables X and Y according to propositions of the form 'the more X is A, the more Y is B', where A and B are fuzzy sets modeling certain symbolic labels. This can also be stated as 'the larger the degree of membership of X in the fuzzy set A, the larger is the degree of membership of Y in B' or, even more precisely, as 'the larger the degree of membership of X in the fuzzy set A, the larger is the guaranteed lower bound to the degree of membership of Y in B'. The intended semantics of such a rule can be expressed in terms of membership degrees[3] by

$$A(X) \leq B(Y) \tag{3.1}$$

---

[2] Reflexive and symmetric relations are sometimes called *proximity relations*, and similarity relations are defined as transitive proximity relations. We shall use the term similarity relation here without assuming transitivity.

[3] For the sake of simplicity we denote degrees of membership of x in a fuzzy set A by $A(x)$, rather than using the notation $\mu_A(x)$ which is predominant in the literature on fuzzy sets. Also we do not distinguish between a fuzzy set and the symbolic label it stands for.

which is equivalent to the collection of constraints

$$\forall 0 < \alpha \leq 1 : X \in A_\alpha \Rightarrow Y \in B_\alpha$$

where A_α denotes the α-cut of the fuzzy set A [15]. Observe that Equation 3.1 induces a $\{0, 1\}$-valued (conditional) possibility distribution $\pi_{Y|X}$, where $\pi_{Y|X}(y|x)$ denotes the possibility of $Y = y$ given that $X = x$:

$$\forall x \in D_X \, \forall y \in D_Y : \pi_{Y|X}(y|x) = A(x) \overset{\text{rg}}{\leadsto} B(y) \qquad (3.2)$$

with $\overset{\text{rg}}{\leadsto}$ being the Rescher–Gaines implication ($a \overset{\text{rg}}{\leadsto} b = 1$ if $a \leq b$, and 0 otherwise) and D_X and D_Y the domains of X and Y, respectively.

More generally, fuzzy gradual rules can be classified as *truth-qualifying rules*, the semantics of which is adequately modeled by means of so-called R(esiduated)-implications [14]. For instance, making use of the implication operator $\leadsto$ defined as

$$a \leadsto b = \begin{cases} 1 \text{ if } a \leq b \\ b \text{ if } a > b \end{cases}$$

the possibility of $Y = y$ is not restricted to the values 0 and 1 but may take any value in the interval $[0, 1]$. Nevertheless, for the rest of the chapter we will adhere to the model (Equation 3.2).

Within the context of our CBR framework, a gradual rule reads 'the more similar two situations are, the more similar are the associated outcomes' or, more precisely, 'the more the similarity of situations is F, the more the similarity of outcomes is G', with F and G being fuzzy sets of 'large similarity degrees' (F and G are non-decreasing functions from $[0, 1]$ to $[0, 1]$.) In connection with Equation 3.1 and an observed case $\langle s_1, r_1 \rangle$, this rule (completely) excludes the existence of other (hypothetical) cases $\langle s, r \rangle$ which would violate

$$F(S_{\mathcal{S}}(s, s_1)) \leq G(S_{\mathcal{R}}(r, r_1)). \qquad (3.3)$$

Thus, given a new situation s_0 and assuming $F = G = \mathrm{id}$,[4] Equation 3.3 becomes

$$\forall \langle s, r \rangle \in \varphi : S_{\mathcal{S}}(s, s_1) \leq S_{\mathcal{R}}(r, r_1) \qquad (3.4)$$

and, hence, leads to the restriction

$$r_0 \in \{r \in \mathcal{R} \mid S_{\mathcal{S}}(s_0, s_1) \leq S_{\mathcal{R}}(r, r_1)\} \qquad (3.5)$$

for the result r_0 associated with s_0. Since corresponding constraints are obtained for all cases of a memory $\mathcal{M}$, we finally derive the prediction [9,10]

$$r_0 \in C_{\mathcal{M}}(s_0) = \bigcap_{1 \leq i \leq n} \{r \in \mathcal{R} \mid S_{\mathcal{S}}(s_0, s_i) \leq S_{\mathcal{R}}(r, r_i)\}. \qquad (3.6)$$

---

[4] id denotes the identical function $x \mapsto x$.

Clearly, the extent to which the CBR hypothesis holds true depends on the respective application. Consequently, the formalization of this principle by means of the constraint (Equation 3.1) might be too strong, at least in connection with the underlying similarity relations S_S and S_R. That is, cases $\langle s, r \rangle, \langle s', r' \rangle$ might exist such that $S_S(s, s') > S_R(r, r')$; i.e., although the situations are similar to a certain degree, the same does not hold for the associated results. This, however, contradicts Equation 3.3. Thus, calling a prediction $C_M(s_0)$ *valid* (with respect to the case $\langle s_0, r_0 \rangle$) if $r_0 \in C_M(s_0)$, the (general) validity of the inference scheme (Equation 3.6) is no longer guaranteed in the sense that it might yield an invalid prediction:

$$\exists \mathcal{M} \in \mathcal{M}^* \, \exists \langle s_0, r_0 \rangle \in \varphi : r_0 \notin C_M(s_0).$$

That is, there is a memory $\mathcal{M}$ and a case $\langle s_0, r_0 \rangle$ such that the set-valued prediction derived from $\mathcal{M}$ does not cover r_0. Note that the complete class φ of cases would have to be known in order to guarantee the validity of Equation 3.6 in the above sense. Needless to say, this condition is usually not satisfied.

3.2.2 Modification of Gradual Rules

More flexibility can be introduced in Equation 3.1 by means of a modifier [45], i.e., a non-decreasing function $m : D_S \to [0, 1]$. This leads to

$$\forall \langle s, r \rangle \in \varphi : m(S_S(s, s_1)) \leq S_R(r, r_1) \tag{3.7}$$

instead of Equation 3.4. Moreover, Equation 3.6 becomes

$$r_0 \in C_{m, \mathcal{M}}(s_0) = \bigcap_{1 \leq i \leq n} \{ r \in \mathcal{R} \mid m(S_S(s_0, s_i)) \leq S_R(r, r_i) \}. \tag{3.8}$$

The application of the modifier m can be seen as 'calibrating' the similarity scales underlying the set of situations and the set of results such that Equation 3.1 is always satisfied. As an extreme example of Equation 3.7 consider the case where $m \equiv 0$, expressing the fact that the CBR hypothesis does not apply at all. In other words, the similarity of situations (in the sense of S_S) does not justify any conclusions about the similarity of outcomes (in the sense of S_R.) Observe, however, that m can be utilized in order to strengthen Equation 3.1 as well. We might take, for instance, $m \equiv 1$ if all outcomes are always perfectly similar according to S_R!

The modification of a gradual rule can be interpreted in different ways. In connection with the linguistic modeling of fuzzy concepts, modifiers such as $x \mapsto x^2$ or $x \mapsto \sqrt{x}$ are utilized for depicting the effect of linguistic hedges such as 'very' or 'almost' [36,45]. Applying the modifier $x \mapsto x^2$ might thus be seen as replacing the hypothesis that 'similar situations induce similar outcomes' by the weaker assumption that '*very* similar situations induce similar outcomes'. More precisely: 'If two situations are *very similar* in the sense of the relation S_S, the respective results are (at least) *similar* in the sense of S_R.' Thus, one interpretation of applying m is to replace the CBR hypothesis (and to maintain the similarity measures). A second interpretation is that of replacing the similarity measure S_S (by the measure $m \circ S_S$) in such a way that the (original) hypothesis is satisfied.[5] That is, the hypothesis is not adapted to similarity, but similarity to the hypothesis.

We call a modifier *admissible* if it guarantees the validity of the inference scheme (Equation 3.8), i.e.,

$$\forall \mathcal{M} \in \mathcal{M}^*, \langle s_0, r_0 \rangle \in \varphi : r_0 \in C_{m,\mathcal{M}}(s_0). \tag{3.9}$$

The modifier m defined by

$$m(x) = \sup \left\{ h(x') \mid x' \in D_{\mathcal{S}}, x' \le x \right\} \tag{3.10}$$

for all $x \in D_{\mathcal{S}}$ where

$$h(x) = \inf_{\langle s,r \rangle, \langle s',r' \rangle \in \varphi : S_{\mathcal{S}}(s,s') = x} S_{\mathcal{R}}(r, r')$$

is admissible. Moreover, it is maximally restrictive in the sense that

$$\forall \mathcal{M} \in \mathcal{M}^* \, \forall s_0 \in \mathcal{S} : C_{m,\mathcal{M}}(s_0) \subseteq C_{m',\mathcal{M}}(s_0)$$

holds true for each admissible (and non-decreasing) $m' : D_{\mathcal{S}} \to [0, 1]$. Taking the upper bound in Equation 3.10 only guarantees that m is non-decreasing. In fact, Equation 3.9 is already valid when using h instead of m. Thus, one could think of a more general approach which allows for the application of non-increasing functions [29,31].[6] The modification by means of a non-decreasing function m corresponds to the 'stretching' and 'squeezing' of the similarity scale underlying $S_{\mathcal{S}}$. Interpreting $m \circ S_{\mathcal{S}}$ as a new (improved) similarity measure, $m \circ S_{\mathcal{S}}$ and $S_{\mathcal{S}}$ are still *coherent* in the sense that

$$S_{\mathcal{S}}(s_1, s_2) \le S_{\mathcal{S}}(s_3, s_4) \Rightarrow m(S_{\mathcal{S}}(s_1, s_2)) \le m(S_{\mathcal{S}}(s_3, s_4)) \tag{3.11}$$

for all $s_1, s_2, s_3, s_4 \in \mathcal{S}$. As opposed to this, a non-increasing function h also puts the similarity degrees $x \in D_{\mathcal{S}}$ in a different order and hence violates Equation 3.11.

Loosely spoken, Equation 3.10 can be seen as a solution to the (optimization) problem of finding a modifier maximally restrictive among all the admissible ones. Estimation (Equation 3.10) from observed data, i.e., using the memory $\mathcal{M}$ instead of φ, can be considered as a problem of *case based learning*. Of course, data in the form of a memory $\mathcal{M}$ will generally not allow for verifying the admissibility of a modifier in the sense of Equation 3.9. In fact, Equation 3.9 can be checked only for the observed cases, which means that the requirement of (global) admissibility has to be weakened. An obvious idea is to look for a maximally restrictive modifier m which is admissible, not for the complete relation φ, but at least for the memory $\mathcal{M}$. That is,

$$\forall \langle s, r \rangle \in \mathcal{M} : r \in C_{m,\mathcal{M}}(s). \tag{3.12}$$

---

[5] One has to be careful with this interpretation, since $m \circ S_{\mathcal{S}}$ does not necessarily inherit all (mathematical) properties of the relation $S_{\mathcal{S}}$.

[6] This amounts to modeling the CBR principle in a form which is less strong than 'the more ... the more ...' version formulated at the beginning of this chapter.

In addition to Equation 3.12, it might appear natural to require

$$\forall s \in \mathcal{S} : C_{m,\mathcal{M}}(s) \neq \emptyset. \tag{3.13}$$

That is, for each situation s which might be encountered, the inference scheme (Equation 3.8) yields a non-empty (even if invalid) prediction [11]. Needless to say, the additional requirement (Equation 3.13) makes the learning of a modifier more complex.[7]

A learning algorithm for the case where $\mathcal{H}$ is not restricted to non-decreasing functions has been proposed in [30]. This algorithm derives a modifying function satisfying Equation 3.12 from a number of observed cases. It is shown that, under certain conditions concerning the (stochastic) occurrence of new situations s_0, the prediction (Equation 3.8) defines a *confidence region* for r_0 in a statistical sense. The probability of an invalid prediction $C_{h_{\mathcal{M}},\mathcal{M}}(s_0) \not\ni r_0$, where $h_{\mathcal{M}}$ denotes the modifying function derived from the memory $\mathcal{M}$, decreases linearly with the number $\mathrm{card}(\mathcal{M})$ of observed cases. The corresponding algorithm is easily adapted to the problem of learning modifying functions which are non-decreasing and, hence, can also be applied within the framework of this section.

It is worth mentioning that the similarity relations do principally play the role of *ordinal* concepts in our approach. According to Equation 3.8, the set $C_{m,\mathcal{M}}(s_0)$ depends only on the relative order of similarity degrees as specified by the modifier m. In other words, the sets $D_{\mathcal{S}}$ and $D_{\mathcal{R}}$ can be interpreted as linearly ordered scales of similarity, for which only the (relative) order of the grades of similarity is important. In fact, the numerical encoding is just a matter of convenience, and the interval $[0, 1]$ could be replaced by any other linearly ordered scale.

Observe also that $F = G = \mathrm{id}$ can be assumed for the fuzzy sets F and G in Equation 3.3 without loss of generality (as long as G is strictly increasing.) This becomes obvious from the constraint (Equation 3.7). Namely, $m(F(S_{\mathcal{S}}(s, s'))) \leq G(S_{\mathcal{R}}(r, r'))$ is equivalent to $m'(S_{\mathcal{S}}(s, s')) \leq S_{\mathcal{R}}(r, r')$ with $m' = G^{-1} \circ m \circ F$.

The inference rule underlying Equation 3.7 can be seen as the (heuristic) 'meta-knowledge' of an agent. This *generic* knowledge, which relates degrees of similarity, is interpreted in the context of observed cases. That is, each observed case $\langle s_1, r_1 \rangle$ leads to an *instantiation* in form of a concrete rule: 'If the similarity between s_1 and some situation s is x and $r \in \varphi(s)$ is the outcome associated with s, the similarity between r_1 and r is at least $m(x)$.'

The modifier m allows for adapting the strength of the CBR hypothesis to the current application. Making use of a modifier can be interpreted in two different ways: (a) as adapting a similarity relation $S_{\mathcal{S}}$, which is natural for comparing situations in $\mathcal{S}$, in order to control the effect of the constraint (Equation 3.7); (b) as modifying a specification of the CBR rule (given by some expert) in order to agree with cases in the memory.

Choosing m from some class $\mathcal{H}$ of functions comes down to considering the class $\{g \circ S_{\mathcal{S}} \mid g \in \mathcal{H}\}$ of similarity relations. In our case $\mathcal{H}$ contains only non-decreasing

---

[7] Verifying Equation 3.13 is closely related to testing the *coherence* of a set of gradual rules [19].

functions.[8] Thus, we do not take arbitrary relations into account but only 'biased' versions which modulate the 'strength' of the original measure S_S and which are coherent to S_S in the sense of Equation 3.11.

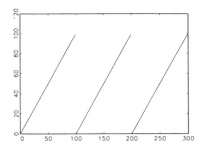

Fig. 3.1. Graph of the function $a \mapsto a \bmod 100$.

Even though the approach (Equation 3.7) enables the adaptation of the formal CBR model based on a gradual rule, this model remains rather restrictive and might lead to imprecise predictions. Consider the following example, to which we shall return occasionally in subsequent sections:

$$S = \mathcal{R} = \mathbb{N} = \{0, 1, \dots\}, \quad D_S = D_\mathcal{R} = \{0, 1\},$$
$$S_S(a, b) = S_\mathcal{R}(a, b) = 1 \Leftrightarrow |a - b| \leq 10, \tag{3.14}$$
$$\varphi : S \to \mathcal{R}, \, a \mapsto a \bmod M.$$

Thus, situations and results correspond to natural numbers, and two situations (results) are either completely similar or not similar at all. Moreover, $\varphi(a) = q \Leftrightarrow (q \in \{0, 1, \dots, M-1\} \wedge \exists p \in \mathbb{N} : a = pM + q)$. Knowing M to be a rather large integer, we can hence say that $\varphi(s)$ and $\varphi(s')$ are 'almost surely' similar whenever s and s' are similar. (See Fig. 3.1, where the graph of φ is illustrated for $M = 100$.) Nevertheless, 'exceptional' pairs of situations s, s' for which $S_S(s, s') = 1$ and $S_\mathcal{R}(\varphi(s), \varphi(s')) = 0$ still exist (e.g., $s = M - 1$, $s' = M$). Thus, one has to take $m \equiv 0$ in order to guarantee the validity of Equation 3.8. Then, however, case based inference via Equation 3.6 becomes meaningless, since $C_{m,\mathcal{M}}(s_0) = \mathcal{R} = \mathbb{N}$ for all $s_0 \in S$.

This example suggests looking for generalized inference schemes which are less restrictive. In this chapter, we consider two possibilities of weakening the formalization of the CBR principle based on gradual rules. Firstly, we give up the requirement of its *global* validity, i.e., the fact that *one* modifier has to be determined such that Equation 3.7 is satisfied for *all* (tuples of) cases. A related approach will be proposed in Section 3.6, where case based inference will be formalized not by means of a single modifier, but by means of a set of ('locally valid') fuzzy rules.

Secondly, Equation 3.7 is obviously not very flexible in the sense that it does not allow for incorporating some tolerance toward exceptions into the inference process.

---

[8] In connection with learning algoritms, $\mathcal{H}$ will generally be restricted further, e.g. to a set of polynomials.

In fact, the above example suggests looking for inference schemes which not only distinguish between the possibility and impossibility of outcomes, but also which are able to derive more expressive predictions, using a graded notion of possibility. For this reason, we shall consider so-called certainty rules in Section 3.3 below.

3.3 Certainty Rules

A certainty rule corresponds to statements of the form 'the more X is A, the more *certain* Y lies in B'. More precisely, it can be interpreted as a collection of rules 'if $X = x$, it is certain at least to the degree $A(x)$ that Y lies in B', where $x \in D_X$. This translates into the following constraint on the conditional possibility distribution $\pi_{Y|X}$ [17]:

$$\forall x \in D_X \forall y \in D_Y :$$

$$\pi_{Y|X}(y|x) \leq \max\{1 - A(x), B(y)\}. \tag{3.15}$$

More generally, rules of this kind can be classified as *(un)certainty-qualifying rules* [14]. The semantics of such rules is adequately captured by means of so-called S(trong)-implication operators, a special case of which is the Kleene–Dienes implication in Equation 3.15.

The upper bound (Equation 3.15) implies that the possibility of $Y = y$ is bounded by $1 - A(x)$ if $X = x$ and $B(y) = 0$, which means that y is outside of the support of B. Thus, the larger $A(x)$, the smaller the possibility that y lies outside of B. Within the framework of possibility theory, *certainty* is closely related to *impossibility*[9] and, hence, Equation 3.15 indeed means that y lies in B with certainty $A(x)$.

Since a certainty rule is thought of as a constraint which holds true in general but still allows for exceptions (see, e.g., [43]), it is more flexible than the approach based on gradual rules and seems to be particularly suitable as a formal model of CBR [28]. In connection with the concept of a certainty rule, the CBR hypothesis can be understood as 'the larger the similarity of two situations, the more *certain* it is that the similarity of corresponding outcomes is large', an interpretation which emphasizes the heuristic nature of this assumption.

Given a new situation s_0, an observed case $\langle s_1, r_1 \rangle \in \mathcal{M}$ constrains the possibility of similarity degrees $y = S_\mathcal{R}(r_0, r_1)$ according to Equation 3.15:

$$\pi(y|x) \leq \pi_C(y|x) = \max\{1 - y, x\} \tag{3.16}$$

where $x = S_\mathcal{S}(s_0, s_1)$ is the similarity between s_0 and s_1. Since $r_0 = r$ implies $y = S_\mathcal{R}(r, r_0)$, we thus obtain

$$\pi(r|s_0) \leq \max\{1 - S_\mathcal{S}(s_0, s_1), S_\mathcal{R}(r, r_1)\} \tag{3.17}$$

---

[9] Formally, the certainty c of an event A and the possibility p of the complement of A are related according to $c = 1 - p$.

for the possibility that $r \in \mathcal{R}$ corresponds to the unknown outcome r_0.[10] The more similar the situations s_0 and s_1 are, the more constrained becomes the possibility of outcomes according to Equation 3.17. If, for instance, $S_{\mathcal{S}}(s_0, s_1)$ is close to 1, the possibility bound $\pi(r|s_0)$ can be large only for outcomes which are very similar to r_1. If, however, $S_{\mathcal{S}}(s_0, s_1)$ is very small, we obtain a large possibility bound also for results hardly similar to r_1. Particularly, Equation 3.17 becomes trivial if $S_{\mathcal{S}}(s_0, s_1) = 0$. The resulting possibility distribution $\pi \equiv 1$ reveals *complete ignorance*. That is, the observed outcome r_1 says nothing about the unknown outcome r_0, because the corresponding situations are not similar at all.

Since Equation 3.17 applies to all cases of the memory we obtain the possibility distribution

$$\pi_C(r) = \pi_C(r|s_0) \tag{3.18}$$

$$= \min_{1 \leq i \leq n} \max \left\{ 1 - S_{\mathcal{S}}(s_0, s_i), S_{\mathcal{R}}(r, r_i) \right\}$$

which emerges from Equation 3.15 under the application of the minimal specificity principle.[11] The constraint (Equation 3.18) can be generalized to

$$\pi_C(r) = \pi_C(r|s_0) \tag{3.19}$$

$$= \min_{1 \leq i \leq n} \max \left\{ 1 - m_1(S_{\mathcal{S}}(s_0, s_i)), m_2(S_{\mathcal{R}}(r, r_i)) \right\}$$

with modifiers $m_1 : D_{\mathcal{S}} \to [0, 1]$, $m_2 : D_{\mathcal{R}} \to [0, 1]$. Again, the approach (Equation 3.19) can be seen as a formalization of the 'meta-knowledge' of an agent, and the functions m_1 and m_2 allow for an adequate adaptation of this knowledge to the application [29].

Observe that Equation 3.19 makes use of two modifiers, whereas only one modifier is used in the model based on a gradual rule. As already mentioned in Section 3.2, similarity of results serves as a *comparative* value in Equation 3.7; i.e., only the order relation between $m(S_{\mathcal{S}}(s, s'))$ and $S_{\mathcal{R}}(r, r')$ is important. In fact, since we are using a binary implication in Equation 3.2, the application of a modifier m_1 to $S_{\mathcal{S}}$ and a (strictly increasing) modifier m_2 to $S_{\mathcal{R}}$ (in the approach of Section 3.2) is equivalent to applying the modifier $m = m_2^{-1} \circ m_1 \circ S_{\mathcal{S}}$ to $S_{\mathcal{S}}$.[12] This is no longer true for Equation 3.19, where the effect of an observed case on the degree of possibility of other (not yet encountered) cases cannot be controlled by modifying $S_{\mathcal{S}}$ alone.

Nevertheless, the second modifier in Equation 3.19 becomes superfluous if possibility is considered as an ordinal concept, i.e., if $D_{\mathcal{S}}$ and $D_{\mathcal{R}}$ are defined as ordinal

---

[10] Subsequently, we use the symbol π (as well as π_C) alternately to denote possibility distributions on $\mathcal{R}$ and $D_{\mathcal{R}}$. However, the context will always become obvious from the argument, which is either an outcome $r \in \mathcal{R}$ or a similarity degree $x \in D_{\mathcal{R}}$.

[11] According to this principle, each element of the domain of a possibility distribution is assigned the largest possibility in agreement with the given constraints. The principle has been discussed under the name *principle of maximal possibility* in [46], and has been introduced as an information-theoretic principle in [12].

[12] Using a modifier m_2 which is not strictly increasing can only be disadvantageous with respect to the precision of predictions.

scales of similarity degrees. Indeed, we have

$$\max\{1 - m_1(x), m_2(y)\} \leq \max\{1 - m_1(x'), m_2(y')\}$$

$$\Leftrightarrow \max\{1 - m(x), y\} \leq \max\{1 - m(x'), y'\}$$

with $m : x \mapsto 1 - m_2^{-1}(1 - m_1(x))$. Then, however, the function $1 - (\cdot)$ in Equation 3.19 has to be replaced by an order-reversing mapping of the ordinal scale. Subsequently, we shall assume (without loss of generality) that the latter is still defined as $1 - (\cdot)$.

A gradual rule is *deterministic* [9] in the sense that an observed case $\langle s_1, r_1 \rangle$ completely rules out the existence of other (hypothetical) cases, namely those which do not obey Equation 3.7. Particularly, the set

$$\{r \in R \,|\, m(S_S(s_0, s_1)) \leq S_R(r, r_1)\}$$

of outcomes regarded as possible for the situation s_0 excludes results which are not similar enough, namely those outcomes $r \in \mathcal{R}$ with $S_R(r, r_1) < m(S_S(s_0, s_1))$. As opposed to this, a certainty rule has a *non-deterministic* character. According to Equation 3.17, it restricts the possibility of a case $\langle s, r \rangle$ only gradually:

$$\pi(s, r) \leq \max\{1 - S_S(s, s_1), S_R(r, r_1)\}. \tag{3.20}$$

Thus, it does not generally exclude other cases completely. In fact, the possibility of a case $\langle s, r \rangle$ is 0 only if both s is perfectly similar to s_1 and r is perfectly different from r_1. Given a new situation s_0, we hence obtain $\pi_C(r|s_0) > 0$ as soon as $S_S(s_0, s_1) < 1$ or $S_R(r, r_1) > 0$. It is just this property which allows for the modeling of exceptional situations, and which seems advantageous in connection with the adaptation of CBR models.

To illustrate this, let us reconsider the example of Equation 3.14. The fact that we have to take $m \equiv 0$ means that a case $\langle s, r \rangle$ no longer constrains the possibility of outcomes associated with a new situation s_0. Now, suppose that we define m_1 by $m_1(0) = 0$ and $m_1(1) = 1 - \varepsilon$ (and $m_2 = $ id) in the certainty rule approach (Equation 3.19), where $0 < \varepsilon \ll 1$. Given a case $\langle s_1, r_1 \rangle$ and a new situation s_0 similar to s_1, we obtain

$$\pi_C(r|s_0) = \begin{cases} 1 & \text{if} \quad S_R(r, r_1) = 1 \\ \varepsilon & \text{if} \quad S_R(r, r_1) = 0. \end{cases} \tag{3.21}$$

Thus, outcomes similar to r_1 are regarded as completely possible, but a positive (even if small) degree of possibility is also assigned to outcomes r which are not similar to r_1. This takes the existence of exceptional pairs of situations into account.

As pointed out in [9], a certainty rule (Equation 3.17) fails to modulate the width of the neighborhood around an observed outcome r_1 in terms of the similarity between s_0 and s_1, which a gradual rule would do. As expressed by Equation 3.17, it only attaches a level of uncertainty (which depends on $S_S(s_0, s_1)$) to the fuzzy set $S_R(r_1, \cdot)$ of values close to r_1. A way of remedying this problem would be to use implication operators (which are obtained from some R-implication $\rightarrow$ by contraposition, i.e., $a \rightsquigarrow b = (1 - b) \rightarrow (1 - a)$) such as

$$a \rightsquigarrow b = \begin{cases} 1 & \text{if} \quad a \leq b \\ 1 - a & \text{if} \quad a > b \end{cases} \tag{3.22}$$

or

$$a \rightsquigarrow b = \begin{cases} 1 & \text{if} \quad a \leq b \\ \max\{1 - a, b\} & \text{if} \quad a > b \end{cases} \tag{3.23}$$

in place of $\max\{1 - a, b\}$ in Equation 3.15.[13]

We then obtain the (generalized) model

$$\pi(r|s_0) = \min_{1 \leq i \leq n} m_1(S_\mathcal{S}(s_0, s_i)) \rightsquigarrow m_2(S_\mathcal{R}(r, r_i)) . \tag{3.24}$$

This approach avoids the following effect which occurs under the application of the constraint (Equation 3.17): if the situations s_0 and s_1 are similar enough, the bound of $\pi_C(r|s_0)$ in Equation 3.17 only reflects the similarity between r and r_1. This, however, means that we generally have $\pi_C(r|s_0) < 1$ even for outcomes r which are rather similar to r_1. In fact, Equation 3.17 reduces the possibility of $r_0 = r$ even if $S_\mathcal{S}(s_0, s_1) \leq S_\mathcal{R}(r, r_1)$. In this situation it appears to be more restrictive than a gradual rule. Observe that Equation 3.22 somewhat combines the effect of gradual and certainty rules since $r_0 \in S_\mathcal{R}(r_i, \cdot)_\alpha$ with certainty $\alpha = m_1(S_\mathcal{S}(s_0, s_i))$ for all $1 \leq i \leq n$ (if $m_2 = \text{id.}$) Now, however, the certainty level and the level of the cut of the similarity relation $S_\mathcal{R}(r_i, \cdot)$ are directly related (through m_1).

3.4 Cases as Information Sources

In this section, we shall look at cases as individual information sources, and consider case based inference as the parallel combination of such information sources. A corresponding (probabilistic) framework allows for a semantic interpretation of the prediction $\pi_C(\cdot|s_0)$ derived from a (modified) certainty rule. This interpretation gives a concrete meaning to a degree of possibility $\pi(r|s_0)$ and hence might be helpful in connection with the acquisition of modifiers (which act on possibility distributions). At the same time, it establishes a connection between the approaches presented in Section 3.2 and Section 3.3, showing that the latter can be seen (from a probabilistic point of view) as a generalization of the former.

3.4.1 A Probabilistic Model

When making use of the CBR hypothesis formalized by means of a fuzzy rule, each observed case provides some evidence concerning the unknown outcome r_0. Given a

---

[13] Equation 3.23 is the R-implication and, at the same time, the S-implication related to a t-norm called the nilpotent minimum. Given a strong negation n, the latter is defined as $t(x, y) = \min\{x, y\}$ if $y > n(x)$, and $t(x, y) = 0$ otherwise [24].

memory $\mathcal{M}$ of n cases, the individual pieces of evidence have to be combined into a global constraint. Seen from this perspective, each case serves as an information source, and one task arising in connection with CBR is the parallel combination of these information sources.[14] In Section 3.2, for instance, the evidence derived from an individual case $\langle s_1, r_1 \rangle$ is given in the form of a set $\mathcal{N}_{m(S_S(s, s_0))}(r)$ of possible candidates, where

$$\mathcal{N}_\alpha(r_1) = \{r \in \mathcal{R} \mid \alpha \leq S_\mathcal{R}(r, r_1)\}$$

denotes the α-*neighborhood* of the outcome r_1. Moreover, the (conjunctive) combination of evidence is realized by the intersection (Equation 3.8).

The problem of combining concurrent pieces of (uncertain) evidence can be considered in a broader context. It arises in many fields such as robotics (sensor fusion) or knowledge-based systems (expert opinion pooling), and it has been dealt with in a probabilistic setting [25,27] as well as alternative uncertainty frameworks [4,6,16,33]. The combination of evidence derived from individual cases is perhaps best compared to that of expert opinion pooling. That is, each case is seen as an expert, and the prediction of the unknown outcome associated with this case is interpreted as an expert statement. The task is to synthesize these statements.

A general framework for the parallel combination of information sources which seems suitable for our purpose has been proposed in [26]. A basic concept within this framework is that of an *imperfect specification*: let Ω denote a set of alternatives, consisting of all possible states of an object under consideration, and let $\omega_0 \in \Omega$ be the actual (but unknown) state. An imperfect specification of ω_0 is a tuple $\Gamma = (\gamma, p_C)$, where C is a (finite) set of *specification contexts*, γ is a function $\gamma : C \to 2^\Omega$, and p_C is a probability measure over C.[15] The problem of combining evidence is then defined as generating an imperfect specification Γ of ω_0 which performs a synthesis among n imperfect specifications $\Gamma_1, \ldots, \Gamma_n$, issued by n different information sources.

From a semantic point of view, a specification context $c \in C$ can be seen as a physical or observation-related frame condition, and $\gamma(c)$ is the (most specific) characterization of ω_0 that can be provided by the information source in the context c. The value $p_C(c) = p_C(\{c\})$ can be interpreted as an (objective or subjective) probability of selecting c as a true context. An imperfect specification is thus able to model *imprecision* as well as *uncertainty*. The probability measure p_C accomplishes the consideration of (probabilistic) uncertainty. Moreover, the modeling of imprecision is possible due to the fact that γ is a *set-valued* function.

Consider again the CBR framework specified in Section 3.1, and suppose $\mathcal{S}$ and $\mathcal{R}$ (and hence $D_\mathcal{S}$ and $D_\mathcal{R}$) to be finite. In Section 3.2, the evidence derived from an individual case $\langle s_1, r_1 \rangle$ is given in the form of the set $\mathcal{N}_{m(x)}(r_1)$, where $m(x) = m(S_S(s_0, s_1))$ specifies the lower similarity bound (Equation 3.10). This corresponds

---

[14] Of course, this is not true for CBR systems using only a single case from the memory for solving a new problem.

[15] Formally, an imperfect specification is nothing but a set-valued mapping on a probability space, a well-known concept in connection with random set approaches [8,38,42].

to a particular imperfect specification, namely

$$\Gamma = (\gamma, p_{C_x}), \quad C_x = D_{\mathcal{R}}, \quad \gamma(c) = \mathcal{N}_c(r_1),$$

$$p_{C_x}(c) = \begin{cases} 1 & \text{if} \quad c = m(x) \\ 0 & \text{if} \quad c \neq m(x). \end{cases} \tag{3.25}$$

A context c is hence thought of as the lower similarity bound $m(x) \in D_{\mathcal{R}}$ associated with the similarity degree $x \in D_{\mathcal{S}}$. Observe that the information source $\langle s_1, r_1 \rangle$ is *correct* in the sense that the prediction $\gamma(c) = \mathcal{N}_c(r_1)$ contains the object $\omega_0 = r_0$ under the assumption that the context c is true (and the modifier m is admissible). It is also of *maximum specificity*, since $\mathcal{N}_c(r_1)$ is the most specific characterization of r_0 that can be inferred by $\langle s_1, r_1 \rangle$ in this context.

The one-point distribution p_{C_x} in Equation 3.25 suggests the lower similarity bound to be precisely known. Generally, however, knowledge about $m(x)$ will be incomplete. Let us therefore assume p_{C_x} to be defined in a more general way, such that $p_{C_x}(c)$, the probability that $m(x) = c$, can take values between 0 and 1. Since $m(x) = c$ means that c defines the (largest) lower similarity bound, it implies $S_{\mathcal{R}}(r_0, r_1) \in [c, 1]$. That is, the true similarity between r_1 and the unknown outcome r_0 is at least c. For $y \in D_{\mathcal{R}}$, the probability that $S_{\mathcal{R}}(r, r_0) = y$ is hence bounded as follows:

$$\Pr(y) \leq \sum_{c \in D_{\mathcal{R}}: c \leq y} p_{C_x}(c).$$

Interpreting a possibility distribution π on $D_{\mathcal{R}}$ as an encoding of upper degrees of probability, by virtue of the correspondence $\pi(y|x) = \Pr(y)$, it is possible to trace the possibility distribution

$$\pi_C(y|x) = m(x) \leadsto y \tag{3.26}$$

derived from a (modified) certainty rule[16] back to a probabilistic specification of the similarity bound $m(x)$. Consider Equation 3.26 for the implication operator (Equation 3.22) as an example:

$$\pi_C(y|x) = \begin{cases} 1 & \text{if} \quad m(x) \leq y \\ 1 - m(x) & \text{if} \quad m(x) > y. \end{cases} \tag{3.27}$$

For $m(x) > 0$, Equation 3.27 corresponds to the probability p_{C_x} defined by

$$p_{C_x}(c) = \begin{cases} 1 - m(x) & \text{if} \quad c = 0 \\ m(x) & \text{if} \quad c = m(x) \\ 0 & \text{if} \quad c \notin \{0, m(x)\}. \end{cases} \tag{3.28}$$

This model can be interpreted as follows: the lower similarity bound is estimated by $m(x)$, but this estimation is correct only with a certain probability. Particularly, Equation 3.28 assigns a positive probability to the value 0; i.e., it does not exclude the

---

[16] In this section, we restrict ourselves to certainty rules with one modifier.

existence of outcomes which are not similar at all (and hence entail $m(x) = 0$). Associating $m(x)$ with the interval $[m(x), 1]$, we might also interpret this model as some kind of confidence interval for a similarity degree $y = S_{\mathcal{R}}(r, r_0)$, supplemented with a corresponding level of confidence.

Since $m(x) = c$ also implies

$$r_0 \in \{r \in \mathcal{R} \mid S_{\mathcal{R}}(r, r_1) \geq c\}$$

the possibility distribution

$$\pi_C(r) = m(S_{\mathcal{S}}(s_0, s_1)) \rightsquigarrow S_{\mathcal{R}}(r, r_1) \tag{3.29}$$

induced by an observed case $\langle s_1, r_1 \rangle$ in connection with a certainty rule, can be interpreted in the same way as the corresponding distribution (Equation 3.26). That is, the value $\pi_C(r)$ can be interpreted as an upper bound for the probability that $r_0 = r$.

The probability (Equation 3.28) reveals a special property of the uncertain prediction derived from a certainty rule. Namely, the certainty level associated with the estimation of a similarity bound is in direct correspondence with the similarity degree itself. That is, the larger the estimation of the similarity bound $m(x)$ is, the larger is the level of confidence attached to the confidence interval $[m(x), 1]$.

3.4.2 Combination of Information Sources

So far, we have considered only one piece of evidence, derived from a single case $\langle s_1, r_1 \rangle$, and the imperfect specification related to the corresponding similarity bound $m(x)$, where $x = S_{\mathcal{S}}(s_0, s_1)$. More generally, the memory $\mathcal{M}$ contains several cases, and uncertainty concerning the complete modifier (Equation 3.10) has to be specified. Thus, let us define the set of specification contexts as $C = D_{\mathcal{R}}^{D_{\mathcal{S}}}$. Each context $c \in C$ corresponds to a function $c : D_{\mathcal{S}} \to D_{\mathcal{R}}$ and, hence, specifies a lower similarity bound $c(x)$ for all $x \in D_{\mathcal{S}}$. Moreover, suppose a certainty rule with modifier m to be given, and let p_C be defined on C in such a way that the marginal distributions correspond to the distributions p_{C_x} ($x \in D_{\mathcal{S}}$) induced by this rule.

The different information sources associated with cases in the memory now share a common set C of specification contexts. Let $\Gamma_i = (\gamma_i, p_C)$ ($1 \leq i \leq n$) denote the imperfect specification associated with the ith case $\langle s_i, r_i \rangle$. The function γ_i is then given by

$$\forall c \in C : \gamma_i(c) = \mathcal{N}_{c(S_{\mathcal{S}}(s_i, s_0))}(r_i).$$

Making use of all cases and assuming the specification context $c \in C$ to be true, we can derive the prediction $r_0 \in C_{c,\mathcal{M}}(s_0)$, where

$$C_{c,\mathcal{M}}(s_0) = \bigcap_{1 \leq i \leq n} \{r \in \mathcal{R} \mid c(S_{\mathcal{S}}(s_0, s_i)) \leq S_{\mathcal{R}}(r, r_i)\}. \tag{3.30}$$

This is in accordance with the gradual rule model, which considers only one modifier and, hence, provides the corresponding set-valued prediction (Equation 3.30). In fact, Equation 3.30 reveals that each context $c \in C$ corresponds to some modified gradual rule. In other words, a certainty rule can be interpreted as a 'random' gradual rule, i.e., a class of (modified) gradual rules with associated probabilities.

When considering the modifier m as a random variable, the prediction of r_0 according to Equation 3.30 becomes a random set, where $C_{c,\mathcal{M}}(s_0)$ occurs with probability $p_C(c)$.[17] The probability that a certain result $r \in \mathcal{R}$ is an element of this set is given by

$$\Pr(r \in C_{c,\mathcal{M}}(s_0)) = \sum_{c:r \in C_{c,\mathcal{M}}(s_0)} p_C(c) \qquad (3.31)$$

and defines an upper bound to the probability that $r_0 = r$. In connection with the idea of a randomized gradual rule model, Equation 3.31 corresponds to the probability of selecting a (modified) gradual rule c which does not exclude the (hypothetical) case $\langle s_0, r \rangle$, i.e., for which Equation 3.30 holds.

The imperfect specification $\Gamma = (\gamma, p_C)$ defined by

$$\forall c \in C : \gamma(c) = C_{c,\mathcal{M}}(s_0)$$

(and C, p_C as above) corresponds to the *conjunctive pooling* of the information sources $\Gamma_1, \dots, \Gamma_n$. This kind of combination is justified by the fact that all information sources are correct with respect to all specification contexts $c \in C$. Within a possibilistic setting, conjunctive pooling comes down to deriving the intersection of possibility distributions. In fact, it is not difficult to show that Equation 3.31 is bounded from above by the possibility distribution π_C derived from a certainty rule in connection with a number of cases. That is,

$$\Pr(r \in C_{c,\mathcal{M}}(s_0)) \leq \pi_C(r) = \min \left\{ \pi_C^1(r), \dots, \pi_C^n(r) \right\} \qquad (3.32)$$

for all $r \in \mathcal{R}$, where π_C^i denotes the possibility distribution derived from the ith case according to Equation 3.29.[18] The interpretation of possibility degrees as upper approximations of probabilities is hence in agreement with the application of the minimum operator in Equation 3.19, i.e., with making use of this operator in order to combine the possibility distributions derived from individual cases.

According to the interpretation proposed in this section, the certainty rule approach can be seen as a generalization of the approach based on gradual rules, in the sense that the lower similarity bounds, which guarantee the validity of the set-valued prediction of r_0, are no longer assumed to be precisely known. The incomplete knowledge concerning these bounds is characterized by means of a probability distribution. This allows for interpreting the case based inference scheme in Section 3.3 as a kind of approximate probabilistic reasoning. More precisely, a prediction $\pi_C(\cdot|s_0)$ specifies possibility degrees $\pi_C(r|s_0)$ which can be seen as upper bounds to the probability that the unknown result r_0 is given by the outcome r.

---

[17] Observe, however, that $c \neq c' \not\Rightarrow C_{c,\mathcal{M}}(s_0) \neq C_{c',\mathcal{M}}(s_0)$.
[18] For certain conditions, it can even be shown that the inequality (Equation 3.32) is actually an equality.

3.5 Exceptionality and Assessment of Cases

Considering cases as individual information sources, as we have done in Section 3.4, suggests rating their contribution to the prediction of outcomes. In fact, the assessment of information sources is supported by most frameworks for the combination of evidence. The basic idea, then, is to realize some kind of weighted aggregation procedure or to modify (discount) the information provided by a source according to its reliability.[19]

Recall that, given the same information in the form of a context $c \in C$, i.e., a modifier specifying lower similarity bounds, different cases provide different specifications of the unknown outcome r_0. Considering this modifier and the new situation s_0, a case $\langle s, r \rangle$ provides a prediction of r_0 in the form of a possibility distribution which supports outcomes in the neighborhood of r. Such a specification might hence be misleading if, e.g., the outcome r is rather 'untypical'.

Consider again the example of Equation 3.14, and suppose that $s_0 = M - 1$ and $s_1 = M + 1$. In accordance with the certainty rule model (Equation 3.21) of this example (cf. Section 3.3), the case $\langle s_1, r_1 \rangle = \langle M + 1, 1 \rangle$ strongly supports the outcomes $\{0, \dots, 11\}$ which are similar to $r_1 = 1$. It almost rules out all other results, including the true outcome $r_0 = M - 1$. Loosely speaking, the (otherwise useful) information about similarity relations, specified by the certainty rule, is 'misinterpreted' by $\langle s_1, r_1 \rangle$. Even though the advice to disqualify outcomes which are not similar to r will lead to good predictions for the majority of cases $\langle s, r \rangle$ it is hardly reasonable when taken up in connection with an 'exceptional' pair of cases such as $\langle s_0, r_0 \rangle$ and $\langle s_1, r_1 \rangle$.

The above example makes clear that exceptionality is not necessarily a property of an individual situation or case. Rather, the label of exceptionality applies to *pairs* of cases. In fact, $\langle s_1, r_1 \rangle$ is exceptional only in connection with situations $s = M - k$, where $1 \leq k \leq 9$, but will lead to correct predictions for all other situations. Moreover, the decision of whether to call two cases exceptional will often not be as obvious as in our example, where only two degrees of similarity are distinguished. Making use of richer scales including intermediate degrees of similarity, exceptionality will become a gradual property.

Interestingly enough, a degree of exceptionality can be computed within the certainty rule framework as follows:

$$\mathrm{ex}(\langle s, r \rangle, \langle s', r' \rangle) = 1 - \pi_C(S_R(r, r') \mid S_S(s, s')). \tag{3.33}$$

That is, the exceptionality of the tuple of cases $\langle s, r \rangle$, $\langle s', r' \rangle$ is inversely related to the possibility of observing $S_R(r, r')$-similar outcomes for $S_S(s, s')$-similar situations, as specified by the certainty rule model. The more $\langle s, r \rangle$ and $\langle s', r' \rangle$ violate the certainty rule, the more exceptional they are in the sense of Equation 3.33.

It is worth mentioning that Equation 3.33 also makes sense in connection with the gradual rule model. Applying Equation 3.33 to the possibility distribution (Equation 3.2) induced by a gradual rule, a tuple of cases is either completely exceptional or

---

[19] See, e.g., [37] for various approaches to the discounting of expert opinions within a generalized probabilistic framework.

not exceptional at all. In fact, Equation 3.33 may also be seen as a reasonable generalization of this rather obvious definition of exceptionality. This again reveals the difference between the gradual and the certainty rule model: the former is indeed not *tolerant* toward exceptions in the sense that each violation of the rule is 'punished' by classifying the involved cases as *completely* exceptional ones. As opposed to this, exceptionality is a gradual property in the certainty rule model.

Even though a gradual or certainty rule can only be violated by *tuples* of cases and, hence, exceptionality should be considered as a property of pairs of cases, it seems intuitively clear in our example that the most unreliable information sources are those cases $\langle s, r \rangle$ with s close to integers kM ($k \in \mathbb{N}$). The closer a situation is to such a point, the more likely the case might be called exceptional. In fact, one possibility of regarding exceptionality as a property of an individual case $\langle s, r \rangle$ is to consider the likelihood or possibility of $\langle s, r \rangle$ to be exceptional with respect to a new case $\langle s_0, r_0 \rangle$. Thus, one might think of generalizing Equation 3.33 as follows:

$$\mathrm{ex}_1(\langle s, r \rangle) = \sup_{\langle s', r' \rangle \in \varphi} \mathrm{ex}(\langle s, r \rangle, \langle s', r' \rangle). \qquad (3.34)$$

Assigning a case a degree of exceptionality in the sense of Equation 3.34 can be interpreted as rating the reliability of this case. Of course, this degree of exceptionality depends on the formalization of the underlying rule. In other words, a case is exceptional not by itself but only with respect to a particular rule: changing the rule by means of a modifier also changes the degree of exceptionality of the case. For instance, the modification of a gradual rule, as proposed in Section 3.2.2, can be interpreted as adapting the rule in such a way that no exceptional cases exist whatever. Likewise, no case is exceptional with respect to the certainty rule in its weakest form, as formalized by $m_1 \equiv 0$ in Equation 3.19. In connection with the certainty rule model (Equation 3.21) for the example of Equation 3.14 we obtain

$$\mathrm{ex}_1(\langle s, r \rangle) = \begin{cases} 1 - \varepsilon & \text{if } \exists k \in \mathbb{N} : |s - kM| \leq 10 \\ 0 & \text{otherwise} \end{cases}$$

for all $\langle s, r \rangle \in \varphi$.

Let us briefly hint at two properties of Equation 3.34. Firstly, this definition of exceptionality is completely independent of any kind of *frequency*; i.e., the value $\mathrm{ex}_1(\langle s, r \rangle)$ should not be understood as a probability of $\langle s, r \rangle$ being exceptional with respect to some other case. Of course, defining exceptionality of an individual case by using an averaging operator in place of the supremum in Equation 3.34 seems intuitively appealing and would clearly make sense within, say, a probabilistic setting. Recall, for instance, the probabilistic interpretation of the certainty rule model proposed in Section 3.4. According to this interpretation, a certainty rule can be seen as a collection of (modified) gradual rules each of which is attached a certain probability. Since a case is either exceptional or not with respect to a fixed gradual rule, it is an obvious idea to derive a corresponding probability of being exceptional with respect to a certainty rule.

Secondly, Equation 3.34 is rather strict in the sense that it implies

$$\mathrm{ex}(\langle s, r \rangle, \langle s', r' \rangle) \leq \min\{\mathrm{ex}_1(\langle s, r \rangle), \mathrm{ex}_1(\langle s', r' \rangle)\} \qquad (3.35)$$

for all cases $\langle s, r \rangle$ and $\langle s', r' \rangle$. In other words, having encountered an exceptional tuple of cases, *both* cases are considered to be exceptional. This principle can obviously be weakened by concluding on the exceptionality of *at least one* of the two cases. This leads to the constraints

$$\mathrm{ex}(\langle s, r \rangle, \langle s', r' \rangle) \leq \max\{\mathrm{ex}_1(\langle s, r \rangle), \mathrm{ex}_1(\langle s', r' \rangle)\} \qquad (3.36)$$

for all $\langle s, r \rangle, \langle s', r' \rangle \in \mathcal{S}$. Indeed, Equation 3.36 will often appear more reasonable than Equation 3.35. For instance, modifying the function φ in the example of Equation 3.14 according to

$$\varphi(s) = \begin{cases} M & \text{if} \quad a \bmod M \neq 0 \\ 0 & \text{if} \quad a \bmod M = 0 \end{cases}$$

suggests calling the cases $\langle 0, 0 \rangle, \langle M, 0 \rangle, \langle 2M, 0 \rangle \ldots$ exceptional, and to consider all other cases as being (completely) normal. As opposed to this, Equation 3.35 does not only qualify a case $\langle kM, 0 \rangle$ itself as exceptional, but also all neighbored cases $\langle kM + a, M \rangle$ such that $1 \leq |a| \leq 10$.

A natural idea is to discount the information provided by a case based on its level of exceptionality. Discounting a fuzzy restriction F over a domain D within the qualitative min–max framework amounts to modifying F into $\max\{\lambda, F\}$, where λ is a discounting factor [16]. Indeed, F remains unchanged if $\lambda = 0$. As opposed to this, the modified restriction becomes trivial (and corresponds to the complete referential D) if the discounting is maximal ($\lambda = 1$). Applying this approach to the result of case based inference by identifying discounting factors with degrees of exceptionality amounts to computing

$$\pi(r|s) = \min_{1 \leq i \leq n} \max\left\{\mathrm{ex}_1(\langle s_i, r_i \rangle), m(S_{\mathcal{S}}(s_0, s_i)) \to S_{\mathcal{R}}(r, r_i)\right\}. \qquad (3.37)$$

If exceptionality is equivalent to complete exceptionality, as in the gradual rule model, Equation 3.37 comes down to removing the exceptional cases from the memory. Apart from that, the usual inference process is realized. In other words, Equation 3.37 corresponds to the gradual rule approach ($\to$ is the Rescher–Gaines implication) restricted to the normal cases. When using the certainty rule model in Equation 3.37, i.e., when modeling $\to$ by implication operators such as Equation 3.22 or Equation 3.23, the level of uncertainty of an individual prediction is increased in accordance with the degree of exceptionality of the corresponding case. The CBR hypothesis underlying the generalized approach might then be characterized as follows: 'The larger the similarity between s and s_0 and the less exceptional the situation s, the more certain we can conclude on the similarity between the associated results r and r_0.'

Interestingly enough, the modifications outlined above suggest a further way of adaptation: not that the strength of the rule is adapted to the class φ of cases, but that the influence of each case is modulated in accordance with its exceptionality relative to the (predefined) rule. In this connection, it seems also worth mentioning that assigning degrees of exceptionality to cases in such a way that Equation 3.36 is satisfied leads to an interesting problem from both a mathematical as well as a semantic point of view. In addition to observed cases, one might think of using an (a priori) expert assessment of the exceptionality of cases (which then correspond to triples $\langle s, r, e \rangle$) in order to solve this problem, all the more since the minimization of some objective function subject to the constraints (Equation 3.36) might not guarantee a unique solution.

3.6 Local Rules

The rule based approaches to CBR outlined in previous sections are *local* in the sense that the information provided by different cases is processed and combined independently. It is, however, *global* in the sense that a (modified) fuzzy rule constitutes a constraint which is assumed to be globally valid. This becomes especially apparent in connection with the gradual rule approach, where an (admissible) modifier m specifies (conditional) lower bounds for the similarity of outcomes which hold true for all (pairs of) cases. It has already been pointed out in Section 3.2 that this requirement often entails rather imprecise predictions, caused by the fact that admissible modifiers might not be very restrictive.

Instead of looking for a global rule, which is valid up to some exceptions as discussed in connection with the certainty rule model in previous sections, one might weaken the principle of a gradual rule by specifying rules which are somehow locally valid. In this section, we follow the idea, not of associating instantiations of a global rule with all observed cases (and perhaps discounting these instantiations in the sense of Section 3.5), but of adapting a fuzzy rule to each case of the memory more directly.

Let us again consider the gradual rule model. The problem that global validity might lead to (local) predictions which are unnecessarily imprecise is already certified by the example of Equation 3.14. In fact, the necessity of taking $m \equiv 0$ leads to the useless predictions $C_{m, \mathcal{M}}(s_0) = \mathbb{N}$. Loosely speaking, a CBR strategy is not applicable because the hypothesis of similar situations having similar outcomes is not globally satisfied. Still, it seems desirable to make use of the observation that the function φ in the example is piecewise linear, i.e., that the CBR hypothesis is satisfied at least *locally*. One possibility of doing this is to partition the set S of situations and to derive corresponding local models. In our example, the idea to partition S into sets of the form $\{kM, kM + 1, \ldots, kM + (M - 1)\}$ ($k \in \mathbb{N}$) suggests itself. However, since φ is generally unknown, the definition of a partition will not always be obvious, all the more if S is non-numerical.

Here, we consider a second possibility, namely, that of associating an individual (local) rule with each case of the memory. Thus, the idea is to define rules of the form 'the more similar a situation is to s, the more similar the associated outcome is to r' for each case $\langle s, r \rangle$ in the memory. The validity of such a (gradual) rule is already guaranteed by the (non-decreasing) modifier

$$m_{\langle s, r \rangle}(x) = \sup \left\{ h_{\langle s, r \rangle}(x') \mid x' \in D_S, x' \leq x \right\} \qquad (3.38)$$

for all $x \in D_S$, where

$$h_{\langle s, r \rangle}(x) = \inf_{\langle s', r' \rangle \in \varphi \, : \, S_S(s, s') = x} S_{\mathcal{R}}(r, r'). \qquad (3.39)$$

Since the infimum in Equation 3.39 is taken over a smaller set of cases, Equation 3.38 is obviously more restrictive than Equation 3.10. Based on Equation 3.38, the inference scheme (Equation 3.8) can be replaced by

$$r_0 \in \bigcap_{1 \leq i \leq n} \{r \in \mathcal{R} \mid m_{\langle s_i, r_i \rangle}(S_S(s_0, s_i)) \leq S_{\mathcal{R}}(r, r_i)\}. \qquad (3.40)$$

In our example, the maximally constraining (admissible) modifier for a case $\langle s, r \rangle - \langle s, \varphi(s) \rangle$ is simply given by

$$m_{\langle s, r \rangle}(x) = \begin{cases} x & \text{if } \quad 10 \leq s \bmod M \leq M - 9 \\ 0 & \text{otherwise.} \end{cases}$$

Based on a sufficiently large number of observations, the function φ can hence be approximated rather accurately. More precisely, the prediction (Equation 3.40) converges toward

$$\widehat{\varphi}(s_0) = \begin{cases} \{\varphi(s_0), \ldots, 20\} & \text{if } \quad 0 \leq \varphi(s_0) < 20 \\ \{\varphi(s_0)\} & \text{if } \quad 20 \leq s_0 \bmod M < M - 20 \\ \{2M - 12 - \varphi(s_0), \ldots, M + 9\} & \text{if } \quad M - 20 \leq \varphi(s_0) < M \end{cases}$$

with an increasing number of observations.

Observe that a local rule can be taken as an indication of the (prediction) quality of a case $\langle s, r \rangle$, and can hence support the design of an optimal case base. The more restrictive a rule can be made by means of a modifier $m_{\langle s, r \rangle}$, the more it will contribute to precise predictions. As in our example, good local rules will generally be provided by 'typical' cases, the outcome of which is somehow representative for similar situations. In this sense, a modifier can also be seen as an assessment of a case (cf. Section 3.5). A modifier $m_{\langle s, r \rangle} <$ id, for instance, brings the discounting of a case about, whereas a modifier $m_{\langle s, r \rangle} >$ id produces the opposite effect. Particularly, letting $m_{\langle s, r \rangle} \equiv 0$ comes down to leaving the corresponding case out of account, i.e., to remove it from the memory.

Let us mention that a (globally admissible) gradual rule can be seen as a collection of rules

$$\alpha(x) : \ S_S(s_1, s_2) = x \Rightarrow$$
$$\forall r_1 \in \varphi(s_1) \, \forall r_2 \in \varphi(s_2) : \ S_{\mathcal{R}}(r_1, r_2) \geq m(x)$$

each of which is an aggregation of more specific (local) rules associated with cases $\langle s, r \rangle \in \varphi$. More precisely, a rule $\alpha(x)$ can be seen as an approximation in the form of a disjunction

$$\alpha(x) = \bigvee_{\langle s, r \rangle \in \varphi} \alpha(\langle s, r \rangle, x) \qquad (3.41)$$

of local rules

$$\alpha(\langle s, r \rangle, x) : \ (\langle s_1, r_1 \rangle = \langle s, r \rangle) \wedge (S_S(s_1, s_2) = x) \Rightarrow \qquad (3.42)$$
$$\forall r_2 \in \varphi(s_2) : \ S_{\mathcal{R}}(r, r_2) \in [m_{\langle s, r \rangle}(x), 1].$$

Since the disjunction in Equation 3.41 is taken over all cases $\langle s, r \rangle \in \varphi$, the global rule $\alpha(x)$ depends on the similarity degree alone. Observe that Equations 3.10 and 3.38 are related through

$$\forall x \in D_S : m(x) = \inf_{\langle s, r \rangle \in \varphi} m_{\langle s, r \rangle}(x)$$

which shows that taking the disjunction of the conclusion parts in Equation 3.42 comes down to bounding similarity degrees from below and again reveals the restrictive nature of the gradual rule model.

Interestingly enough, a certainty rule can be seen as a more general fusion of local rules (Equation 3.42), taking into account that some conclusions might be less plausible (or might occur less often) than others and hence may lead to a *weighted* union of antecedents instead of a disjunction.

Let us finally mention that the idea of adapting a rule-based formalization of the CBR hypothesis to individual cases applies to certainty rules in the same way as to gradual rules. Observe that local certainty rules can be seen as a combination of the aforementioned generalizations of the gradual rule model. In fact, these rules are local and tolerant toward exceptions at the same time.

3.7 Summary

The objective of this chapter was to discuss fuzzy rules as a basic model of the inference process in CBR. It has been shown that different types of rules correspond to different interpretations and formalizations of the CBR hypothesis. In this connection, we have distinguished between two types of rules. The first type (gradual rules) assumes a kind of closeness relation between the similarity of situations and the similarity of outcomes which is not tolerant toward exceptions. Given a new situation, the observed cases which constitute the memory are taken as evidence for either allowing or completely excluding certain outcomes. A second type of rule (certainty rules) uses case based information only for deriving conlusions about the *possibility* of outcomes. They are more expressive and allow for the *partial* exclusion of results. Moreover, they can formalize situations in which the CBR hypothesis holds true 'in general', up to some exceptions to the 'similar problem–similar solution' rule.

The use of modifiers has been proposed for modulating the 'strength' of fuzzy rules. This way, it becomes possible to adapt the formal model according to the extent to which the CBR hypothesis actually holds true for the respective application. The realization of concrete (learning) methods for the determination of appropriate modifiers is an important aspect of future work. As already mentioned above, the algorithm proposed in [30] can easily be adapted to the learning of modified gradual rules from observed cases. This algorithm may also serve as a point of departure for learning modifiers of local gradual rules (cf. Section 3.6). According to the interpretation in Section 3.4, the certainty rule model is closely related to the probabilistic characterization of lower similarity bounds. This relationship may provide the basis for developing algorithms which learn certainty rule models from data.

The meaning of exceptionality of cases has been discussed in connection with the idea of discounting cases which might be seen as somewhat unreliable or misleading information sources. The discounting of cases, in conjunction with a modification of the basic inference scheme, presents a further possibility of model adaptation. This approach gives rise to learning algorithms which estimate the degree of exceptionality of cases with respect to some (fixed) underlying rule. Elaborating on these ideas is a further topic of future work.

Local rules have been introduced as a second direction of generalizing the basic model. There are different motivations for this step: in the gradual rule model, it is true that the instantiation of a (globally) admissible rule by different cases leads to valid predictions. However, inference results might be poor, since this rule will often be hardly constraining. In the certainty rule model, the multiple instantiation of the same global rule leads to difficulties in connection with exceptional (still not discounted) cases. This might cause inconsistencies and an exaggerated exclusion of (rather possible) cases. We have also pointed out a close relation between local rules and the assessment of cases. In fact, the determination of a modifier for an individual case can be seen as a rating of the typicality or prediction quality of that case. Particularly, a modifier can make a local rule completely ineffective, which amounts to removing the corresponding case from the memory. Next to the idea of exceptionality with respect to a global rule, the concept of local rules thus presents a further possibility of rating and discounting cases.

Let us finally mention that case based inference can also be formalized by means of so-called *possibility rules* [9,10], a type of rule quite different from those discussed in this chapter. In fact, gradual and certainty rules belong to the class of *implicative* fuzzy rules entailing a *constraint-based* approach: already encountered cases are looked at as evidence of (partially) ruling out other (hypothetical) cases, not similar enough to the observed ones. As opposed to this, a possibility rule is a *conjunctive* rule, and gives rise to an *example-oriented* approach: observed cases are considered as pieces of data which provide evidence for the possibility of observing similar cases. Using implicative and conjunctive rules jointly in order to improve the informational contents of (possibilistic) predictions in case based inference has been proposed in [32].

In summary, it can be said that the potential of fuzzy sets to combine the concepts of similarity and uncertainty, in conjunction with the possibility of fuzzy rules to model various kinds of inference strategies, provides the basis of a flexible tool for modeling and formalizing parts of the CBR methodology within the framework of approximate reasoning [47]. In fact, it should be possible to use the different types of models proposed in [32] and in this chapter for realizing some kind of possibilistic case based approximation of an underlying class of (potential) cases (corresponding to some relation φ) which goes beyond the simple interpolation of observations or the adaptation of a parametrized function. Elaborating on this idea and developing concrete learning and approximation algorithms are central topics of future work.

Acknowledgements

One of the authors (E. Hüllermeier) greatfully acknowledges financial support in the form of a TMR research grant funded by the European Commission.

References

1. A. Aamodt and E. Plaza. Case-based reasoning: Foundational issues, methodological variations, and system approaches. *AI Communications*, 7(1):39–59, 1994.
2. D. Aha. Case-based learning algorithms. In R. Bareiss, editor, *Proceedings of the DAPRA Workshop on Case-Based Reasoning*, pages 147–158. Morgan Kaufmann Publishers, 1991.
3. D. Aha, D. Kibler, and M.K. Albert. Instance-based learning algorithms. *Machine Learning*, 6(1):37–66, 1991.
4. D.A. Bell, J.W. Guan, and S.K. Lee. Generalized union and project operations for pooling uncertain and imprecise information. *Data & Knowledge Engineering*, 18:89–117, 1996.
5. P. Bonissone and W. Cheetman. Financial applications of fuzzy case-based reasoning to residential property valuation. In *Proceedings of the 6th IEEE International Conference on Fuzzy Systems* (FUZZ-IEEE-97), pages 37–44, Barcelona, 1997.
6. B. Bouchon-Meunier, editor. *Aggregation and Fusion of Imperfect Information*. Physica-Verlag, Heidelberg, 1998.
7. B. Bouchon-Meunier and L. Valverde. Analogy relations and inference. In *Proceedings of the 2nd IEEE International Conference on Fuzzy Systems*, pages 1140–1144, San Francisco, CA, 1993.
8. A.P. Dempster. Upper and lower probability induced by a random closed interval. *Annals of Mathematical Statistics*, 39:219–246, 1968.
9. D. Dubois, F. Esteva, P. Garcia, L. Godo, R. Lopez de Mantaras, and H. Prade. Fuzzy set modelling in case-based reasoning. *International Journal of Intelligent Systems*, 13:345–373, 1998.
10. D. Dubois, F. Esteva, P. Garcia, L. Godo, R.L. de Mantaras, and H. Prade. Fuzzy modelling of case-based reasoning and decision. In D.B. Leake and E. Plaza, editors, *Case-based Reasoning Research and Development, Proceedings* ICCBR-97, pages 599–610. Springer-Verlag, 1997.
11. D. Dubois, F. Esteva, P. Garcia, L. Godo, R.L. de Mantaras, and H. Prade. Case-based reasoning: a fuzzy approach. In A.L. Ralescu and J.G. Shanahan, editors, *Proceedings of the IJCAI-97 Workshop on Fuzzy Logic in Artificial Intelligence*, number 1566 in Lecture Notes in Artificial Intelligence, pages 79–90. Springer-Verlag, 1999.
12. D. Dubois and H. Prade. The principle of minimum specificity as a basis for evidential reasoning. In B. Bouchon and R.R. Yager, editors, *Uncertainty in Knowledge-Based Systems*, number 286 in Lecture Notes in Computer Science, pages 75–84. Springer-Verlag, Berlin, 1987.
13. D. Dubois and H. Prade. A typology of fuzzy 'if ... then ...' rules. In *Proceedings of the 3rd International Fuzzy Systems Association (IFSA) Congress*, pages 782–785, Seattle, WA, 1989.
14. D. Dubois and H. Prade. Fuzzy sets in approximate reasoning, part 1: Inference with possibility distributions. *Fuzzy Sets and Systems*, 40:143–202, 1991.
15. D. Dubois and H. Prade. Gradual inference rules in approximate reasoning. *Information Sciences*, 61(1,2):103–122, 1992.

16. D. Dubois and H. Prade. On the combination of evidence in various mathematical frameworks. In J. Flamm and T. Luisi, editors, *Reliability Data Collection and Analysis*, pages 213–241. Kluwer Academic Publishers, 1992.

17. D. Dubois and H. Prade. What are fuzzy rules and how to use them. *Fuzzy Sets and Systems*, 84:169–185, 1996.

18. D. Dubois and H. Prade. The three semantics of fuzzy sets. *Fuzzy Sets and Systems*, 90(2):141–150, 1997.

19. D. Dubois, H. Prade, and L. Ughetto. Checking the coherence and redundancy of fuzzy knowledge bases. *IEEE Transactions on Fuzzy Systems*, 5(3):398–417, 1997.

20. S. Dutta and P. Bonissone. Integrating case- and rule-based reasoning. *International Journal of Approximate Reasoning*, 8:163–203, 1993.

21. F. Esteva, P. Garcia, L. Godo, and R. Rodriguez. A modal account of similarity-based reasoning. *International Journal of Approximate Reasoning*, 16:235–260, 1997.

22. B. Faltings. Probabilistic indexing for case-based prediction. In D.B. Leake and E. Plaza, editors, *Case-based Reasoning Research and Developement, Proceedings ICCBR-97*, pages 611–622. Springer-Verlag, 1997.

23. H. Farreny and H. Prade. About flexible matching and its use in analogical reasoning. In *ECAI-82, European Conference on Artificial Intelligence*, pages 43–47, Orsay, France, July 1982.

24. J. Fodor. Contrapositive symmetry of fuzzy implications. *Fuzzy Sets and Systems*, 69(2):141–156, 1995.

25. S. French. Group consensus probability distributions: A critical survey. In J.M. Bernardo et al., editor, *Bayesian Statistics 2*, pages 183–201. North-Holland, Amsterdam, 1985.

26. J. Gebhardt and R. Kruse. Parallel combination of information sources. In D.M. Gabbay and Ph. Smets, editors, *Handbook of Defeasible Reasoning and Uncertainty Management Systems, Vol. 3*, pages 393–439. Kluwer Academic Publishers, 1998.

27. C. Genest and J.V. Zidek. Combining probability distributions: A critique and an annotated bibliography. *Statistical Science*, 1(1):114–148, 1986.

28. E. Hüllermeier. A possibilistic formalization of case-based reasoning and decision making. In *Proceedings of the 6th International Conference on Computational Intelligence*, Dortmund, Germany, May 1999.

29. E. Hüllermeier. A probabilistic approach to case-based inference. Technical Report 99-02 R, IRIT – Institut de Recherche en Informatique de Toulouse, Université Paul Sabatier, January 1999.

30. E. Hüllermeier. Similarity-based inference as constraint-based reasoning: Learning similarity hypotheses. Technical Report 64, Department of Economics, University of Paderborn, September 1999.

31. E. Hüllermeier. Toward a probabilistic formalization of case-based inference. In *Proceedings IJCAI-99*, pages 248–253, 1999.

32. E. Hüllermeier, D. Dubois, and H. Prade. Fuzzy rules in case-based reasoning. In *Proceedings RàpC, Raisonnement à partir de Cas*, pages 45–54, Paris, July 1999.

33. R. Hummel and L. Landy. Evidence as opinions of experts. In J.F. Lemmer and L.N. Kanal, editors, *Uncertainty in Artificial Intelligence 2*, pages 43–53. North-Holland, 1988.

34. M. Jaczynski and B. Trousse. Fuzzy logic for the retrieval step of a case-based reasoner. In *Proceedings of the European Workshop on Case-Based Reasoning (EWCBR-94)*, pages 313–321, 1994.

35. D. Kibler and D. Aha. Learning representative exemplars of concepts: An initial study. In *Proceedings of the Fourth International Workshop on Machine Learning*, pages 24–29, University of California–Irvine, 1987.

36. G. Lakoff. Hedges: A study in meaning criteria and the logic of fuzzy concepts. *Journal of Philosophical Logic*, 2:458–508, 1973.

37. S. Moral and J. del Sagrado. Aggregation of imprecise probabilities. In B. Bouchon-Meunier, editor, *Aggregation and Fusion of Imperfect Information*. Physica-Verlag, Heidelberg, 1998.

38. H.T. Nguyen. On random sets and belief functions. *Journal of Mathematical Analysis and Applications*, 65:531–542, 1978.

39. E. Plaza and R. Lopez de Mantaras. A case-based apprentice that learns from fuzzy examples. In Z. Ras, M. Zemankova, and M. Emrich, editors, *Methodologies for Intelligent Systems*, pages 420–427. Elsevier, 1990.

40. E. Plaza, F. Esteva, P. Garcia, L. Godo, and R. Lopez de Mantaras. A logical approach to case-based reasoning using fuzzy similarity relations. *Journal of Information Sciences*, 106:105–122, 1998.

41. H. Prade. Raisonner avec des règles d'inférence graduelle: Une approche basée sur les ensembles flous. *Revue d'Intelligence Artificielle*, 2(2):29–44, 1988.

42. V. Strassen. Meßfehler und Information. *Zeitschrift für Wahrscheinlichkeitstheorie und verwandte Gebiete*, 2:273–305, 1964.

43. L. Ughetto, D. Dubois, and H. Prade. Implicative and conjunctive fuzzy rules: A tool for reasoning from knowledge and examples. In *Proceedings AAAI-99*, Orlando, FL, 1999.

44. R.R. Yager. Case-based reasoning, fuzzy systems modelling and solution composition. In D.B. Leake and E. Plaza, editors, *Case-Based Reasoning Research and Development, Proceedings of the Second International Conference on Case-Based Reasoning, ICCBP-97*, pages 633–643, Providence, RI, 1997. Springer-Verlag.

45. L.A. Zadeh. A fuzzy-set theoretic interpretation of linguistic hedges. *Journal of Cybernetics*, 2(3):4–32, 1972.

46. L.A. Zadeh. The concept of a linguistic variable and its application to approximate reasoning, parts 1–3. *Information Science*, 8/9, 1975.

47. L.A. Zadeh. A theory of approximate reasoning. In J.E. Hayes, D. Mitchie, and L.I. Mikulich, editors, *Machine Intelligence, Vol. 9*, pages 149–194. Wiley, New York, 1979.

4. Hybrid Approaches for Integrating Neural Networks and Case Based Reasoning: From Loosely Coupled to Tightly Coupled Models

Maria Malek

Abstract. This chapter describes integration schemes for neuro-case based reasoning (neuro-CBR) systems. Three major schemes are distinguished: the neural networks can be used to implement a complete CBR system, to implement a special phase of the CBR cycle as retrieval or adaptation, and it can also be used separately with a CBR system in order to contribute to the accomplishment of a given task. We show example systems of the different schemes; we then present in detail a hybrid tightly coupled model for memory organization called ProBIS which was validated on different applications (diagnosis, control, classification).

4.1 Introduction

Research on hybrid neurosymbolic models has been considerably developed in recent years both for intelligent systems and cognitive modeling. Motivations for this research are [32]:

- Cognitive processes are not homogeneous – a wide variety of representations and mechanisms are employed.
- The development of intelligent systems for practical applications can benefit from a combination of different techniques, since no one single technique can do everything [22].

Classical neurosymbolic approach deals with integration schemes of neural networks and rule based reasoning [21]. The goal of this chapter is to study a particular neurosymbolic integration which has a case based reasoning (CBR) component. We present a brief survey on integration strategies and coupling degrees in classical neurosymbolic systems.

We then analyze the particularity of a CBR component and propose a taxonomy of neuro-CBR systems. We distinguish three principal cases:

- The neural network is used to implement a complete CBR system. This type of system is considered as a parallel implementation of CBR.
- The neural network is used to implement a special phase in a CBR system in order to optimize a certain needed criterion during the accomplishment of this phase, such as the efficiency of the retrieval or the computing of the similarity.
- The neural network and the CBR system are two separate components and contribute in a different manner to achieve a certain goal.

We then present and analyze examples of each category. We detail finally a fully integrated hybrid model for CBR memory which is a tightly coupled one. We show how the integration of a neural network for memory organization has enhanced the retrieval efficiency and simplified the learning process. We show the validation of this model on three different applications: toxic coma diagnosis, thermoplastic injection control, and detection of false alarms in the field of forest fires.

4.2   Strategies for Neurosymbolic Integration

Two main categories of strategy are distinguished in classical neurosymbolic systems [11]:

- *Unified strategies,* which aim at reaching neural and symbolic capabilities using neural networks alone [6,8,28].
- *Hybrid strategies,* which combine neural networks with symbolic models.

Unified strategies can be subdivided into two distinct trends: neuronal symbol processing and connectionist symbol processing. The term neuronal denotes a close identification with the proprieties of biological neurons.

Hybrid neurosymbolic models can be either transitional or functional:

- *Transitional models* rely on neural networks as processors but they can start from and end with symbolic structures. The objective is to translate or transform symbolic structures into neural networks before processing or extract symbolic structure from neural networks after processing. More often, the symbolic structures used are rules [5].
- *Functional models* incorporate complete symbolic and connectionist components: in addition to neural networks, they comprise both symbolic structure and their corresponding processors (like rule interpreters, parser, etc.)

A taxonomy of functional hybrid systems based on *the degree and mode of integration of the neural and symbolic components* is proposed in [11].

To simplify, we can distinguish between two main *degrees of integration*. In *loosely coupled systems,* interaction between the two components is localized: control and data can be transferred directly between the two components, or via an agent (or supervisor) and this interaction is always initiated by one of the components or by an external agent. In *tightly coupled systems,* knowledge and data are not transferred but shared by the two components via common internal structures.

Now, the *integration mode* refers to the way in which the neural and symbolic components are configured. Four integration schemes have been defined (see Fig. 4.1) [21]:

- *In chain-processing mode,* one of the components is the main processor whereas the other takes charge of pre or post-processing tasks.
- *In subprocessing mode,* one of the two modules is embedded in and subordinated to the other, which acts as the main problem solver.
- *In metaprocessing mode,* one module is the base level problem solver and the other is a metalevel processor (monitor, supervisor, etc.)

- *In coprocessing mode,* the two components are equal partners in the problem solving process, each can interact directly with the environment and can transit/receive information to/from the other.

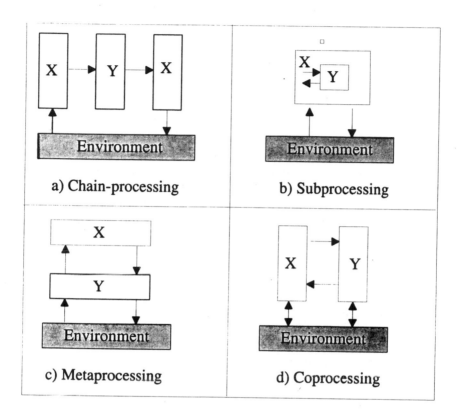

Fig. 4.1. Integration modes in neurosymbolic systems.

4.3 Neuro-CBR models

We study in this section integration strategies of neural networks and CBR. CBR is a methodology [1,12,36] to solve problems by retrieving similar cases from the memory or the case base and adapting them. The CBR is described by the CBR cycle containing the following phases:

- Retrieval phase: retrieve similar cases to the problem description.
- Reuse phase: reuse or adapt the solution to better fit the new problem.
- Revise phase: revise the solution.
- Retain phase: learn the new case.

Note that different techniques can be used for each of the phases. For example, rules can be used during the adaptation phase [14], induction or nearest neighbor technique can be used to assess the similarity measurement [35], etc.

On the other hand, neural network models are techniques based on learning and resolving algorithms to achieve given tasks (classification, approximation, prediction) [10].

This leads us to distinguish between two cases:

- The neural network (NN) technique is used by the CBR method.
- NN is considered at the same level of the case base reasoner and contributes equally to the resolution of the problem.

We define a new hierarchy for neuro-CBR integration strategies as follows (see Fig. 4.2):

- *Two strategies of functional neuro-CBR hybrid systems are possible*:
    - *Separated components*: The case based reasoner and the neural network are considered here as two different components that contribute to accomplish a given task. They can communicate. Three integration modes can be envisaged: coprocessing, metaprocessing and chain-processing.
    - *NN incorporated into the CBR cycle*: NN is used by one or many of the CBR cycle phases. This corresponds to a subprocessing integration mode.
- *One strategy of unified CBR-NN system is possible:*
    - *Connectionist implementation of a CBR system*: A neural network is used to produce exactly a CBR reasoner aiming at achieving a given task.
- *No transitional neuro-CBR hybrid configuration is possible* because such an architecture supposes that the NN is the only processor. Remember that a case based reasoner is a complete method for processing. As a consequence, using an NN to extract cases or case structure has no significance if these cases are not processed by the case based reasoner later.

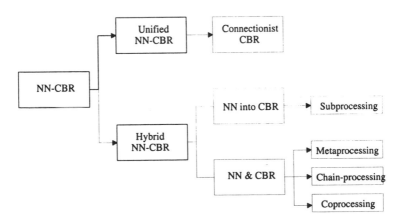

Fig. 4.2. Neuro-CBR integration strategies.

In the following sections, we will show examples of each type of neuro-CBR hybrid system.

4.3.1 Hybrid Neuro-CBR systems

4.3.1.1 Separate component

We present in this section examples of neuro-CBR systems where CBR and NN are considered as separate components.

CBR as a pre-processor:

In [13], a hybrid model for wastewater treatment, WATTS, is proposed. This model integrates several learning and reasoning techniques and methods:

- The ID3 algorithm [25] is used to extract knowledge from the data base in the form of rules that will be added to the knowledge base.
- A heuristic search method based on the A* algorithm is used to reduce the influential concentration of the water.
- A Hopfield NN model [10] (which constitutes an alternative method to the heuristic search one) is used to minimize a cost function in order also to reduce the influential concentration. Thus, the problem is considered here as an optimization problem with an energy equation whose minimal values correspond to the best solution.
- A CBR system containing a memory of old treated cases. New cases are added automatically to the case base. The retrieval method is domain dependent and based on a heuristic search method for finding the optimal method.

CBR is either integrated with the heuristic search method or with the Hopfield NN. In the neuro-CBR configuration, the CBR is viewed as *a preprocessor model which produces the most similar case and transfer it to the NN.* The solution of the found case is not adopted immediately but used to initialize the Hopfield NN. The NN can then reach (converge to) the optimal solution rapidly. In other words, the CBR helps the NNs to start processing from an initial solution which is sufficiently close to the optimal one.

It is obvious that this type of coupling is a tight one, because no shared structure exists between the CBR and the NN.

Note that the optimization process done by NN can be considered as an *adaptation strategy* to the final found solution. *From this point of view, the NN is considered to be incorporated into the CBR cycle.*

In [27], a neural network is constructed from a set of training examples. The knowledge is then extracted from the NN and discriminating attributes are discovered. This knowledge is represented explicitly by symbolic structures (diagnostic descriptors). The role of these descriptors is to guide the CBR module during the retrieval phase and to perform explications.

The NN used is a forward-propagation network composed of three layers:

- An input layer that contains neurons whose activation values are in $[0, 1]$. These values correspond to trust degrees given to each attribute.
- A hidden layer that makes the combination of attributes.
- An output layer which contains the different diagnoses.

Connections between the hidden layer and the input layer can be excitatory or inhibitory. An excitatory connection propagates the input signal reduced by its weight; an inhibitory connection makes the logical negation of the input signal. Each neuron in the hidden layer makes a fuzzy logical AND computation and each output neuron makes a fuzzy logical OR computation. The learning rule is based on the retropropagation one [30].

The NN is used here as a *preprocessor module* to the CBR. It produces knowledge that will be used later by the CBR. It is obvious that this coupling is a tight one.

Two types of knowledge are extracted from the network:

- The general knowledge of the domain represented by three types of features: triggers, primary features and supporting features. These features are used to represent prototypical cases.
- Two types of features which can be used as indexes to the case base when the general knowledge is not sufficient. These two types of indexes are positive and negative features which can be used to index atypical cases.

During the reasoning process, when a new problem is presented to the system, if the general knowledge gives more than one hypothesis of diagnosis the CBR module with the positive and negative feature is used to determine a set of candidate cases.

4.3.1.2   NN Incorporated into the CBR Cycle

Using an NN for retrieval:
In [37] a back-propagation NN is used for case retrieval. Each neuron of the output layer represents one case. When an output neuron is active it is considered as an index to find the corresponding case in the case base. A big drawback of this model is its incapacity for learning. Cases are determined at the beginning and each one is represented by a neuron.

Using an NN for adaptation:
In [4], an NN based on radial basis function (RBF) is used during the adaptation phase. It acts as a function that obtains the most representative solution from a number of cases which are the ones most similar to the current solution. In RBF NNs [7,23], the hidden layer performs a non-linear transformation from the input space to the hidden layer space. The output computes a linear combination of the hidden neurons' outputs. Units or centers in the hidden layer are associated with a Gaussian function.

Training of the network is done by presenting pairs of inputs and desired outputs (adaptation cases) vectors. Two types of neural weight adaptations are envisaged. The center closest to each particular input vector is moved toward the input vector, and the delta rule is used to adapt the weighted connections from the centers to the output neurons.

4.3.2   Unified Neuro-CBR Systems

4.3.2.1   *Connectionist implementation of a CBR system*
We present in this section a parallel implementation of CBR systems.

In [3], a connectionist implementation of CBR is proposed (see Fig. 4.3). Three types of neuron are used:

- PAV corresponds to input neurons which contain the attribute values. There is a neuron for each attribute value.
- OC corresponds to stored cases in the hidden layer of the NN.
- DAC corresponds to output neurons which contain decision features to be undertaken.

Two types of connections exist between the input and the hidden layer:

- No weighted connections (symbolized by * on the figure): this connection means that the attribute value is necessary for the determination of the case represented by the neuron.
- Weighted connections: the associated weights correspond to the degree of importance of an attribute for the determination of a case.

When a new case is introduced into the network, the activation of a case in the hidden case is computed by the weighted sum of input signals. If this activation is bigger than a given threshold, the associated decision features in the output layer will be activated.

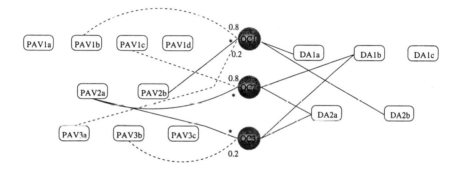

Fig. 4.3. Connectionist implementation of CBR: Becker and Jazayeri model.

In [33], a similar model is proposed to implement CBR using a three-layer network. The main difference is that the learning rule is based on retro-propagation of the gradient. In addition, new neurons that play the role of adapters are added to the hidden layer.

In [24] a connectionist implementation of a CBR system which performs a probabilistic reasoning is proposed. The NN contains three layers (see Fig. 4.4):

- The input layer contains a neuron for each attribute value.
- The hidden layer contains m groups of neurons. Each group contains l neurons and each neuron A_{ik} has n_i connections from the neurons $a_{i1}, .., a_{in_i}$ in the input layer. Weights connecting A_{ik} to neuron a_{ij} are given by

$$W(A_{ik})_j = P(A_i = a_{ij}|C = c_k). \tag{4.1}$$

$W(A_{ik})_j$ corresponds to the probability that the attribute A_{ik} takes the value a_{ij} for an observation belonging to class c_k. The activation of A_{ik} is computed by

$$S(A_{ik}) = \sum_{j=1}^{n} W(A_{ik})_j \times S(a_{ij}). \tag{4.2}$$

- The output layer contains l neurons and each one corresponds to a class. The activation of c_k is computed by

$$S(c_k) = \theta_k \times \Pi_{i=1}^{m} S(A_{ik}) \tag{4.3}$$

where $\theta_k = P(C = c_k)$ is a constant stocked in the neuron c_k.

This forward propagation allows to perform retrieval of similar cases. The activation of the hidden layer corresponds to the similarity measurement.

On the other hand, probabilities can be retro-propagated. This allows memorized cases to contribute to the adaptation process in function of their similarity to the new problem presented to the network. The retro-propagation implies updating activations in the hidden layer as follows:

$$S(A_{ik}) = \frac{S(c_k)}{S(A_{ik})}. \tag{4.4}$$

Activations of input layer neurons are updated using the following formula:

$$S(a_{ij}) = S(a_{ij}) \times \sum_{k=1}^{l} W(a_{ij})_k \times S(A_{ik}) \tag{4.5}$$

where $W(a_{ij})_k$ is the weight from A_{ik} to a_{ij}, with a value of $P(a_{ij}|c_k)$.

This modification can be interpreted as a correction of the original values of the attributes.

4.4   ProBIS: A Tightly Coupled Hybrid Model for Memory

In this section, we detail a tightly coupled hybrid model for CBR memory. The NN is incorporated into the CBR cycle and contributes to many phases (retrieval, retention or learning and memory organization). In addition neurons (or prototypes) are treated as common structures to the two components.

The origin of ProBIS was the study of memory organization in CBR systems [16,19]. In the literature, two widely used approaches are distinguished: flat memory systems and hierarchical organization of cases [12].

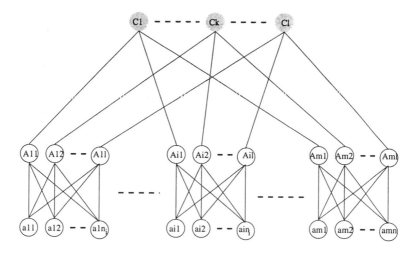

Fig. 4.4. Connectionist implementation of CBR: Myllymaki and Tirri model.

In a *flat memory system*, cases are stored sequentially in the case base. They are retrieved by applying a matching function sequentially to each case in the list. The advantage of this approach is that the whole case base is searched, so accuracy is a function of the matching function quality. In addition, adding new cases is cheap. However, the retrieval process becomes very expensive in time when the case base becomes rather large.

Hierarchical organization of cases provides a means of clustering cases so that cases that share many features are grouped together. Building such a hierarchy takes a lot of time, but it can be used very efficiently during the retrieval phase. Now, adding cases is a complex operation. Besides, it is hard to keep the structure optimal as cases are added.

ProBIS makes the retrieval process efficient and at the same time maintains a continuous learning process. The proposed case hierarchy contains two memory levels. At the lower one, cases are gathered into groups by similarity. The upper level contains prototypes, each of which represents one group of cases of the lower levels. This upper level memory is used as an indexing system during the retrieval phase. Prototypes are constructed using an incremental prototype based NN.

The hybrid memory model has two essential components, which are the symbolic component and the connectionist one (Fig. 4.5). The symbolic component contains the lower memory level and non-connectionist methods used during the CBR retrieval and learning (as the k-nearest neighbour). The connectionist component contains a prototype-based incremental NN.

The control part of the system is composed of two modules: the interaction administrator and the knowledge transfer module. The interaction administrator supervises the two components during both *learning and retrieval modes*. The knowledge transfer module controls data exchange between the two components.

In the next sections we detail the used NN and the control part.

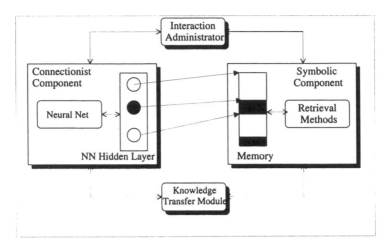

Fig. 4.5. General architecture of ProBIS.

4.4.1 Prototype-Based Incremental Neural Networks

Learning a given class of objects by accumulating representative exemplars of the class and slightly modifying existing ones is the approach used by prototype-based incremental networks. Each hidden network unit represents a *prototype*. These prototype units are grouped into their corresponding classes, and each class is identified by a category label. The first implemented model using this method commercially known as the Nestor Learning System (NLS) is described in [29].

We describe in this section the incremental prototype-based NN model used in ProBIS [2,9]. Fig. 4.6 shows the architecture of the basic model. The network is composed of three layers:

- The input layer, which contains one unit for each attribute.
- The output layer, which contains one unit for each class.
- The hidden layer, which contains one unit for each prototype and whose value is represented by the reference vector w_i^t.

This model operates either in *supervised learning mode* or in *operating mode*. The input vector at cycle t is denoted by X^t and is associated with a class unit C_x^t when the network is in supervised learning mode. Comparison between the current input and the different prototypes is achieved by means of a similarity measure m_i^t which computes, using some pre-defined measure $M(X^t, w_i^t)$, the similarity between the input vector and the individual reference vectors.

An influence region of a reference vector w_i^t having n components is defined as the locus of points in the space that register a measure of similarity equal to or greater than a given threshold Θ. In *learning mode*, the network learns to associate a training example to its correct class. Let U^t be the set of prototype units having the current input X^t within their influence regions:

- If U^t is empty, then a new prototype is created (we call this *assimilation*).

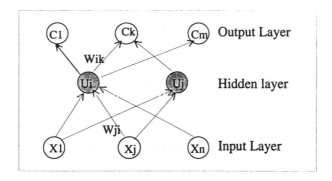

Fig. 4.6. General architecture of a prototype-based network.

- Otherwise a winner-take-all competition strategy selects the winning prototype U_s which registers the highest measure of similarity:

  1. If the wining prototype belongs to the same category then the network fine-tunes itself to make the winning prototype even more similar to the training input (we call this *accommodation*). This is achieved by applying the Grossberg learning law to this prototype [10].
  2. Otherwise, the influence region of the activated unit is decreased in order to exclude the wrong classified example (we call this *differentiation*). This example is then reintroduced to the network.

4.5 The Control Module

Memory Organization: The idea is to construct a simple indexing system that contains two levels of memory:

1. Memory that contains *prototypical cases*.
2. Memory that contains *instances* or real cases.

The *prototype* memory is used during retrieval phase as an indexing system in order to decrease retrieval time.

The first memory level is composed of the hidden layer of the incremental prototype-based network described in the previous section. The second memory level is a simple flat memory in which cases are organized into zones of similar cases. These two levels are linked together: with each prototype unit is associated a low memory zone which contains all instances belonging to this prototype. This makes the model a very tightly coupled one.

In addition, a memory zone is reserved for *atypical* cases which belong to an uncertain region[1] as well as for cases that are not classified elsewhere (Fig. 4.5).

---

[1] An uncertain region is an intersection of many prototypes which not belong to the same class.

4.5.1   The Interaction Administrator

The interaction administrator controls the learning process and the retrieval process [18].

4.5.1.1   Learning Process
Initially, the network contains no prototypes and the case base contains one zone: the *atypical zone*. Let us suppose that one wants to construct the prototype memory given a training set S. Instances of S are initially placed in the atypical zone. *No boundary* instances[2] are learned by the network, and *boundary* instances are kept in the atypical zone. In fact, the network can forget many previously learned instances after each epoch. These *lost* instances are then retrieved from their memory zones and are replaced in the atypical zone. The learning procedure is re-executed until stabilization of the atypical zone or a maximum number of times has been attained.

Once a case *i* is presented to the NN, the following supervised learning procedure is applied:

- If no prototype unit is activated then
  - Create a new prototype unit (*assimilation*)
  - Associate to this prototype a new memory zone
  - Add this case to this memory zone
- If **i** belongs to an uncertain region then (this is a boundary case)
  - Add **i** into the atypical memory zone.
- If **i** belongs to the activated prototype then
  - fine-tune this prototype (*accommodation*).
  - add **i** to the associated memory zone.
- if **i** does not belong to the activated prototype
  - Decrease the influence region of the activated unit to exclude **i** (*differentiation*).
  - Relearn **i** to the network .

4.5.1.2   Retrieval Process
Let us suppose that a new problem is presented to the system. The interaction administrator proceeds as follow:

1. First it searches a case in the atypical memory which is similar *enough* to the current problem (this is achieved by using a threshold). If such a case exists then it is retrieved.
2. If such a case does not exist then the new problem is presented to the network and the following procedure is executed:
   - If only one class unit is activated then
     - Retrieve the most activated prototype.
   - If many class units are activated
     - Determine the memory zones associated with the activated prototypes.
     - Retrieve the k-most similar cases from these memory zones.
   - If no prototype is activated
     - Retrieve the k-most similar case from the *atypical* memory zone.

---

[2] An instance which does not belong to an uncertain region.

4.5.2 The Knowledge Transfer Module

The knowledge transfer module controls data exchange between the two components. The knowledge transfer can be done from the symbolic component to the connectionist one or vice versa. During the learning process, prototypes are modified by accommodation, differentiation or assimilation. Consequently, many old atypical cases could become typical and vice versa. In addition, some prototypes can be reduced to approximately a single point in the input space.

Cases which are in the atypical zone and which are no longer atypical are transferred to the connectionist component during the learning process. On the other hand, prototype units whose influence radius is less than a given threshold are considered as single cases and thus are removed from the network and added to the atypical zone.

Thus, the role of the knowledge transfer module is to maintain prototypical cases in the connectionist module and boundary and particular cases in the atypical memory zone.

The utility problem: Before training the system with the new case, the utility of the new case must be studied [31]. If the case does not contribute to increase the knowledge of the system, it is not useful to add it to the memory. The following strategy is adopted:

- If the new case is very close to the prototype center (according to a given threshold), the case is not memorized because it is well represented by the prototype in the memory of the system.
- Otherwise, it is necessary to memorize the case. The prototype is modified to better suit this new case (by accommodation).

4.6 Validation of the hybrid approach

We present in this section three real applications used to validate ProBIS.

4.6.1 Psychotrope-Induced Comas

When a comatose patient is admitted as an emergency, the clinician makes an early tentative diagnosis by collecting clinical and biological parameters. The diagnosis may be later confirmed or rejected by toxicological analysis. Thus, for the initial therapeutic action to be as adequate as possible, there is a need for an accurate assessment of the toxic cause, without waiting for the toxicological analysis.

The case base contains 505 pre-analyzed patient cases [16]. Each one is described by:

- The problem description: there are 13 parameters selected by the physicians which are classified into three main groups – general symptoms, neurological symptoms and cardiological symptoms.
- The diagnosis: the poison or the composition of poisons that were injested by the patient. There are 28 toxic coma causes in the case base that represent a combination of seven possible poisons.

We construct from the initial case base seven case bases with each one treating a given poison. Each case can belong to one of two possible classes. The positive class indicates that the poison exists whereas the negative one indicates its absence from the combination.

Seven sub-systems based on the ProBIS model have been constructed. Each one is trained to detect one poison. We show in Table 4.1 the results obtained for alcohol:[3]

Table 4.1. Results obtained for alcohol: NbP is the number of prototypes, NbE is the epoch number, App is the learning accuracy, Test is the generalization accuracy, and NbN is the number of nodes in the decision trees

	ProBIS				K-PPV		C4.5		
k	NbP	NbE	App%	Test%	App%	Test%	NbN	App%	Test%
1	107.4	21	98.07%	70.71%	100%	65.52%	131.8	92.64%	64.2%
3	94.4	18.2	89.63%	68.94%	82.2%	66.56%	70	88.08%	65.4%

ProBIS is compared to C4.5 [26] and to the k-nearest neighbor algorithm. For each poison, five tests have been carried out, and for each one 70% of cases were randomly selected for training. The generalization test is then performed on the rest of the case base.

The first line of each table contains results for $k = 1$ for the k-NN and ProBIS. It also contains results of the initial decision tree used without pruning. The second line of each table contains results for $k = 3$ for the k-NN and ProBIS. It also contains results of the pruned decision tree.

k allows to determine the classification precision. When k is increased, the precision is decreased because more similar cases are tolerated to be taken into consideration. Pruning the decision tree also has the same effect of decreasing the precision. This explains why the training accuracies are better in general in the first lines of tables. However, the generalization accuracies become better in general in the second lines.

4.6.2 Plastic Molding Injection Process

The main way to produce plastic parts is the injection molding process. It consists of using an injection molding machine (IMM) which transforms granules of polymer into product ready for use.

During the fabrication of molded parts, an operator has to monitor the IMM and checks if the part *quality is correct*. Fluctuations in the process (modification of the raw material, i.e. polymer used, increase in ambient temperature or humidity, etc.) affect the quality of the molded parts. In the case of bad quality, *the operator has to change the setting parameters of the IMM in order to re-obtain good quality parts*. Finding the new setting parameters of the machine is not trivial since we lack a total understanding of the process. The operation depends heavily on operator expertise.

---

[3] 137 patient cases contain alcohol in the absorbed combination.

Part quality is evaluated according to different criteria (or defects), such as flashes, gloss, shrinkage, and burns.

The goal is to develop an operator support system which is able to help and to guide the operator in decision making during *control of the process*. The main objective is to optimize the injection process in order to decrease defects as much as possible (increase the quality) [20,34].

Creating a new case for each produced part is time consuming and leads to creation of a great number of cases as long as parts are injected. Thus, one solution is to build a *new case each time we modify the quality* (appearance of a new defect or modification of an existing one, etc.). This helps to reduce the number of cases to only those that are useful and informative. Consequently, a case can be related to a given part or to a set of parts having the same defects and the same parameters. A case representing a set of parts is characterized by the set of average values of the different parameters. A case (we will call it *the general case*) contains a problem component and a solution component [12]. The set of descriptors of the problem component are:

1. A set of defects which allows to define the quality of a given part. Each defect is described by a value between 0 and 3 indicating the degree to which the part is defective (e.g. for flashes the value 0 means that there is no flash, while 3 means that there are many flashes). A function of quality should be defined on the set of defects. We classify the different possible defects (we have identified 16) into three categories: aspect defects (e.g. bulls, flashes and burn, dimensional defects (e.g. shrinkage) and mechanical defects (e.g. weld lines).

2. A set of features describing the problem. Now, we consider only *injection parameters*. Environmental and mold parameters (like the surface of the mold and the environmental temperature) are supposed to have constant values during the same production phase.[4]

The set of descriptors of the solution component are as follows:

1. The considered action is described by the set of modification of some injection parameters which was undertaken by the operator in order to enhance the quality. This modification can be done on one (or many) of the injection parameters. This action can have two sources, which are the operator's personal experience and his or her general knowledge concerning the domain.

2. The effect of the application of an action is memorized into the case to indicate how much the quality is enhanced. This effect will be presented as a vector, each element of this vector corresponding to the effect on one defect.

To simplify our task, we divide the main problem into many sub-problems, each treating one defect for a given production (a production is characterized by a given mold and a given material). This is justified by the fact that each defect is the result of a certain setting of a subset of injection parameters. The whole system is composed of a number of *specialized case memories*, each one treating one defect by using its own retrieval and learning processes.

---

[4] Injection parameters are parameters related to the injection cycle such as the injection temperature and injection speed.

We call *general memory* the memory containing the set of all cases, each case containing the whole set of parameters shown in the case representation. However, cases of each *specialized case memory* contain only a subset of the whole set of parameters. This subset is composed of the necessary parameters for the diagnosis of the related defect.

ProBIS is used to construct *specialized memory*. Fig. 4.7 shows the system cycle. When a new problem is introduced into the system (a problem is characterized by a set of defects and a complete set of injection parameters), the *problem decomposition process* constructs 16 different problems for each specialized memory. The plausible parameters of each problem are determined. For each defect we obtain a list of the k-similar cases. The *re-composition and adaptation process* proposes a new *general case* which is added to the general memory and decomposed into 16 specialized cases. Each of them is trained to the corresponding specialized memory.

4.6.2.1   Experimental studies

We present in this section the case and memory structures corresponding to the defect: flashes. The material used is *granulated polymer* and we have chosen an experimental one. The flash values can range from 0 to 3 according to the level of flashes (0 means there are no flashes, and 3 means there are many flashes). The subset of parameters chosen as plausible parameters is shown in Table 4.2. We then applied the mutual information theory to a set of 255 experimental cases containing different flash levels. The most discriminate parameter was the *General-injection-speed*, the second one was *Temperature-zone-2* and the third one was *Melt-cushion*. This subset of parameters has been taken into consideration for the following test.

Table 4.2. Subset of plausible injection parameters for the diagnosis of flashes: the expert point of view

Parameter	Value range
Temperature-zone-1	[0,300] deg. C
Temperature-zone-2	[0,300] deg. C
General-injection-speed	[0,99] mm/s
Switch-over-point-hydraulic-pressure	[0,200] bar

Now, to construct the specialized memory for the defect *Flashes* we pick up randomly 70% of cases from the initial complete set (255 cases) to build a *training set*. The training set is initially stocked into the atypical zone. The knowledge transfer process has the charge to transfer knowledge from the atypical zone to the NN. After each training epoch,[5] the forgotten cases are extracted and put in the atypical zones. After four training epochs, only one case still stocked in the atypical zone and the prototypes are stabilized. We obtain seven prototypes (thus seven memory zones). Table 4.3 shows the distribution of the cases in the different zones and the flash levels associated with the different prototypes.

---

[5] The training epoch corresponds to one passage of the atypical zone into the NN for training.

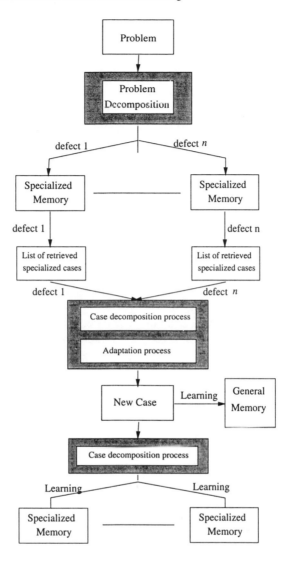

Fig. 4.7. The system cycle.

This means that from the initial training set (178 cases), only one case is considered as atypical; the others are regrouped into zone according to the similarity measurement induced by ProBIS. The size of the first level of memory is relatively small (seven prototypes) in comparison with the whole case size (178 cases). This accelerates the retrieval processes because the K-NN algorithm is only applied to certain memory zones (those which are associated with the activated prototypes units). The other subset (30% of cases) has been used to test the capacity of generalization of ProBIS.[6] The results obtained are 100%.

---

[6] The ration of cases which belong to the prototypes associated with the right flash levels.

Table 4.3. The distribution of cases in the different zones and flash levels associated with the different prototypes

Flash levels	Prototypes	Case numbers
0	1	15
	2	18
1	1	48
	2	15
2	1	21
	2	30
3	1	30

4.6.3   Alarm Reduction in the Field of Forest Fire

The AFFIRM project[7] had as an objective the development and demonstration of a system for early and reliable wild fire detection. The system consists of a network of autonomous terminals disseminated in the forest area and linked to an operations center through a satellite communications link. The terminals contain video cameras and image acquisition and processing equipment to detect the smoke plumes associated with starting fires as soon as the smoke is in the field of view of the camera. Early detection of the smoke plumes associated with starting fires allows taking fire-fighting action when the fire is still small in size [15]. Satellite communications are used to minimize the need for infrastructure in the terminal locations. In the operation center a ProBIS is used as an incremental classifier in order to filter out false alarms.

In case a smoke cloud is detected by the terminal, it sends the corresponding alarm to the operations center, where it is processed in order to filter out false alarms. Alarms contain parameters derived from the fire detection algorithm that, together with the meteorological data sent by the terminals and the data obtained from a geographical information system (GIS), help the classifier subsystem in the decision process. A *fire-alarm case* is composed of a *problem description part and a solution part* [17]:

- *The problem description part* contains a set of pertinent parameters discriminating false alarms from real fires. We can distinguish four types of parameters:
    - Environmental parameters (general, land, visibility).
    - Vegetation parameters like the vegetation kind and appearance.
    - Measurable parameters as the meteorological ones (humidity, wind speed, temperature, wind direction).
    - Detection parameters such as smoke size, color and shape.
- *The solution part* which determines the kind or class of the fire (forest or false alarm).

To detect the two classes (false alarms and real fires) we use ProBIS for constructing representative prototypes for each class. Each prototype represents a set of similar examples.

---

[7] AFFIRM IS A DGXII European project.

The similarity measurement we use is based on computing the Euclidean distance between two examples. To refine this measurement, the different parameters are weighted according to their importance of discrimination between the two classes.

When an alarm is received by the classifier component from the detection algorithm, an example is constructed as follows:

- Environmental parameters (general parameters and vegetation features) are entered (actually by the watcher).
- Meteorological parameters are requested from terminals (via a communication protocol) to complete the example.
- Some optional parameters about the detection can be taken into account in the example.

Once the case is constructed, the prototype(s) containing this example are activated and the probability of the appurtenance to each class (false alarm or real fire) is computed. This information is made available to the user.

4.6.3.1 Training Campaign, 11 – 15 September 1998, Tower of Courmettes

The aim of this short campaign is to collect cases in order to test the capacity of the classifier to detect false alarms . One camera has been installed and oriented to the region where a maximum number of garden fires is expected. A meteorological station was installed. One PC was installed and connected to the camera and the meteorological station. The software used during this campaign consisted of the meteorological application, the detection application, the terminal and system controllers, and ProBIS as a classifier.

The fact that the system was installed for only five days and that the probability of real fires was not significant, we decided to train the system to distinguish between two classes: garden fires and false alarms. Fifty-seven examples were collected during this campaign: 28 corresponded to garden fire examples and 29 to false alarms.

To evaluate ProBIS classification capacity we carried out five different tests. For each test we proceeded as follows: 80% of examples (45 examples) were picked at random from the whole set of examples. This subset is called training set. This set was used to train the system and to construct the prototypes. The remaining examples (20%) were used to evaluate the capacity of the system to classify new (unseen) examples.

After the training, we checked the number of prototypes constructed by the system, the number of examples contained in each prototypes and the stabilization epoch. We then tested the training and generalization capacities. Table 4.4 gives an idea of how much the classifier enhanced the original detection algorithm.

Table 4.4. Classification performances: means of 5 tests

Mean	Learning ratio	Generalization ratio	Prototypes Nbr	Stabilization
	99.1%	86.65%	15.6	5.6

4.7   Conclusion

We have shown in this chapter different schemes for neuro-CBR integration. We have
described a taxonomy for a neuro-CBR system based on the role of the NN besides
a CBR system. An NN can be used to implement completely a CBR system, or a
specific phase, and it can be considered also as a separate module that contributes to
the CBR in the task resolution.

We have analyzed different systems and we have detailed a tightly coupled hybrid
memory model which was used and validated in many applications such as medical
and industrial domains.

Until now, the term neuro-symbolic has referred naturally to the integration between NN and rule based systems. That these two approaches are complimentary is
more than obvious. We show, however, that NNs can be used in many phases in order to enhance the efficiency of retrieval, to accomplish adaptation or to offer new
methods for learning new cases.

The use of prototype-based NNs in ProBIS has led to a complete memory model
with a dynamic indexing system able to auto-adapt itself according to new cases. Pro-
BIS has been the kernel of many CBR systems in the domain of diagnosis, classification and control.

References

1. A. Aamodt and E. Plaza. Case-based reasoning: Foundational issues, methodological variations, and system approaches. *AICOM*, 7(1):39–59, March 1994.
2. A. Azcarraza and A. Giacometti. A prototype-based incremental network model
   for classification task. In *Fourth International Conference on Neural Networks
   and their Applications*, Nimes, France, 1991.
3. L. Becker and K. Jazayeri. A connectionist approach to case-based reasoning. In
   Proceedings of the DARPA Case-Based Reasoning Workshop, Pensacola beach,
   FL, Morgan Kaufmann, San Mateo, CA, 1989.
4. J. Corchado, B. Lees, C. Fyfe, N. Rees, and J. Aiken. Neuro-adaptation for a
   case-based reasoning system. *Computing and Information Systems*, 5(1):15–20,
   1998.
5. P. Domingos. Instance-based and rule-based learning. *Machine Learning*, 70:
   119–165, 1994.
6. G. Edelman. *Bright Air, Brilliant Fire. On the Matter of the Mind.* Basic Books,
   New York, 1992.
7. B. Fritzke. Growing cell structure: a self organizing network for unsupervised
   and supervised learning. *Neural Networks*, 7(9):1441–1460, 1994.
8. S.I. Gallant. *Neural Network Learning and Expert Systems.* Bradford/MIT, Cambridge, MA, 1993.
9. A. Giacometti. *Modèles Hybrides de l'Expertise.* PhD thesis, Telecom, Paris,
   1992.
10. R. Hecht-Nielsen. *Neurocomputing.* Addison-Wesley, Reading, MA, 1990.
11. M. Hilario. An overview of strategies for neurosymbolic integration. In *Connec-
    tionist Symbolic Integration*, chapter 1. Lawrence Erlbaum, Hillsdale, NJ, 1997.

12. J. Kolodner. *Case-Based Reasoning*. Morgan Kaufmann, San Mateo, CA, 1993.

13. S. Krovvidy and W.G. Wee. *Hybrid Architecture for Intelligent System*, chapter 17, pages 357–377. CRC Press, Boca Raton, FL, 1992.

14. D.B. Leake, A. Kinley, and D. Wilson. Acquiring case adaptation knowledge: A hybrid approach. In *Fourteenth National Conference on Artificial Intelligence*, Providence, RI, 1997.

15. X. Lobao, J. Sempere, J.L. Wybo, M. Malek, K. Schutte, E. den Breejen, and L.Torres. Affirm: A system for autonomous early and reliable forest fire detection. In *International Conference on Forest Fire Research*, Portugal, November 1998.

16. M. Malek. *Un modèle hybride de mémoire pour le raisonnement à partir de cas*. PhD thesis, Université Joseph Fourier, 1996.

17. M. Malek. Un classificateur incrémental á base de prototypes pour la détection des fausses alarmes dans le domaine des feux de forêts. In *Septiémes journée de la Société Francophone de classification*, INRIA, Nancy, September 1999.

18. M. Malek. Une approche d'apprentissage multi-stratégique intégrant induction et analogie pour l'organisation de la mémoire. In *Actes de RáPC'99: Raisonnement á Partir de Cas*, Palaiseau, June 1999.

19. M. Malek and B. Amy. A preprocessing model for integrating case-based reasoning and prototype-based neural network. In *Connectionist Symbolic Integration*, chapter 8. Lawrence Erlbaum, Hillsdale, NJ, 1997.

20. M. Malek, M.Ph. Toitgans, J.L. Wybo, and M. Vincent. An operator support system based on case-based reasoning for the injection moulding process. In *Advances in Case-Based Reasoning: (EWCBR-98), 1998, Lecture Notes in Artificial Intelligence (1488)*, Springer, pages 402–413, September 1998.

21. K. McGarry, S. Wermter, and J. MacIntyre. Hybrid neural systems: From simple coupling to fully integrated neural networks. *Neural Computing Surveys*, (2).62–93, 1999.

22. L. Medsker. *Hybrid Neural Networks and Experts Systems*. Kluwer, Boston, MA, 1994.

23. J. Moody and C.J. Darken. Fast learning in networks of locally-tuned processing units. *Neural Comutation*, 1:281–294, 1989.

24. P. Myllymaki and H. Tirri. Massively parallel case-based reasoning with probabilistic similarity metrics. In *First European Workshop on CBR*, Berlin, November 1993.

25. J.R. Quinlan. Induction of decision trees. *Machine Learning*, (1):81–106, 1986.

26. J.R. Quinlan. *C4.5: Programs for Machine Learning*. Morgan Kaufmann, San Mateo, CA, 1992.

27. E. Reategui, J.A. Campbell, and S. Borghetti. Using a neural network to learn general knowledge in a case-based system. In M.Veloso and A. Aamodt, editors, *Case-Based Reasoning: Research and Development*, number 1010, pages 528–537. Springer, Berlin, 1995.

28. G.N. Reeke and G.M. Edelman. Real brains and artificial intelligence. In *The Artificial Intellgence Debate*. S. Graubard, editor, 1988.

29. D.L. Reilly, L.N. Cooper, and C. Elbaum. A neural model for category learning. *Biological Cybernetics*, (45):35–41, 1982.

30. D.E. Rumelhart, G.E. Hinton, and J.L. McCelelland. Learning internal representation by error propagation. *Parallel Distributed Processing: explorations in the microstructures of cognition*, 1:318–362, 1986.

31. B. Smyth and M.T. Keane. Remembering to forget: A competence-preserving case deletion policy for case-based reasoning systems. In *14th International Joint Conference on Artificial Intelligence (IJCAI)*, Montreal, volume 1, pages 377–382, August 1995.

32. R. Sun and F. Alexandre. *Connectionist–Symbolic Integration: From Unified to Hybrid Approaches*. Lawrence Erlbaum, Hillsdale, NJ, 1997.

33. P. Thrift. A neural network model for case-based reasoning. In *Proceedings of the DARPA Case-Based Reasoning Workshop*, Pensacola beach, FL, Morgan Kaufmann, San Mateo, CA, May 1989.

34. M.Ph. Toitgans, M. Malek, J.L. Wybo, and M. Vincent. Control of the injection molding process. In *15th Annual Congress of the Polymer Processing Society*, Hertogenbosch, Netherlands, 1–4 June 1998.

35. I. Watson. *Applying Case-Based Reasoning: Techniques for Enterprise Systems*. Morgan Kaufmann, San Mateo, CA, 1997.

36. I. Watson. CBR is a methodology not a technology. In *Research and Development in Expert Systems*. Springer, Berlin, 1998.

37. Baogang Yao and Yongbao He. A hybrid system for case-based reasoning. In *World Congress on Neural Networks*, San Diego, CA, July 1994.

5. Towards Integration of Memory Based Learning and Neural Networks

Chung-Kwan Shin and Sang Chan Park

Abstract. We propose a hybrid prediction system of neural network (NN) and memory based learning (MBR). NN and MBR are frequently applied to data mining with various objectives. NN and MBR can be directly applied to classification and regression without additional transformation mechanisms. They also have strength in learning the dynamic behavior of the system over a period of time. In our hybrid system of NN and MBR, the feature weight set which is calculated from the trained NN plays the core role in connecting both learning strategies and the explanation on prediction can be given by obtaining and presenting the most similar examples from the case base. Experimental results show that the hybrid system has a high potential in solving data mining problems.

5.1 Introduction

Artificial neural networks (ANNs) have been considered as the most powerful and universal predictor of all. It has proved highly effective in resolving complex problems. However, neural networks (NNs) are not so commonly used in real data mining problems as other learning strategies such as the decision tree technique. This is partly due to its shortcoming of being a 'black box', meaning that the NN provides end users with little comprehensible knowledge about how it arrived at a given result [1]. Actually, the knowledge obtained in the learning process is embedded in the form of connection weights. This is a significant weakness in its application to the data mining process, which requires comprehensible and persuasive information for making critical decisions. To address this problem considerable efforts have been made in supplementing ANNs with the requisite capability of explanation. Researchers mainly suggest various algorithms that are able to extract symbolic rules from trained NNs [1–5].

We approach the comprehensible knowledge problem of NNs in a memory aid perspective. In the data mining community there has been growing interest in learning techniques using cases or instances directly, such as instance based learning or memory based learning. In this framework, similar case (or instance) retrieval plays an important role, and the k-nearest neighbor (k-NN) method or its variants are widely used as the retrieval mechanism.

However, the most important assumption of k-NN is that all of the features presented are equally important, which is not true in most data mining problems. This handicaps k-NN by allowing redundant or irrelevant features to influence the prediction. Thus, k-NN may perform poorly when such irrelevant features are present. Many variants of k-NN have been proposed that assign higher weights to the (presumably) more relevant features for case retrieval. Though many feature-weighted variants of

k-NN have been reported to improve its retrieval accuracy on some tasks [6–9], none is used in conjunction with NN learning in any form.

Our hybrid approach begins with an analogy to the human information processing system. Since its appearance, the NN has been well known for its analogy to the human neural system. After training, the NN keeps its knowledge in the connection weights among the neurons. Confronted with a new instance, the NN calculates the prediction value based on the connection weights. The NN is expected to contain the intrinsic nature of the training dataset completely, and once the network is trained properly the training dataset itself is no longer utilized. However, the thinking process of the human brain is apparently aided by the memory (the training dataset in the machine learning case) as well as the connection weights between neurons. Although the nature of the human memory process is not fully explicated yet, cognitive scientists recognize that the human memory is one of the most important components in human information processing [10].

In data mining 'memory' is realized in the form of a database, which can store, query, and retrieve large amounts of data in a short time. Now the database is the fundamental information resource in corporate information systems. It means that, with proper case retrieval methods, we can easily benefit from the abundant database.

Our hybrid approach has synergetic advantages other than its quite interesting biological analogy. It can give example based explanations together with prediction values of the NN. Though previous examples may not provide enough knowledge as other symbolic learning techniques, providing an example is an essential prerequisite in explaining the prediction.

Our hybrid system is designed to take full advantage of the vast amount of memory. It is also able to deal with other problems of practical data mining. One of the typical problems is that the behavior of the target system may change in time. This dynamic behavior is frequently observed in many application areas including manufacturing, financing and marketing. In the instance of semiconductor manufacturing [11], the manufacturing process is constantly altered and calibrated by engineers to achieve a higher manufacturing yield quickly. The knowledge extracted from data of the previous month may not correctly predict the present state of the manufacturing system. In such dynamic situations, the on-line learning property is crucial. An on-line learning system can update its knowledge with the data that is additionally acquired in real time, once it has built the knowledge base from the initial training data. The on-line learning property can be simply realized in the hybrid system of the NN and memory based learning.

The chapter is organized as follows. In Section 5.2, we review memory based reasoning (MBR) and NN learning. We focus on the feature weighting methods, which utilize trained NNs. We then present the hybrid strategy of our system in the data mining setting. The methods of extracting feature weight from NNs are discussed in Section 5.2.1, and MBR with the feature weight set is reviewed in Section 5.2.2. The overall structure of the hybrid system is then presented in Section 5.2.3. In Section 5.3, illustrative experimental results are presented. We use datasets from the UCI machine learning archive for experiments [12]. We conclude the chapter by briefly discussing limitations of the study and future research directions.

5.2 Hybrid System of Neural Networks and Memory Based Learning

5.2.1 Feature Weighting Algorithms Using a Trained Neural Network

The brief procedure of learning and prediction is as follows. First, the NN is trained completely with the given dataset. With the trained NN and the training data, we calculate the feature weight set according to the methods presented in this section. Then, when a new query comes in, we can point out k-NNs in the training data based on the feature weight sets. The prediction value of the NN may also be utilized in conjunction with the neighborhood information. This provides extended information for the query with most similar cases in the database.

In surveying the literature on NN pruning, we recognize that pruning mechanisms might be adopted as methods of feature weighting as well as feature selection. Network pruning is a practical method to minimize the size of the network while maintaining good performance. Detailed discussions on pruning and feature selection methods using NNs are found in [13–15].

Based on the pilot experimental results, we set up a framework for classifying feature weighting methods along two dimensions: information source and measure. According to this framework, we derived the four feature weighting methods: sensitivity, activity, saliency, and relevance. We describe these methods in detail below.

The information source dimension is composed of signal perspective and structural perspective. With the signal perspective, we intend to seek to what degree the input feature contributes to the difference of the output pattern of the NN. In this perspective, a trained NN is viewed as a signal processing system which resembles the given data mining problem.

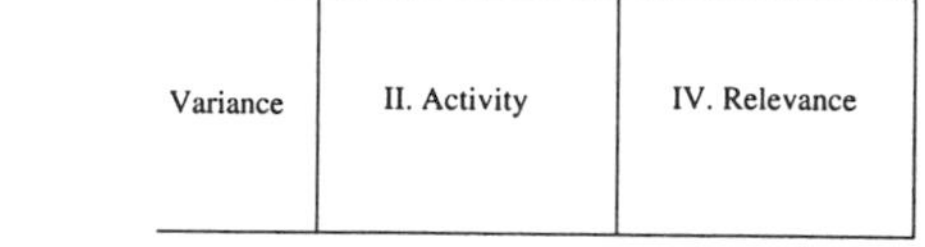

		Information Source	
		Signal	Structure
Measure	Intensity	I. Sensitivity	III. Saliency
	Variance	II. Activity	IV. Relevance

Fig. 5.1. Framework of extracting feature weight from neural networks.

We evaluate the importance of an input feature by refeeding the training data onto the trained network. Sensitivity and activity methods fall into the signal perspective. With the structural source, we examine the significance of network elements such as connection weights and threshold value of nodes. For example, input nodes with large connecting weights might be considered as important features. Research which discovers something useful in the structure of the weight set was originally carried out with the purpose of deleting less useful weights, that is, network pruning. On the other side, some tried to construct the *modus operandi* as sets of symbolic rules. Most of this research deals with the structure of the trained NN as the major information source. A well-organized summary of this approach is provided in [5]. Of our four methods, saliency and relevance fall into the structural perspective.

The measure dimension is about what to measure in the information source. For example, for a given signal source, we may examine the amplitude of output patterns of the node or, on the other hand, we may examine the variance of output patterns. If one node generates a high amplitude output signal, it is considered as an important node. However, if the node always produces high and equal signals for all the training data, the importance of the node should be regarded as low, though its absolute value of weight is high. As to the structural analysis, a node which has connection weights of various levels can have more significant importance to the output than a node which passes equally high weights to the next layer. Thus, both intensity and variance must be included in assessing the feature weights for a given source. Figure 5.1 shows the dimensions of our framework and locates the four feature weighting methods respectively.

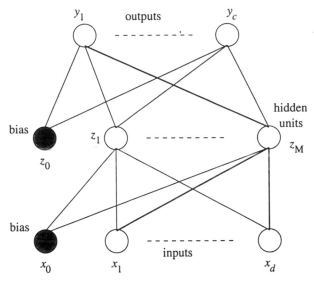

Fig. 5.2. A fully connected feed-forward network with one hidden layer.

Basically, we intend to obtain a vector of feature weights $\{w_1, w_2, \ldots, w_n\}$ (where n is the number of input features) from trained NNs. Let us consider a fully connected network with a single hidden layer depicted in Fig. 5.2. In this network there are d inputs ($x_i, i = 1, \ldots, d$), M hidden units ($z_j, j = 1, \ldots, m$) and c output units ($y_k, k = 1, \ldots, c$). For simplicity of discussion, we deal with the problem with one output variable. The input of the jth-hidden unit, a_j, is obtained by first forming a weighted linear combination of the d input values, and then adding a bias. The input of the kth output unit, b_k, is obtained in the same manner. They are given as

$$a_j = \sum_{i=0}^{d} w_{ji}^{(1)} x_i, \tag{5.1}$$

$$b_k = \sum_{j=0}^{m} w_j^{(2)} z_j. \tag{5.2}$$

Here $w_{ji}^{(1)}$ denotes a connecting weight from x_i to z_j, and $w_{kj}^{(2)}$ is also the connecting weight between z_j and y_k. The bias terms of hidden and output units are treated by the inclusion of extra variables $x_0 = 1$ and $z_0 = 1$. The activation of hidden unit j and output unit k is then obtained by transforming the linear sum in (5.1) and (5.2) using an activation function. The typical activation function is the sigmoid function $g(a) = 1/(1 + e^{-a})$. Here we obtain an explicit expression for the output function in Fig. 5.2 as

$$y = g\left(\sum_{j=0}^{M} w_j^{(2)} g\left(\sum_{i=0}^{d} w_{ji}^{(1)} x_i\right)\right). \tag{5.3}$$

See [16] for further discussion on training methods for the feed-forward NN. We now move on to detailed algorithms for calculating each feature weight from a trained NN. Following is the calculation method of each feature weighting method. The feature weight vector $\{w_1, w_2, \ldots, w_n\}$ may be normalized without distorting the evaluation results.

5.2.1.1 Sensitivity

Sensitivity of an input node is calculated by removing the input node from the trained NN. An input node might be removed by setting all the connected weights to zero. A measure of sensitivity of an input feature is the difference in the prediction value between when the feature is removed and when it is left in place. The sensitivity S_i of input feature x_i is given by

$$S_i = \frac{\left(\sum_L \frac{|P^0 - P^i|}{P^0}\right)}{n} \tag{5.4}$$

where P^0 is the normal prediction value for each training instance after training and P^i is the modified prediction value when the input node i is removed. L is the set of training data and n is the number of training data records. To measure the sensitivity, feeding zero input to the network is suggested instead of actually removing the weights and directly calculating the sensitivity [17].

5.2.1.2 Activity

Activity of a node is measured by the variance of activation level in the training data. When the activation value of a node varies much according to its input value, the activity of the node may be considered to be high. On the contrary, if the activation value of a node keeps constant over the training data, the activity of the node becomes zero. Hence, the activity of a hidden node z_j is

$$A_j = \left(w_j^{(2)}\right)^2 . \text{var}(g(\sum_{i=0}^{d} w_{ji}^{(1)} x_i)) \tag{5.5}$$

where var(.) is the variance function. Weights are squared because variance of linear combination can be transformed as $\text{var}(cx) = c^2 \text{var}(x)$ where c is a constant. The activity of an input node x_i is defined as

$$A_i = \sum_{j=1}^{M}((w_{ji}^{(1)})^2 . A_j). \tag{5.6}$$

5.2.1.3 Saliency

The saliency of a weight is measured by estimating the second derivative of the error with respect to the weight. It is used in [18] to prune NNs in an iterative fashion: training within a reasonable error level, computing saliency, deleting low saliency weights, and resuming the training. The saliency measure of a weight is proportional to the squared value of the weight. We adopt it to measure the importance of an input node. The saliency of an input node is given as

$$\text{Saliency}_i = \sum_{j=1}^{M}((w_{ji}^{(1)})^2 . (w_j^{(2)})^2). \tag{5.7}$$

5.2.1.4 Relevance

It is reported that the variance of weights into a node is a good predictor of the node's relevance and that the relevance of a node is a good predictor of the increase in error expected when the node's largest weight is deleted [19]. Following this notion, the relevance of a hidden node z_j is given as

$$R_j = (w_j^{(2)})^2 . \text{var}(w_{ji}^{(1)}) \tag{5.8}$$

and the overall relevance of input node x_i is

$$R_i = \sum_{j=1}^{M}((w_{ji}^{(1)})^2 . R_j). \tag{5.9}$$

5.2.2 MBR with the Weighted Features

Variants of the k-NN method are frequently used for case retrieval in MBR settings. k-NN assumes that each case $x = \{x_1, x_2, \ldots, x_n, x_c\}$ is defined by a set of n features, where x_c is x's class value (discrete or numeric). Given a query q and a case library L, k-NN retrieves the set K of q's k most similar (i.e., of least distance) cases in L and predicts their weighted majority class value as the class value of q. Distance is defined as

$$\text{Distance } (x, q) = \sqrt{\sum_{j=1}^{n} w_f \times \text{difference}(x_f, q_f)^2} \qquad (5.10)$$

where w_f is the parametrized weight value assigned to feature f, and

$$\text{difference } (x_f, q_f) = \begin{cases} 0 & \text{if feature } f \text{ is symbolic and } x_f = q_f \\ |x_f - q_f| & \text{if feature } f \text{ is numeric} \\ 1 & \text{otherwise.} \end{cases} \qquad (5.11)$$

In Equation 5.10, k-NN generally assigns equal weights to all features (i.e., $w_f = 1$ for all f). Many methods have been proposed which assign higher weights to the more relevant features for case retrieval. It should be noted that feature weighting methods for real-value forecasting problems are seldom found. Differences in probability distributions across classes are used to modify the distance metric for nominal attributes [6], or mutual information is used to compute coefficients on numeric attributes [7,20]. An incremental scheme is reported to alter feature weights according to their distance and the predicted class [21]. All of this research reports improvement over the simple version of nearest neighbor that gives equal weights to all attributes. However, these methods are applicable only to classification problems. More discussions on MBR and feature weighting methods are found in [6–9, 21, 22]. Possible approaches are suggested for learning general knowledge in a diagnostic case based system using NNs [23].

Feature weighting methods can be described along five dimensions: feedback, weight space, representation, generality and knowledge [7]. Here, we review our feature weighting method in this perspective.

1. *Feedback*: This dimension concerns whether the feature weighting method receives feedback from the k-NN variant to assign weights. Feedback methods modify feature weights to increase the similarity between a query and nearby cases in the same class, and decrease its similarity to nearby cases in the other classes. In these methods, each training case is processed once and is thus sensitive to the presentation ordering. Feedback methods usually adopt optimization techniques such as the incremental hill-climbing and genetic algorithm. Non-feedback methods extract the intrinsic importance factor of the features using the information in the training set. Conditional probability, class projection, and mutual information

may be the measure for weighting features. In general, it is known that feedback methods produce more accurate weights, yet the learning time is usually longer than non-feedback methods. The feature weighting method presented in this chapter may be regarded to be a feedback method. Though any explicit feedback is not directly made in the weight set, feedback is the core mechanism of NN learning, which generates the weight set in our system. Our weight set can be used as a starting point for other feedback based feature weight search strategies.

2. *Weight space*: It is known that the continuous weighting scheme increases accuracy when features vary in their relevance, though it requires searching of a much larger space [23]. Our method provides a continuous feature weight rather than constraining the search space to binary values.

3. *Representation*: NN learning restricts the presentation of the input feature set. The symbolic features have to be transformed into binary features; that is, each feature defined over v values has to be replaced with v binary features. Continuous features are better transformed to fall into a more restricted range, for example [0,1], for the NN to learn the patterns effectively. Our method can be applied to either classification or regression while many feature weighting methods may be used only in the classification problem.

4. *Generality*: Our feature weight method generates a single set of global weights. The assumption is that feature relevance is invariant over the domain. While most feature weighting methods commonly hold this assumption, it is sometimes inappropriate. In our system, if the variant feature relevance clearly exists, several NNs can be trained for each region and generate different feature weighting sets.

5. *Knowledge*: Domain specific knowledge is not explicitly used in our system as many automated algorithms do not receive much task specific knowledge. However, if it is possible to encode the domain knowledge in the training process, the weight set may also reflect the domain knowledge.

5.2.3   Integration of Memory and Neural Network Based Learning

The framework of the memory and NN based learning system is shown in Fig. 5.3. The feature weight discussed in Section 5.2.1 plays the role of kernel in keeping the prediction power of MBR. Once the neural network is trained, it can provide the feature weight set to MBR module by the methods presented in Section 5.2.1.

In the perspective of integration, NN and MBR have two important properties in common. First, they can be used for both classification and regression tasks without any converting mechanism. The NN generally generates one real value per output node. In a classification problem, it is possible to set some threshold values to interpret the value as a predicted class. MBR retrieves a set of k most similar previous cases and the most frequent class is selected as the prediction. For the regression task, the output of the NN can be directly interpreted as the predicted value. MBR generally averages output values of the similar cases for regression tasks.

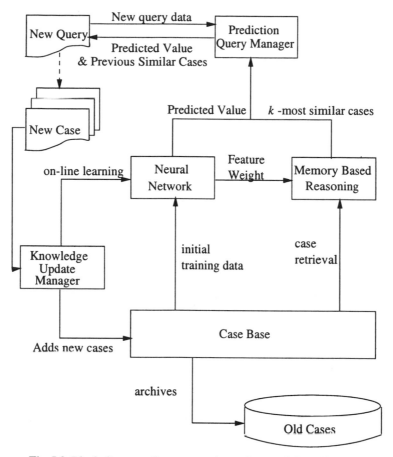

Fig. 5.3. Block diagram of memory and neural network based learning.

Secondly, both methods have an on-line learning property. As the NN is trained with new cases after initial training, the feature weight set for memory based learning is also updated. The case base also updates itself as new data is stored and old data discarded. The feature weight set may serve for a feature selection task, which is indispensable in the preprocessing stage of data mining.

In our architecture of memory and NN based learning system, integration of prediction results is carried out by the prediction query manager (PQM). The PQM receives new query requests and consults NN and MBR concurrently. When both predictors agree in prediction value, the PQM normally returns the predicted value. When the results produced are considerably different, the PQM reports that a reliable decision cannot be made for the case and further investigation by human experts should be required for the 'rejected' cases. In a classification task, the rule of PQM rejection is simply defined as

$$\textbf{If } P_M \neq P_{NN} \textbf{ Then } \text{`Reject to Answer'}$$
$$\textbf{Else } \text{`Answer with } P_M \text{ (or, identically, } P_{NN} \text{)'}$$

where P_M is the predicted value of MBR and P_{NN} is that of the NN. The rejection rule for the regression setting is

$$\textbf{If } |P_M - P_{NN}| \geq \varepsilon \textbf{ Then } \text{'Reject to Answer'}$$
$$\textbf{Else } \text{'Answer with average of } P_M \text{ and } P_{NN}\text{'}$$

where ε is some threshold value (say, 0.1). The rejection ratio can be defined as

$$\text{Rejection ratio} = \frac{\text{Number of unanswered queries}}{\text{Total number of queries}} \qquad (5.12)$$

Though the PQM does not guarantee the validity of prediction within some rejection ratio, a more accurate decision is gained for the answered queries. This rejecting function of the PQM is crucial in mission critical tasks which, however, should be automated because of the vast amount of queries. A self-warning system should also be devised with the rejecting function of the PQM. If the rejection ratio becomes large, PQM sends a warning message that indicates abnormality is going on either in the manufacturing process or in the prediction system itself. It is an important component in predictive data mining systems. This means our system may be suitable for processing monitoring tasks such as semiconductor manufacturing processes [24]. The knowledge update manager takes the role of providing new cases for on-line learning. Old cases may take up unnecessary storage space in the case base and thus cause delay in searching similar cases. In a dynamic situation like semiconductor manufacturing, old cases may even hinder MBR from correct prediction.

Table 5.1. Datasets used in the experiments and their neural network learning settings

Datasets used for the experiments						Neural network settings		
Dataset	Instances		Attributes		Output classes	# of hidden nodes	Mean iterations	Prediction error
	Learning	Testing	Original	Random				
Odd parity	350	150	4	7	2	6	727±1528	0.0 ±0.0
Sinusoidal	350	150	2	0	2	18	8442±1163	35.5±6.3
WDBC	468	101	30	0	2	20	3017±1495	3.7 ±0.0
WDBC+15				15			2826±2221	5.7 ±0.0
WDBC+30				30			3284±814	5.9 ±0.0
Credit	500	153	43	0	2	5	8820±1454	20.20 ±3.86
Credit+20				20		8	7553±2143	22.43 ±2.45
Credit+43				43		20	6870±1915	24.2 ±3.17
Sonar	104	104	60	0	2	6	6230±1565	16.5±2.15
Sonar+30				30		8	5995±2158	26.2±2.04
Sonar+60				60		9	8159±1927	27.1±3.54
MPG	300	92	9	0	real	9	5709±2902	3.11 ±0.41
MPG+4				4			5764±3432	3.42 ±0.52
MPG+9				9			3278±2530	3.73 ±0.32

5.3 Experimental Results

5.3.1 Methods

This section reports an empirical comparison of our feature weighting methods. We begin with two artificial datasets (odd parity, sinusoidal) to ensure our methods work properly. Experimental results in Aha [9] are also compared for the same datasets. Secondly, four standard datasets from the UCI collection are used in the experiments: three for the classification task and the other for the regression task. We compare the prediction accuracy to the other methods found in the literature as well as the simple k-NN and the NN. To ensure that our system was working properly when irrelevant features were present in the input, we added random noise features in the dataset. For example, WDBC+15 and WDBC+30 are identical to the WDBC dataset with the addition of 15 and 30 continuous irrelevant features, respectively. The level of irrelevant features is 50% and 100% of the number of its original features, respectively. Datasets were randomly partitioned 10 times into disjoint training and test sets. Table 5.1 summarizes the experimental settings of each dataset. Since our approach initially demands a trained NN, an NN is trained first at the beginning of each experimental session. We use a back-propagation learning setting; the resulting prediction error of trained NNs is also presented in Table 5.1. We then calculate the feature weight set using the algorithms described in Section 5.2.1. For the real world data sets, we calculate the feature weights by averaging the four proposed methods. The PQM rule is set as described in Section 5.2.3. The PQM classifies a case as 'no decision' when the predictions of MBR and NN are different from each other. For the regression problem (Auto-mpg), we set the threshold $\varepsilon = 0.1$. We devised an automated experimental environment to analyze the weight set and extract the feature weights. It has been reported that the performance of the classifier improves as k increases and starts to deteriorate on reaching its maximum [25]. In general, it is hardly possible to specify the optimum value for k beforehand. We present the experimental results with various k's for the artificial datasets and used optimal k's for the real world datasets; k's optimal range may be determined for each feature weighting method after experiments, but it does not break the generality of the experiments because the same range is applied whenever any comparison is made.

5.3.2 Problems

5.3.2.1 Odd Parity Problem

The odd parity problem is on 11 binary features where positive cases have an odd number for the first four features. For binary inputs $I_1, I_2, \ldots, I_{11}$, the output O is defined by

$$O = \mathbf{mod}\left(\sum_{j=1}^{4} I_j, 2\right) \tag{5.13}$$

where $\mathbf{mod}(.)$ means the modulus operator. The odd parity problem is frequently used in validating feature weighting methods [7, 26].

Table 5.2. Odd parity problem. (a) Mean weights of relevant features ($I_1 \ldots I_4$) and irrelevant features ($I_5 \ldots I_{11}$). (b) Mean error of feature weighting algorithms

	Sensitivity	Activity	Saliency	Relevance
$I_1 - I_4$	1.91 ± 0.60	2.06 ± 0.56	2.06 ± 0.42	2.04 ± 0.41
$I_5 - I_{11}$	0.48 ± 0.46	0.40 ± 0.60	0.39 ± 0.58	0.40 ± 0.62

(a)

k	Uniform	Sensitivity	Activity	Saliency	Relevance
1	30.8 ± 3.4	0.9 ± 1.30	0.8 ± 1.4	1.0 ± 1.8	0.2 ± 0.4
3	31.7 ± 2.6	1.8 ± 2.50	1.3 ± 2.3	1.7 ± 2.7	0.7 ± 1.2
5	72.0 ± 1.5	9.3 ± 11.1	4.5 ± 6.7	6.9 ± 9.5	4.3 ± 5.5
7	69.0 ± 1.0	10.1 ± 12.2	4.8 ± 7.0	8.3 ± 11.4	5.2 ± 7.0
9	67.9 ± 2.6	14.1 ± 15.0	6.9 ± 7.3	11.5 ± 12.7	8.4 ± 8.3
11	65.8 ± 2.6	19.7 ± 15.5	13.1 ± 9.7	16.3 ± 13.0	13.4 ± 10.2
13	66.7 ± 3.1	22.1 ± 16.6	16.7 ± 9.1	19.1 ± 11.2	17.9 ± 9.3
15	83.1 ± 2.0	41.1 ± 21.3	33.1 ± 13.7	37.3 ± 11.0	38.1 ± 10.4

(b)

5.3.2.2 Sinusoidal

The decision boundary in the sinusoidal task is a sine curve. It has two real features and one binary output. More specifically, the output is defined by

$$Y = \begin{cases} 1 & \text{if } x_2 \leq \frac{1}{2} + \frac{1}{2}\sin\left(16\pi.\mathbf{mod}\left(x_1, \frac{1}{8}\right)\right) \\ 0 & \text{otherwise.} \end{cases} \tag{5.14}$$

where x_1, x_2 are the input features and Y is the output. The distribution of examples is shown in Fig. 5.4. x_1 and x_2 are generated randomly on [0,1]. The second feature, x_2, is nearly completely irrelevant [9].

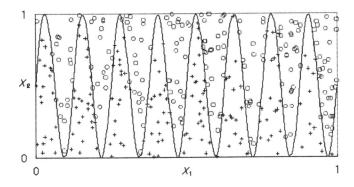

Fig. 5.4. The distribution of samples from the sinusoidal problem.

5.3.2.3 Wisconsin Diagnostic Breast Cancer (WDBC) Dataset

WDBC is a classification problem on breast cancer diagnostic data [27]. It has 30

Table 5.3. Sinusoidal problem. (a) Mean weights of relevant feature (I_1) and less relevant feature (I_2). (b) Mean error of feature weighting algorithms

	Sensitivity	Activity	Saliency	Relevance
I_1	1.68 ± 0.25	1.84 ± 0.09	1.85 ± 0.10	1.75 ± 0.14
I_2	0.32 ± 0.25	0.16 ± 0.09	0.15 ± 0.10	0.25 ± 0.14

(a)

k	Uniform	Sensitivity	Activity	Saliency	Relevance
1	22.4 ± 2.2	14.2 ± 4.4	11.7 ± 1.3	12.1 ± 1.3	14.0 ± 1.7
3	27.6 ± 3.5	15.8 ± 6.1	13.1 ± 2.9	14.2 ± 3.7	15.9 ± 3.2
5	34.0 ± 4.9	19.1 ± 6.7	15.0 ± 3.7	16.5 ± 3.8	19.2 ± 4.5
7	36.3 ± 4.3	22.8 ± 8.2	17.9 ± 2.6	18.3 ± 4.3	20.7 ± 5.7
9	37.1 ± 4.9	25.3 ± 8.4	20.1 ± 3.7	21.1 ± 4.0	23.2 ± 6.3
11	36.9 ± 5.0	25.5 ± 9.5	19.9 ± 3.2	20.9 ± 4.5	24.6 ± 5.2
13	37.0 ± 3.5	27.3 ± 9.0	21.9 ± 4.1	23.3 ± 5.1	26.1 ± 6.6
15	37.5 ± 3.9	28.3 ± 8.6	24.0 ± 5.3	25.1 ± 6.5	28.5 ± 7.1

(a)

continuous inputs and one binary output ('benign' and 'malignant') and there are 569 observations in the dataset. We randomly selected 468 training instances and 101 testing instances for each trial. We also prepared two noise-added datasets to examine the prediction power of each method in a noisy environment.

5.3.2.4 Credit

This task concerns credit card applications. Credit approval is one of the major applications for data mining. All attribute names and values have been changed to meaningless symbols to protect confidentiality of the data by the donor of the dataset. There is a good mix of attributes: continuous, nominal with small numbers of values, and nominal with larger numbers of values. We scaled the attributes for NN learning. For example, the 'A6' attribute in the original dataset has one of 14 possible values: c, d, cc, i, j, k, m, r, q, w, x, e, aa, ff. It is transformed into 13 binary attributes and only one of them is 1 in each instance.

Quinlan [28] used this dataset with a modified version of C4.5. We added randomly generated binary features to Credit+20 and Credit+43, respectively.

5.3.2.5 Sonar

This is the dataset used by Gorman and Sejnowski [29] in their study of the classification of sonar signals using an NN. The task is to discriminate between sonar signals bounced off a metal cylinder and those bounced off a roughly cylindrical rock. This example has 60 features, two classes ('mines' and 'rocks') and 104 cases in both the training and testing dataset.

5.3.2.6 Auto-MPG

This is a regression problem. The data concerns city-cycle fuel consumption in miles

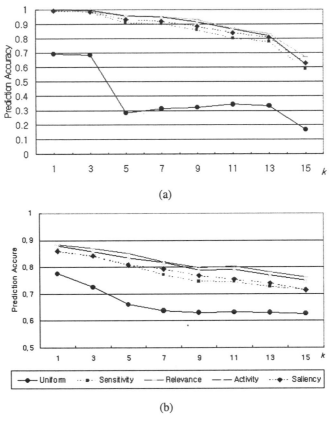

(a)

(b)

Fig. 5.5. Classification accuracy of the feature weighting methods for the odd parity problem (a) and sinusoidal problem (b).

per gallon, to be predicted in terms of one multi-valued discrete and six continuous attributes [30]. One multi-valued attribute (origin country of manufacturing: either of United States, Japan and Europe) is transformed into three binary attributes and this makes nine input features. The output is one real value MPG, of which the range is from 9 to 46.6. We linearly scaled the MPG feature into [0.1] for NN learning. The total number of instances is 392, which we randomly divided into 300 training data and 92 testing data for each trial.

5.3.3 Discussion of Results

For artificial problems (Sections 5.3.2.1 and 5.3.2.2), we focus on whether our feature weighting methods can outperform previously suggested feature weighting methods. We generated 500 cases respectively and randomly divided them into one training set of 350 cases and one testing set of 150 cases for each trial. The experimental results over 10 trials are depicted in Fig. 5.5, where we can observe that the four feature weighting methods presented in this chapter predict the target concept successfully with a small k (less than 3). In addition, our methods perform relatively well

Table 5.4. Comparison of feature weight learning algorithms on parity and sinusoidal problem

Max. prediction accuracy (%)	Parity	Sinusoidal
k-NN	69.2	77.6
Sensitivity	99.1	85.8
Activity	99.2	88.3
Saliency	99.0	87.9
Relevance	99.8	86.0
Relief-F	100.0	80.1
k-NN (VSM)	100.0	88.6
CCF	70.5	68.5
VDM	70.9	68.5
MVDM	71.1	68.4
MI	71.4	73.0

Table 5.5. Comparison of MANN and other experiments in real world datasets

	MANN error rate (rejection ratio)	Other experiment
WDBC	2.1% (5.0%)	2.5% (Bennett [31]), MSM tree
Credit	8.3% (9.1%)	14.13% (Quinlan [28]), Bagged C4.5
Sonar	1.2% (17.3%)	4.8% (Hastie and Tibshirani [8]), DANN
		6.2% (Setiono and Liu [15]), selected features
MPG	2.09 (10.1%)	2 11 (Quinlan [30]), model tree

with suboptimal k (say, 9), whereas the performance of uniform weight setting degrades quickly as k increases. The individual weight values for the original features are significantly higher than those of irrelevant features as seen in Tables 5.2(a) and 5.3(a). In Table 5.4, we compare our results to other feature weighting methods that are discussed in [9]. Our four methods are among the top five of 11 methods in both problems.

The experimental results of the real world datasets (Sections 3.2.3–3.2.6) are shown in Fig. 5.6. We see that our method outperforms the k-NN and NN learning with a reasonable range of rejection ratio (RR). In most of the predictive data mining settings, it is not required (or should be avoided) to fully automate the decision making process. For the example of the credit evaluation process, the human analyst can focus on the small portion of the loan requests whose decisions are not made by the automated data mining system, while the automated procedure processes the large part of the loan requests with higher accuracy than if it were to make the decisions of all the request [32].

We can observe that the error rate of our method is maintained low while RR rises moderately as the number of irrelevant features increases. Our method shows robust

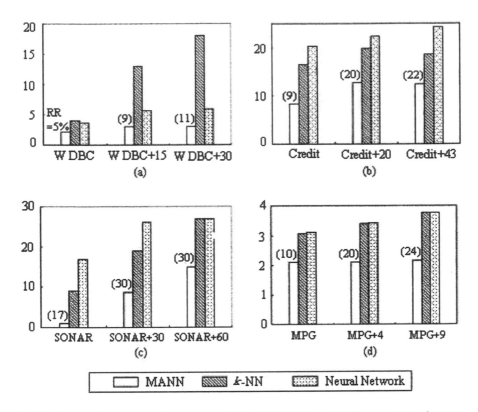

Fig. 5.6. Grouped bar graphs of error rates (%) for WDBC (a), credit (b), sonar (c) and average error of auto-MPG (d). The numbers in parentheses are the rejection ratio ('no decision') of MANN learning.

behavior in the noisy datasets, which has irrelevant features in the input. This implies that our method is particularly useful to large dimensional problems.

We add a regression problem to demonstrate that our method can be used in the regression setting. Most existing feature weighting methods are applicable only to classification problems. The feature weight profile of MPG+9 is presented in Fig. 5.7. Weights for the original features are shown to the left of the dotted line, which are evaluated higher than weights for the random features. Comparison to previous researches is shown in Table 5.5. The previous experiments are the best results found in the literature for the same datasets. Our method shows better prediction accuracy within a reasonable rejection ratio. When the rejection function of the PQM is removed, however, the error rates are maintained lower than the benchmarks except for the WDBC and MPG problems.

We proposed and tested four feature weighting methods: sensitivity, activity, saliency, and relevance. With many irrelevant input features, the sensitivity method does not show such good properties as the other three methods. The sensitivity measure performs worse than the uniform weights even in some experiments. However, activity, saliency and relevance methods produce good feature weight sets and they are sim-

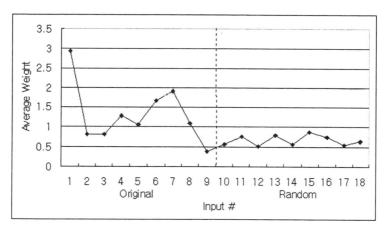

Fig. 5.7. Average feature weights computed in the auto-MPG task (with nine irrelevant features).

ilar in their values. They generally perform better than the uniform weights in any experiments.

5.4   Conclusion, Limitations and Future Work

The NN is generally blamed for its lack of understandability of knowledge representation. Our hybrid system provides the most similar cases for the prediction query, which, to some extent, demonstrates its explaining capability. On the other hand, MBR suffers from the feature weighting problem. Feature weighting has been one of the most debated subjects for MBR. Many researchers have tackled the problem using the information theoretic approach. However, most existing feature weighting methods are only applicable to classification problems. Our method suggests a hybrid approach to the feature weighting problem with techniques from NN pruning studies and it provides feature weights to regression problems as well as classification problems. In adaptive learning problems, which show dynamic behavior over time, the NN provides an on-line learning property. On-line learning can also be accomplished for MBR by updating the case base with new data and discarding old data. We set up a framework for extracting feature weights from trained NNs and defined four feature weighting mechanisms based on the framework.

Memory and NN based reasoning require a number of exemplary cases to operate properly. Therefore, our system may not be appropriate to situations that require a short learning time. In addition, our system does not explicitly provide any symbolic knowledge. It just presents previous cases that are similar to the present query. The non-symbolic knowledge feature may be reinforced if the system is operated in conjunction with other symbolic knowledge learning systems.

The memory and NN based expert system has a few design parameters: length of the case lifetime, treatment of old cases, point where to renew the feature weight, and so forth. It is natural to assume the target system is dynamically changing its behavior in many applications. To cope with the dynamic behavior, two adaptive learning mechanisms are embedded in our system: one is discarding old cases and the other is updating the feature weight. To exclude and archive old cases automatically, it is necessary to set up the criterion of 'old' cases and the strategy on how to treat those old cases. Updating the feature weight is adaptively and gradually performed via the on-line learning capability of the NN. Further research on the design parameters is required for practical guides on details of operating the memory and NN learning system in the data mining environment.

This work is related to many research fields in the data mining community such as hybrid learning strategy, feature selection, feature weighting in CBR and rule extraction. The hybrid strategy is accepted as a valid approach to data mining, because no single method has enough capability to deal with various data mining settings. Memory based learning has often been integrated with many other learning techniques, for it is essential to look for similar cases in inductive learning and data mining process. However, a hybrid system of the NN and the memory based learning is first proposed in this research. Further integration is still possible. It would seem that the support vector machine (SVM) is very close to our research, with the support vectors providing the memory-based component, and the kernel function replacing the NN. Though SVMs have an advantage in the far more rigorous and principled framework, our approach may have practical advantages in scalability and learning speed.

Feature weighting and selection are active areas of data mining. The proposed system may be used in feature weighting and/or feature selection problems. For situations where performance measure is vague in defining accurately the feature weights and selection algorithms, this application needs a close investigation. Rule extraction is the task of converting learned NN models into more easily understood representations. Though the problem of understanding trained NNs has been widely considered an important area of research in the last decade, it has had less influence on the data mining, machine learning and NN community than it deserves. Knowledge extraction from trained NNs is now a challenge for the NN community to make better applications in data mining in many business and industrial fields. Our method can be viewed as an alternative approach to make use of trained NNs by integrating NN learning and MBR.

References

1. Benitez JM, Castro JL, Requena I. Are Neural Networks Black Boxes? IEEE Trans. Neural Networks 1997; 8(5): 1156–1164.
2. Towell G, Shavlik W. Refining Symbolic Knowledge Using Neural Networks. In: Machine Learning: A Multistrategy Approach. Morgan Kaufmann, San Mateo, CA, 1994; 405–429.
3. Park SC, Lam SM, Gupta A. Rule Extraction from Neural Networks: Enhancing the Explanation Capability. Journal of Expert Systems 1995; 2: 57–71.
4. Liu H, Setiono R. Effective Data Mining Using Neural Networks. IEEE Trans. on Knowledge and Data Engineering 1996; 8(6): 957–961.
5. Tickle AB, Andrews R, Golea M, Diederich J. The Truth will Come to Light: Directions and Challenges in Extracting the Knowledge Embedded Within Trained Neural Networks. IEEE Trans. on Neural Networks 1998; 9(6): 1057– 1068.

6. Cost S, Salzberg S. A Weighted Nearest Neighbor Algorithm for Learning with Symbolic Features. Machine Learning 1993; 10(1): 57–78.
7. Wettschereck D, Aha DW. In: Weighting Features. Proceedings of ICCBR 1995; 347–358.
8. Hastie T, Tibshirani R. Discriminant Adaptive Nearest Neighbor Classification. IEEE Trans. on Pattern Analysis and Machine Intelligence 1996; 18(6): 607–616.
9. Wettschereck D, Aha DW, Mohri T. A Review and Empirical Evaluation of Feature Weighting Methods for a Class of Lazy Learning Algorithms. AI Review 1997; 11: 273–314.
10. Shneiderman B. Designing the User Interface: Strategies for Effective Human–Computer Interaction. Addison-Wesley, Reading, MA, 1997.
11. Kang BS, Lee JH, Shin CK, Yu SJ, Park SC. Hybrid Machine Learning System for Integrated Yield Management in Semiconductor Manufacturing. Expert System With Applications 1998; 15: 123–132.
12. Blake C, Keogh E, Merz CJ. UCI Repository of Machine Learning Databases [www. ics. uci. edu]. University of California, Department of Information and Computer Science, Irvine, CA, 1999.
13. Weigend AS, Rumelhart DE, Huberman BA. Generalization by Weight- Elimination with Application to Forecasting. Advances in Neural Information Processing Systems 1991; 3: 875–882.
14. Reed R. Pruning Algorithms: A Survey. IEEE Trans. on Neural Networks 1993; 4(5): 740–747.
15. Setiono R, Liu H. Neural-Network Feature Selector. IEEE Trans. on Neural Networks 1997; 8(3): 654–662.
16. Bishop CM. Neural Networks for Pattern Recognition, Clarendon Press, Oxford, 1997.
17. Karnin ED. A Simple Procedure for Pruning Back-Propagation Trained Neural Networks. IEEE Trans. on Neural Networks 1990; 1(2): 239–242.
18. Cun YL, Denker JS, Solla SA. Optimal Brain Damage. In: Advances in Neural Information Processing (2). MIT Press, Cambridge, MA, 1989; 598–605.
19. Segee BE, Carter MJ. Fault Tolerance of Pruned Multilayer Networks. In: Proc. Int. Joint Conf. Neural Networks, vol. II, 1991; 447–452.
20. Daelemans W, Gillis S, Durieux G. The Acquisition of Stress: A Data Oriented Approach. Computational Linguistics 1994; 20(3): 421–455.
21. Rachlin J, Kasif S, Salzberg S, Aha D. Towards a Better Understanding of Memory Based and Bayesian Classifiers. In: Proc. Internatl. Conf. on Machine Learning, New Brunswick, 1994; 242–250.
22. Kohavi R, Langley P, Yun Y. The Utility of Feature Weighting in Nearest- Neighbor Algorithms. In: Proceedings of ECML-97, 1997.
23. Reategui E, Campbell JA, Borghetti S. Using a Neural Network to Learn General Knowledge in a Case-Based System. In: Proceedings of ICCBR-95, 1995; 528–537.
24. Shin CK, Park SC. Memory and Neural Network Based Prediction System. Expert Systems with an Application 1999; 16: 145–155.
25. Okamoto S, Satoh K. An Average-Case Analysis of k-Nearest Neighbor Classifier. In: Proceedings of ICCBR-95. 1995; 254-264.

26. Dash M, Liu H. Feature Selection for Classification. Intelligent Data Analysis 1997; 1(3).
27. Street WN, Wolberg WH, Mangasarian OL. Nuclear Feature Extraction for Breast Tumor Diagnosis. In: IS&T/SPIE 1993 International Symposium on Electronic Imaging: Science and Technology, 1993; 861–870.
28. Quinlan R. Bagging, Boosting, and C4.5. In: Proceedings on the AAAI-96. 1996; 725–730.
29. Gorman RP, Sejnowski TJ. Analysis of Hidden Units in a Layered Network Trained to Classify Sonar Targets. Neural Networks 1988; 1: 75–89.
30. Quinlan R. Combining Instance-Based and Model-Based Learning. In: Proceedings on the Tenth International Conference of Machine Learning, 1993; 236–243.
31. Bennett KP. Decision Tree Construction Via Linear Programming. In: Proceedings of the 4th Midwest Artificial Intelligence and Cognitive Science Society, 1992; 97–101.
32. Shin CK, Hong HK, Park SC. A Hybrid Machine Learning Strategy in Credit Evaluation. In: Proceedings of the 2nd Asia–Pacific Industrial Engineering and Management Systems, 1999, 331–334.

6. A Genetic Algorithm and Growing Cell Structure Approach to Learning Case Retrieval Structures

Werner Dubitzky and Francisco Azuaje

Abstract. Designing suitable case retrieval mechanisms in case base reasoning can amount to a significant knowledge engineering task. Time pressures, lack of domain knowledge, and high-dimensional, incomplete, and inconsistent case descriptions often add to the problem. This chapter presents a neural and a genetic learning approach to the automated construction of case retrieval structures.

6.1 Introduction

Given the description of a new problem, called query case, the first and arguably most crucial step in case based reasoning (CBR) is to retrieve those cases from the case base that are most *relevant* to solving the problem at hand or most *similar* to the problem. The two most frequently employed retrieval models in CBR are based on the approximation of relevance or similarity via a *computational* or a *representational* approach [1]. Generally, both approaches may require a significant knowledge engineering effort when actual systems are built. We argue that soft computing techniques, such as *evolutionary* and *neural* computing, may be usefully put to work to automate some of the processes involved [2]. Within this discussion we present two approaches to (introspective) learning of case retrieval knowledge structures: (a) learning of global and local feature weights using an evolutionary computing approach, and (b) learning of useful case groupings using a *growing cell structures* neural computing model. Approach (a), can be considered a so-called *feedback method* since it uses feedback of a system's performance during the learning process. Method (b), on the other hand, can be considered a so-called *ignorant method*, for no performance feedback of the system is analyzed in the learning process. Before we present the actual methods, we take a brief look at four general case retrieval models, namely, computational, representational, partitioning, and model based.

6.2 Case Retrieval Models

Prompted by the description of a new problem or situation, called *query case*, the task of the *case retrieval* process is to identify those cases in the case library that are most *relevant* or *similar* to the current situation [3]. Generally, it is assumed that the degree to which a query case, x, is relevant or similar to a (base) case, y, can be expressed as a quantity, $rel(x, y)$.

Definition 1. Given the *universe of cases*, U, and the case base, CB, the relevance, $rel(x, y)$, of a case, x, to a case y, is defined as follows:

$$rel(x, y) : U \times CB \rightarrow \mathbf{R}$$

such that $CB \subset U$, and $x, y \in U$.

Generally, it is assumed that the degree of relevance or similarity between two cases, x and y, can be expressed as a quantity, $rel(x, y)$, such that

1. $0 \leq rel(x, y) \leq 1$, that is, $rel(x, y) : U \times CB \rightarrow [0, 1]$ *(normalization)*; and
2. $rel(x, y) = 1, for x = y$ *(reflection)*.

Sometimes, the properties of *symmetry* and *triangular equality* (under a geometric, distance-like interpretation of the terms $1 - rel(x, z), 1 - rel(x, y)$, and $1 - rel(y, z)$, which may be considered to represent *irrelevance*), are also assumed, such that

3. $rel(x, y) = rel(y, x)$ *(symmetry)*; and
4. $(1 - rel(x, z)) \leq (1 - rel(x, y)) + (1 - rel(y, z))$ *(triangular equality)*.

In CBR, researchers have implemented case retrieval structures based on different models or approximations of relevance and similarity. For the purpose of this discussion we distinguish four different approaches, namely *computational, representational/indexing, partitioning,* and *knowledge based/model based* approaches. This distinction should not be seen as absolute, for in actual CBR systems it is often not possible to say that the system is 'pure' in terms of any of these approaches. Therefore, a fifth category, namely *hybrid* approaches, is not explicitly discussed, as it is seen as a combination of the other four general models.

6.2.1 Computational Retrieval Models

Computational retrieval models calculate a relevance or similarity score on the basis of an explicit, pre-defined similarity (or distance) measure or metric. Normally, the combined or *global similarity*, $sim(x, y)$, between two cases, x and y, is computed by a function, f, from the feature-to-feature or *local similarities*, $sim(x_1, y_1)$, $sim(x_2, y_2), \ldots, sim(x_n, y_n)$, as follows:

$$sim(x, y) = f(sim(x_1, y_1), sim(x_2, y_2), \ldots, sim(x_n, y_n)) \qquad (6.1)$$

such that $x_1, x_2, \ldots, x_n \in x$, and $y_1, y_2, \ldots, y_n \in y$ refer to two corresponding features in the cases.

Typical representatives of (weighted) global similarity measures are the *Euclidean* similarity (Equation 6.2), the *Hamming* similarity (Equation 6.3), and the *nearest neighbor* similarity (Equation 6.4).

$$sim(x, y) = \sqrt{\sum_{i=1}^{n} w_i^2 sim^2(x_i, y_i)} \qquad (6.2)$$

$$sim(x, y) = \sum_{i=1}^{n} w_i \, sim(x_i, y_i) \qquad (6.3)$$

such that $w_i \in [0, 1]$ and $\sum_{i=1}^{n} w_i = 1$ (normalized weights) for Equations 6.2 and 6.3.

$$sim(x, y) = \frac{\sum_{i=1}^{n} w_i sim(x_i, y_i)}{\sum_{i=1}^{n} w_i} \qquad (6.4)$$

such that $w_i \in [0, 1]$.

The weight, w_i, in the global similarity measures discussed above, reflects the relative importance of corresponding feature (index i) within the cases. Section 6.3 discusses an approach to case retrieval, which automatically determines the global and local weights of case features based on evolutionary techniques.

For numerical attributes, typical general-purpose feature-to-feature or local relevance of similarity measures are the *Canberra metric* (Equations 6.5–6.7).

$$sim(x_i, y_i) = 1 - \frac{|x_i - y_i|}{|x_i| + |y_i|} \qquad (6.5)$$

$$sim(x_i, y_i) = 1 - \frac{|x_i - y_i|}{|max(x_i, y_i)|} \qquad (6.6)$$

$$sim(x_i, y_i) = 1 - \frac{|x_i - y_i|}{max(x_i, y_i) - min(x_i, y_i)} . \qquad (6.7)$$

For example, given the attribute values of $x_i = 3$ and $y_i = 5$, $sim(x_i, y_i) = 0.75$ (using Equation 6.5), $sim(x_i, y_i) = 0.60$ (using Equation 6.6), and $sim(x_i, y_i) = 0.00$ (using Equation 6.7).

Typical measures used for symbolic attributes are shown in Equation 6.8 (nominal values; no particular order of values) and Equation 6.9 (ordinal values; values are ordered on a scale).

$$sim(x_i, y_i) = \begin{cases} 1 & \text{for } x_i = y_i \\ 0 & \text{otherwise,} \end{cases} \qquad (6.8)$$

$$sim(x_i, y_i) = \begin{cases} 1 & \text{for } x_i = y_i \\ 1 - (d/N) & \text{otherwise} \end{cases} \qquad (6.9)$$

such that N denotes the total number of symbolic values used for that particular attribute, and d denotes the number of values separating the values x and y.

For example, given a set, V, of possible values, $V = \{red, green, blue, black, yellow\}$, for the attribute type *ColorOfCar*, and two specific values, x and y, with $x_i = red$ and $y_i = blue$, the similarity $sim(x_i, y_i) = 0$, according to Equation 6.8, and given the range or scale, S, of possible values, $S = \{very\ low, low, high, very\ high\}$ (i.e., $N = 4$), of symbolic values for the attribute type *BloodPressure*, and two specific values, a and b, with $a = low$ and $b = high$, the similarity $sim(a, b) = 1 - (1/N) = 1 - 0.25 = 0.75$, according to Equation 6.9.

Of course, similarity measures do not need to be general like those outlined above. They may exploit and incorporate existing domain knowledge [4,5].

6.2.2   Representational or Indexing Retrieval Models

The term *indexing* in CBR can mean different things to different people. Perhaps in its most general and comprehensive interpretation, indexing refers to the efforts involved in

- The *labeling* of cases in the case library. The labels of a case designate in what circumstances the case should be retrieved [6]. A good index or label is one that is predictive, makes useful predictions, is easy to recognize, and is generally applicable. A critical problem here is the choice of the *indexing vocabulary*. Generally speaking, an indexing vocabulary consists of descriptive dimensions (feature or attribute *types*), and a definition of the values each dimension is allowed to assume (feature or attribute *instances*).
- *Organizing* the cases in the case library so that case retrieval is done efficiently and accurately. This aspect is concerned also with the case retrieval algorithms themselves.

On the other side of the spectrum, indexing is interpreted in a similar way to the indexing mechanisms used in conventional databases. Indexing in databases is concerned with balancing the organizational structure and improving access *performance*; an index divides datasets into partitions. In CBR, on the other hand, indices are used to distinguish cases from one another for some purpose, namely, to make sure that a case is retrieved whenever it is appropriate, i.e., *relevant* to the current problem.

When referring to indexing based retrieval models within this discussion, we have in mind a structure composed of a set of *nodes*, N, a set of *arcs*, A, and a set of *cases*, C, that constitute the cases in the case library. A node in such an indexing structure represents a case descriptor or feature; an arc either reflects a relationship between case features or it connects a feature with a case. Given the set of descriptors used to describe a query case, the retrieval procedure (e.g., using a *spreading- activation* or *marker-passing* algorithm) in such a model *traverses* the indexing structure to determine the relevance of the cases in the case library. The indexing retrieval model, then, is similar to Schank's and Kolodner's early retrieval models based on various types of *memory organization packages* (MOPs, T-MOPs, E-MOPs, etc.) [7,8], and to more recent developments such as the *case retrieval nets* (CRNs) [9] and *ontology-based approaches* [10].

6.2.3   Retrieval Models Based on Partitioning

In partitioning based case retrieval models, the case library is subdivided into sets or groups of cases. In general, the cases within each group have a high degree of similarity (reflecting some concept in the domain) and the similarity between the groups themselves is high. Mathematically, such an organization constitutes a *partition*.

Definition 2. Let a case library contain the cases, $CB = \{x_1, x_2, \ldots, x_m\}$. Then the collection of non-empty sets, $P = \{C_1, C_2, \ldots, C_n\}$, is a partition of CB, if, and only if,

1. $CB = C_1 \cup C_2 \cup \ldots \cup C_n$ (all clusters together yield CB); and
2. $C_1, C_2, \ldots, C_n$ are mutually disjoint such that, for all $i, j = 1, 2, \ldots, n$, $C_i \cap C_j = \emptyset$, whenever $i \neq j$.

Partitioning methods are interesting for CBR because if one can group together the cases in the case library that are similar to one another, and one can find a way to figure out which group best matches a new query case, then only cases in that group need to be considered. For very large case bases, this could be the only practical approach to retrieving cases within acceptable time limits.

The key requirement for a case retrieval model based on partitioning is a knowledge structure (set of rules, decision tree, etc.), $r(x)$, which effectively selects a class or cluster of cases, $Y \in P = \{C_1, C_2, \ldots, C_n\}$, from the case library, CB, based on the description of a query case, x.

Definition 3. Let P denote a partition of the case library, $CB = \{x_1, x_2, \ldots, x_m\}$, such that $P = \{C_1, C_2, \ldots, C_n\}$, and let U define the *universe of cases*, such that $CB \subseteq U$. Then the knowledge structure, $r(x)$, is defined as follows:

$$r(x) : U \to P$$

such that $r(x) = Y \in P$, and $x \in U$.

Notice that assigning a new query case, x, to its relevant class or cluster, $Y \in P$, in the case base may only form the first part of the actual retrieval process. The set of cases in Y may be subject to further processing, for example, a nearest neighbor, similarity based selection process.

Of course, the question that arises in partitioning based case retrieval models is *how* to partition the case library in the first place.

A common scheme is to form groups or classes according to a pre-defined classification based on a deeper understanding of the domain. For example, one might partition a case base containing patients with a particular disease according to various aspects of the disease, e.g., stage of disease, severity, perceived pain, and so on. The point here is that in such approaches it is required that the cases in the case base are given a label designating their class at *design time*. The labeling is then used to group cases marked with the same label in a single group. However, although it might well be possible to manually assign such labels, in many applications it may be difficult to explicitly define a set of rules or a knowledge structure, $r(x)$, that accurately determines the classification label for an unclassified case. Without such knowledge structure it is not possible to take advantage of the organization in the case base. Two principal ways for establishing such a knowledge structure are possible:

- *Knowledge engineering.* Within a knowledge acquisition exercise, the required knowledge structure, $r(x)$, is elicited from a domain expert and encoded in some representation scheme. This option is not discussed further in this section.
- *Supervised (machine) learning.* The cases, CB, together their pre-defined classification, P, are used with an inductive machine learning method to generate the required knowledge structure, $r(x)$. This scenario is depicted in diagram (a) of Fig. 6.1.

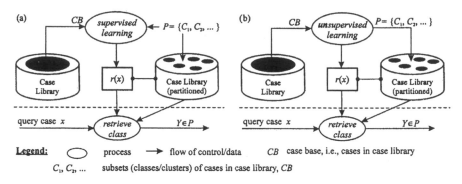

Fig. 6.1. Case retrieval based on partitioning.

Consider diagram (a) in Fig. 6.1. The part above the dashed line depicts how the design time process labeled *supervised learning* interacts with the system components. The interesting point to note is that the partitioning or classification of the cases in the case library is a prerequisite to the supervised or directed learning process. Based on this input the learning process generates the knowledge structure, $r(x)$, used at run-time (process labeled *retrieve* class shown beneath the dashed line) to determine the class or set of cases, $Y \in P$, for the query case, x. Typical machine learning approaches to supervised learning of this kind are *kd-trees* [11], *shared- feature* and *discrimination* networks [6,12], *decision trees* [9], and (artificial) neural networks. Approaches based on decision trees and similar constructs have the advantage that their structures can be converted into human-understandable rules, and, as a by-product of the learning process, can pinpoint the importance of features. The problem with these approaches is that relearning is required if new cases are added to the case library. The problem with neural network approaches is that the learned classification rules – which lie buried in the network's topology and weight settings – can normally not be made explicit so that humans can understand them.

In addition to partitioning based on a set of predetermined classes, there exists a method which can usefully divide up the cases in the case library without an a priori classification of the cases. This approach is referred to as *unsupervised learning* or *clustering* (or *automatic cluster detection*); it is depicted in diagram (b) of Fig. 6.1. Generally, clustering methods look for similarities over a series of objects or instances and form categories (clusters) based on these similarities. Common strategies to determine which clusters are right are:

- to cluster on features or features sets that are shared among a large number of objects (in the training set);
- to cluster based on features that divide the resulting clusters into sets of equal size;
- to cluster in individual features (as opposed to sets of features) to differentiate small groups of items from the others; and
- to cluster such that a pre-defined set of cluster will result (e.g., k-means clustering).

Consider diagram (b) in Fig. 6.1. The key difference to the supervised learning approach is that the unsupervised learning approach generates both the actual grouping of cases into classes or clusters, and a knowledge structure, $r(x)$, used by the run-time retrieval process to identify the relevant cluster of cases in the partitioned case library. Typical approaches to clustering include *k-means*, *hierarchical*, and *single linkage* clustering [13,14]. An advantage of clustering methods is that they more amenable to incremental modification in the light of newly added cases. Clustering approaches to case retrieval are perhaps most interesting for more open structured decision support or case completion tasks, where it is not known at design time which part of the case is used as outcome or solution. Section 6.3 discusses a clustering approach to case retrieval based on growing cell structure neural networks.

One general problem associated with inductive machine learning approaches to case retrieval is that they normally require a fixed, flat vector representation.

Notice that the way the retrieval structures (trees, rules) of inductive (supervised and unsupervised learning) retrieval models are being processed at retrieval time is somewhat different from the processing in indexing models. In the indexing approach, a kind of activation marker *traverses* the indexing structure and 'spreads' activation to the connected cases; those cases that accumulate the highest activation are retrieved. In inductive models, on the other hand, the retrieval process effectively

- searches through a set of classification rules until a match is found; or
- proceeds from the root node of a tree to nodes lower down the hierarchy until a single leave node is reached; at each intermediate node local rules are used to decide which path of the tree to chose.

Also, in indexing based schemes an explicit a priori partitioning of the case base is normally not required.

6.2.4 Model Based Retrieval Approaches

Ideally, all case based retrieval models should be based on a deep model of the *background knowledge* of the underlying application. Deep, general domain knowledge (also referred to as background knowledge or model based knowledge) describes the *concept definitions* and the *principles* underlying the more operational knowledge (heuristic rules, specific experiences or cases). Typically, general domain knowledge reflects a thorough model of a domain in terms of *relationships* (structural, causal, temporal, functional, etc.) between the *concepts* (classes, objects, components, processes, etc.) of the domain [15]. Many real-world domains are characterized by an incomplete or partial body of general background knowledge, which arises from uncertain relationships between the concepts of a domain. Such domains are also referred to as *weak-theory* domains. Typical weak-theory domains include medical diagnosis, engineering domains, investment planning, and geological interpretation. Domains with relatively strong domain theory include mathematical domains (e.g., Euclidean geometry) and games such as chess. Strong or complete domain theories may still be *intractable*. The notion of an intractable domain theory refers to very strong or complete domain theories and the *complexity* involved in deriving correct solutions based on the associated background knowledge. For example, in principle it is possible to determine the best move in any given chess position, but the underlying algorithm may have to analyze too many (an intractable number of) possible board positions to do so within reasonable time limits.

In a way, all case based retrieval models incorporate, directly or indirectly, some form of domain-specific background knowledge. For example, the selection of the features (and their relative importance) used to represent the cases themselves is usually based on some deeper insight into the domain in question. Simple similarity schemes rely on such feature/weight case models to define the corresponding distance functions. More sophisticated domain models embody explicit descriptions about feature-to-feature dependencies and relationships [10]. Such descriptions could be exploited by retrieval models to select among various similarity measures (or weight settings) based on the description of the query case and/or the source case. Other model based approaches to case retrieval explicitly model the relationships between feature values [5]. Yet other approaches employ model based knowledge in the retrieval phase to anticipate the subsequent work (adaptation, explanation) that needs to be done once a case is retrieved [16,17].

6.3   Learning Local and Global Weights Using Genetic Techniques

This section discusses a case feature weight learning model for CBR that automates the difficult and time-consuming case engineering task of defining effective feature weights. The model covers the discovery or learning of both global and local feature weights from data. It is based on the concept of introspective learning and the methods from genetic algorithms and genetic or evolution programming.

A critical design decision for many case based systems is that of determining the relative importance or *weight* of case features. In CBR, feature weights are used to express how predictive or important the features within a case are with respect to the solution of a case.

For example, a measure for heart rate variability (HRV) may be more indicative for estimating a subject's risk of getting coronary heart disease than, say, his blood pressure. For a concrete model this situation may be expressed as illustrated in Table 6.1.

Table 6.1. Global feature weights (HRV = heart rate variability)

	HRV	Blood pressure	...
	weight=0.35	*weight=0.45*	...
Case number	Value	Value	...
123	*low*	105	...
124	*high*	140	...
...	...	...	...
200	*low*	120	...

Two types of feature weights are generally distinguished: *global* and *local* feature weights. A global feature weight assigns the relative importance or predictiveness to a particular feature, and this weight is the same for all cases in the case base. This means that a particular feature always has the same relative impact regardless of which case is being considered. It has been argued that the global weights assumption may not always hold, and that feature weights should be considered within the context of the information contained within individual cases – features that are predictive or important in one case may not be so in another [18,19]. The idea, then, is that the relative importance of features should be determined for each individual case. Such case-specific feature weights are referred to as local weights.

To illustrate the concept of local case feature weights consider the three case snippets depicted in Table 6.2.

Table 6.2. Local feature weights (HRV = heart rate variability)

Case number	HRV		Blood pressure		...	
	Value	Weight	Value	Weight	...	...
123	low	0.45	105	0.30	...	...
124	high	0.30	140	0.80	...	...
. ...	...	...	...	...	...	...
200	low	0.05	120	0.25	...	...

The process of manually eliciting useful feature weights can be a difficult and time-consuming knowledge acquisition exercise. Establishing global weights for cases with many features or local weights for case bases of moderate size could become prohibitively complex. In such a situation the obvious choice is to automate the process of finding good feature weights. A general framework for the automatic setting of system parameters like feature weights is that of *introspective learning*.

6.3.1 Introspective Learning of Case Feature Weights

Introspective learning refers to a learning approach (learning of problem-solving knowledge) that monitors the progress of a problem solver [18,19]. This approach is also referred to as the feedback method [19], as opposed to so-called ignorant methods, because feedback about the performance of the overall system is used within the learning process.

The basic idea behind the learning of feature weights within the CBR framework using the feedback or introspective learning model is to increase or decrease the weight of selected features in the light of problem-solving performance. The assumption of this model is that, in CBR, poor or good problem-solving performance can be, at least partially, attributed to the underlying model of similarity, and in particular to the weighting of case features.

Fig. 6.2 illustrates the basic structure and components for introspective weight learning in CBR. (This architecture applies to both global as well as local weights.) The entire set of available cases is randomly split into three sets: training cases (case library), test cases, and evaluation cases. Within the learning phase feature weights for the training cases are established. In each cycle the newly determined weights are used to test the performance of the case base by applying a set of test cases (feedback). Once a satisfactory performance has been reached the case base can be evaluated against a set of evaluation cases that played any part in the learning procedure.

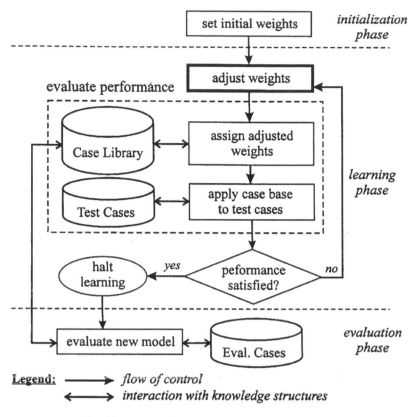

Fig. 6.2. Introspective learning of case feature weights.

A critical element in the weight learning architecture outlined above is that of weight modification or weight adjustment within each learning cycle. Here, it must be decided what strategy should be used to change or update the weights. This is highlighted in the diagram by the bold-lined box labeled *adjust weights*.

A conventional, deterministic approach to feature weight learning must define a policy (set of rules) according to which feature weights are updated or modified. Generally, such policies are governed by two criteria: retrieval failure and retrieval success. Such approaches update feature weights as a result of retrieval failure or as a result of retrieval success respectively. For each model, the feature weights of non- matching and matching features are decreased and increased accordingly. Two distinct general strategies exist [18]:

- **Retrieval failure:** *increase* the weights of *non-matching* features, and *decrease* the weights of *matching* features; and

- **Retrieval success:** *increase* the weights of *matching* features, and *decrease* the weights of *non-matching* features.

Of course, whatever combination of the above strategies is being adopted, there is still the need to define by what amount the selected weights should be updated, and to make sure that the feature weight update is consistent (convergence). Incidentally, the concept of *elitist selection*, i.e., the 'carrying along' of the best current solution from one population to the next, is often used in genetic algorithms to ensure convergence (see Section 6.3.2).

6.3.2 Genetic Techniques

The field of *evolutionary computation* has been growing rapidly over the last few years. Generally, three evolutionary techniques are distinguished: *genetic algorithms, genetic programming*, and *evolutionary programming*. A genetic algorithm (GA) is a search algorithm that is modeled on the mechanics of natural selection and natural genetics [20,21]. It combines survival of the fittest among individuals or string structures (e.g., bit strings) with a structured yet randomized information exchange to form a search algorithm. GAs belong to the class of probabilistic algorithms, but they differ from random algorithms in that they combine elements of directed and stochastic (non-deterministic) search. Because of this GAs are more robust than directed search methods. Another advantage of GAs is that they maintain a population of potential solutions while other search methods process a single point of the search space.

A GA is an algorithm which maintains a *population, $P(t)$*, of individuals or *chromosomes $S_1^t, S_2^t, \ldots, S_n^t$*, for each iteration or *generation, t*, such that $P(t) = \{S_1^t, S_2^t, \ldots, S_n^t\}$. Each individual, S_i^t, represents a potential solution to the problem at hand and is implemented as some string structure, S. Each solution, S_i^t, is evaluated by some *fitness* function, $f(S_i^t)$, to give some measure of its 'goodness' or 'fitness'. Then, a new population (generation or iteration $t+1$), $P(t+1)$, is generated by selecting the more fit individuals from $P(t)$. Some members of this new population undergo alterations by means of *mutation* and *crossover* operations, to form new solutions. The basic procedure of the GA is illustrated in Fig. 6.4. Mutation arbitrarily alters one or more genes (i.e., string elements) of a selected chromosome by a random change with a probability equal to the *mutation rate*.

For example, if a chromosome, S, is represented as a 5-digit binary string based on the finite alphabet $A = \{1, 0\}$, then a single mutation transformation, $m(S)$, may have changed the chromosome $S = 10001$ as follows: $S^{new} = m(10001) = 10000$ (see Fig. 6.3a). The mechanism that actually selects the digit or bit (bit 0 in this case) that is mutated is also based on a probabilistic or 'random' scheme.

Crossover combines the features (i.e., substrings) of two or more *parent* chromosomes to form two similar *offspring* chromosomes by swapping corresponding segments of the parents' chromosomes. For example, let $S_1 = 10001$ and $S_2 = 11111$ denote two 5-digit parent chromosomes. By combining the first 3 bits of parent $S_1(\underline{100}01)$ and the last 2 bits of $S_2(111\underline{11})$ into the offspring chromosome O_1, and the first 3 bits of $S_2(\underline{111}11)$ and the last 2 bits of $S_1(100\underline{01})$ into O_2 as follows: $O_1 = c(S_1, S_2) = \underline{100} + \underline{11} = \underline{10011}$, and $O_2 = c(S_1, S_2) = \underline{111} + \underline{01} = \underline{11101}$;

where c symbolizes the crossover operation and '+' the concatenation operation (see Fig. 6.3b). Note, the mechanism that actually decides the dividing point (between bit 1 and 2) in the parent chromosome is also based on a probabilistic or 'random' scheme.

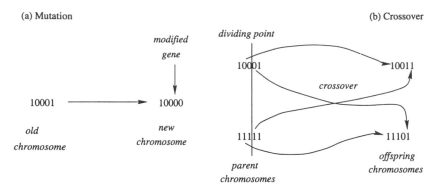

Fig. 6.3. Mutation and crossover operations.

The diagram in Fig. 6.4 depicts the basic control structure of the problem-solving model based on genetic algorithms. The cloning operator, depicted in the lower part of the diagram, complements the *mutation* and the *crossover* operators. It is used to copy entire chromosomes from one population to the next without modification. This operator is used, for instance, to transfer 'elitist' chromosomes, that is, those with the highest fitness scores, from one generation to the next.

Recently, there has been increased interest in genetic and evolutionary programming [21,22]. Genetic and evolutionary programming techniques carry on the principal ideas from GAs with the exception that individuals or chromosomes are no longer represented by simple string structures but by more complex data structures such as trees, graphs, arrays, and so on, or even entire computer programs. Although some people make a distinction between genetic programs and evolution programs, the terms are used interchangeably within this discussion. With such chromosomes the choice of what constitutes a gene and how such genes should be manipulated by the genetic mutation and crossover operators is not obvious. The approach presented in this chapter uses an array (the chromosome) of bit strings to represent a set of case feature weights. Each element (bit string) in this *array* is called a macro gene, and each particle (bit) within such a *macro* gene is referred to as *micro* gene. The genetic operations are carried out by manipulating the chromosome at macro gene level and at micro gene level.

6.3.3 Introspective–Genetic Feature Weight Learning

The feature weight learning approach discussed in this chapter is based on a combined genetic algorithm and genetic programming approach. Thus, by definition, it is a feedback or introspective learning approach, since it uses a mechanism commonly employed by genetic methods called *fitness function* to determine the performance

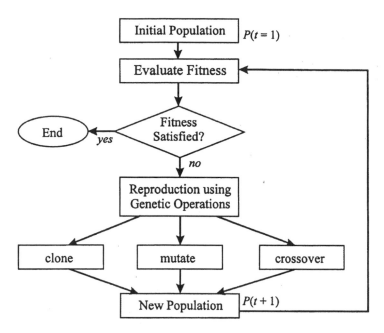

Fig. 6.4. Basic GA components and control structure.

during learning. However, the way feature weights are being updated is very different from the deterministic family of models described in Section 6.3.1.

- Firstly, within each iteration of the learning phase (see Fig. 6.2) both poor and good weight settings may be modified.
- Secondly, the modification (increase, decrease) of a weight is performed by means of the two genetic operations of mutation and crossover in a non- deterministic fashion (the weight may be increased or decreased by a small or a large amount). Hence, there is no need for spelling out, that is, defining a priori, the details of the amount and the 'direction' by which the weights should altered.

The diagram in Fig. 6.5 illustrates the basic architecture for learning case feature weights through a combined introspective/evolutionary learning approach. This general framework is used for both the learning of global and local weights. The box labeled 'adjust weights' shows clearly the role of the genetic operators for modifying the weights.

For both the learning of global and local case feature weights, the approach taken in this work is to represent an individual or chromosome by a vector, $\mathbf{W}$, of n 10-digit binary bit strings, S_i, such that $\mathbf{W} = (S_1, S_2, \ldots, S_n)$, where n is the number of features used to describe a case. Each bit string, S_i, is used to represent the weight, w_i, of a case feature, $w_i \in [0.000, 0.001, \ldots, 1.000]$, in the usual way. Based on the normalized weight range of $[0, 1]$, and on the requirement of a precision of three places after the decimal point, the range $[0,1]$ must be divided into at least $1 \times 1000 = 1000$ equal-sized ranges. This means that 10 bits are required to represent a feature weight,

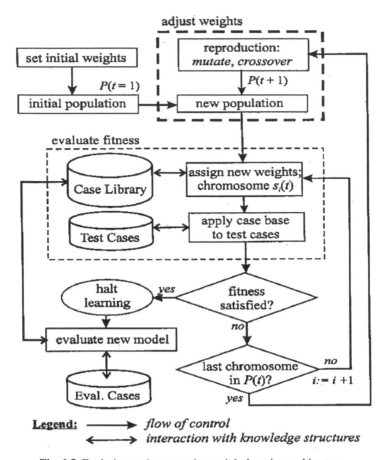

Fig. 6.5. Evolutionary introspective weight learning architecture.

since $512 = 2^9 < 1000 < 2^{10} = 1024$. Converting a bit string, $S_i = \langle b_i^9, \dots, b_i^1, b_i^0 \rangle$, into a feature weight, w_i, is done in two steps: (1) conversion of the bit string into an integer number, w_i', with base 10 using Equation 6.10; and (2) mapping of that integer into the corresponding real number, the weight w_i, using Equation 6.11.

$$w_i' = \sum_{j=0}^{9} b_i^j 2^j; \ \forall b_i^j \in \{0, 1\}, \tag{6.10}$$

$$w_i = 0 + 1\frac{w_i'}{2^{10} - 1}. \tag{6.11}$$

For example, the 10-digit 1/0-string $S = 0000010101$ would be converted to the integer w', and then to the real-numbered weight, w, as follows:

$$w' = 0 \times 2^9 \dots + 1 \times 2^4 + 0 \times 2^3 + 1 \times 2^2 + 0 \times 2^1 + 1 \times 2^0 = 16 + 4 + 1 = 21,$$

and
$$w = 0 + w'/(2^{10} - 1) = 21/1023 = 0.021.$$

The representation of the feature weights of a case within a single data structure (chromosome) – a vector, $\mathbf{W}$, of n 10-digit binary bit strings – gives rise to a somewhat more complex regime for the mutation and crossover operations.

The mutation operation on the feature weight vector chromosome, $\mathbf{W}$, is divided into a *macro-mutation* and a *micro-mutation* operation. Which of the two schemes is applied when mutation is applied to a particular chromosome is determined by a random selection scheme.

Micro-mutation randomly (no bias) selects a single macro gene, S_i, from the feature chromosome – the vector, $\mathbf{W}$, that represents all feature weights – and modifies (mutates) the macro gene according to the scheme described in Section 6.3.2. So here only a single bit, that is a micro gene, is randomly altered, such that $S_i^{new} = m(S_i^{old})$, where m denotes micro-mutation.

Macro-mutation randomly selects a single feature weight or macro gene, S_i, from the chromosome, $\mathbf{W}$, and replaces the macro gene by a new, randomly generated one. That is, $S_{i=rand(\{1,...,m\})}^{new} = M(r([0, ...00, 1...11]))$, where M denotes the macro-mutation operation, r a function, which randomly generates a 10-digit binary bit string, and $rand$ a function that randomly generates an index between 1 and m (random selection of macro gene). The macro-mutation operation is illustrated in Fig. 6.6.

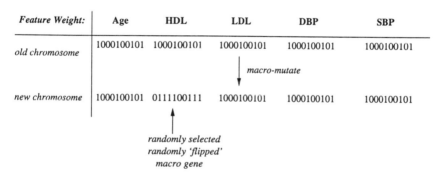

Fig. 6.6. Macro-mutation (HDL/LDL: high/low density lipoprotein cholesterol; DBP/SBP: diastolic/systolic blood pressure).

In contrast to mutation, crossover is simpler, as there is no macro version of this operation,[1] but only a micro-crossover. Once two chromosomes, $\mathbf{W}$ and $\mathbf{V}$, have been selected for crossover, a random scheme selects a feature weight or macro gene, S_i in $\mathbf{W}$, and the corresponding macro gene, R_i in $\mathbf{V}$. The new macro genes, S_i^{new} and R_i^{new}, are then obtained from S_i and R_i respectively by applying the micro- crossover

---

[1] A macro-crossover operation would generate a new weight vector, for example, by deriving the new weights of age and blood pressure by replacing them with the weights cholestrol and diabetes from the previous generation. Clearly, unlike with its counterpart for mutation, this operation doesn't make sense

scheme as described in Section 6.3.2. The newly obtained macro genes are then put back into the chromosomes, $\mathbf{W}$ and $\mathbf{V}$, to yield the two new chromosomes $\mathbf{W}^{new}$ and $\mathbf{V}^{new}$. This micro-crossover mechanism is illustrated in Fig. 6.7 (in the diagram the white and black bars correspond to case feature weights or macro genes of the chromosome).

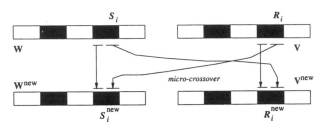

Fig. 6.7. Micro-crossover.

The aspects considered above apply to both feature weight learning architectures. The main differences between the two learning approaches lie mainly in the following features:

- *Added complexity of the local-weights model:* The complexity arises because for each of the n cases in the training set (case base) a population of m chromosomes (weight sets) is established, manipulated, and evaluated over a maximum of k generations; whereas in the global-weights model only m global weights (chromosomes) are established, manipulated, and evaluated over a maximum of k generations.
- *Evaluation of fitness:* For the global-weights model it is straightforward to assign to the training cases, i.e., the case base, m times the weights corresponding to the chromosomes of each generation, and determine the overall error (or fitness). With the local-weights model it is not obvious how the performance (or fitness) should be measured.

6.3.3.1 Learning of Global Feature Weights

Within the local-weights model a base or training case, c, within the case base, CB, is described by a pair, which consists of a feature vector, $\mathbf{F} = \langle f_1, f_2, \ldots, f_m \rangle$, and a solution, s, as follows: $c = (\mathbf{F}, s)$. The query cases within the test set, $TEST$, are defined as a pair, q, as follows: $q = (\mathbf{F}, ?)$, where the symbol '?' donates the solution that has to be found for q.

Definition 4. Based on the definition for cases, the case base, CB, is defined by a set of training cases, $TR = \{c_1, c_2, \ldots, c_i, \ldots, c_n\}$, a similarity metric, δ, a set of solution adaptation rules, A, and a set of feature weights vector, $\mathbf{w}_{glob} = \langle w_1, w_2, \ldots, w_m \rangle$, as follows:

$$CB = (TR, w_{glob}, \delta, A)$$

such that $\delta : T \times U \to [0, 1]$, where U refers to the *universe of cases* or possible cases, and the feature weights, $\mathbf{w}_{glob}$, correspond to the features such that w_1 is weight of

f_1, w_2 is weight of f_2, and so on, and $w_1, w_2, \ldots \in [0, 1]$. For the experiments the feature-to-feature similarity metric defined in Equation 6.6 and combined similarity rule defined in Equation 6.4 were used. The adaptation rules, A, are dependent on the application at hand. For the evaluation of the proposed learning models a regression task has been chosen (prognosis of risk change over time). The adaptation (solution transformation) rules for this task are realized by the formula given in Equation 6.12:

$$s(q) = \frac{1}{k} \sum_{i=1}^{k} s(c_i) \qquad (6.12)$$

where $s(q)$ denotes the solution (coronary heart disease risk change over a certain period of time) of a new case based on the solutions, $s(c_i)$, of the k most similar past cases (k is a pre-defined constant).

The general control architecture for the global-weights algorithm is depicted in Fig. 6.5. However, that architecture does not say much about the intrinsic mechanics of the algorithm; these are now discussed.

The first part of the algorithm consists of a procedure, realized by a case base message or method called $learnGlobalWeights$, which takes as parameters a set of test cases, $TEST$, the size of the populations, $popsize$, the maximal number of generations, g_{max}, that will be explored, and a threshold value for the maximal, t_{max}, fitness required (see Algorithm 6.1). Upon termination, the procedure returns an object called $fittest = (\mathbf{w}_{glob}, fit)$ which is a pair containing a feature weight vector, $\mathbf{w}_{glob}$, representing the global weights and the degree, fit, of fitness for that vector. The algorithm terminates if either the t_{max} is reached or the number of generations is exhausted. In line 04 the case base passes the message $assignFitnessGlobal$ to itself; this will have the result that each chromosome in the current population is assigned a fitness score.

Notice that in the algorithm we use an object-based notation. Also, the symbol '$\leftarrow$' denotes an assignment or copy of set-valued objects, and '$\leftarrow_{rep}$' denotes a 'copy' under the reproduction transformation rules discussed above.

CB::learnGlobalWeights($TEST, popsize, g_{max}, t_{max}$): **fittest**
01   Initialize: population counter: $t := 1$
02   Randomly create set, $P(t)$, of $popsize$ chromosome/finess pairs
03   **repeat**
04 $fittest := this.$assignFitnessGlobal$(P(t), TEST)$
05 $fitness := fittest.$getFitness$()$
06   **if** $fitness > t_{max}$ **then goto DONE**
07   Create next generation, $P(t+1)$, from $P(t)$ using genetic operators:
         $P(temp) \leftarrow_{rep} P(t); P(t) \leftarrow P(temp)$
08 $t = t + 1$
09   **until** $t \geq g_{max}$
10   **DONE:**
11   **end.**

Algorithm 6.1. Learning of global weights.

   The second part of the algorithm is realized by a case base message or method called $assingFitnessGlobal$ (see Algorithm 6.2) which determines the fitness of each chromosome in the current population, $P(t)$. Basically, this procedure fetches each chromosome in the current population (line 04), converts the chromosome into a set of global weights and assigns it to the case base (line 05), and then 'runs' a set of test cases against the case base to determine an error (line 06), which is then converted into a fitness score (line 07). The current chromosome is then assigned its fitness value (line 08), and the fittest chromosome is tracked (lines 09 to 10). Notice that we assume a pass-by-reference model similar to Java or Object Pascal in the algorithmic descriptions; thus the assignments made in lines 04 and 08 in Algorithm 6.2 result in the corresponding updates within the calling procedure $learnGlobalWeights$ (Algorithm 6.1).

6.3.3.2   Learning of Local Feature Weights
Within the local-weights model a base or training case, c, within the case base, CB, is described by a triple, which consists of a feature vector, $\mathbf{F} = \langle f_1, f_2, \ldots, f_m \rangle$, the associated weight vector, $\mathbf{w}_{loc} = \langle w_1, w_2, \ldots, w_m \rangle$, and a solution, s, as follows: $c = (\mathbf{F}, \mathbf{w}_{loc}, s)$. For each case there is a direct correspondence between the feature and its local weight, such that $\leftrightarrow$. The query cases within the test set, $TEST$, are defined as before.

Definition 5. Apart from the weights at the global level, the case base has a similar definition to the case base in Definition 4. Based on the definition for cases, the case base, CB, is defined by a set of training cases, $TR = \{c_1, c_2, \ldots, c_i, \ldots, c_n\}$, a similarity metric, δ, and a set of solution adaptation rules, A, as follows:

$$CB = (TR, \delta, A).$$

CB::assignFitnessLocal($P(t), TEST$): **fittest**
01   Initialize: $fitness := 0; error := 0; fittest$.setFitness(0)
02   Randomly create set, $P(t)$, of $popsize$ chromosome/finess pairs
03   **for** $i := 1$ **to** $|P(t)|$ **do**
04   Get ith chromosome/fitness pair: $current := P(t)$.getChromFitnessPair(i)
05   Set case base's weights based on ith chromosome:
         this.setGlobalWeights($current$.getChromosome())
06   Run case base against test cases to obtain error: $error := this$.run($TEST$)
07   Compute fitness from error: $fitness := f(error)$
08   Assign fitness to ith chromosome: $current$.setFitness($fitness$)
09   **if** $current$.getFitness() $>$ $fittest$.getFitness() **then**
10          $fittest := current$
11   **next** i
12   **end.**

Algorithm 6.2. Fitness function for global weights model.

   The first part of the local-weights learning algorithm consists of a procedure, realized by a case base message or method called $learnLocalWeights$, which takes as parameters a set of test cases, $TEST$, the size of the populations, $popsize$, the maximal number of generations, g_{max}, that will be explored, and a threshold value for the maximal, t_{max}, fitness required (see Algorithm 6.1). Upon termination, the procedure returns an object called FT, which is a set containing triples of the form $(c, \mathbf{w}_c, fit_c)$, where c represents the identifier of a case in the case base (training set), $\mathbf{w}_c$ reflects the local weights for c, and fit_c represents the weight vector's degree of fitness. The algorithm terminates if either the t_{max} is reached or the number of generations is exhausted. In line 04 the case base passes the message $assingFitnessLocal$ to itself, this will have the result that each chromosome in the current population is assigned a fitness score.

Notice that in this algorithm a population, $P_c(t)$, represents the different weights of a single case. Also, the variable fittest refers to an object containing a triple of the form $(c, \mathbf{w}_c, fit_c)$ as discussed above.

The second part of the algorithm is realized by a case base message or method called $assingFitnessLocal$ (see Algorithm 6.4) which determines the fitness of each chromosome in the current population, $P_c(t)$. Basically, this procedure fetches each chromosome in the current population (line 04), converts the chromosome into a set of global weights and assigns it to the case base (line 05), and then 'runs' a set of test cases against the case base to determine an error (line 06), which is then converted into a fitness score (line 07). The current chromosome is then assigned its fitness value (line 08), and the fittest chromosome is tracked (lines 09 to 10). Notice that we assume a pass-by-reference model similar to Java or Object Pascal in the algorithmic descriptions; thus the assignments made in lines 04 and 08 in Algorithm 6.4 result in the corresponding updates within the calling procedure $learnGlobalWeights$ (Algorithm 6.3).

CB::learnLocalWeights$(TEST, popsize, g_{max}, t_{max})$: **FT**
01   **For each** Case c in the case base CB
02   Initialize: population counter: $t := 1$
03   Randomly create set, $P_c(t)$, of $popsize$ chromosome/finess pairs
04   **repeat**
05       $fittest := this.$assignFitnessLocal$(P_c(t), c, TEST)$
06       $fitness := fittest.$getFitness$()$
07   **if** $fitness > t_{max}$ **then goto** DONE
08   Create next generation, $P_c(t+1)$, from $P_c(t)$ using genetic operators:
09       $P_c(temp) \leftarrow_{rep} P_c(t); P_c(t) \leftarrow P_c(temp)$
10       $t = t + 1$
11   **until** $t \geq g_{max}$
12   DONE:
13   Remember weights, $\mathbf{w}_c$, for case $c : FT \leftarrow fittest$
14   **Next** case
15   Assign all local weights to case base: $this.$setLocalWeights(Q)
16   **end.**

Algorithm 6.3. Learning of local feature weights.

CB::assignFitnessLocal $(P(t), c, TEST)$: **fittest**

01   Initialize: $fitness := 0; error := 0; fittest.\text{setFitness}(0)$

02   Randomly create set, $P(t)$, of *popsize* chromosome/fitness pairs

03   **for** $i := 1$ **to** $|P_c(t)|$ **do**

04   Get ith chromosome/fitness pair: $current := P(t).\text{getChromFitnessPair}(i)$

05   Set individual base case's weights, $\mathbf{w}_c$, based on ith chromosome:
             $this.\text{setLocalWeights}(current.\text{getChromosome}(), c)$

06   Run case base against test cases to obtain error: $error := this.\text{run}(TEST)$

07   Compute fitness from error: $fitness := f(error)$

08   Assign fitness to ith chromosome: $current.\text{setFitness}(fitness)$

09   **if** $current.\text{getFitness}() > fittest.\text{getFitness}()$ **then**

10 $fittest := current$

11   **next** i

12   Reset case c's weights to defaults: $this.\text{setDefaultLocalWeights}(c)$

13   **end.**

Algorithm 6.4. Fitness function for local weights model.

6.3.4   Results and Evaluation

The two weight learning schemes have been implemented and applied to a medical data set to predict change in *coronary heart disease* (CHD) risk of individuals over a certain period of time. CHD is a degenerative disease which is the result of an increase of *atheroma* (degeneration of artery walls caused by the formation of fatty plaques or scar tissue) in the coronary artery walls leading to total or partial *occlusion* (blockage). The resulting clinical feature is *myocardial infarction* (heart attack) and subsequently sudden death [23]. The main risk factors related to this condition involve physical inactivity, smoking, hypertension (high blood pressure), stress, and hypercholesterolemia (high cholesterol). A total of 83 middle-aged, male subjects undertook standard screening tests in order to identify selected modifiable and non-modifiable CHD risk factors [24]. The screening tests were carried out twice, in 1993 and in 1996. At both times a CHD risk score for each patient was established using the *Anderson* scheme [25]. Based on a small set of recognized CHD risk factors, the task of this application is to predict the *change* of Anderson CHD risk of asymptomatic individuals over a three-year period.

   The purpose of this study is *not* to establish a complete working model for predicting CHD risk change. Rather, in the light of the available data, we are concerned with a comparison between various models. For our studies, we have based our prognostic model on the so-called *Markovian assumption*. Basically, this assumption states that all patients in a given state at a given time have the same prognosis, no matter how they got to the present state. We admit that this is a very strong assumption. But as indicated above, this study is not so much concerned with trying to build a system that is best suited, in terms of absoluteness and completeness, to the medical task at hand. The data available for this study and the resulting case model are described below.

- *Case features* (data gathered in 1993): Age (in years), total cholesterol, HDL (high density lipoprotein cholesterol), cigarette smoking (in years), and SBP (systolic blood pressure); and

- *Case solution:* Risk change (change of *Anderson CHD risk score*) from 1993 to 1996. The *Anderson CHD risk score* is defined by a set of equations and a worksheet that allows users to estimate their current CHD risk by assigning a point score to a number of recognized risk factors.
- A total number of 83 cases was available for this study.

Thus the task of the resulting CBR prognostic model is to predict the risk change (case solution) of a patient or query case, q, over a period of three years based on k best-matching cases from the case base.

In order to gain insight into the performance of both feature weight learning models within the context of risk change prognosis, three reference models have been built and implemented:

- a CBR model with global feature weight settings that were obtained from a participating CHD domain expert (to manually generate *local* feature weights in this way was considered too unfeasible a task);
- a neural network model based on a standard back-propagation approach; and
- a standard multiple linear regression statistical model.

To evaluate the various prognostic models, the entire set of 83 cases was randomly partitioned nine times into a disjoint training set (71 cases) and an evaluation set (12 cases). The nine training/test set combinations served then as a basis for a nine-fold cross-validation procedure. For each of the nine training sets, the three reference models as well as several global and local feature weight learning models were then generated. All models – including the non-CBR models – were then applied to the corresponding evaluation sets, and the prediction errors (predicted risk change minus actual risk change recorded for the subjects in the evaluation set) were obtained. For all CBR models, the prediction was generated from $k = 6$ nearest neighbors according to Equation 6.12. The retrieval model used Equations 6.6 and 6.4 to determine the similarity between cases taking into account the global and local weights, respectively.

From a series of test runs using different population and generation size settings, the two best-performing global-weight and local-weight models have been chosen. For the global-weight models, population/generation size combinations of 100/50 and 100/100 performed best; these are abbreviated in Table 6.3 by 'gw GA 100/50' and 'gw GA 100/100' respectively. For the local-weight learning models, the best performing population/generation size combination was 100/25, hence the abbreviations 'lw GA 100/25'. On a 233 MHz/32 MB Pentium PC/NT4 platform, the training of a single local-weight model took approximately 4 hours! By comparison, the learning time for the global-weight approach was in the region of 15–20 minutes per training set.

The results of the experiments are concisely presented in Table 6.3. The second column shows the mean absolute error obtained from applying the nine models for each approach to the corresponding evaluation sets. Informal analysis-by-observation shows that the all models, except for the two global-weight models, are roughly the same in terms of the mean absolute error they produced (i.e., in the region of 2.37–2.46). The errors obtained with the global-weight models are in the range of 2.24–2.28, so they appear to be 'significantly' lower than the errors of the other models.

Table 6.3. Results of the various prognostic models

Model	Mean of MAE	Standard error	Significance
gw expert-defined*	2.46	0.00	n/s
gw GA 100/50	2.24	2.79	< 0.025
gw GA 100/100	2.28	2.05	< 0.050
MLR	2.37	0.87	n/s
lw 100/25/1	2.44	0.34	n/s
neural network	2.44	0.13	n/s

gw: global weights; lw: local weights; MLR: multiple linear regression; MAE: mean absolute
error; n/s: not significant; * reference model.

To evaluate these results more formally, the performances (errors) of all seven models
have been compared to a reference CBR model whose global feature weights were
manually established with the aid of the domain expert. This model is labeled 'gw
expert-defined' in the table.

On the basis of the nine mean errors for each model, a two-tailed t-test has been
performed to establish how significant the error differences are. In contrast to typical medical studies, which frequently rely on independent random *samples*, the experiments described in this chapter take repeated random samples (nine-fold cross-
validation) from the same base dataset. In such circumstances, the computation for
the *combined standard error*, SE, of two distributions A and B (here: nine mean errors of the 'gw expert-defined' reference model against the nine mean errors of all
other models) is defined by the combined or joint variance, VAR, and the sample size,
n, as follows [26]:

$$SE = \sqrt{\frac{VAR}{n}} \tag{6.13}$$

such that

$$VAR = \frac{1}{n} \sum_{i=1}^{n} [(\bar{x}_A - \bar{x}_B) - (x_{i,A} - x_{i,B})]^2 \tag{6.14}$$

where $\bar{x}_A$ and $\bar{x}_B$ represent the means of the sets A and B respectively, and $x_{i,A}$ and
$x_{i,B}$ refer to corresponding individual entries in the respective sets.

The third and fourth columns in Table 6.3 illustrate the obtained results. The third
column shows the standard error of the corresponding model against the 'gw expert-
defined' reference model, and the fourth column shows the resulting significance values. For an entry in the t-distribution table with $n = 9$ (nine cross-validations), we get
the following cut-off points for the standard significance level:

$$p < 0.05 \leftrightarrow SE > 1.83; \text{ and}$$

$$p < 0.01 \leftrightarrow SE > 2.82.$$

The empirical results obtained from this study indicate that the global-weight learning approach performs (prediction accuracy) much better than local-weight variations,

back-propagation neural networks, and multiple linear regression when compared with a CBR reference model with expert-defined, global case feature weights. Also, the efficiency (learning time) of the global-weight approach was clearly superior to that of its local-weight counterpart. This being the case, we feel that there is still room to further explore the local-weight model in particular with regard to the way fitness is determined. One approach could be to keep the learned weights for case features when proceeding to the next case in the learning phase. Another, obvious, aspect for future work is to apply the models to case bases of higher complexity with regard to the number of cases and the number of case features.

6.4   Learning Case Retrieval Models with Growing Cell Structures

As outlined in the introduction, the second soft computing approach to case retrieval is one based on a more recent neural computing model, called *growing cell structures* neural networks. This approach belongs to the unsupervised learning, partitioning based retrieval model category discussed above.

6.4.1   Growing Cell Structure Neural Networks

Growing cell structure (GCS) neural networks [27,28] are a variation of Kohonen's self-organizing maps (SOM) [29]. GCS offers several advantages over both non-self-organizing neural networks and the Kohonen self-organizing feature maps [30]. They have provided the basis for powerful information retrieval applications and similarity visualization tools [31,32]. Some the advantages are summarized as below:

- The network architecture or topology is automatically determined from the domain data and thus reflects the underlying characteristics of the domain more accurately than an ad hoc user-defined topology of a standard back-propagation network.
- In contrast to Kohonen SOMs and classical back-propagation configurations, the self-organizing model of GCS networks requires a small set of constant parameters; there is no need to define time-dependent or decay schedule parameters.
- In contrast to Kohonen SOMs, the adaptation rules of a GCS network permit the processing of data with changing probability distributions.
- The ability of GCS networks to resume a previously interrupted learning process enables *incremental* learning.
- Unlike back-propagation models, GCS networks have demonstrated their capacity to process data both of small and high dimensionality.
- GCS neural networks can be operate in both unsupervised as well as supervised learning mode.
- Because the final topology of a GCS network depends on the underlying data, it can be used for multiple data analysis and knowledge discovery tasks such as visualization, clustering, and navigation.

The type of GCS network used in this work is characterized by a two-dimensional space, where the units (cells) are connected and organized in triangles. The initial topology is a single (two-dimensional) triangle as illustrated in diagram (a) of Fig. 6.8. Each cell in the network is associated with a weight vector, w, which is of the same dimension as the input data. At the beginning of a learning process, the weight vector of each cell is initialized with random values. The basic learning process consists of topology modification (call insertion and deletion) and weight vector adaptations [27]. Based on a set, CB, of n *training cases* or *training input vectors*, learning is carried out as a sequence of k *input presentation epochs* (or simply epochs). Within a single epoch, the network is presented with all training cases, CB, in a sequential fashion. Thus an epoch is characterized by the number, n, of training cases. For each individual case presentation, the network performs a so-called *learning cycle*, which may result in topology modification and weight adaptation. Fig. 6.8(b) illustrates the GCS network topology after a number of learning cycles. The cell connections (lines between cells) reflect the weight vector difference of the corresponding cells.

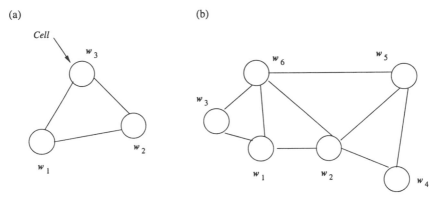

Fig. 6.8. (a) Initial topology of GCS. (b) GCS topology after learning.

In the first step of an individual learning cycle, the cell, c, with the *smallest* difference of its weight vector, w_c, and the actual input vector or case, x, is chosen (recall, weight vector and input vector dimensions are the same). This cell is referred to as the *winner cell* or best-match cell. This selection process is defined by Equation 6.15, where O denotes the set of all cells in the GCS topology. It may be implemented using for example *Euclidean distance* as defined in Equation 6.16, where O denotes the set of all cells in the GCS topology.

$$c : ||x - w_c|| \leq ||x - w_i|| \; ; \forall i \in O \qquad (6.15)$$

$$||x - y|| = \sqrt{\sum_{i=1}^{n}(1 - sim(x_i, y_i))^2} . \qquad (6.16)$$

The second step consists of the adaptation of the weight vectors of the winning cell and the winning cell's neighboring cells. This weight adaptation process is defined by Equations 6.17 and 6.18. The terms ε_c and ε_n represent the *learning rates* for the winning cell and its neighbors respectively. Both learning parameters are constant during learning, and $\varepsilon_c, \varepsilon_n \in [0, 1]$. The set of cells within the direct neighborhood of the winning cell, c, is denoted by N_c.

$$w_c(t + 1) = w_c(t) + \varepsilon_c(x - w_c) \qquad (6.17)$$

$$w_n(t + 1) = w_n(t) + \varepsilon_n(x - w_n) \; ; \forall n \in N_c \; ; N_c \subset O. \qquad (6.18)$$

The diagram in Fig. 6.9 illustrates the overall architecture for GCS based learning of case retrieval structures. The selection of the winning cell (Equation 6.15) and the weight adaptation process (Equations 6.17 and 6.18) are shown in the upper part of the diagram.

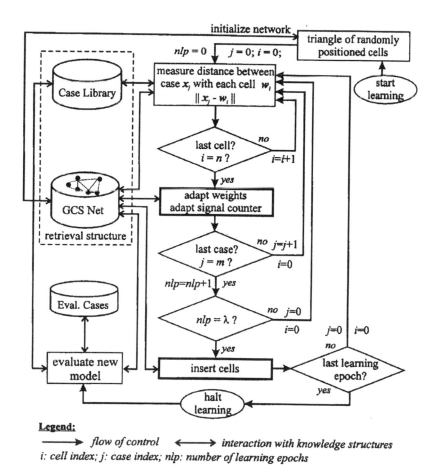

Fig. 6.9. GCS-based learning of case retrieval structures.

In the third step of a learning cycle, each cell is assigned a *signal counter*, τ, that reflects how often a cell has been chosen as winner. Equations 6.19 and 6.20 define the update procedure for the signal counter with regard to the winning cell (subscript c) and all other cells in the network (subscript i). The parameter α reflects a constant *rate of counter reduction* for the rest of the cells at the current learning cycle, t, where $\alpha \in [0, 1]$.

$$\tau_c(t + 1) = \tau_c(t) + 1 \tag{6.19}$$

$$\tau_i(t + 1) = \tau_i(t) - \alpha\tau_i(t) \; ; \; i \neq c. \tag{6.20}$$

Growing cell structures also modify the overall network structure by *inserting* new cells into those regions that represent large portions of the input data (see box labeled insert cells in Fig. 6.9). This form of structure modification is herein referred to as cell *insertion update*. In some cases, when higher statistical accuracy is of interest or when the probability density of the input space consists of several separate regions, a better model can be achieved by *removing* cells that do not contribute to the input data representation. This form of structure modification is herein referred to as cell *deletion update*. For reasons of limited space, only the cell insertion update is discussed here.

The frequency of cell insertion update is controlled by the parameter λ, which represents the number of learning epochs between two cell insertions. A learning epoch refers to the learning process carried out over all cases in the training set. If a training case consists of n cases then a learning epoch consists of n learning cycles. For example, for 100 training cases and a $\lambda = 5$, cell insertion will occur every 500 learning cycles. The equations that govern the cell insertion update process are given by Equations 6.21 to 6.23. The parameter h_i represents the relative counter value of cell i. When cell insertion is carried out, the new cell is inserted between cells q and r.

$$h_i = \frac{\tau_i}{\sum_j \tau_j} \; ; \; \forall i, j \in O, \tag{6.21}$$

$$q : h_q \geq h_i \; ; \; \forall i \in O, \tag{6.22}$$

$$r : \|w_r - w_q\| \geq \|w_p - w_q\| \; ; \; \forall p \in N_q. \tag{6.23}$$

The first step in the cell insertion update process is to determine the cell, q, with the highest relative counter value, h_q, according to Equation 6.22. The neighboring cell, r of q, with the most dissimilar weight vector is determined using Equation 6.23, and a new cell, s, is inserted between cells q and r. Fig. 6.10 illustrates the insertion of a new cell, s (black circle), between cells q and r after λ epochs of input presentations, that is, after $\lambda \times m$ learning cycles (m = *number of training cases*). The new cell, s, is connected to its neighbor cells, i, in such a way that s forms a triangle structure with any two of its neighbors.

Initially, the weight vector, w_s, of the new cell, s, is assigned a value equal to the mean of the corresponding element in the two existing weight vectors, w_r and w_q, of

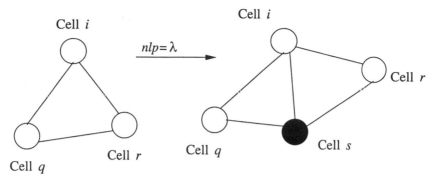

Fig. 6.10. Cell insertion update process.

the cells r and q. Finally, the signal counters, τ_i and τ_s, in the topological neighborhood, N_s, of s are adjusted. The topological *neighborhood*, N_s, of s is defined by the cell s itself and its neighboring cells, N_p, that is, $N_s = N_p \cup \{s\}$, and $\forall i \in N_p$. For reasons of limited space, the equations that govern the signal counter update are not presented here (see [28] for more detail).

After the entire GCS learning process is completed, each case (input vector, x_j) is represented by exactly, one cell, i, in the network structure whose weight vector, w_i, best matches the case's data, x_i. However, more than one case can share exactly the same cell as the best-match cell. There may be cells in the network which are not associated with any case in the training set. To put this another way, after completion of the learning process, each cell, i, in the network represents zero or more cases from the set, CB, of training cases, such that $CB \rightarrow C$ (where the set C represents all 'non-empty' cells in the network, and $x_j \in CB, i \in C$). This is already very close to what is required for partitioning based case retrieval as defined by Definition 2 and Definition 3. Furthermore, because the learning process has also associated a weight vector, w_i, with each cell, $i \in C$, in the network, it has effectively learned a knowledge structure, $r(x)$ (the component labeled GCS Net in Fig. 6.9). With this structure it is possible to assign a new case, $x \in U$, drawn from the universe, U, to a cell (or case group or cluster), $i \in C$. As outlined above, this structure serves as a basis to retrieve cases at run-time.

The abstract ideas and concepts discussed above are explained by means of the following example. The diagrams in Fig. 6.11 depict a GCS topology, which has emerged after learning based on the set of seven training cases, $CB = \{x_1, x_2, \ldots, x_7\}$. These cases may represent the stored past cases of a simple case base. The final cell structure is composed of five cells, Cell 1, Cell 2, . . ., Cell 5, as depicted by circles in the diagram. Each cell is associated with zero or more cases; for example, Cell 5 represents the case cluster consisting of the cases x_4, x_5, and x_6, Cell 2 consists only of one case (x_3), whereas Cell 3 is not associated with any cases at all. This organization of cells and their associate weight vectors (not shown in the diagram), w_i, effectively represents the retrieval knowledge structure, $r(x)$, for the underlying case base. This structure is used at run-time by the CBR system to locate relevant cases. At run-time, when the system is presented with a new query case, x, the distance $\|x - w_i\|$ between the query case weight vector, w_i, of each of the existing cells is calculated (see Equations 6.15 and 6.16). The cell with the shortest distance (highest similarity) to the query case is considered as the winning cell. All the cases represented with this cell are considered as most relevant to the problem reflected by the query case. For example, the query case, x, depicted in diagram (a) in Fig. 6.11 is assigned to Cell 1, thus, the cases x_1 and x_2 are retrieved for further analysis. In the event that there are no cases associated with the best-match cell, the cell closest to the best-match cell is considered. This situation is depicted in diagram (b) of Fig. 6.11, where the query case, y, is closest to Cell 3, which is 'empty'. In this case, the cell nearest to the best-match cell is chosen. In the example, it is Cell 4, which is associated with a single case, x_7.

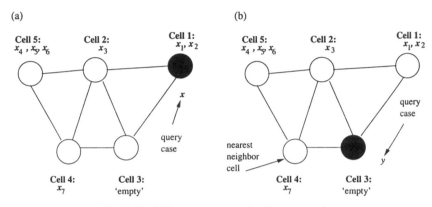

Fig. 6.11. GCS-based case retrieval, an example.

A GCS learning process continues until a desired network size (number of inserted cells) is reached. There is no standard for defining a priori the number of learning epochs and the exact number of cells required for the final GCS topology. Such values depend on the selection of the other learning parameters, the size of the database, and the number of classes (clusters) that are expected. Furthermore, it is expected that a high number of learning epochs may over-train the network and its capacity for generalization will be diminished. On the other hand, the GCS would not be able to 'learn' from the stored cases if a very low number of learning cycles are performed. With regard to the number of cells required to implement the most effective GCS something similar is expected: a very low number of cells would tend to classify the cases into a very small number of clusters (classes), a situation that may affect negatively the estimation performance of the GCS. At the same time, massive structures may contain a very few number of cases per cluster (cell), which also may influence negatively the prediction performance of the GCS.

According to Kohonen's theory of self-organizing maps (which form the basis for the GCS model), a winning cell is the most responsive cell to the input vector (case) under consideration. Thus a case is represented on the ordered spatial topology by the cell with the strongest activation. Moreover, at the end of the learning process, the cells of the network are spatially correlated, in such a way that cells at nearby points on the resulting structure are more similar than those widely separated (the proximity is based on the difference of their respective weight vectors). Therefore, cases represented at nearby points are more similar than those widely separated. In the case retrieval algorithm proposed in this chapter, when a winning cell does not contain any cases during the retrieval phase, its nearest cell is selected. This guarantees that the most similar cases will be retrieved.

6.4.2 Evaluating the GCS-Based Case Retrieval Model

In order to evaluate the potential of the proposed case retrieval scheme within CBR, an experiment based on real-world medical data was conducted. The underlying task of the experiment is that of prognosis, namely, prediction of *survival* of colorectal cancer patients after surgery. Note that the prognostic model is based on the so-called *Markovian assumption* [33]. Basically, this assumption states that all patients in a given state at a given time have the same prognosis, no matter how they got to the present state.

This study is concerned with post-surgery survival prognosis of colorectal cancer (cancer of the large bowel) patients. Each case is represented by 15 attributes, namely, sex, pathological type, polarity, tubule configuration, tumor pattern, lymphocytic infiltration, fibrosis, venous invasion, mitotic count, penetration, differentiation, Dukes stage, obstruction, and site, plus the number of months the patient survived after the operation (case solution). The number of cases in the training dataset (case base) and test set (query cases) was 158 and 30 respectively. A 12-fold cross-validation procedure was carried out.

A normalized version of the case description data described above served as the input value vector, x, for the GCS system. The overall task of the resulting CBR system is to predict the survival of a patient after surgery. For each of the 12 cross-validations, the GCS based learning procedure described above was carried out on each training set, and then applied to the corresponding test set. For each individual the *survival prediction*, $sur_{pred}(x)$, was derived, based on k retrieved cases, $C = \{x_1, x_2, \ldots, x_k\}$, by averaging the actual k survival figures, $sur_{act}(x_i)$, as follows (see also Equation 6.12):

$$sur_{pred}(x) = \frac{1}{k} \sum_{i}^{k} sur_{act}(x_i). \tag{6.24}$$

Notice that for the GCS based retrieval experiments the number of retrieved cases, k, is not constant, but depends on the number of cases in the retrieved cluster.

To evaluate the GCS model, a series of experiments with the classical similarity based CBR retrieval model has been performed using Equation 6.7 for local similarity and the weighted (uniform weight of 1.00 for each feature) k-nearest neighbor (k-NN) method with various constant settings for k. The total average absolute errors (TAAE in second row) for all experiments are presented in Table 6.4. The parameter settings for the GCS approach were as follows: 200 learning epochs, $\lambda = 10$, $\alpha = 0.095$, $\varepsilon_w = 0.095$, and $\varepsilon_n = 0.01$.

The result of this experiment shows that the GCS approach outperformed all standard fixed k-NN models. Taking the best-performing k-NN (the one with $k = 10$) as

Table 6.4. Errors based on GCS- and k-NN-based retrieval

Method	GCS based	4-NN	6-NN	8-NN	10-NN
TAAE	29.33	40.63	40.44	40.17	39.94

a reference model, and analyzing each individual cross-validation in more detail, we can see in Table 6.5 that the GCS model's superior performance was statistically significant (based on Equations 6.13 and 6.14) in seven out of the 12 cross-validation runs.

Table 6.5. GCS compared with 10-NN model

Test set	Average absolute error			
	GCS	10-NN	SE	Significance, p
1	26.83	36.27	1.45	n/s
2	24.37	38.91	2.18	$p < 0.025$
3	28.14	42.32	2.09	$p < 0.025$
4	36.86	44.11	1.32	n/s
5	26.82	32.61	1.03	n/s
6	31.64	42.96	1.64	n/s
7	29.01	39.97	2.19	$p < 0.025$
8	30.81	42.96	2.15	$p < 0.025$
9	27.53	34.43	1.34	n/s
10	33.17	46.82	2.00	$p < 0.025$
11	30.32	39.89	2.15	$p < 0.025$
12	25.52	37.97	2.12	$p < 0.025$
Tot. average	29.33	39.94	–	–

SE: combined standard error; n/s: not significant.

The results clearly demonstrate that such a network can be effectively used for CBR, particularly in applications where more than one best-match case is of interest. The prognostic model in the cancer domain showed a statistically significant improvement over the standard method in seven out of 12 tests, and the model was also superior in the remaining five test runs. The proposed case retrieval method performs both learning and retrieving tasks in a very short period of time. Moreover, on the basis of the implemented algorithm, visualization and searching applications can be realized in addition to the tested decision support (estimation) tasks.

6.5   Conclusions

Discussing a case retrieval framework, revolving around computational, representational, partitioning, and model based approaches, we proposed (a) an evolutionary approach to learning case retrieval structures in the computational model, and (b) a growing cell structure approach to learning case retrieval structures in the partitioning model. Perhaps the most interesting result of this study is that the incremental learning of useful case retrieval structures can be done, without a feedback of the system's performance, by clustering cases together with a unsupervised learning model (approach (b)).

References

1. T.W. Liao, Z. Zhang, C.R. Mount, Similarity Measures for Retrieval in Case-Based Reasoning Systems, *Applied Artificial Intelligence*, 12, 267–288, 1998.
2. D. Patterson, W. Dubitzky, S.S. Anand, J.G. Hughes, On the Automation of Case Base Development from large Databases, in *Proc. AAAI 1998 Workshop: Case-Based Reasoning Integrations*, pp 126–130, US, 1998.
3. M. Lenz, B. Bartsch-Spörl, H-D. Burkhard, S. Wess (eds), *CBR Technology: From Foundations to App lications*, Springer-Verlag, Berlin, 1998.
4. F. Gebhardt, Survey on Structure-Based Case Retrieval, in *Knowledge Engineering Review*, 12(1), 41–58, 1997.
5. W. Dubitzky, A. Schuster, D.A. Bell, J.G. Hughes, K. Adamson, How Similar is VERY YOUNG to 43 Years of Age? On the Representation and Comparison of Polymorphic Properties, in *Proc. 15th Int. Joint Conf. on Artificial Intelligence, IJCAI-99*, Nagoya, Japan, pp 226–231, 1997.
6. J.L. Kolodner, *Case-Based Reasoning*, Morgan Kaufmann, San Mateo, CA, 1993.
7. R.C. Schank, *Dynamic Memory: A Theory of Learning in Computers and People*, Cambridge University Press, 1982.
8. J.L. Kolodner, C.K. Riesbeck, *Experience, Memory, and Reasoning*, Lawrence Erlbaum Associates, Hillsdale, NJ, 1986.
9. M. Lenz, E. Auriol, M. Manago, Chapter 3: Diagnosis and Decision Support, in M. Lenz, B. Bartsch-Spörl, H-D. Burkhard, S. Wess (eds), *CBR Technology: From Foundations to Applications*, Springer-Verlag, Berlin, 1998.
10. N.G. Lester, F.G. Wilkie, W. Dubitzky, D.W. Bustard, A Knowledge-Guided Retrieval Framework for Reusable Software Artefacts, in *Proc. 17th Annual Association of Management/Int. Association of Management Conf. on Computer Science*, San Diego, US, pp 206–211, 1999.
11. S. Wess, K-D. Althoff, G. Derwand, Improving the Retrieval Step in Case-Based Reasoning, in *1st European Workshop on CBR (EWCBR-93)*, Otzenhausen, Germany, vol. I, pp 83–88, 1993.
12. K.J. Hammond, *Case-Based Planning: Viewing Planning as a Memory Task*, Academic Press Harcourt Brace Jovanovic, New York 1989.
13. M.J.A. Berry, G. Linoff, *Data Mining Techniques for Marketing, Sales, and Customer Support*, Wiley, New York, 1997.
14. T.M. Michell, *Machine Learning*, McGraw-Hill, New York, 1997.
15. A. Aamodt, A Knowledge-Intensive App roach to Problem Solving and Sustained Learning, PhD dissertation, University of Trondheim, Norwegian Institute of Technology, 1991.
16. C. Bento, E. Costa, A Similarity for Retrieval of Cases Imperfectly Explained, in *1st European Workshop on CBR (EWCBR-93)*, Otzenhausen, Germany, vol. I, pp 8–13, 1993.

17. M.T. Keane, B. Smyth, Retrieving Adaptable Cases: The Role of Adaptation Knowledge in Case Retrieval, in *1st European Workshop on CBR (EWCBR-93)*, Otzenhausen, Germany, vol. I, pp 76–82, 1993.
18. A. Bonzano, P. Cunninghan, B. Smyth, Using Introspective Learning to Improve Retrieval in CBR: A Case Study in air Traffic Control, in D.B. Leake and E. Plaza (eds), *Proc. Case-Based Reasoning: Research and Development, 2nd Int. Conf. on Case-Based Reasoning*, Springer, pp 291–302, 1997.
19. D. Wettschereck, D.W. Aha, T. Mohri, A Review and Empirical Evaluation of Feature Weighting Methods for a Class of Lazy Learning Algorithms, in D.W. Aha (ed.), *Lazy Learning*, Kluwer, Dordrecht, pp 273–314, 1997.
20. D.E. Goldberg, *Genetic Algorithms in Search, Optimization, and Machine Learning*, Addison-Wesley, Reading, MA, 1989.
21. Z. Michalewicz, *Genetic Algorithms + Data Structures = Evolution Programs*, 3rd edition, Springer-Verlag, Berlin, 1996.
22. J.R. Koza, *Genetic Programming: On the Programming of Computers by Means of Natural Selection*, MIT Press, Cambridge, MA, 1992.
23. Study Group, European Atherosclerosis Society, Strategies for the Prevention of Coronary Heart Disease: A Policy Statement of the European Atherosclerosis Society, *European Heart Journal*, 8, 77, 1987.
24. P. Lopes, R.H. Mitchell, J.A. White, The Relationships Between Respiratory Sinus Arrhythmia and Coronary Heart Disease Risk Factors in Middle-Aged Males, *Automedica*, 16, 71–76, 1994.
25. K. Anderson, P. Wilson, P. Odell, W. Kanel, An Updated Coronary Risk Profile: A Statement for Health Professionals, *Circulation*, 83, 356–361, 1991.
26. S.M. Weiss, N. Indurkhya, *Predictive data Mining: A Practical Guide*, Morgan Kaufmann, San Mateo, CA, 1998.
27. B. Fritzke, A Self-Organizing Network that Can Follow Non-Stationary Distributions, in *Proceedings of International Conference on Artificial Networks (ICANN-97)*, Laussane, Switzerland, pp 613–618, 1997.
28. B. Fritzke, Growing Self-Organizing Networks–Why?, in *ESANN'96: European Symposium on Artificial Neural Networks*, M. Verleysen (ed.), Brussels, pp 61–72, 1996
29. T. Kohonen, *Self-Organizing Maps*, Springer, Heidelberg, 1995.
30. B. Fritzke, Growing Cell Structures: A Self-Organizing Network for Unsupervised an Supervised Learning, *Neural Networks*, 7, 1441–1460, 1994.
31. M. Köhle, D. Merkl, Visualizing Similarities in High Dimensional Input Spaces with a Growing and Splitting Neural Network, in *Proc. of Int. Conf. on Artificial Neural Networks (ICANN'96)*, Bochum, Germany, pp 581–586, 1996.
32. J. Zavrel, Neural Navigation Interfaces for Information Retrieval: Are they More than an Appealing Idea?, *Artificial Intelligence Review*, 10, 477–504, 1996.
33. G. Kemeny, J.L. Snell, *Finite Markov Chains*, Springer-Verlag, New York, 1976.

7. An Architecture for Hybrid Creative Reasoning

Amilcar Cardoso, Ernesto Costa, Penousal Machado, Francisco C. Pereira and Paulo Gomes

Abstract. Creativity is one of the most remarkable characteristics of the human mind. It is thus natural that artificial intelligence research groups have been working towards the study and proposal of adequate computational models to creativity. Artificial creative systems are potentially effective in a wide range of artistic, architectural and engineering domains where detailed problem specification is virtually impossible and, therefore, conventional problem solving is unlikely to produce useful solutions. Moreover their study may contribute to the overall understanding of the mechanisms behind human creativity.

In this text, we propose a *computational hybrid architecture for creative reasoning* aimed at empowering cross-contributions from case based reasoning (CBR) and evolutionary computation (EC). The first will provide us a long-term memory, while the later will complement its adaptive ability. The background knowledge provided by the memory mechanism can be exploited to solve problems inside the same domain or problems that imply inter-domain transfer of expertise.

The architecture is the result of a synthesis work motivated by the observation that the strong similarities between the computational mechanisms used in systems developed so far could be explored. Moreover, we also propose that those mechanisms may be supported by a common knowledge representation formalism, which appears to be adequate to a considerable range of domains. Furthermore, we consider that this architecture may be explored as a unifying model for the creative process, contributing to the deepening of the theoretical foundations of the area.

7.1 Introduction

Creativity is consensually viewed as one of the most remarkable characteristics of the human mind. Its study has been a challenge for many scientists and researchers, especially for those of areas such as cognitive science and psychology. During recent years, a growing number of artificial intelligence (AI) groups have been working towards the study and proposal of adequate computational models to creativity. As a result of this endeavor, a new AI area is emerging, usually named creative reasoning (CR). Artificial creative systems are potentially effective in a wide range of artistic, architectural and engineering domains, where detailed problem specification is virtually impossible and, therefore, conventional problem solving is unlikely to produce useful solutions. Moreover their study may contribute to the overall understanding of the mechanisms behind human creativity.

Several explanation models, originated in the psychology and cognitive science fields, have been proposed for the creative process, like those suggested by Dewey [1], Guilford [2], and Wallas [3]. Generally, they split the process into steps, which may be summarized (with more or fewer differences) into the following ones: problem formulation and knowledge assimilation; conscious or unconscious search for a solution; proposal of a solution; and verification of the proposed solution. These models may constitute an important source of inspiration to computational models of creativity. Also relevant are the studies of De Bono [4] around the concepts of lateral and vertical thinking and their relation with creativity.

We may also look for other sources of inspiration besides human creativity. When we look to nature we see that all living species struggle permanently for life. The Neo-Darwinist theory, revising Darwin's first ideas in the light of modern genetics, gives us a scientific framework that explains how life forms survive by adapting themselves to environmental changes. In the center of this process is a mechanism that selects the fittest individuals and recombines their genetic material. Putting together 'good' parts of different individuals can give rise to a new and better one. This is clearly a way of producing innovative solutions [5]. But is nature capable of producing creative solutions? This is a more difficult question to answer. In fact the biological adaptive processes have a limitation: they do not have a long-term memory (although we can view multiploidy as a limited memory mechanism), and memory is an important part of the creative process. Thus, if we want to have a computational model of creativity, inspired in nature, we must introduce a memory element. This points to hybrid solutions.

In the past some creative systems based either on case based reasoning (CBR) or evolutionary computation (EC) techniques were proposed. CBR approaches can explore previous knowledge and have good explanatory capabilities. Nevertheless, they have difficulties exploring large search spaces. On the other hand, EC approaches are efficient in dealing with complex search spaces and explore parallelism in a natural way. However, they lack long-term memory and the incorporation of problem-specific knowledge and the interpretation of results is problematic.

In this text, we propose a *computational hybrid architecture for creative reasoning* aimed at empowering cross-contributions from CBR and EC. The first will provide us a long-term memory, while the latter will complement its adaptative ability. The background knowledge provided by the memory mechanism can be exploited to solve problems inside the same domain or problems that imply inter- domain transfer of expertise.

The architecture is the result of a synthesis work motivated by the observation that the strong similarities between the computational mechanisms used in systems developed so far could be explored. Moreover, we also propose that those mechanisms may be supported by a common knowledge representation formalism which appears to be adequate to a considerable range of domains. Furthermore, we consider that this architecture may be explored as a unifying model for the creative process, contributing to the deepening of the theoretical foundations of the area.

The remainder of this chapter is organized as follows. In Section 7.2 we give a synthetical presentation of the background concepts of CBR and EC. Those who are familiar with these two techniques may safely skip this section. In Section 7.3 we present a state of the art on creative systems, as well as on hybrid systems which resort to CBR and EC. In Section 7.4 we give an overview of some systems developed by our team using CBR and EC approaches. These systems motivate the presentation, in Section 7.5, of a common representation formalism and a unifying hybrid architecture. Section 7.6 is devoted to the presentation of an example which illustrates the application of the proposed architecture to creative reasoning. In Section 7.7 we present some improvements to the architecture which we are currently exploring. In Section 7.8 we draw some conclusions.

7.2 Background

This section is intended for readers who are not familiar with CBR and/or EC. We will briefly present the basic concepts behind CBR and EC, focusing on the main steps of their basic cycles and on the main issues concerning representation.

7.2.1 Case Based Reasoning

CBR uses past experience to solve new problems [6,7]. In a CBR system, experience is stored by way of cases, which form a case library. *Cases* are episodic chunks of knowledge that are used in the resolution of a new situation. The problem-solving process in CBR is based on the premise that identical problems have identical solutions. When a CBR system has a new problem to solve, it *retrieves* cases with similar problem descriptions. If the selected cases are different from the target problem, they must be modified in order to fit it. This modification of a retrieved case is called *adaptation*. Finally, the new case created by adaptation is *evaluated* and may be stored in the case base. The reasoning steps are illustrated in Fig. 7.1, where the iterative nature of the process is outlined.

Case representation is crucial in CBR, since the case representation delimits the CBR steps. For example, cases can only be efficiently retrieved if the important features of the problem description are represented. Cases can be represented by attribute/value pairs, hierarchies of concepts, objects (object-oriented style), textual description, causal models, or a combination of them.

In the case retrieval phase, the CBR systems must decide which cases are the best candidates to solve the target problem. There are several ways of doing it, but the most used ones are: using an indexing scheme, where there is a set of indexes associated to each case that are used to retrieve the case; and using a metric function like K-nearest neighbor to assess the similarity of the target problem and the case problem's description. Both have their advantages and disadvantages.

Case adaptation is one of the most unexplored phases of CBR. This may be explained by the complex and domain dependent nature of the adaptation process. In general terms, during adaptation, the CBR system must first identify the differences between the target problem and the cases' problem description, and then apply modification operators to change the case solution. These operators can be production rules, formulas, heuristics, or specific procedures.

The evaluation of the solutions generated by adaptation is important to provide feedback to the system. In this phase, the new solution is evaluated and, according to the evaluation's result, is stored in the case library and presented to the user; or it is rejected, which leads the system back to the adaptation phase. The evaluation can be done automatically or by a human.

The case learning step introduces flexibility and also the capability to adapt to new situations. In this phase, the feedback gathered from the evaluation phase can be stored, in order to be used again in similar situations. Several things can be learned, and the new case created to solve the target problem is the more basic and obvious of them. Other things can be learned; for instance, new adaptation operators, cases where the solution failed, and so on.

In summary, CBR provides a fast reasoning mechanism, specially suited for domains where there is no causal model; it can be used for evaluation where no algorithmic methods exist, and can avoid previous failure situations. Cases are also useful for interpretation of ill-defined concepts. One of the main drawbacks of CBR is that it is difficult to make the right index selection. Also, the solution space is focused around the case points, thus constraining the possible solutions.

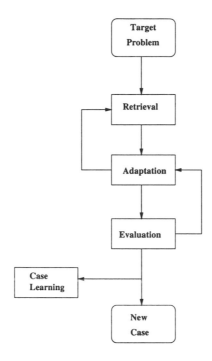

Fig. 7.1. The CBR cycle.

7.2.2 Evolutionary Computation

In recent years, a new paradigm for problem solving, called evolutionary computation (EC), has emerged. EC can be viewed as a set of stochastic search procedures inspired by the biological principles of natural selection and genetics [8]. Historically, these sets can be divided into four families, namely, evolution strategies [9,10], evolutionary programming [11], genetic algorithms [12] and genetic programming [13]. In spite of their differences they are all instances of the following general algorithm:

Procedure EC
  t=0;
  Intialize P(t);
  Evaluate P(t);
  While stoping_criterion_false **do**
      t = t+1;
      P'(t) = select_from P(t-1);
      P"(t) = use_op_modification P'(t);
      Evaluate P"(t);
      P(t) = merge P"(t) , P(t-1)
End_do

We start with a set of candidate solutions, called a *population*, usually defined randomly. Each element of that initial population, called an *individual*, is then evaluated using a *fitness function* that gives a measure of the quality of that element. Each individual is in fact an aggregate of smaller elements or units, which are called genes. Each gene can have different values or *alleles*. The algorithm then enters a cycle in order to generate a new population. We start by probabilistically selecting the fittest individuals. Then they undergo a modification process, using genetic inspired operators like *crossover* or *mutation* that will eventually alter the alleles of some genes. Finally, the old and new populations are combined and the result becomes the next generation that will in turn be evaluated. The cycle stops when a certain condition is achieved (for instance, a pre-defined number of generations). The selection mechanism introduces the possibility of *exploiting* promising parts of the search space. The crossover operator works by exchanging genetic material between two individuals, while the mutation operator modifies the alleles of some individuals. That way they promote the *exploration* of different areas of the search space. A good balance between exploitation and exploration is essential for the success of the EC algorithm. Another important aspect is the question about what is manipulated. The algorithm just described works, generally, with a low-level representation of each individual called its *genotype*. Nevertheless, in complex problems, the fitness function acts upon a high-level representation of an individual, its *phenotype*. It is thus necessary to have *decoders* from genotypes to phenotypes.

It is outside the scope of this text to refer all the variants of an EC algorithm. The interested reader can gain a deeper idea about the many EC algorithms that were proposed and their practical applications in Back et al. [8].

The success of EC algorithms is linked to their ability to solve difficult problems – problems where the search space is large, multi-modal and when domain knowledge is scarce and/or difficult to obtain. When this is the case EC proves to be more efficient than traditional algorithms.

7.3   Creative Systems and Hybrid Systems: State of the Art

There are multiple approaches to CR, and a diversity of applications have been explored by researchers of the area. In this section we will first give an overview of the present state of the art in computational creativity, focusing on the paradigms used, the domains in which they were applied and some successful experiences.

Afterwards, we will also present an overview of works that combine CBR and EC in a hybrid way.

7.3.1 Creative Systems

Several AI techniques have already been applied to tasks that are usually considered to require creativity, such as design, music composition, image generation, scientific discovery, and architecture. One of the paradigms that has been used with this purpose is CBR. It has been thoroughly applied, for example, in creative design, which is generally defined as a cognitive task where some knowledge of the mapping process between the problem and solution spaces is missing [14,15]. The solutions generated in creative design define new classes of artifacts, thus expanding the space of known designs. In this exploration process, designers often use old solutions to solve new problems - which suggests the suitability of CBR to this problem. In creative design, the old solutions are changed in novel ways or used in novel situations. Several researchers have used the CBR paradigm as a framework for building systems to tackle this task. Some very interesting CBR based works in this area are those of: Kolodner and Wills [16], which applies case indexing accordingly to various perspectives, in order to allow the search of the case memory for reminders that might be represented in a different way in the light of the current problem; Simina and Kolodner [17], which proposes a computational model that accounts for opportunistic behavior, which is considered to be characteristic of creative behavior; and Sycara and Navinchandra [18,19], which uses a thematic abstraction hierarchy of influences as a retrieval method. In this framework, case organization provides the main mechanism for cross-contextual reminding, which is very important in creative design. It also stresses the importance of composition of multiple cases and case parts.

Still in the CBR area, we can find works in music composition, such as Pereira et al. [20], presented later in this chapter, which applies musical analysis structures to build new musical pieces. Each of these structures is considered a decomposable case. The work of Arcos et al. [21] on expressive performance based on CBR is also interesting. Its cases consist of information extracted from spectral analysis of performances and the scores themselves. From this set of cases, the system infers a set of possible expressive transformations for a given new phrase.

CBR has also been applied in architecture [22], and we believe it is a promising paradigm to other kinds of creativity-demanding tasks. As nature by itself is known to be creative, it is not surprising that EC paradigms have also been used as a means to implement computational creativity. The difficulty of creating an evaluation function in domains such as image or music generation has led, frequently, to the use of interactive evolution (IE). In these systems the user evaluates the individuals, thus guiding evolution. IE has great potential as the countless already developed applications show. In the field of music, it has been applied in the evolution of rhythmic patterns and melodies [23]; in jazz improvisations [24]; and in composition systems [25]. The work of Dawkins [26], which uses IE to evolve artificial creatures based on the esthetic preferences of the user, Sims [27], Todd [28], Rooke [29] and Machado et al. [30], which resort to IE to evolve images, and Baker [31], where IE is used to evolve human faces, are some examples of the application of IE in the field of image generation. IE has also been successfully applied in the fields of design [32,33] and animation [27,34,35].

As far as we know, in the field of image generation there has been only one attempt to automate fitness assignment: the work of Baluja et al. [36]. However, the results produced by this system, which uses neural networks to evaluate images, were disappointing.

There have been several attempts to automate fitness assignment in the musical field. Some examples of this type of work are: Horner and Goldberg [37], which use genetic algorithms (GAs) to evolve thematic connections between melodies; McIntyre [38], which uses GAs to generate musical harmonization; Spector [39,40] which resorts to genetic programming to evolve programs that generate jazz melodies from an input jazz melody; and Papadopoulos and Wiggins [41] use GAs to evolve jazz melodies based on a progression of chords. However, and in spite of the numerous applications, Wiggins et al. [42], who have studied the performance of this type of system, defend that these approaches are not ideal for the simulation of human musical thought.

CBR and EC are not the only approaches to the resolution of tasks demanding creativity. Other techniques currently used are knowledge based systems, as in Harold Cohen's AARON[43] and Ed Burton's ROSE [44] in visual arts, and the work of Pachet and Roy [45] in music; mathematical models (e.g., the Markov chains of Cambouropoulos [46] to assist with music composition); and grammars (e.g., the work of Cope [47] in music, and of Stiny [48] in architecture).

7.3.2   Hybrid Systems Based on CBR and EC

There are a few systems that try to combine CBR and EC. Most of the work was done by Sushil Louis and his co-workers [49–52], who built the CIGAR system, and by Ramsey and Grefensttete [53]. The main idea of CIGAR was to use a base of cases to initialize the population, and then let the EC algorithm do its typical adaptation work. The first cases are former solutions of old problems obtained by running the GA alone (see Fig. 7.2).

Louis used his system to solve a similar problem or a set of similar problems. He also studied how many cases to inject into the population, coming from the base of cases, and which ones should be chosen. Finally, he also studied the possibility of injecting cases not only into the initial population but also in intermediate ones. Some of the problem domains used to test these ideas were combinational circuit design, open shop scheduling and rescheduling and function optimization. The results presented showed that with a judicious choice the combination CBR and EC gave better results. Other authors had also used the idea of injecting new, random generated, individuals into a population at certain times. For instance, Eshelman [54], in his algorithm named CHC, replaces the mutation operator, used in the standard GA to insure population diversity, by a restarting process applied to the population. Once again, the definition of when to do it, how many new individuals should be generated randomly and which

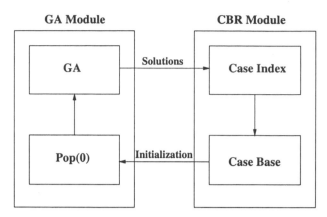

Fig. 7.2. The CIGAR system.

ones should be kept from the previous generation is an important issue and is most relevant when we deal with creative systems.

As far as we know, nobody has tried to use a hybrid system to produce creative solutions. Nevertheless, Goldberg [5] states that there are forms of adaptation which go beyond innovation. He suggests two ways by which this can be achieved: *remapping the primitives*, that is, changing the representation; and performing *metaphorical transfer*, that is, the transfer of a solution from a known problem domain to another.

7.4   Creative Reasoning

During recent years, the authors have centered most of their research work on the development of CBR based and EC based approaches to CR. In this section we will present in some detail the main applications developed so far. Some common characteristics of the work, particularly those which concern the adoption of a tree-like knowledge representation, will constitute the basis for the hybrid architecture that we will propose in subsequent sections.

7.4.1   Creative Reasoning with CBR

The capability of reminding previous experiences to draw analogies with the current situation has made CBR a good framework to support creative design [16,55]. In the following subsections we present several approaches to CR with CBR which we have developed so far. There are three main systems: IM-RECIDE, a generic CR shell; CREATOR and CREATOR II, creative design systems in the area of digital circuit design; and SICOM/INSPIRER, a system that uses CBR for creating new musical pieces.

7.4.1.1   IM-RECIDE
IM-RECIDE [55] is a generic creative reasoning shell that uses CBR as the main reasoning mechanism. Its reasoning cycle comprises several steps: problem definition, space initialization, problem solving, verification and evaluation. The first step

comprises problem specification, where the user states a new problem in terms of goals and constraints. In the initialization phase the system clusters cases in different sets, each one called a reasoning space. These spaces allow a gradual exploration of the case library enabling the system to generate new designs. In the problem-solving phase, reasoning operators are applied to old solutions for generation of new ones. If no solution is generated within a specific space, the system switches to the next space from the list that was created during the initialization phase. When a solution cannot be generated, and there are no more spaces to search for, the user is asked to give a solution for the problem. After a solution has been generated it has to be verified and evaluated. In a first step, it is internally validated by failure cases (verification). Failure cases represent constraints in the generation of new solutions. If a failure case is triggered by the new solution, then the solution is rejected. If a solution passes the internal validation, the user is asked to accept or reject the new case. If she/he rejects the new solution, then the user is asked to explain this rejection in terms of failure cases. After this, the process returns to the problem-solving step. This last phase is called evaluation because the user has to make a decision about the originality and validity of the case.

Case representation is very important for a CBR system, because it determines the capabilities of the system. Within IM-RECIDE, a case is represented by a triple $< P, S, R >$ with P and S, respectively, a set of facts representing the problem and solution descriptions, and R a set of rules representing a causal justification (for a more detailed description see [56]). A fact is composed by a function name (functor), and n arguments, with n equal to or greater than zero. The justification is a causal tree, linking problem facts to solution facts through rules. The case library also comprises failure cases representing design constraints.

For case retrieval, we consider four spaces of knowledge: Space I, Space II, Space III and Space IV. Each space comprises the cases possessing a set of common properties concerning the target problem. Each space forms a cluster in the case library. The definition of each space is done in terms of the characteristics that the cases within this space share with the target problem. Creativity can be seen as the result of reasoning on spaces of cases increasingly further away from the target problem. As the system goes from Space I to Space IV, it drifts away from the problem, trying to find non-trivial solutions. The retrieval process starts with the cases in Space I, going from space to space, until it reaches Space IV.

Space I comprises the cases for which all functor/argument pairs belonging to the problem description match the new problem. Space I is considered the space normally associated with the current problem. Most of the current CBR systems use cases from this space. Cases for which all functors describing the problem component match the new problem belong to Space II. This space is related to problems similar to the target problem. This space is often called the innovation space, where parametric adaptations are usually done, sometimes resulting in using a novel value for a well-known functor. Space III contains the cases which have explanation rules with all functor/argument pairs matching the target problem. Space III is defined using causal knowledge, which makes similarities between cases and the target problem more abstract, but also more important. This space is usually associated with creative solutions, but also with bizarre ones.

Space IV gathers all cases that contain at least one explanation rule with at least one functor/argument pair matching the target problem. Space IV is like a speculation space where cases have remote similarities to the target problem, because constraints were relaxed. This relaxation allows the system to explore cases considered distant from the target problem. Once again, the knowledge used to do this is the causal knowledge comprised in the explanations.

We now describe the adaptation mechanisms used in IM-RECIDE, called adaptation operators. These operators modify cases in the current space in order to solve the new problem. The cases that are used for generation of the new case are called the source cases. The selection of the cases for adaptation is performed through a metric [57]. These cases are selected from the set of cases in the current working space.

Each space possesses a set of pre-defined adaptation operators. These operators are used accordingly to the type of cases that the space comprises. The operators in Space IV are more powerful than the operators in Space I. This is an obvious situation, because cases in Space IV have fewer similarities to the problem. In order to reach a valid solution, more difficult adaptation operations must be done. Associated with the operator capabilities is the complexity of the computational process originated by each operator, the cognitive risks involved, and the probability of generating a more creative solution.

A solution of one case belonging to Space I does not need to be modified in order to become a solution to the target problem. Therefore, a metric is used for selection of the best case, and its solution is the one for the target problem. Cases in Space II have only some different values regarding the problem description. In order to meet the target problem requirements, it is necessary to modify the old case solution. This solution is derived from the old case by the propagation of the differences in the old problem to the old solution. The causal knowledge is used to guide the propagation process. The selected case is chosen using a metric function, which measures the similarity of cases against the target problem. Space III generates new solutions by splitting and merging of case pieces. IM-RECIDE starts selecting the most similar case from the set of episodes comprising Space III. Then it splits the case into pieces, selecting the pieces that match part of the target problem. These pieces are then merged to form a new case. If the problem description in the new case has some missing parts in regard to the target problem, other cases are selected to contribute case pieces to complete it. Pieces from these cases that are relevant for the new case are merged with it. In Space IV there are several adaptation operators, and they can be applied in sequence. Splitting and merging is one of the operators within this set. The other operators are elaboration, reformulation, substitution, and generalization. Elaboration comprises relaxing and/or strengthening of constraints described in a case problem, in order to match the target problem description. The case solution is suggested as the new solution. Reformulation involves changing the new problem description according to constraints imposed by failure cases. Substitution comprises replacing a functor/argument pair in the past case in order to make it similar to the new problem. The solution that results from this substitution is given as the one for the new problem. Generalization involves considering values initially not considered in the problem description of a past case, and assuming the case solution remains unchanged.

After a solution is created, it is verified by the failure cases. If the solution matches one failure case, then it is rejected. Only solutions that the system assumes to be correct, by its current knowledge, are shown to the user.

7.4.1.2   CREATOR and CREATOR II

CREATOR is a case based creative design system in the domain of digital circuit design. CREATOR comprises four different modules: reasoning, knowledge base, evaluation and meta-control. The system was developed having SBF models [58,59] as the case representation formalism. The reasoning module is responsible for problem elaboration, retrieval of relevant cases and adaptation of cases. The knowledge base comprises the case base, general domain knowledge and memory structure. Hierarchies of functions, structures and substances are used as general domain knowledge. This is important for several purposes, one of which is the construction of the memory structure. The memory structure has two main goals: to index cases and to allow space exploration. The evaluation module verifies and validates the generated solutions, while the meta-control module controls and coordinates all the other modules. The evaluation module and adaptation processes are being implemented in CREATOR II, which is the successor of CREATOR.

Within our framework, design cases are represented in the form of SBF models. These models are based on the component-substance ontology developed by Bylander and Chandrasekaran [60]. A case comprises three parts: (1) problem specification; (2) explanation; (3) design solution. The explanation is in the form of a causal chain, representing the design behavior. The case solution describes the design structures that accomplish the functionalities described in the target problem. Thus the problem specifications are related to the design function, the explanation to the design behavior, and the solution to the design structure.

The problem specification comprises a set of high level functionalities (HLFs) and a set of functional specifications (FSs) which must be held by the design. HLFs are abstract functionalities, used to help the user in specifying the design problem. While an HLF is a function that can be decomposed into several subfunctions, an FS is undecomposable. An FS is defined in detail in accordance with input and output substances. A design problem is represented by a tree of functionalities, where leaves are FSs and the high levels in the tree represent HLFs. Each leaf in the tree represents an FS in a schema comprising the initial behavior state, the final behavior state, behavioral constraints, external stimulus to the design, and structural constraints.

The design solution is in the form of a hierarchy of device structures. Each structure can be viewed as a set of device structures where substances can flow through. The structure schema comprises information such as: structure class, sub- structures, super-structures, relations, properties and functions. Figure 7.3 shows the high level representation of an arithmetic and logic unit (ALU), where each node in the tree represents a structure. Each of these structures has a corresponding structure schema.

A case explanation describes the causal behavior of the design in terms of directed graphs (DGs). The nodes of a DG represent behavioral states and the edges represent state transitions. One or more substance schemas can compose a behavioral state. A substance schema characterizes the properties and the property values of a substance.

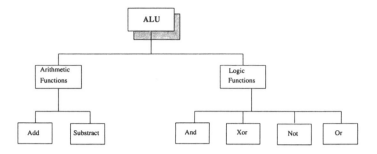

Fig. 7.3. A representation for an arithmetic and logic unit (ALU) in CREATOR.

A state transition represents the conditions under which the transition between behavioral states occurs.

The memory structure that supports case retrieval comprises two substructures: (1) a hierarchy of HLFs and FSs; and (2) a graph, whose nodes represent cases, and whose links describe functional differences between cases. The hierarchy of functions is used as an index structure for selection of the starting cases. The starting cases have at least one FS in common with the target problem. These cases are then used as starting points for exploration of the case graph. The leaves of the hierarchy are nodes that describe an HLF instance. These nodes are called list of functions (LF) and they comprise a set of HLFs and/or FSs. These nodes are extracted from cases and index the case they belong to, thus connecting the hierarchy of functions to the graph of cases. Two cases can be connected by difference links, which represent the differences between the problem description of the cases linked. A difference link is created only when the cases it connects have at least one FS in common. A difference link connecting two cases comprises three parts:

- the set of FSs that belong to the first case but don't belong to the second one;
- the set of FSs that belong to the second case but don't belong to the first one;
- the set of FSs common to both cases.

The reminding of useful experiences in a case based system is a critical issue. The accuracy of case retrieval in case based CR is important, but even more important than that is the capability to explore several solutions. Within our framework, accuracy is achieved by the use of functional indexes, and space exploration takes place through the use of difference links in the graph of cases. The FSs defined in the target problem are used as probes to retrieve the set of starting cases. Then, a best starting case is selected as a starting point in the search space. The search space is represented by the graph of cases. Exploration is performed using the difference links necessary to go from one case to another.

An important feature of the exploration algorithm is the selection of cases according to the adaptation strategy that will be used for generation of the new solution. The retrieval algorithm explores the case graph, searching for cases with features suitable for the adaptation method that will be applied. This makes retrieval an adaptation-guided process as defined by Smyth and Keane [61], although there are some differences to their process. Two of the adaptation strategies considered within our framework are thematic abstraction and composition. Thematic abstraction is an adaptation strategy that generates a new solution from a single case. It consists of the transfer of knowledge from a case to the target problem, in order to create a new design. The composition strategy deals with one or multiple cases. It splits and/or merges case pieces generating new solutions – it is a multi-case strategy.

7.4.1.3 SICOM/INSPIRER

Following some of the features from IM-RECIDE, we designed INSPIRER [62] for creative problem solving in domains in which knowledge can be represented by hierarchically structured cases. This framework was deeply tested in the music domain, and its implementation, SICOM [20], generated some pieces of music from a small case base with three compositions from a seventeenth century Portuguese baroque composer, Carlos Seixas. In SICOM, each case consists of a highly detailed analysis with several layers of abstraction, in which a piece of music is progressively subdivided according to thematic groupings (following harmonic, melodic and rhythmic principles from music theory). The result is a strictly hierarchical structure complemented by causal links that establish non-hierarchical relations (see Fig. 7.4). This kind of structured organization is common within music and some other artistic domains like architecture, literature and visual arts.

Generally, each case in SICOM is a complete piece of music, represented by a set of interrelated nodes (case pieces) extracted from music analysis.

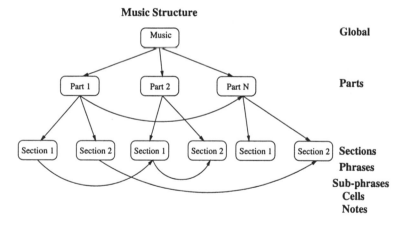

Fig. 7.4. Representation of a musical piece in SICOM.

The generation of a composition consists of the creation of a new structure applying case pieces from the case base. This generation is taken in a top-to-bottom and left-to-right sequence, as illustrated in Fig. 7.5 (i.e., it starts by choosing the more abstract and temporally preceding nodes).

One key point of systems such as INSPIRER/SICOM is that of the similarity metric. It is according to this measurement that it selects which nodes to apply or to avoid

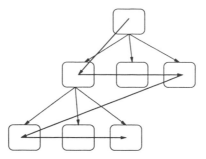

Fig. 7.5. Sequence of generation of a musical piece in SICOM.

in a new composition. Unfortunately (or fortunately), there are no formulas to evaluate a good solution in the musical domain. Moreover, we don't have a clear definition of what is or is not a good choice for any specific situation during the composition of a new piece of music. We do have the clear notion that context and structure can be determinant to the success of a choice and we have a set of composition rules to help with evaluation and adaptation. The similarity metric that we apply in SICOM [63] takes two main aspects of a node into account: its intrinsic properties (e.g., its internal attributes, like the melodic contour it defines) and its context (e.g., the causal links connected to it, the attributes of its parents, its position in the whole structure). After applying this similarity metric, SICOM can use one of several orderings to select the node (e.g., choosing the most similar; the least similar; avoid the first 20% of the candidate list, etc.).

The output compositions of the project SICOM/INSPIRER, although not being comparable to those of a professional composer, are nevertheless very interesting, especially taking into account that it has a library with only three cases. A particular example of its performance is the introductory part of its compositions. Each of the three Carlos Seixas' pieces had a similar introductory part, but SICOM was able to generate several new structures with different and correct (according to the style) solutions.

7.4.2   Creative Reasoning with Genetic Programming

As stated before, EC has great potential for creative reasoning. In this section we will make a brief yet comprehensive description of NEvAr (neuro-evolutionary art).

NEvAr is an evolutionary art tool, inspired in the work of Sims [27] and Dawkins [26], that allows the evolution of populations of images from an initial one using iterative evolution. The presentation of the underlying model will follow. We will finish this section by showing some experimental results and drawing some overall conclusions.

7.4.2.1   Representation
As in most GP applications, in NEvAr the individuals are represented by trees. Thus, the genotype of an individual is a symbolic expression, which can be represented by a tree.

The trees are constructed from a lexicon of functions and terminals. The internal nodes are functions and the leaves terminals. In NevAr, we use a function set composed mainly by simple functions such as arithmetic, trigonometric and logic operations. The terminal set is composed of the variables x and y, and of constants which can be scalar values or 3d-vectors.[1]

The interpretation of a genotype results in a phenotype, which in NEvAr is an image. The easiest way to explain how this is achieved is through an example. Let us consider the function $f(x, y) = (x + y)/2$ with $x, y \in [-1, 1]$. This function can be represented by the tree presented in Fig. 7.6.

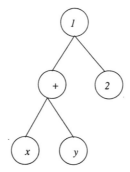

Fig. 7.6. Representation of $f(x, y) = (x + y)/2$ in the form of a tree.

How can we visualize this function? One hypothesis is making a tridimensional graphic such as the one presented in Fig. 7.4a. Another option would be to view this graphic from the top and indicate the value of the function through a color. The value -1 could correspond to 0% luminance (black) and 1 to 100% luminance (white); the values in between -1 and 1 would be represented by intermediate luminance values. This approach yields an image similar to the one presented in Fig. 7.7b. In Fig. 7.8 we present some examples expressions and the images generated by them.

7.4.2.2 Genetic Operators

In NEvAr we use two kinds of genetic operators: recombination and mutation. As recombination operator we use the 'standard' GP crossover operator [13] which exchanges sub-trees between individuals (see Fig. 7.9): given two individuals A and B, we select randomly two crossover points (one node of A and one of B) PA and PB; these nodes are the roots of two sub-trees; then we swap the sub-trees, thus obtaining two new individuals A' and B'.

We use five mutation operators that are similar to those used in [27]:

- Sub-tree swap – randomly select two mutation points and exchange the corresponding sub-trees.
- Sub-tree replacement – randomly select a mutation point and replace the corresponding sub-tree by a randomly created one.

---

[1] The three-dimensional vectors are necessary to produce color images: each dimension of the vector corresponds to a color channel (red, green and blue)

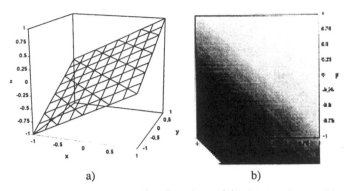

a)   b)

Fig. 7.7. (a) Tridimensional graphic of $f(x, y) = (x + y)/2$. (b) A color graphic of the same function.

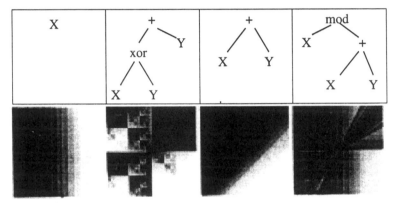

Fig. 7.8. Some simple functions and the corresponding images.

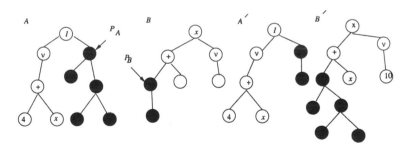

Fig. 7.9. Example of crossover between the individuals A and B.

- Node insertion – randomly select an insertion point for a new, randomly chosen, node. If necessary, create the required arguments randomly.
- Node deletion – the dual of node insertion.
- Node mutation – randomly select a node and change its value.

These operators induce changes at the phenotype level. In Fig. 7.10, we show examples of the application of the crossover operator. As can be seen, the crossover between two images can produce interesting and unexpected results. Additionally, there are cases in which the images seem to be incompatible, i.e. images that, when combined, result in 'bad' images.

Fig. 7.10. In the top row, the progenitor images. In the bottom row, some examples of the results generated by the crossover among them (color images available at http://www.dei.uc.pt/~amilcar/softcompbook/fig10.htm).

In Fig. 7.11 we give examples of images generated through mutation. Once again, the results of this operation can give quite unexpected results.

7.4.2.3 Model

In NevAr, the assignment of fitness is made by the user and, as such, she/he has a key role. The interaction of human and computer poses several problems. For instance, we cannot use populations with a large number of individuals, or make big runs. It would be unfeasible to expect that a human would be willing to evaluate one hundred individuals per population over a period of one thousand or more populations. Thus, to produce appealing images, NevAR must do it in a few evolutionary steps and in a low number of individuals' evaluations.

The fact that NEvAr is an interactive tool also has the advantage that a skilled user can guide the evolutionary process in an extremely efficient way. She/he can predict

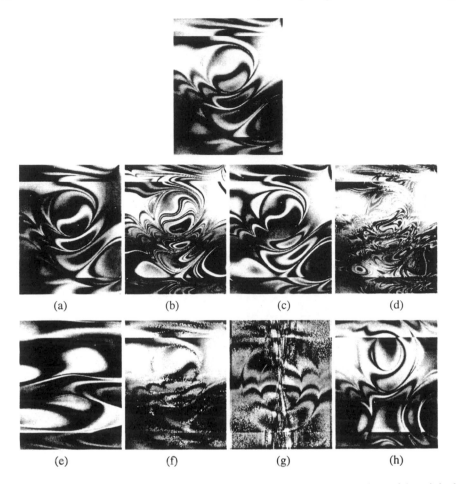

Fig. 7.11. In the top row, the original image. In the bottom rows, several mutations of the original image. The images a and b where generated through node mutation, c and d through node insertion, e through node deletion, f and g through sub-tree swap, h by sub-tree replacement (color images available at http://www.dei.uc.pt/~amilcar/softcompbook/fig11.htm).

which images are compatible, detect when the evolutionary process is stuck in a local optimum, etc. In other words, the user can change its evaluation criteria according to the specific context in which the evaluation is taking place. In the design of NevAr, we took these aspects into consideration.

Fig. 7.12 shows the model of NEvAr. In the following we will refer to the set of all populations, from the initial to the last, of a particular GP run as the *experiment*.

NEvAr implements a parallel evolutionary algorithm, in the sense that we can have several different and independent experiments running at the same time. It is also asynchronous, meaning that we can have an experiment that is in population 0, for example, and another one that is in population 100. Additionally we can transfer individuals between experiments (migration) and can also transfer individuals from one population to another.

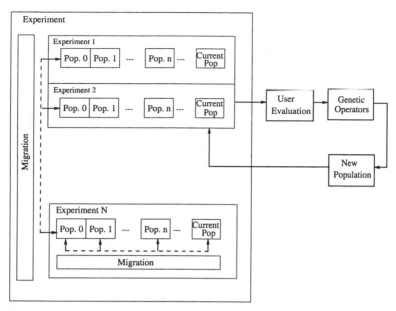

Fig. 7.12. The evolutionary model of NEvAr. The active experiment is depicted in gray.

We will illustrate the utilization of this model through an example. Let's suppose that the user creates, to start, two different experiments, a and b, the initial population of a is randomly generated and has size N, and the initial population of b has size 0. The user focuses her/his efforts in experiment a and evaluates the individuals of successive populations generated by NEvAr. When the user finds images that she/he likes, she/he adds these images to the current population (in this case the population 0) of experiment b. If at a given point the user feels that the evolutionary process would benefit if the next population was generated by the combination of the individuals of the current population with individuals previously transferred to population b, she/he adds those individuals to the current population and the evolutionary process continues.

If the user, at a certain point, chooses to focus on experiment b, NEvAr will generate a new population from the current one (population 0), which is composed, exclusively, of individuals transferred from a. Thus, the initial population of experiment b is not random, but exclusively composed by fit individuals that were originally generated in other experiments. In fact, experiment b can be seen as a database of images, which may be used to initialize future experiments. We may generalize this approach by organizing a gallery of images.

As stated before, NEvAr also allows migration within experiments. This feature is important because of the limited size of each population, since it allows the revival of images from previous populations. It is also possible to go back to a previous population and change the evaluation of the individuals, which allows the exploration of different evolutionary paths.

In Fig. 7.13 we give some examples of images generated by NEvAr). These images were presented in the exhibit *Art and Aesthetics of Artificial Life* by Nicholas Gesseler (curator), which took place at the Center for the Digital Arts of the UCLA.

Fig. 7.13. Some of the images presented the *'Art and Aesthetics of Artificial Life'* exhibit (color images available at http://www.dei.uc.pt/~amilcar/softcompbook/fig13.htm).

The results achieved with NEvAr clearly show the power and potential of interactive evolution techniques, and the advantages of the reuse of past solutions (images). The galleries of images play an increasingly important role in the generation of new images. The chosen representation allows the recombination of images in interesting ways yielding unexpected, yet fit, images.

The results also show that it isn't necessary to resort to complex primitives, such as fractals or other complex functions, to generate complex and interesting images. What is necessary is a set of simple functions that can be combined in complex ways.

7.5   The Unifying Architecture

The analysis of our previous work, described in the last section, took us to a point where we realized that it was possible to settle a common framework (representation language) for the objects manipulated by the algorithms in different domains. The common representation language which emerged is a set of hierarchical structured objects (HSOs). It can be defined more precisely by means of a grammar that we partially show below using the traditional BNF formalism:

<structure> ::= <node> | <node>({< structure >}$^+$)
<node> ::= <name> | <name>({< attribute >}$^+$)
<attribute> ::= <type-attrib>(<name>)
<type-attrib> ::= link-in(<value>) | link-out(<value>)

It is possible to use the same common language to represent objects from different domains. The objects represented in Figs. 7.3, 7.4 and 7.6 are, in fact, instantiations of the above described HSOs, and only the non-terminals <name> and <value> depend on the domain. The main advantages of the adoption of such a representation are that it permits a full integration of EC and CBR mechanisms in the same architecture, and also the inclusion of objects from different domains in the same knowledge base. This last characteristic makes the implementation of metaphorical transfer mechanisms possible, which will be further explored in Section 7.7.

The proposed architecture (Fig. 7.14) builds upon this representation and models the creative process as an iterative sequence of steps, which resembles some models proposed by psychologists like by Guilford [2], Dewey [1], Mansfield and Busse [64], Poincare [65], Rossman [66], Wallas [3] and others. The main goal is to propose new ideas, which are transformations of hierarchical structured objects contained in a knowledge base (KB). The quality of a new idea depends on its novelty and on its suitability to solve a given problem. Two key modules play a central role in the process: the selector and the generator. The first one is intended to produce ideas (which are also hierarchical structured objects) by exploring the knowledge space. The second one manipulates the selected ideas and proposes new ones to the user (typically, a human user). To conveniently feed the generator, the first module must be fluent (i.e., must have the capability to produce a wide variety of ideas), even if at the expense of taking cognitive risks. The second module, which must contribute to control the overall quality of the proposed ideas, may adopt two strategies: it may try to increase the overall novelty of the proposed ideas (e.g., by recombining them) or act towards an increase of their overall appropriateness (e.g., by adapting them to the problem to solve).

The KB is initially set up through a knowledge filler, which may be controlled by a human user or act autonomously. It also may fill the KB with domain knowledge or randomly create the necessary structures. The KB may evolve during the process. This is done through a feedback controller, which may feed the KB with new ideas proposed by the generator. Similarly to the knowledge filler, the feedback controller may or may not act autonomously.

We can draw a parallelism between the proposed architecture and the way EC and CBR solve problems (see Table 7.1). In EC, a population (KB) is evaluated and individuals (ideas) are selected according to a fitness function. This may be seen as a *selection* process. Afterwards, genetic operators play the role of the generator and proposed ideas are fed back to the KB. In CBR, cases (ideas) from a case base (KB) are

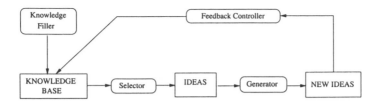

Fig. 7.14. The proposed architecture.

selected according to a metric. Adaptation operators transform (generate) the selected cases. Proposed cases may be fed back to the KB.

Table 7.1. Similitude between the hybrid architecture, EC and CBR

Proposed architecture	Evolutionary computation	Case based reasoning
Knowledge base	Population	Case base
Selector	Evaluation/selection (w./fitness function)	Selection (w./ metric)
Generator	Genetic operators (crossover, mutation, ...)	Adaptation operators

The architecture may be explored in many ways. The objects may be produced, used and manipulated either by CBR and EC mechanisms. We may use CBR in the selector and apply genetic operators in the generator to improve diversity. We may also use the fitness function to select ideas and adaptation operators to gain adequacy. We may even change the mechanisms for the selector and the generator in each cycle; the choice for each combination of them may depend on the evaluation of the intermediate results and/or on the specific goals in mind.

In the next section, we will show an example of how this architecture may deal with creative problem solving using the proposed common knowledge representation.

7.6   Example

The following example illustrates a possible way of combining EC with CBR in the framework of the proposed hybrid architecture, showing how a case library and a retrieval metric can be coupled with an EC system. Consider that we have a case library of images and that the user chooses one of these images (see Fig. 7.15). Using a similarity metric, the system compares the chosen image with the other images in the database. In this example, and for the sake of simplicity, we decided to use the root mean square error as similarity metric.

It is worth noting that this measure isn't the most adequate for our goals. It would probably be best to use a metric that takes into account the similarity between the genotypes of the individuals. Considering that the individuals are represented by graphs (trees in this particular case), we could use, for instance, the Hamming distance or the maximal common sub-graph as metrics [67].

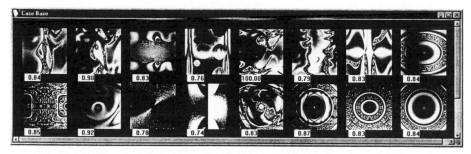

Fig. 7.15. Some of the cases in the case library. The selected image has the score of 100 (color image available at http://www.dei.uc.pt/~amilcar/softcompbook/fig15.htm).

The most similar images will be used to initialize de EC algorithm. Thus, these images will be added to the initial population. In this example the number of images added was five, including the image selected by the user. The first population (see Fig. 7.16) will therefore be composed of five images from the case library and 11 randomly created images (population size was set to 16).

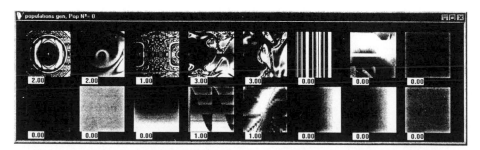

Fig. 7.16. The initial population. The first five images were retrieved from the case library using the similarity metric; the other images were randomly created (color image available at http://www.dei.uc.pt/~amilcar/softcompbook/fig16.htm).

From this point on, the system uses the EC process to create new populations of images. The process is similar to the one described earlier: the user makes the assignment of fitness, and the genetic operators are the ones previously described.

In Fig. 7.17, we can see the first generated population. The numbers below the images indicate the fitness score assigned to each image by the user. In Fig. 7.18, we show the twentieth population, yet to be evaluated.

While the evolutionary process is taking place, images that have a fitness score above a given threshold value are added to the case library, thus feeding the case library with the best individuals found. In Fig. 7.19 we show a partial snapshot of the

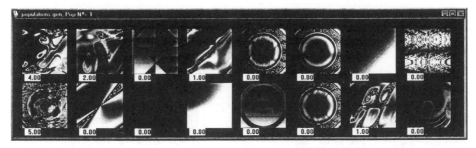

Fig. 7.17. Population number 1 (color image available at http://www.dei.uc.pt/~amilcar/softcompbook/fig17.htm).

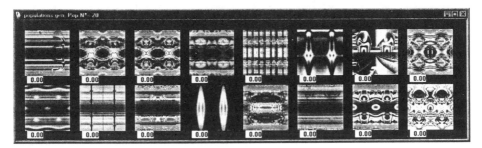

Fig. 7.18. Population 20, not yet evaluated (color image available at http://www.dei.uc.pt/~amilcar/softcompbook/fig18.htm).

case library after 20 populations. The first row of images comprises the images that were added to the case library from the generated populations.

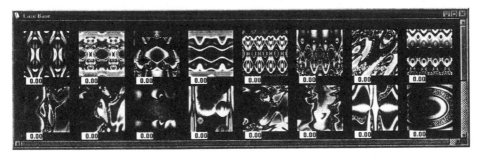

Fig. 7.19. Snapshot of the case library after 20 populations (color image available at http://www.dei.uc.pt/~amilcar/softcompbook/fig19.htm).

We verify that by using the proposed model in this way we speed up significantly the process of image generation.

7.7 Improvements

The proposed architecture opens an exciting range of research opportunities. We are currently exploring ways of taking the best of it to produce creative systems with improved capabilities.

The unifying characteristics of the architecture leads us to a situation in which there can be several different domains represented through the same principles and coexisting in the same environment. According to many creativity researchers (e.g., Guilford [68]) and to our own intuition, the ability to interrelate ideas from different domains can be determinant to a creativity outcome. In fact, the core of many creative products (be they artistic, scientific or other) lies exactly in the association of apparently unrelated ideas. Moreover, the human being inhabits a heterogeneous world and his own survival depends upon the understanding and processing of such complex and widespread information. This takes us to the conclusion that our architecture can be much improved (i.e., be more creative) if we add a process to interrelate different domains that can coexist in the same knowledge base.

Metaphor theories [69,70] center mainly on the understanding of metaphors, establishing correspondences between concepts of the domains involved (e.g., in the metaphor 'Star Wars is the King Arthur Saga', Veale and Keane establish correspondences between the concepts that are present in both stories). In a project named Dr Divago, Pereira and Cardoso [71] explore these metaphor theories to search for cross-domain mappings that are used to make translations of concepts between domains. These translations are necessary to apply cases (Dr Divago is also a CBR project) from one domain onto the other.

We think the ability to establish cross-domain transfer of knowledge is a vital future development for our work. With this feature, our systems will be able to explore wider and more varied spaces, and get ideas from apparently sterile ground. Another improvement that we are exploring comes from the observation that, in our framework, cases may be represented as partonomic hierarchies, whose leaf nodes can be represented as trees, thus making a two level case representation. This makes the representation more flexible to solve problems at different levels of granularity. It also provides the possibility to exploit the case representation from evolutionary and adaptation viewpoints, allowing these different representation levels to be used in more complex reasoning processes. The more abstract level of representation is associated with the functional description of a case, while the less abstract level is associated with the structural and/or behavioral aspect of the node it is associated with.

As an example of this kind of representation, we return to the case already presented in Section 7.4, describing an arithmetic and logic unit (ALU). In Fig. 7.3 we have shown the more abstract level representation that describes how the ALU is divided. The leaf nodes of this hierarchy can have attached a tree representing the function implementation. For instance, Fig. 7.20 describes the implementation of the XOR, which is used in the ALU. This dual representation enables us to carry out a two stage evolutionary process. We can first evolve the functional description of the case and then evolve the structure associated with each function node. In the ALU example, we can reach a different ALU, while at a finer level we can also evolve the XOR implementation.

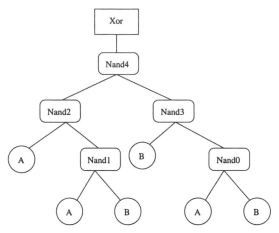

Fig. 7.20. The representation of the XOR node in Fig. 7.3.

7.8   Conclusions

Creative reasoning is increasingly challenging research groups mainly from the area of AI. Several computational models have been proposed, mostly inspired on cognitive and biological models, and a wide range of artistic, architectural and engineering domains of application are being explored. There is a diversity of computational approaches to the problem, but CBR and EC are the most common techniques and, in our opinion, the most promising ones. EC techniques offer diversity while adapting to environmental changes, are efficient in dealing with complex search spaces and explore parallelism in a natural way. CBR techniques can explore previous knowledge in versatile ways and have good explanatory capabilities. We argue that CR will benefit from the cross-contribution of these techniques.

During recent years we have separately explored CBR and EC based computational approaches to creativity. In Section 7.4 we have briefly presented some of the results achieved, focusing on four developed applications in the domains of design, music composition and image generation. From these efforts two key ideas emerged: first, the representation formalisms we were using could be generalized into one common knowledge representation; second, there were strong similarities between the computational mechanisms we were using.

As a result of this synthesis work we proposed in Section 7.5 a hybrid architecture which empowers cross-contributions from CBR and EC. The architecture builds on the above mentioned common representation language.

The proposed architecture, as was illustrated by the example in Section 7.6, fully integrates EC and CBR techniques: we may use the typical mechanisms of both paradigms in each of its core modules, the selector and the generator. The generic characteristics of the representation language and the computational mechanisms we use allow its application to a wide range of domains. Moreover, in spite of being a creativity-oriented architecture, its features lead us to believe that it may prove useful in other problem-solving tasks.

This framework also enables the coexistence of objects from multiple domains in the same knowledge base, providing the means to explore advanced creativity-related concepts like metaphoric transfer.

References

1. Dewey, J. (1919). *How we Think*. D. C. Heath, Boston, MA.
2. Guilford, J. P. (1968). *Intelligence, creativity and their educational implications*, Robert Knapp, San Diego, CA.
3. Wallas, G. (1926). *The Art of Thought*, Harcourt Brace, Nova Iorque.
4. De Bono, E. (1986). *El pensamiento lateral. Manual de la creatividad*. Paidós, Barcelona, Spain (in Spanish).
5. Goldberg, D. (1998). The design of innovation: lessons from genetic algorithms, lessons for the real world, IlliGAL Report no. 98004, February 1998, Department of General Engineering, University of Illinois at Urbana–Champaign.
6. Kolodner, J. (1993). *Case-Based Reasoning*. Morgan Kaufmann, San Mateo, CA.
7. Aamodt, A. and Plaza, E. (1994). Case-based reasoning: foundational issues, methodological variations, and systems approaches. *AICOM* 17(1), 39–59.
8. Back, T., Fogel, D., Michalewicz, Z. (eds) (1997). *Handbook of Evolutionary Computation*, Oxford University Press, New York.
9. Rechenberg, I. (1965). Cybernetic solution path of an experimental problem. Library Translation no. 1122, Royal Aircraft Establishment, Farnborough, UK.
10. Schewefel, H-P. (1965). Kybernetishe evolution als strategie der experimentallen forschung in der stromungstechnik. Diplomarbeit, Tecnische Universitat Berlin.
11. Fogel, L. (1962). Autonomous automata. *Industrial Research* 4, 14–19.
12. Holland, J. (1975). *Adaptation in Natural and Artificial Systems*. University of Michigan Press, Ann Arbor, MI.
13. Koza, J. R. (1992). *Genetic Programming: On the Programming of Computers by Means of Natural Selection*. MIT Press, Cambridge, MA.
14. Gero, J. (1994). Computational models of creative design processes. In Dartnall, T. (ed.), *Artificial Intelligence and Creativity*, pp. 269–281. Kluwer Academic Publishers, Dordrecht.
15. Gero, J. (1994). Introduction: creativity and design. In Dartnall, T. (ed.), *Artificial Intelligence and Creativity*, pp. 259–267. Kluwer Academic Publishers, Dordrecht.
16. Kolodner, J. and Wills, L. (1993). Case-based creative design. In *AAAI Spring Symposium on AI+Creativity*, Stanford, CA.
17. Simina, M. and Kolodner, J. (1997). Creative design: reasoning and understanding. In *Proceedings of the International Conference on Case Based Reasoning (ICCBR'97)*, Providence, RI.
18. Sycara, K., and Navinchandra, D. (1991). Influences: a thematic abstraction for creative use of multiple cases. In *Proceedings of the First European Workshop on Case-Based Reasoning*. Springer-Verlag, Washington, DC.
19. Sycara, K. and Navinchandra, D. (1993). Case representation and indexing for innovative design reuse. In *Proceedings of the Workshop of the 13th International Joint Conference on Artificial Intelligence*, Paris, France. Morgan Kaufmann, San Mateo, CA.

20. Pereira, F. C., Grilo, C., Macedo, L. and Cardoso, A. (1997). Composing music with case-based reasoning. In *Proceedings of Computational Models of Creative Cognition (Mind II)*, Dublin, Ireland.

21. Arcos, J. L., Mantaras, R. L. and Serra, X. (1997). SAXEX: a case-based reasoning system for generating expressive musical performances. In *Proceedings of the 1997 International Computer Music Conference*. Thessaloniki, Greece.

22. Do, E. and Gross, M. D. (1995). Supporting creative architectural design with visual references. In J. Gero et al. (eds), *3rd International Conference on Computational Model of Creative Design (HI'95)*, Heron Island, Australia.

23. Ralley, D. (1995). Genetic algorithm as a tool for melodic development. In *International Computer Music Conference*, Alberta, Canada.

24. Biles, J. (1994). A genetic algorithm for generating jazz solos. In *International Computer Music Conference*, Aarhus, Denmark.

25. Jacob, B. L. (1995). Composing with genetic algorithms. In *International Computer Music Conference*, Alberta, Canada.

26. Dawkins, R. (1987). *The Blind Watchmaker*. W.W. Norton, New York.

27. Sims, K. (1991). Artificial evolution for computer graphics. *ACM Computer Graphics* 25, 319–328.

28. Todd, S. and Latham, W. (1992). *Evolutionary Art and Computers*. Academic Press, Winchester, UK.

29. Rooke, S. (1996). *The evolutionary art of Steven Rooke*, http://www.azstarnet.com/~srooke/.

30. Machado, P. and Cardoso, A. (1999). NEvAr. In *Evolutionary Design by Computers CD- ROM*, Bentley, P. (ed). Morgan Kaufmann, San Francisco, CA.

31. Baker, E. (1993). *Evolving Line Drawings*. Harvard University Center for Research in Computing Technology, Technical Report TR-21-93.

32. Bentley, P. (ed.) (1999). *Evolutionary Design by Computers*. Morgan Kaufmann, San Francisco, CA.

33. Graf, J. and Banzhaf, W. (1996). Interactive evolution for simulated natural evolution. In *Artificial Evolution*, Alliot, J.-M., Lutton, E., Ronald, E., Schoenauer, M. and Snyers, D. (eds), Vol. 1063. Springer-Verlag, Nimes, France, pp. 259–272.

34. Angeline, P. J. (1996). Evolving fractal movies. In *Genetic Programming 1996: Proceedings of the First Annual Conference*, Koza, J. R., Goldberg, D. E., Fogel, D. B. and Riolo, R. L. (eds). MIT Press, Stanford University, CA, pp. 503–511.

35. Ventrella, J. (1999). Animated artificial life. In *Virtual Worlds – Synthetic Universes, Digital Life, and Complexity*, Heudin, J. C. (ed.). New England, Complex Systems Institute Series on Complexity. Perseus Books, pp. 67–94.

36. Baluja, S., Pomerlau, D. and Todd, J. (1994). Towards automated artificial evolution for computer-generated images. *Connection Science* 6, 325–354.

37. Horner, A. and Goldberg, D. (1991). Genetic algorithms and computer-assisted composition. In *Genetic Algorithms and their Applications: Proceedings of the Fourth International Conference on Genetic Algorithms*, Urbana-Champaign, IL, pp. 427–441.

38. McIntyre, R. A. (1994). Bach in a box: the evolution of four-part baroque harmony using genetic algorithms. In *IEEE Conference on Evolutionary Computation*, Orlando, FL.

39. Spector, L. and Alpern, A. (1994). Criticism, culture, and the automatic generation of artworks. In *Proceedings of the Twelfth National Conference on Artificial Intelligence*. AAAI Press/MIT Press, Seattle, WA, pp. 3–8.

40. Spector, L. and Alpern, A. (1995). Induction and recapitulation of deep musical structure. In *Proceedings of International Joint Conference on Artificial Intelligence, IJCAI'95 Workshop on Music and AI*, Montreal, Quebec, Canada.

41. Papadopoulos, G. and Wiggins, G. (1999). AI methods for algorithmic composition: a survey, a critical view and future prospects. In *AISB Symposium on Musical Creativity*, Wiggins, G. (ed.), Edinburgh, UK.

42. Wiggins, G., Papadoupoulos, G., Phon-Amnuaisuk, S. and Tuson, A. (1999). Evolutionary methods for musical composition. *International Journal of Computing Anticipatory Systems*.

43. McCorduck, P. (1991). *AARON's Code: Meta-Art, Artificial Intelligence and the Work of Harold Cohen*. W.H. Freedman, New York.

44. Burton, E. (1997). Representing representation: artificial intelligence and drawing. In Mealing, S. (ed.), *Computers & Art*. Intellect Books, Exeter, UK.

45. Pachet, F. and Roy, P. (1998). Formulating constraint satisfaction problems on whole–part relations: the case of automatic harmonisation. In *Workshop at ECAI'98. Constraint Techniques for Artistic Applications*, Brighton, UK.

46. Cambouropoulos, E. (1994). Markov chains as an aid to computer assisted composition. *Musical Praxis* 1(1), 41–52.

47. Cope, D. (1992). Computer modeling of musical intelligence with EMI. *Computer Music Journal* 16(2), 69–83.

48. Stiny, G. (1976). Two exercises in formal composition. *Environment and Planning B: Planning and Design* 3, 187–210.

49. Louis, S., McGraw, G. and Wyckoff, R. (1992). CBR assisted explanation of GA results, *Journal of Experimental and Theoretical Artificial Intelligence* 5, 21-37.

50. Louis, S. and Xu, Z. (1996). Genetic algorithms for open shop scheduling. In *Proceedings of ISCA, 11th Conference on Computers and their Applications*, Raleigh, NC. International Society for Computers and their Applications, pp. 99–102.

51. Louis, S. and Johnson, J. (1997). Solving similar problems using genetic algorithms and case based memory. In Back., T. (ed.), *Proceedings of the 7th International Conference on Genetic Algorithms, ICGA'97*, East Lansing, MI. Morgan Kaufmann, San Mateo, CA, pp 283– 290.

52. Louis, S. and Zhang, Y. (1999). A sequential metric for case injected genetic algorithms applied to TSPs. In Banzhaf W. et al. (eds), *Proceedings of the Genetic and Evolutionary Computation Conference, GECCO'99*, Orlando, FL. Morgan Kaufmann, San Mateo, CA, pp. 377–384.

53. Ramsey, C. and Grefensttete, J. (1993). Case based initialisation of genetic algorithms. In Forrest, S. (ed.), *Proceedings of the Fifth International Conference on Genetic Algorithms, ICGA'93*, Urbana-Champaign, IL. Morgan Kaufmann, San Mateo, CA, pp. 84–91.

54. Eshelman, L. (1991). The CHC adaptive search algorithm: how to have a safe search when engaging a non-traditional genetic recombination. In Rawlings, G. (ed.), *Foundations of Genetic Algorithms (FOGA-1)*. Morgan Kaufmann, San Francisco, CA, pp. 265–283.

55. Gomes, P., Bento, C., Gago, P. and Costa, E. (1996). Towards a case based model for creative processes. In Wahlster, W. (ed.), *Proceedings of the 12th European Conference on Artificial Intelligence*. Wiley, Chichester, UK, pp. 122–126.

56. Bento, C., Macedo, L. and Costa, E. (1994). Reasoning with cases imperfectly described and explained. In Wess, S., Althoff, K-D. and Richter, M. M. (eds), *Topics in Case-Based Reasoning: Selected Papers from the First European Workshop on Case-Based Reasoning*. Springer-Verlag, Kaiserslautern.

57. Bento, C. and Costa, E. (1994). A similarity metric for retrieval of cases imperfectly explained. In Wess, S., Althoff, K-D. and Richter, M. M. (eds), *Topics in Case-Based Reasoning: Selected Papers from the First European Workshop on Case-Based Reasoning*. Springer-Verlag, Kaiserslautern.

58. Goel, A. (1992). Representation of design functions in experience-based design. In Brown, D., Waldron, M. and Yoshikawa, H. (eds), *Intelligent Computer Aided Design*. Elsevier Science, Amsterdam, pp. 283–308.

59. Stroulia, E., Shankar, M., Goel, A. and Penberthy, L. (1992). A model-based approach to blame assignment in design. In *Proceedings of the 2nd International Conference on AI in Design*, Kluwer, Dordrecht, pp. 519–537.

60. Bylander, T. and Chandrasekaran, B. (1985). Understanding behaviour using consolidation. In *Proceedings of the Ninth International Joint Conference on Artificial Intelligence*, Los Angeles, CA. Morgan Kaufmann, San Mateo, CA, pp. 45–454.

61. Smyth, B. and Keane, M. (1995). Experiments on adaptation-guided retrieval in case-based design. In Veloso, M. and Agnar A. (eds), *Topics in Case-Based Reasoning: Proceedings of the International Conference on Case-Based Reasoning*. Springer-Verlag, Berlin, pp. 313–324.

62. Macedo, L., Pereira, F. C., Grilo, C. and Cardoso, A. (1998). A computational model for creative planning. In Schmid, U., Krems J. F. and Wysotzki, F. (eds), *Mind Modelling: A Cognitive Science Approach to Reasoning, Learning and Discovery*. Pabst, Lengerich, Germany, pp. 193–208.

63. Macedo, L., Pereira, F. C., Grilo, C. and Cardoso, A. (1997). Experimental study of a similarity metric for retrieving pieces from structured plan cases: its role in the originality of plan case solutions. In *Proceedings of the 2nd International Conference on Case Based Reasoning, ICCBR-97*, Brown University, Providence, RI. Lecture Notes in Artificial Intelligence, LNAI-1266, Springer-Verlag, Berlin.

64. Mansfield, R. and Busse, T. (1981). *The Psychology of Creativity and Discovery*. Nelson-Hall, Chicago, IL.

65. Poincare, H. (1913). *The Foundations of Science*. Science Press, Lancaster, PA.

66. Rossman, J. (1931). *The Psychology of the Inventor: A Study of the Patentee*. Inventors Publishing, Washington, DC.

67. Macedo, L. and Cardoso, A. (1999). Labelled adjacency matrices for labelled, directed multigraphs: their algebra and Hamming distance. In *Proceedings of the 2nd. IAPR-TC15 Workshop on Graph-Based Representations, GbR'99*. Castel of Haindorf, Austria.

68. Guilford, J. P. (1967). *The Nature of Human Intelligence*. McGraw-Hill, New York.

69. Veale, T. and Keane, M. T. (1994). Metaphor and memory: symbolic and connectionist. issues in metaphor comprehension. In *Proceedings of the European Con-*

ference on Artificial Intelligence Workshop on Neural and Symbolic Integration, Amsterdam.

70. Indurkhya, B. (1992). *Metaphor and Cognition*. Kluwer, Dordrecht, The Netherlands.

71. Pereira, F. C. and Cardoso, A. (1999). Dr. Divago: searching for new ideas in a multi- domain environment. In *Proceedings of the 8th Cognitive Science Conference of Natural Language Processing (CSNLP-8)*, Ireland.

8. Teacher: A Genetics Based System for Learning and Generalizing Heuristics

Benjamin W. Wah and Arthur Ieumwananonthachai

Abstract. In this chapter, we present the design of Teacher (an acronym for TEchniques for the Automated Creation of HEuRistics), a system for learning and for generalizing heuristics used in problem solving. Our system learns knowledge-lean heuristics whose performance is measured statistically. The objective of the design process is to find, under resource constraints, improved heuristic methods (HMs) as compared to existing ones. Teacher addresses five general issues in learning heuristics: (1) *decomposition* of a problem solver into smaller components and *integration* of HMs designed for each together; (2) *classification* of an application domain into subdomains so that performance can be evaluated statistically for each; (3) *generation* of new and improved HMs based on past performance information and heuristics generated; (4) *evaluation* of each HM's performance; and (5) *performance generalization* to find HMs that perform well across the entire application domain. Teacher employs a genetics based machine learning approach and divides the design process into four phases. In the classification phase, the application domain is divided into subspaces (based on user requirements) and problem subdomains (based on the performance behavior of HMs). In the learning phase, HMs are generated and evaluated under resource constraints with a goal of discovering improved HMs. In the performance-verification phase, good HMs from the learning phase are further evaluated to acquire more accurate and more complete performance information. Finally, in the performance-generalization phase, HMs most likely to provide the best performance over the entire application domain are selected. We conclude the chapter by showing some experimental results on heuristics learned for two problems used in circuit testing.

8.1 Introduction

The design of heuristics is an important issue in machine learning. Today, many application problems are too complex for us to find optimal algorithms analytically. Rather, we rely on heuristics designed by experts to find high quality solutions. The effectiveness of these heuristics, however, depends on the domain knowledge and past experience of these experts. When little domain knowledge is available, as in the applications we study in this chapter, it is important to develop automated learning methods for generating improved heuristics systematically, evaluating their performance on realistic test cases, and generalizing their performance to test cases not seen in learning.

The goal of this chapter is to present, for a given application, a system that can *find improved HMs over existing HMs with respect to some average objective measures*. The applications we are interested have the following characteristics:

- a large number, and possibly infinitely many, test cases;
- a knowledge-lean application domain with little domain knowledge to relate the controls of HMs to their performance;

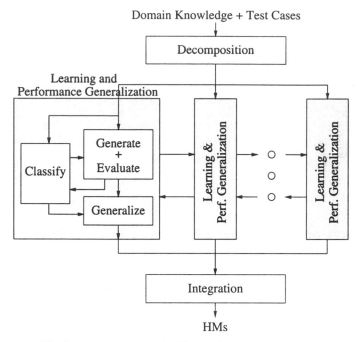

Fig. 8.1. A general model of the heuristics design process.

- performance-related HMs whose performance can be evaluated by the cost of applying them and the quality of the solutions found;
- HMs that are too costly to be tested extensively; and
- a large (and possibly infinite) pool of possible HMs.

In this chapter, we first summarize the process of designing heuristics. We then present a classification of the approaches in the automated learning of heuristics. This is followed by examples on the strengths and weaknesses of various learning methods. Finally, we summarize how our work is related to previous approaches and the type of application problems we have studied.

8.2 Process of Designing Heuristics

A *heuristics-design process* is a process for *learning* improved heuristic methods (HMs) for a problem solver. These HMs, when used to solve an application problem, can provide better and/or less costly solutions.

There are five major issues in developing HMs for an application as outlined in Fig. 8.1.

(1) **Decomposition and integration of problem-solver components.** For a complex problem solver with multiple heuristic components, there are many combinations of

heuristics that can be developed. Oftentimes, it is not possible to find improved heuristics for all the components simultaneously.

A feasible approach is to improve these heuristics in a piecewise fashion. This involves decomposing the problem solver into a number of groups with a smaller number of components in each, designing improved heuristics for each group, and integrating improved heuristics from each group into the problem solver.

There are several difficulties with this approach. First, it is hard to find the best way to group heuristics components in order to have the best overall performance. Second, heuristics in a problem solver may interact with each other, and the design of heuristics for one group may depend on the heuristics designed for others. Without the domain knowledge on the effects of heuristics in one group on others, it is hard to design heuristics for these groups independently.

One simple approach that minimizes the interactions is to design heuristics for different groups sequentially. In this approach, we first design an improved HM_A for group A. This is followed by the design of HM_B for Group B after HM_A is in place. The process is then repeated until HMs for all groups have been designed.

(2) **Classification of application domain.** When the performance of an HM is *nondeterministic* and the cost for evaluating it on a test case is expensive, we can only afford to evaluate each HM on a small number of test cases. In general, it is valid to estimate the true performance of an HM based on a subset of tests when the performance values are independent and identically distributed (IID).

We have found that HMs can behave differently on different subsets of test cases of an application [26]. When this happens, it is necessary to partition the application domain into smaller subsets (called subdomains) so that each can be evaluated independently.

In this chapter, we define a *problem subdomain* as a subset of the application domain so that performance values of HMs, when evaluated on test cases in the subdomain, satisfy the IID property.

Sometimes, it may be more efficient to have different groups of subdomains solved by different HMs. In this case, subdomains may need to be partitioned into groups and an HM be learned for each. We refer to this partitioning of the application domain as the *classification problem*.

(3) **Generation of heuristics.** This refers to the generation of improved HMs based on HMs generated already. This issue has been studied extensively in machine learning. Section 8.3 overviews the previous work in this area.

The generation of improved HMs is difficult for knowledge-lean problem solvers as there are no models that relate the specifications of an HM to its performance. In this case, the problem solver must be treated as a black box, and heuristics generation has to rely on weak (domain-independent) methods.

(4) **Evaluation of heuristics.** To obtain improved HMs, we must be able to compare their performance. The performance of HMs is generally obtained by evaluating them on one or more test cases. When the performance of an HM is non-deterministic, this process may need to be repeated multiple times.

The key issue is to be able to compare the performance of different heuristics using a small number of tests. This is especially important in our research since we are dealing with heuristics that are expensive to evaluate.

(5) **Generalization of performance on heuristics learned.** When the performance of an HM is non-deterministic and varies across different test cases, only a subset of test cases are usually used in evaluating its performance. However, we expect the HM selected to be generalizable; that is, it must perform well not only on test cases tested during learning but also on test cases not seen in learning. We call this the *performance-generalization problem* in this chapter.

Performance generalization is difficult when the application domain is large, and HMs have different (and possibly inconsistent) performance behavior across different regions (or subdomains) in the application domain.

The next section presents an overview of the work in automated learning of heuristics, which has been studied extensively in artificial intelligence. There has also been some work on the evaluation and generalization of heuristics in genetics based learning [28,30,68]. The remaining issues on decomposition/integration and classification have been mostly ignored in the literature since they exist only in complicated application problems. Unfortunately, many real-world applications may fit in this category, and it is highly desirable to have some solutions to address these issues.

The approach presented in this chapter addresses all these issues except decomposition and integration. We currently require the decomposition/integration process to be performed manually by designers, who develop improved heuristics for each group sequentially. This is necessary because decomposition and integration cannot be studied until all the other issues have been addressed and a good system for designing improved heuristics for each component has been developed. We plan to address this issue in our future work.

We present in Section 8.5 the design of Teacher, a system that implements our heuristics design process. Our system has four phases of operation, each of which is isolated to deal with a unique design issue. The first phase dealing with the classification issue is discussed in Section 8.6. Section 8.7 presents the second phase that addresses the generation of good heuristics for a subdomain and their evaluation. The operation in this phase is the one referred to by most researches as the learning process. Our approach in this phase is based on the genetics based machine learning paradigm presented in Section 8.4. Section 8.8 discusses the third phase that deals with the verification of performance of heuristics. Section 8.9 presents the final phase that deals with the performance-generalization issue. In Section 8.10, we report our experience on learning HMs for two problems used in circuit testing.

8.3   Background on Heuristics Learning

8.3.1   Classification of Heuristics Learning Methods

Learning is carried out for application domains that are either knowledge-rich or knowledge-lean. In a *knowledge-rich domain*, there is domain knowledge on a world

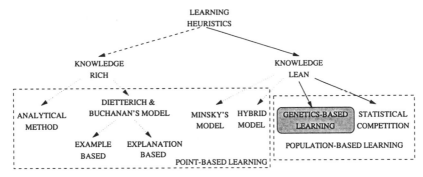

Fig. 8.2. Classification of methods for learning heuristics.

model that relates the controls/inputs of an HM to its performance. Such a model can reduce learning time tremendously because new HMs can be derived with very little or no testing of previous HMs. In contrast, when the domain is *knowledge-lean*, there is no world model, and heuristics derived must be tested to find their performance. These are the domains that we study in this chapter.

Fig. 8.2 shows a classification of the methods for learning heuristics. We classify these methods based on the number of heuristics maintained by each during the design process – whether it is *point based* or *population based* [1,66].

8.3.1.1 Point Based Learning Paradigm
In this paradigm, a learning system maintains one incumbent HM that is modified in place by the learning system. Since each modification of the HM destroys the original HM, there must be high confidence that the new HM is better than the old one. This learning paradigm works well for learning knowledge-rich heuristics because the world model can be used to guide the generation of improved HMs [38,42].

There are three models in traditional machine-learning studies that fit in this paradigm. Fundamental work in this area was addressed by Mitchell [43,56], Minsky [39], and Dieterich and Buchanan [16]. The basic principle is based on a generate-and-test paradigm that generates plausible HMs, performs limited tests, and modifies the HMs according to the feedback signals obtained. Each of these models is described briefly in this section. Many existing machine-learning systems fit in one of these models.

A general point based learning paradigm used by the three point based models is shown in Fig. 8.3 [66]. The general model includes the learning performance database and preprocessor, credit assignment unit, and learning element. The problem solver and its initial conditions are shown as components outside the learning system.

The *learning performance database and preprocessor* captures the effects of decisions made by the problem solver on the application environment. The preprocessed data are used for *credit assignments* that include both *temporal* and *structural* credit assignments. The *learning element* then modifies the HM based on recommended actions from the credit assignment unit.

8.3.1.2 Population Based Learning Paradigm
In contrast to the point based approach, a population based paradigm maintains mul-

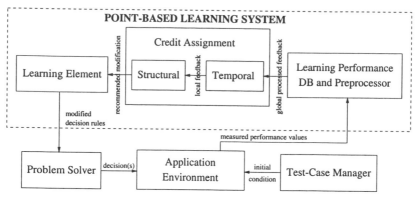

Fig. 8.3. A general point based learning model.

tiple competing HMs and tries to find the best HM within the pool. During learning, new HMs are added to the pool and poor ones removed. This paradigm is useful for learning knowledge-lean heuristics, as the weak methods used in generating new HMs do not have to depend on a good world model [9,23]. Moreover, it is not necessary for every new HM to perform well since a number of alternative HMs are generated.

One important characteristic of the population based approach is the potential need for scheduling the available computational resources among competing HMs. Related issues on scheduling are presented in Sections 8.4 and 8.7.

8.3.2   Learning Knowledge-Rich Heuristics

Several general methods have been proposed for learning knowledge-rich heuristics. These include analytic methods, learning by examples, and explanation based learning. Learning by examples and explanation based learning are examples of Dietterich and Buchanan's model of learning.

8.3.2.1   Analytic Method
An *analytic method* is based on comprehensive analysis on the problem solver with respect to its particular representation [15,17]. This approach is knowledge-intensive and very application-specific.

8.3.2.2   Dietterich and Buchanan's Model
This point based learning model [5,16,66] and similar models proposed by Smith et al. [57] and Langley [34] belong to a class of models for learning HMs of target problems with well-defined objectives. They learn by supervised learning with *prescriptive feedback* that carries explicit information to guide the modification of the HM tested. This learning model fits within the framework of the general point based model shown in Fig. 8.3.

Learning by examples narrows the scope of possible heuristics by specialization and generalization [42]. *Explanation based learning* exercises domain knowledge to explain the relationship between an HM and its performance [40,41].

In learning knowledge-rich heuristics, extensive domain knowledge must be available. As our focus is on learning heuristics without such knowledge, methods developed for learning knowledge-rich heuristics cannot be used.

8.3.3   Learning Knowledge-Lean Heuristics

Several general methods have been proposed for learning knowledge-lean heuristics. These include Minsky's learning model, hybrid point based learning model, genetics based learning, and statistical methods.

8.3.3.1   Minsky's Model
This model [39,66] is an older and perhaps less restricted model of point based learning systems. It applies well for learning HMs of target applications with undefined objectives in knowledge-lean environments, which tend to produce evaluative and possibly delayed feedback signals.

An *evaluative feedback* carries only implicit information about the desired behavior but explicit evaluation of the observed behavior. Such behavior is *a posteriori*, being measured or generated after the behavior has occurred. It requires a critic [70] that has some prior knowledge of the objective function and can assess the goodness of external states or sequences thereof. Scalar evaluative feedback signals are called *reinforcements* [39] and learning from such signals, *reinforcement learning*.

In order to simplify temporal credit assignment, the Markovian property has to be satisfied; namely, the current state of the system depends only on the last action performed by the HM and not on the sequence of actions before it. This property is generally hard to satisfy in complex applications. Examples of systems in this class include Klopf's drive reinforcement model [32] and Sutton and Barto's reinforcement model [61].

8.3.3.2   Hybrid Learning Model
This point based learning model [66] combines aspects of Dietterich and Buchanan's model and Minsky's model. It uses an approximate temporal model instead of the Markovian model. It is intended for dealing with a knowledge-lean learning environment with an ill-defined objective, evaluative feedback, and a non-Markovian temporal scope.

Examples of this type of learning system include EURISKO [35], Samuel's Checker Player [53,54], Williams' REINFORCEMENT model [71], classifier system (the Michigan approach) [25], and the truck-backer-upper problem of Widrow et al. [45]. This type of learning does not address the lack of domain knowledge for structural credit assignment.

8.3.3.3   Genetics Based Machine Learning
This is a population based approach based on generate-and-test and the application of genetic algorithms [19,21] to machine-learning problems. In generate-and-test methods, new heuristics to be tested are generated by applying operators to existing heuristics that perform well [9,23]. The new heuristics are potentially better as they were

generated from heuristics that perform well. The reproduction operators applied include crossover and mutation. More details about this approach are presented in Section 8.4.

Examples of genetics based machine learning include genetic programming [33] and the Pittsburgh approach to classifier systems [23].

8.3.3.4 Statistical Competition

One form of statistical competition uses statistics to translate data into concepts so that concept learning can be applied [49]. Another form uses statistics to decide which heuristics to test more, given a pool of candidate heuristics [11,27]. This method is especially useful for learning heuristics whose exact performance cannot be determined by a limited number of tests.

This approach is limited in its usefulness as it only tests a a fixed pool of heuristics and excludes the introduction of new heuristics based on past evaluations.

8.3.4 Summary

In learning knowledge-lean heuristics, genetics based machine learning is the most suitable approach. The two point based learning models to learning knowledge-lean heuristics are too restricted and cannot be applied to the type of applications we address in our research. Minsky's model requires a Markovian temporal model that is hard to satisfy in general, and the hybrid model requires some domain knowledge for structural credit assignment. The statistical competition approach can only handle a fixed pool of heuristics and does not allow incremental improvements through mutations and crossovers.

We have adopted a genetics based learning approach that can operate in a knowledge-lean environment and can generate new and potentially improved heuristics based on past performance information. Since tests are expensive, we have incorporated some aspects of statistical competition to improve resource scheduling in our learning framework. In the next section, we examine the genetics based approach in more detail and identify some key issues to be studied. Section 8.7 presents the architecture of a population based learning system.

8.4   Background on Evolutionary Computing

Genetics based machine learning, the approach we have selected for our heuristics design process, is a part of a bigger field called evolutionary computing [24,59].

Evolutionary computing (EC) includes *genetic algorithms (GAs), evolutionary programming (EP), evolution strategies (ES), classifier systems (CFSs), genetic programming (GP)*, and several other problem-solving strategies. They are based on the means of natural selection, the survival of the fittest and the theories of evolution [24]. They provide the evolution of individual structures through the processes of selection, mutation, and reproduction. These processes depend on the perceived performance of the individual structures as defined by an environment [59].

In this section, we first present a brief overview of genetic algorithms before proceeding to genetics based machine learning, an extension of genetic algorithms to machine-learning problems.

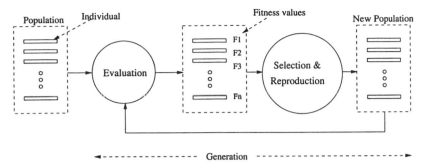

Fig. 8.4. General model of the evolution process in a genetics based approach.

8.4.1 Genetic Algorithms

Genetic algorithms (GAs) are adaptive methods that may be used to solve search and optimization problems. Since the development of GA by Holland [25], GAs have been extensively studied [12,19,22]. They are based on the genetic processes of biological organisms described first by Charles Darwin in *The Origin of Species*. Populations of competing individuals evolve over many generations according to the principle of natural selection and 'survival of the fittest'.

GAs work with a *population* of 'individuals' and a set of biologically based operators (such as mutation and crossover). Each individual represents a possible solution to a given problem. Based on the theory of evolution, only the most suited elements in a population are likely to survive and generate offspring [19].

In GAs, each individual is represented as a string of binary values (0 or 1). This uniform representation is application-independent, allowing various studies to focus on the general approach.

A *fitness level* is assigned to each individual based on how good the problem has been solved. Those with high fitness levels will reproduce by recombining with other individuals in the population. New offspring generated share some features taken from each parent. Those with low fitness levels are less likely to be selected for reproduction and so die out.

A new generation is, therefore, produced by selecting the best individuals from the current *generation* and mating them to produce a new set of offspring. Over many generations, good characteristics are spread throughout the population. This process allows the most promising areas of the search space represented by the population to be explored [6].

Fig. 8.4 shows the overall process within GAs that can be viewed as iterating over two different steps: (1) evaluation of individuals of a population in the current generation, and assigning fitness levels to each individual, and (2) generation of a new population for a new generation by selecting existing individuals based on their fitness values and by using selected individuals to reproduce.

In most traditional GAs, the fitness of each individual is exact and can be computed with negligible costs. However, there are cases in which there are 'noises' in the evaluation process, resulting in multiple evaluations and in uncertainties over the fitness of each individual [3,18,20]. This condition can significantly increase the amount of fitness evaluations performed during each generation. Such is the case in the applications we have studied. Here, the performance of an HM on a test case is governed by a statistical distribution, and testing the HM once is equivalent to drawing a random value from the distribution.

There are many issues in GAs that have been and continue to be studied, including issues on representation, population size, fitness evaluation, selection of individuals for reproduction, and reproduction methods [6,7,13,59].

8.4.2   Genetics Based Machine Learning

Genetics based machine learning is an extension of GAs to solve machine-learning problems [19]. The term is used in this chapter to cover applications of the idea behind GAs in order to develop HMs used in a problem-solving process.

Genetics based machine learning is based on the same idea of evolution and natural selection as in GAs (see Fig. 8.4). Such a system maintains a population of individuals, evaluates their fitness values, and generates a new population by selecting existing individuals for reproduction based on their fitness values. However, the representation of HMs is generally more complex [19,33]. Some example representations of an individual include an if–then rule [19], a set of rules [31], a Lisp expression [33], and a vector of numbers [67].

Genetics based learning applied to learn improved HMs are more complex computationally as compared to GAs. First, because the structure of each individual can be complex, reproduction operators, such as mutation and crossover, can also be more complex. In addition, more domain knowledge may be needed in order to create knowledge-intensive reproduction [7,19], such as those used in GIL [31]. Second, since the evaluation of an HM on a test case is non-deterministic (or noisy), evolutionary computing applied to learn improved HMs must also deal with 'noisy' conditions. This means that the fitness of each individual may not be exact, and that multiple evaluations of each individual may be necessary.

Existing work in genetics based machine learning can be divided into two approaches: (a) treating the entire population as the HM to be learned and (b) treating each individual as a complete HM.

(A) *Population as HM:* This approach, known as the Michigan approach in the GA community [12,72], treats each individual in the current population as a component contributing to the entire population. It requires all components of a solution to be homogeneous across the population. To achieve better performance for the entire population, there must be cooperation among individuals. This is similar to the hybrid point based learning paradigm discussed earlier. It requires credit assignments to apportion credits or debits to various contributing individuals in an episode. The most common credit assignment strategy is the *bucket-brigade* algorithm [19].

Examples of this approach include most classifier systems such as CS-1 [19] and CFS-C [50]. This approach can be applied in online learning to improve a problem solver during the problem-solving process.

(B) *Individual as HM:* This approach, known as the Pittsburgh approach in the GA community [12,72], treats each individual as a solution that competes with other individuals in the population. In this case, each individual can be entirely different from one another, leading to more complex systems as compared to the Michigan approach.

This approach does not require credit assignments to apportion credits or debits, since each performance feedback is directed to only one individual. However, feedbacks usually come less often to each individual, leading to more evaluations in order to reach a final result.

Examples of this type of approach include the Pittsburgh approach [12,72] to classifier system (such as LS-1 [58], GABIL [14], and GIL [31]) and genetic programming (GP) [33].

This approach is more suitable for our system because HMs in our applications are usually non-uniform with different structures and do not have good models of interactions among their components to allow credit assignments.

There are some systems that use a hybrid of the Michigan and the Pittsburgh approaches. In this case, each individual is treated as a potential solution with components that can contribute to the problem-solving process. It is also necessary to use credit assignment within each individual to assign credits/debits to each component. An example of this hybrid approach is SAMUEL [23].

In summary, genetics based learning can be used to learn knowledge-lean HMs in the applications that we study in this chapter. A population of HMs can be maintained; each will be tested, evaluated, mutated, and crossed over with other HMs to form new HMs in the next generation. Existing genetics based methods, however, do not address the issues when performance data of HMs do not belong to one common statistical distribution and when tests are expensive to conduct. When HMs behave differently across different subsets of test cases of an application, it is possible for an HM to perform well in one subset but poorly in another. Hence, the generalization of test results to test cases not evaluated must be considered. The problem is further complicated when tests are expensive to carry out. In this case, the learning system must decide how many HMs to be tested and the amount of testing to be carried out on each. These issues are addressed in Teacher, described in the next section.

8.5   The Teacher System

In this section, we discuss Teacher, a genetics based learning system we have developed in the last six years [66]. Its objective is to learn, under limited computational resources, good HMs for solving application problems and to generalize the HMs learned to unlearned subdomains. We choose to use the average metric for comparing HMs, and examine the spread of performance values when HMs have similar average performance. When there are multiple objectives in comparing HMs, we constrain all but one objective during learning and optimize the unconstrained objective. Our learning system is capable of proposing more than one HM, showing trade-offs among these objectives.

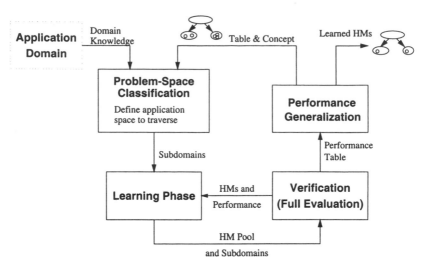

Fig. 8.5. Organization of the heuristics design process in Teacher.

8.5.1 Key Characteristics of Teacher

Our present prototype is unique as compared to other genetics based learning studies because it combines the following three features:

- Our learning environment is noisy so that the performance of each HM may have to be evaluated using multiple tests.
- We consider applications in which HMs behave differently in different subdomains (Section 8.2). Existing methods generally ignore this problem and focus on only one set of statistically related test cases.
- We assume that the cost of evaluating an HM on a test case is expensive. In the applications presented in Section 8.10, a fast workstation takes a few days to perform one to two thousand tests. Hence, it is not feasible to perform millions of tests as assumed in other genetics based learning systems [33]. For simplicity, we consider logical time in this chapter in which one unit of time is needed for each test of an HM.

These conditions are more realistic for complicated real-world applications for which we want to design improved heuristics.

8.5.2 Four Phases of Teacher

The operations of Teacher are divided into four phases: classification, learning, performance verification, and performance generalization. Each phase is designed to deal independently with a separate issue discussed in Section 8.2.

Currently, the classification phase is performed manually while the other three phases are automated [29]. We have plans to incorporate strategies for automated classification, decomposition and integration of HMs in Teacher in the future. Fig. 8.5 shows the overall design process in Teacher. We describe the objectives and the key issues of each phase in this section and our solutions to these issues in the following sections.

8.5.2.1 Classification phase

This first phase of the design process partitions test cases in an application into distinct subsets. Its goal is to partition a target application domain into smaller subsets in order to (a) identify different regions within the application domain that may require different HMs, and (b) make sure that performance values from test cases used in learning are representative and can be used for statistical estimation of the true performance of unseen test cases.

There are two steps in this phase.

(a) *Subspace classification:* Within an application domain, different regions may have different characteristics, each of which can best be solved by a unique HM [48]. Hence, regions should be identified whenever possible so that unique HMs can be developed. This involves partitioning the application domain into a small number of distinct subspaces so that improved HMs are learned for each.

We define an *application subspace* as a user-defined partition of an application domain so that HMs for one subspace can be learned independently of HMs in other subspaces. Subspace partitioning is important when test cases in an application have vastly different behavior.

(b) *Subdomain classification:* A *problem subdomain* in this chapter is defined as a subset of the application domain (or application subspace) so that the performance of HMs in each subdomain can be estimated statistically based on a subset of test cases in this subdomain. In other words, the performance values of an HM in a subdomain are *independent and identically distributed* (IID), but may not be IID across subdomains. Since the performance distribution of an HM may be different across different subdomains, the performance of HMs cannot be compared or combined across subdomains in a learning experiment.

8.5.2.2 Learning phase

The goal in this phase is to find effective HMs for each of a limited set of subdomains. Besides being the most complicated phase in the design process, it is the only phase in which new HMs are introduced and tested under resource constraints. Fig. 8.6 shows the tasks in the learning, performance-verification, and performance-generalization phases.

To perform learning, the system first selects a subdomain, generates good HMs (or uses existing HMs from users or previous learning experiments) for this subdomain, and schedules tests of the HMs based on the available computational resources. When learning is completed, the resulting HMs need to be fully verified, as HMs found during learning may not be tested adequately. Note that learning is performed on one subdomain at a time.

There are three key issues in this phase.

(a) *Heuristics generation:* This entails the generation of good HMs, given the performance information of 'empirically good' HMs. As discussed in Section 8.3, we use

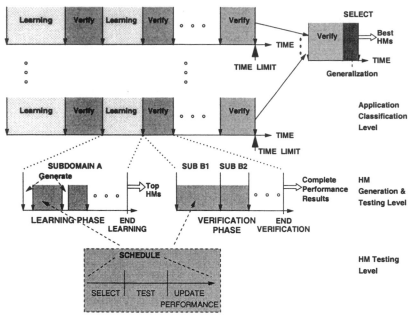

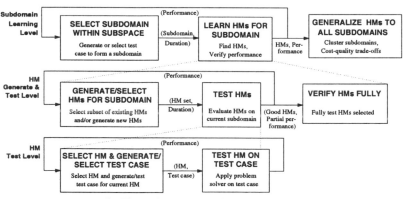

(a) The learning, performance-verification and performance-generalization process.

(b) The actions in each phase of Teacher.

Fig. 8.6. The process and actions in each phase in Teacher.

weak genetics based operators here [9,33].

(b) *Performance evaluation:* This is related to the performance evaluation of HMs during learning, given that there may be multiple performance measures, that there is no defined relationship among them, and that HMs may have different performance across different subdomains.

(c) *Resource scheduling:* Given the performance information of HMs under consideration, resource scheduling entails the selection of HMs for further testing, the termination of the current generation, and the initiation of the next generation. These problems are important when limited computational resources are available and tests of HMs are expensive and noisy. We schedule computational resources rationally by choosing (i) the number of tests on each HM, (ii) the number of competing HMs to be maintained at any time, and (iii) the number of problem subdomains to be used for learning and for generalization. We have studied two related issues in resource scheduling in genetics based learning algorithms: *sample allocation* and *duration scheduling* [2–4,27,67].

8.5.2.3 Performance-Verification Phase

The goal of this phase is to fully evaluate the set of HMs with good performance found at the end of previous learning phases. As mentioned previously, the performance of HMs evaluated during learning is only estimated based on incomplete and possibly inadequate performance data. In order to select HMs that can be generalized to unlearned subdomains, we need to carry out full evaluation of each HM selected at the end of a learning phase. This involves evaluating each selected HM fully on all subdomains from all learning phases and any additional subdomains provided by users. The main potential issue in this phase is the scheduling of limited computational resources to test a given set of HMs.

8.5.2.4 Performance-Generalization Phase

The goal of the last phase is to determine which HMs, found in previous learning phases, perform consistently well on all subdomains, including those not studied in learning. This notion of performance generalization is slightly different from that in point based learning, as we generalize the performance of HMs found to unseen test cases rather than generalizing the HMs found to better HMs. There are two key issues to be studied here.

(a) *Performance of HMs across different subdomains:* As discussed in Section 8.2, HMs may have different performance behavior in different subdomains; hence, performance values of an HM from different subdomains cannot be combined directly. Oftentimes, an HM may perform well in some subdomains but worse in others. One approach we have studied is to find HMs that are consistently better than others with a high probability across all the subdomains [30,68].

(b) *Cost–quality trade-offs:* This involves determining efficient HMs that perform well in an application. Should there be multiple HMs to be applied (at a higher total cost and better quality of results), or should there be one HM that is costly to run but generates high-quality results? Some results on these trade-offs are shown in Section 8.10.

8.6 Strategies in the Classification Phase

Recall from the previous section that quantitative comparison of performance is difficult when test cases are of different behavior. Hence, before learning begins, the application domain should be broken into smaller subspaces and subdomains.

In subspace partitioning, the attributes needed for partitioning may not be defined, or the number of attributes may be too large. When this happens, non-parametric clustering methods, such as those based on neural networks, may have to be used. Another possibility is to always apply multiple HMs for each test case, resulting in a higher computational cost for a better solution.

We show two examples to demonstrate the idea of application subspaces.

Example 1. Consider solving a vertex-cover problem that finds the minimum number of nodes to cover all the edges in a graph. In designing a decomposition HM to decide which vertex to be included in the covered set, previous experience on other optimization problems indicates that HMs for densely connected graphs are generally different from those for sparsely connected ones. Consequently, the application domain of all graphs can be partitioned (in an ad hoc fashion) into a small number of subspaces based on graph connectivities.

Example 2. As another example, in generating test patterns for testing VLSI circuits, previous experience shows that sequential circuits require tests that are different from those of combinatorial circuits. Hence, we can partition the application domain into two subspaces: one for sequential circuits and another for combinatorial circuits. However, we are not able to partition the subspace of sequential circuits into smaller subspaces as it is not clear which attributes (like the length of the longest path, the number of flip-flops, etc.) should be used in this partitioning.

In our current implementation, subspace partitioning is guided by common-sense knowledge or by user experience in solving similar application problems. It requires knowing one or more attributes to classify test cases and is driven by a set of decision rules that identify the subspace to which a test case belongs. When such attributes cannot be identified, we simply assume that the entire application domain is in one subspace.

In classifying test cases in a subspace into subdomains, some domain knowledge, such as previous experience on similar problems, may be required. After subdomains have been classified, it is important to test the HMs in each subdomain to make sure that their performance data are IID. Examples of methods for testing for identical distributions are the Kolmogorov–Smirnov two-sample test [26,44,47], the Mann–Whitney test [65] and the Wald–Wolfowitz two-sample runs test [44]. On the other hand, testing for independence is difficult, if not impossible [65]. Currently, there do not exist methods to guarantee that all performance values are independent. However, it is possible to evaluate the randomness of *a given sequence of test cases*, which is a necessary condition for data to be independent. For instance, test of randomness can be found by computing the total number of runs up and down [44,69], the total number of runs above and below the median [65,69], and the total number of runs above and below the mean [44]. Other randomness tests include Kendall's rank correlation coefficient test [69] and the circular serial correlation coefficient test [69]. Results on applying these tests are discussed in the references [26].

Continuing with Example 1 on the vertex-cover problem, a problem subdomain can be defined as a collection of random graphs with a certain degree of connectivity. As another example, in generating test patterns for testing VLSI circuits (Example 2),

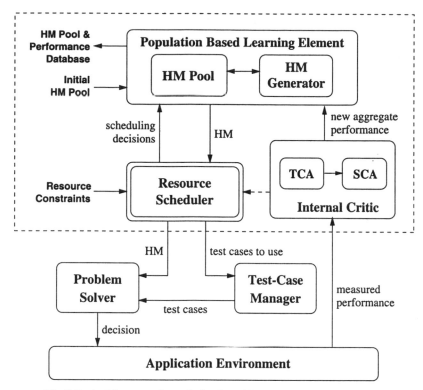

Fig. 8.7. Architecture of population based learning for one subdomain.

each circuit may be treated as an individual subdomain, as we do not know the best set of attributes to group different circuits into subdomains.

8.7 Learning Heuristics in One Subdomain

In this section, we present our approach to learn improved HMs under resource constraints for a single subdomain. Fig. 8.7 shows the architecture of our resource-constrained learning system for one subdomain [66]. This population based learning system is based on the genetics based machine-learning paradigm. There are five main components in the system:

(a) *Resource Scheduler* that determines the best way to use the available computational resources;
(b) *Internal Critic* that provides feedback, based on measured performance, to indicate how well a particular HM has performed;
(c) *Population-Based Learning Element* that generates new HMs and maintains a pool of existing ones and their past performance;
(d) *Test-Case Manager* that generates and maintains a database of test cases used in HM evaluation; and

(e) *Problem Solver* that evaluates an HM using a test case.

In this research, we assume that the application-specific Problem Solver and Test-Case Manager are user-supplied. The remaining three components are designed to deal with the three key issues in Section 8.5: heuristics generation, performance evaluation, and resource scheduling.

8.7.1 Problem Solver

This component is simply the target problem solver whose heuristics we want to improve. The performance of applying a problem solver on a test case is in terms of the quality of the solution found and the cost of the problem-solving process.

In our learning strategy, the problem solver accepts (a) the specification of the HM to be used in problem solving, and (b) the test case to be solved. It also has a mechanism to return the measured performance of the problem-solving process as feedback to the learning system.

8.7.2 Test-Case Manager

This provides test cases to be used in learning. These test cases are either generated randomly or retrieved from a database.

In our current implementation, each HM is evaluated on a pre-defined sequence of user-specified test cases. When a test case is requested for testing a particular HM, the Test-Case Manager returns the first test case in the sequence that has not been evaluated by the chosen HM. This strategy allows performance data of two HMs to be normalized against each other and is useful when performance data have large variances.

8.7.3 Population Based Learning Element

The *Population Based Learning Element* maintains a pool of active HMs. At the end of each generation, a new set of HMs are generated to replace existing HMs. Several top active HMs are usually retained along with the new HMs while other HMs are removed from the active pool.

The Population Based Learning Element in Teacher generates new HMs using weak domain-independent operators, such as crossover, mutation, and hill-climbing. These are traditional operators used in GAs for generating new HMs [9,22]. The process for selecting existing HMs for reproduction is also the same as in traditional genetics based machine learning.

More advanced generation methods that require additional domain knowledge are left for future study. They are currently not necessary because our application domains are knowledge lean.

8.7.4 Internal Critic

In general, this performs credit assignment [60] that apportions credit and blame on components of an HM using results obtained in testing (see Fig. 8.3). Credit assignments can be classified into temporal credit assignment (TCA) and structural credit assignment (SCA). TCA is the first stage in the assimilation of feedback and precedes SCA. TCA divides feedback between the current and the past decisions. Methods for TCA depend on whether the state space is Markovian: non-Markovian representations often require more complex TCA procedures. The second stage is SCA that translates the (temporally local but structurally global) feedback associated with a decision point into modifications associated with various parameters of the decision process.

Since the knowledge-lean applications considered here do not have a world model that relates states, decisions, and feedback signals generated by the learning system or measured in the environment, credit assignment has a much weaker influence on performance improvement. Note that the lack of a world model for credit assignment is the main reason for maintaining competing HMs in our learning system.

In our current prototype, the Internal Critic normalizes the performance value of an HM on a test case against the performance value of the same test case evaluated by the baseline HM. It then updates the performance metrics of the candidate HM. This step is similar to updating fitness values in classifier-system learning.

We have chosen to use a fixed baseline HM during each learning phase and compare different HMs based on their estimated average normalized performance. This baseline HM is usually the best existing HM before learning begins.

Our approach in normalization may cause performance anomalies. For instance, different ways of normalization may lead to different ordering of HMs by their performance data. Anomalies in ordering may also occur when baselines are changed. Strategies to address some of these anomalies have been presented elsewhere [26,66,67].

Although anomalies may happen, it is not critical to have perfect ordering of HMs during learning, as the HMs will eventually be evaluated fully in the Performance Verification Phase.

8.7.5 Resource Scheduler

This schedules tests of HMs based on the available computational resources. It is critical when tests are computationally expensive. There are two problems in scheduling during each learning phase.

The *sample-allocation problem* involves the scheduling of tests of HMs in a generation, given a fixed number of tests in the generation and HMs to be tested. This problem is known in statistics as the (sequential) *allocation problem* [8,64] and the scheduler, the *local scheduler*.

The *duration-scheduling problem* involves deciding when to terminate an existing generation and to start a new one. The part of the resource scheduler that deals with this problem is known as the *global scheduler*.

These two problems, as well as the scheduling of tests under multiple performance objectives, are presented elsewhere [2–4,27,66,67].

VERIFICATION

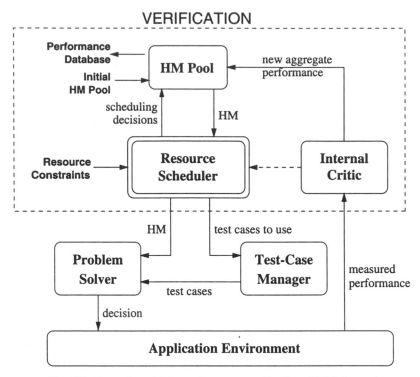

Fig. 8.8. General model for performance verification of HMs learned.

8.8   Strategies in Performance Verification

In this phase, we like to find more complete performance information about the HMs we have generated during the learning phase(s). This is necessary for two reasons. First, the performance information obtained during each learning phase pertains to only one subdomain and is usually incomplete due to resource constraints. Second, the performance-generalization phase (to be described in the next section) requires performance information of each HM on every subdomain. Hence, we need to evaluate thoroughly the HMs selected at the end of learning.

The operations in this phase (see Fig. 8.8) are very similar to those in the learning phase except for the following differences. (a) A fixed pool of HMs is maintained in this phase and no new HMs are generated. (b) More than one subdomain of test cases can be maintained by the Test-Case Manager. (c) The performance of HMs from different subdomains is evaluated separately and independently by the Internal Critic. (d) Resource scheduling in this phase has a different goal of minimizing uncertainties in the performance of all HMs across all subdomains. (e) Only temporal credit assignment is done in the Internal Critic since we do not use structural credit assignment to modify the HMs tested.

Currently, our prototype does not address the issue on resource scheduling in this phase. It evaluates each HM fully on all test cases in each problem subdomain. Such a strategy may be inefficient because it tests good HMs as well as poor HMs to the same extent. We plan to study resource scheduling in the future.

8.9   Strategies in Performance Generalization

As discussed in Section 8.5.2, an application domain (or application subspace) can have many subdomains, and HMs may behave differently in different subdomains. As a result, it is possible for an HM to perform well across all the subdomains, but its performance data from different subdomains cannot be aggregated statistically. Our objective in generalization is, therefore, to find one or more HMs in a given application domain that has a high probability of performing better than other competing HMs on a randomly chosen test case in the problem domain.

The performance-generalization process is difficult because (a) performance data from different subdomains must be treated separately and independently, and (b) there are usually many more subdomains than the ones we can test. Since we may not be able to characterize the subdomains we test to be representatives of the entire application domain, the process is heuristic in nature.

Example 3. To illustrate the difficulties in performance generalization, we show in Fig. 8.9 the average symmetric speedups.[1] of four decomposition HMs used in a branch-and-bound search to solve vertex-cover problems. We treat all test cases as belonging to one subspace, and graphs with the same degree of connectivity are grouped into a subdomain. We apply genetics based learning to find the five best HMs for each of three subdomains with connectivities 0.1, 0.35, and 0.6.

Fig. 8.9 shows the performance of the best HMs learned in each subdomain across all the subdomains. We have also identified a single generalized HM among the 15 HMs learned and show its performance in Fig. 8.9. We find that the generalized HM is not the top HM learned in each subdomain, indicating that the best HM in each subdomain may be too specialized. We have also found that performance generalization is possible in terms of average performance. We must point out that the average performance should not be used as the sole indicator, as performance variances may differ from one subdomain to another.

Our current work on generalization is to ensure that HMs generated in learning perform well across multiple subdomains. This is done by testing each HM on multiple subdomains in a generation and by selecting those that perform well across all the

---

[1] The symmetric-improvement measure, S^{sym+}, is defined as follows [26,66,67]:

$$S^{sym+} = \begin{cases} S^+ - 1 & \text{if } S^+ \geq 1 \\ 1 - \dfrac{1}{S^+} & \text{if } 0 \leq S^+ < 1 \end{cases}$$

where S^+ is the improvement ratio of the new HM with respect to the original baseline HM. Symmetric improvement ratios have the properties that they range from negative infinity to positive infinity, and that the baseline has a value of zero. On the other hand, improvement ratios range from zero to positive infinity, and the baseline HM has a value of one

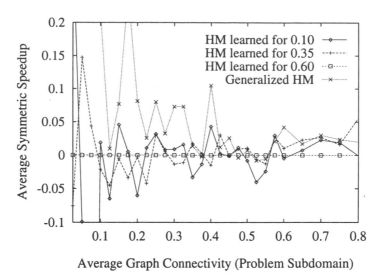

Average Graph Connectivity (Problem Subdomain)

Fig. 8.9. Average symmetric speedups (over 15 test cases) of three decomposition HMs to solve the vertex-cover problem, where subdomains are manually selected based on graph connectivity. The HM learned for 0.6 connectivity is the same as the baseline HM.

subdomains to be candidates for reproduction in the next generation. Our preliminary results indicate the need of a better fitness function to measure the merits of HMs that do not perform well across all the subdomains. Our current fitness function, based on the minimum average performance across all the tested subdomains, is too weak and may prune all the candidate HMs in a generation.

8.10 Experimental Results

Teacher has been applied in learning improved process-placement strategies on a network of workstations [37], more efficient process-placement strategies on distributed-memory multicomputers [27], more robust parameters in a stereo-vision algorithm [55], smaller feed-forward neural networks [62,63], improved heuristics for a branch-and-bound search [36,73], better and less costly strategies in circuit testing [30,67,68] and cell placement and routing [30,67,68], and improved parameters in channel equalization [28,30].

In this section, we report our experience in applying Teacher to learn improved HMs in two problem solvers, CRIS [52] and GATEST [51], for circuit testing. These are two GA software packages for generating patterns to test sequential VLSI circuits. In our experiments, we used sequential circuits from the ISCAS89 benchmarks [10] plus several other larger circuits. Since these circuits are from different applications, it is difficult to classify them by some common features. Consequently, we treat each circuit as an individual subdomain. As we like to find one common HM for all circuits, we assume that all circuits are from one subspace.

8.10.1 CRIS

CRIS [52] is based on continuous mutations of a given input test sequence and on analyzing the mutated vectors to select a new test sequence. Hierarchical simulation techniques are used in the system to reduce memory requirements, thereby allowing its application to large VLSI circuits. The package has been applied successfully to generate test patterns that can detect nearly all the detectable faults (high fault coverage) for large combinatorial and sequential circuits.

CRIS in our experiments is treated as a problem solver in a black box, as we have minimal knowledge in its design. An HM targeted for improvement is a set of eight parameters used in CRIS (see Table 8.1). Note that parameter P_8 is a random seed, implying that CRIS can be run multiple times using different random seeds in order to obtain better fault coverages. (In our experiments, we used a fixed sequence of 10 random seeds from Table 8.2.)

Table 8.1. Parameters in CRIS treated as an HM in learning and in generalization. (The type, range, and step of each parameter were recommended to us by the designer of CRIS. The default parameters were not given to us as they are circuit dependent)

Parameter	Type	Range	Step	Definition	Learned value
P_1	integer	1–10	1	related to the number of stages in a flip-flop	1
P_2	integer	1–40	1	related to the sensitivity of changes of state of a flip-flop (number of times a flip-flop changes its state in a test sequence)	12
P_3	integer	1–40	1	selection criterion – related to the survival rate of a candidate test sequence in the next generation	38
P_4	float	0.1–10.0	0.1	related to the number of test vectors concatenated to form a new test sequence	7.06
P_5	integer	50–800	10	related to the number of useless trials before quitting	623
P_6	integer	1–20	1	number of generations	1
P_7	float	0.1–1.0	0.1	how genes are spliced in the genetic algorithm	0.1
P_8	integer	any	1	seed for the random number generator	–

A major problem in using the original CRIS is that it is hard to find proper values for the seven parameters (excluding the random seed) for a particular circuit. The designer of CRIS manually tuned these parameters for each circuit, resulting in HMs that are hard to generalize. This tuning was done because the designer wanted to obtain the highest possible fault coverage for each circuit, and computation cost was only a

Table 8.2. Sequence of random seeds used in learning experiments for CRIS, GATEST, and TimberWolf

Sequence of random seeds				
61801	98052	15213	48823	55414
60203	43212	08540	94702	92715

secondary consideration. Note that the times for manual tuning were exceedingly high and were not reported in the reference [52].

Our goal is to develop one common HM that works across all the benchmark circuits and that has similar or better fault coverages as compared to those of the original CRIS. The advantage of having one HM is that it can be applied to new circuits without further tuning.

8.10.2 GATEST

GATEST [51] is another test-pattern generator based on GAs. It augments existing techniques in order to reduce execution times and to improve fault coverages. The GA component evolves candidate test vectors and sequences, using a fault simulator to compute the fitness of each candidate test. To improve performance, the designers manually tuned various GA parameters in the package, including alphabet size, fitness function, generation gap, population size, and mutation rate as well as selection and crossover schemes. High fault coverages were obtained for most of the ISCAS89 sequential benchmark circuits [10], and execution times were significantly lower in most cases than those obtained by HITEC [46], a deterministic test-pattern generator.

The entire GA process was divided into four phases, each with its own fitness function that had been manually tuned by the designers. The designers also told us that Phase 2 of their package had the largest impact on performance and recommended that we improved it first. As a result, we treated GATEST as our problem solver, and the fitness function (a symbolic formula) in Phase 2 as our HM. The original form of this fitness function is

$$fitness_2 = \#\_faults\_detected \qquad\qquad (8.1)$$
$$+ \frac{\#\_faults\_propagated\_to\_flip\_flops}{(\#\_faults)(\#\_flip\_flops)}$$

In learning a new fitness function, we have used the following variables as possible arguments of the function: $\#\_faults$, $\#\_faults\_detected$, $\#\_circuit\_nodes$, $\#\_flip\_flops$, $\#\_faults\_propagated\_to\_flip\_flops$, and $sequence\_length$. The operators allowed to compose new fitness functions include $+$, $-$, $*$, and $/$.

8.10.3 Results

In our experiments, we chose five circuits as our learning subdomains. In each of these subdomains, we used Teacher to test CRIS 1000 times with different HMs, each represented as the first seven parameters in Table 8.1. At the end of learning, we picked the top 20 HMs and evaluated them fully by initializing CRIS by 10 different random seeds (P_8 in Table 8.1 with values from Table 8.2). We then selected the top five HMs from each subdomain, resulting in a total of 25 HMs supplied to the generalization phase. We evaluated the 25 HMs fully (each with 10 random seeds) on the five sub-domains used in learning and five new subdomains. We then selected one generalized HM to be used across all 10 circuits. Since there is no incumbent HM, we use the median performance value of each test case as the baseline performance for that test case. The elements of the generalized HM found are shown in Table 8.1.

For GATEST, we applied learning to find good HMs for six circuits (s298, s386, s526, s820, s1196, and s1488 in the ISCAS89 benchmark). We then generalized the best 30 HMs (five from each subdomain) by first evaluating them fully (each with 10 random seeds from Table 8.2) on the six subdomains and by selecting one generalized HM for all circuits. Since there is an incumbent HM, we use the performance of the incumbent HM as our baseline for improvement. The final fitness function we got after generalization is

$$fitness_2 = 2 \times \#\_faults\_propagated\_to\_flip\_flops \qquad (8.2)$$
$$- \#\_faults\_detected$$

Table 8.3 shows the results after generalization for CRIS and GATEST. For each circuit, we present the average and maximum fault coverages (over 10 random seeds) and the corresponding computational costs. These fault coverages are compared against the published fault coverages of CRIS [52] and GATEST [51] as well as those of HITEC [46]. Note that the maximum fault coverages reported in Table 8.3 were based on 10 runs of the underlying problem solver, implying that the computational cost is 10 times the average cost.

Table 8.4 summarizes the improvements of our learned and generalized HMs as compared to the published results of CRIS, GATEST, and HITEC. Each entry of the table shows the number of times our HM wins, ties, and loses in terms of fault coverages with respect to the method(s) in the first column. Our results show that our generalized HM based on CRIS as the problem solver is better than the original CRIS in 16 out of 21 circuits in terms of the maximum fault coverage and better than 11 out of 21 circuits in terms of the average fault coverage. Furthermore, our generalized HM based on GATEST as the problem solver is better than the original GATEST in 7 out of 19 circuits in terms of both the average and the maximum fault coverages. Note that the average fault coverages of our generalized HM are better than or equal to the original GATEST in all subdomains used in the heuristics-design process. Our results show that our generalization procedure can discover good HMs that work better than the original HMs.

Table 8.4 also indicates that HITEC is still better than our new generalized HM for CRIS in most of the circuits (in 14 out of 21 in terms of the maximal fault coverage and in 17 out of 21 in terms of the average fault coverage). The poor performance of our generalized HM as compared to HITECH is attributed to the limitations in CRIS and by our HM generator. Such limitations cannot be overcome without using HITECH as our problem solver or without using more powerful HM generator.

Finally, we plot the distributions of symmetric fault coverages of our generalized HMs normalized with respect to the average fault coverages of the original CRIS

Table 8.3. Performance of HMs in terms of computational cost and fault coverage for CRIS and GATEST. (Learned subdomains for CRIS are marked by '*' and generalized subdomains by '+'). Performance of HITEC is from the literature [46,52]. Costs of our experiments are running times in seconds on a Sun SparcStation 10/51; costs of HITEC are running times in seconds on a Sun SparcStation SLC [51] (a computer around four to six times slower than a Sun SparcStation 10/51).

Circuit ID	Total faults	Fault coverage				Cost		CRIS Gen. HM			GATEST Gen. HM		
		HITEC	CRIS	Avg. GATEST	Max. GATEST	HITEC	Avg. GATEST	Avg. FC	Max. FC	Avg. Cost	Avg. FC	Max. FC	Avg. Cost
*s298	308	86.0	82.1	85.9	86.0	15984.0	128.6	84.7	86.4	10.9	85.9	86.0	126.4
s344	342	95.9	93.7	96.2	96.2	4788.0	134.8	96.1	96.2	21.8	96.2	96.2	133.3
s349	350	95.7	–	95.7	95.7	3132.0	136.9	95.6	95.7	21.9	95.7	95.7	128.3
+s382	399	90.9	68.6	87.0	87.5	43200.0	203.3	72.4	87.0	7.2	87.0	87.5	208.9
s386	384	81.7	76.0	76.9	77.9	61.8	67.6	77.5	78.9	3.5	78.6	79.3	78.6
*s400	426	89.9	84.7	85.7	86.6	43560.0	229.3	71.2	85.7	8.4	85.7	86.6	215.1
s444	474	87.3	83.7	85.6	86.3	57960.0	259.4	79.8	85.4	9.3	85.6	86.3	233.8
*s526	555	65.7	77.1	75.1	76.4	168480.0	333.4	70.0	77.1	10.0	75.5	77.3	302.7
s641	467	86.5	85.2	86.5	86.5	1080.0	181.2	85.0	86.1	19.5	86.5	86.5	195.0
+s713	581	81.9	81.7	81.9	81.9	91.2	219.9	81.3	81.9	23.0	81.9	81.9	256.5
s820	850	95.6	53.1	60.8	68.0	5796.0	266.4	44.7	46.7	51.3	69.3	80.9	225.4
*s832	870	93.9	42.5	61.9	66.8	6336.0	265.8	44.1	45.6	44.6	66.9	72.8	251.0
s1196	1242	99.7	95.0	99.2	99.5	91.8	292.1	92.0	94.1	20.0	99.2	99.4	421.7
*s1238	1355	94.6	90.7	94.0	94.4	132.0	380.5	88.2	89.2	23.0	94.0	94.2	585.2
s1488	1486	97.0	91.2	93.7	96.0	12960.0	512.3	94.1	95.2	85.6	94.3	96.5	553.4
+s1494	1506	96.4	90.1	94.0	95.8	6876.0	510.4	93.2	94.1	85.5	93.6	95.6	584.3
s1423	1515	40.0	77.0	81.0	86.3	–	3673.9	82.0	88.3	210.4	81.3	87.3	4325.7
+s5378	4603	70.3	65.8	69.5	70.1	–	9973.3	65.3	69.9	501.8	69.6	71.9	8875.7
s35932	39094	89.3	88.2	89.5	89.7	13680.0	184316.0	77.9	78.4	4265.7	89.4	89.7	184417.0
am2910	2573	85.0	83.0	–	–	–	–	83.7	85.2	307.6	–	–	–
+div16	2147	72.0	75.0	–	–	–	–	79.1	81.0	149.9	–	–	–
tc100	1979	80.6	70.8	–	–	–	–	72.6	75.9	163.8	–	–	–

Table 8.4. Summary of results comparing the performance of our generalized HMs with respect to those of HITEC, CRIS, and GATEST. (The first number in each entry shows the number of wins out of all applicable circuits, the second, the number of ties, and the third, the number of losses. A second number in the entry on wins indicates the number of circuits in which the test efficiency is already 100%. For these circuits, no further improvement is possible)

Our HM wins/ties/loses with respect to the following systems	CRIS generalized HM			GATEST generalized HM		
	Total	Max. FC	Avg. FC	Total	Max. FC	Avg. FC
HITEC	22	6, 2, 14	4, 0, 18	19	5+2, 2, 10	4+2, 1, 12
Original CRIS	21	16, 1, 4	11, 0, 10	18	18, 0, 0	17, 0, 1
Original GATEST	19	4, 3, 12	3, 0, 16	19	7+2, 7, 3	7+2, 8, 2
Both HITEC and CRIS	21	5, 2, 14	3, 0, 18	18	5+2, 1, 10	3+2, 1, 13
Both HITEC & GATEST	19	3, 3, 13	1, 0, 18	19	3+2, 4, 10	2+2, 2, 13
HITEC, CRIS, & GATEST	18	2, 3, 13	1, 0, 17	18	3+2, 3, 10	1+2, 1, 14

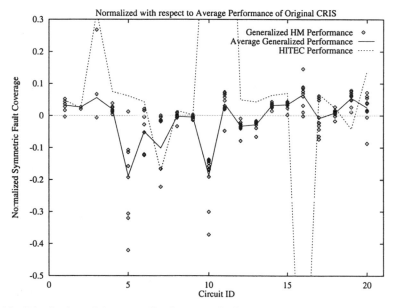

Fig. 8.10. Distribution of the normalized symmetric fault coverages of our generalized HM with respect to the average fault coverages of the original CRIS on 20 benchmark circuits (s298, s344, s382, s386, s400, s444, s526, s641, s713, s820, s832, s1196, s1238, s1488, s1494, s1423, s5378, am2910, div16, and tc100 in that order).

(Fig. 8.10) and GATEST (Fig. 8.11). These plots clearly demonstrate improvements over the original HMs.

8.11 Conclusions

In this chapter, we have studied the following five issues in learning improved knowledge-lean heuristics using a genetics based machine learning approach:

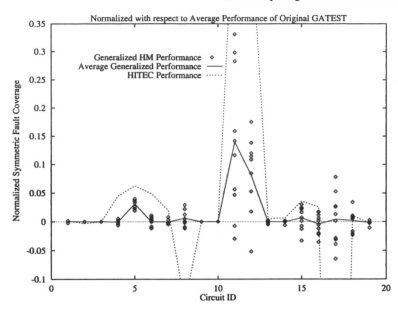

Fig. 8.11. Distribution of the normalized symmetric fault coverages of our generalized HM with respect to the average fault coverages of the original GATEST on 19 benchmark circuits (s298, s344, s349, s382, s386, s400, s444, s526, s641, s713, s820, s832, s1196, s1238, s1488, s1494, s1423, s5378, and s35932 in that order).

- Decomposition of a problem solver into components so that heuristics can be learned for each, and integration of the heuristics learned into the problem solver.
- Partitioning of test cases in an application domain into subdomains so that performance data of heuristics within each subdomain are independent and identically distributed.
- Generation of new heuristics based on performance of existing heuristics evaluated in the past.
- Full evaluation of heuristics to verify their performance.
- Generalization of performance of heuristics to find heuristics that perform well across the entire application domain.

To address these issues, we have developed Teacher, a genetics based system for learning knowledge-lean heuristics. Teacher has four phases in its operation: (a) classification of test cases into subdomains, (b) learning improved heuristics for one subdomain at a time under resource constraints, (c) verification of performance of heuristics learned to augment partial evaluation results obtained during learning, and (d) finding heuristics whose performance behavior can be generalized to subdomains not studied in learning.

Finally, we have shown improved heuristics for two GA packages used in VLSI test-pattern generation and have demonstrated that improved heuristics learned can be generalized to new circuits. Our approach allows designers to apply circuit-independent heuristics in these systems, eliminating the time-consuming process to find good heuristics for each circuit.

Acknowledgement

Research was supported by National Science Foundation Grants MIP 96-32316.

References

1. Ackley, D. H. (1987) *A Connectionist Machine for Genetic Hillclimbing*. Kluwer Academic Pub., Boston, MA.
2. Aizawa, A., and Wah, B. W. (1993) Scheduling of genetic algorithms in a noisy environment. In *Proc. Int. Conf. on Genetic Algorithms*, Morgan Kaufman, Int. Soc. for Genetic Algorithms, 48–55.
3. Aizawa, A. K., and Wah, B. W. (1994) Scheduling of genetic algorithms in a noisy environment. *Evol. Comput. 2*(2), 97–122.
4. Aizawa, A. N., and Wah, B. W. (1994) A sequential sampling procedure for genetic algorithms. *Comput. Math. Appl. 27*(9/10), 77–82.
5. Barr, A., and Feigenbaum, E. A. (1981) *The Handbook of Artificial Intelligence*, vols. 1, 2, and 3. William Kaufmann, Los Altos, CA.
6. Beasley, D., Bull, D. R., and Martin, R. R. (1993) An overview of genetic algorithms: Part 1, fundamentals. *Univ. Comput. 15*(2), 58–69.
7. Beasley, D., Bull, D. R., and Martin, R. R. (1993) An overview of genetic algorithms: Part 2, research topics. *Univ. Comput. 15*(4), 170–181.
8. Bechhofer, R. E. (1954) A single-sample multiple decision procedure for ranking means of normal populations with known variances. *Ann. Math. Statist. 25*(1), 16–39.
9. Booker, L. B., Goldberg, D. E., and Holland, J. H. (1990) Classifier systems and genetic algorithms. In *Machine Learning: Paradigm and Methods*, J. Carbonell, Ed., MIT Press, Cambridge, MA.
10. Brglez, F., Bryan, D., and Kozminski, K. (1989) Combinatorial profiles of sequential benchmark circuits. In *Int. Symposium on Circuits and Systems*, 1929–1934.
11. Chien, S., Gratch, J., and Burl, M. (1995) On the efficient allocation of resources for hypothesis evaluation: A statistical approach. *IEEE Trans. Pattern Anal. Mach. Intell. 17*(7), 652–665.
12. DeJong, K. (1988) Learning with genetic algorithms: An overview. *Machine Learn. 3*(2/3), 121–138.
13. DeJong, K., and Spears, W. (1993) On the state of evolutionary computation. In *Proc. Fifth Int. Conf. Genetic Algorithms*, Int. Soc. for Genetic Algorithms, 618–623.
14. DeJong, K. A., Spears, W. M., and Gordon, D. F. (1993) Using genetic algorithm for concept learning. *Machine Learn. 13*(2/3), 161–188.
15. Desimone, R. (1987) Learning control knowledge within an explanation-based learning framework. In *Progress in Machine Learning*, I. Bratko and N. Lavrac, Eds. Sigma Press, Cheshire, UK, 107–119.
16. Dieterich, T. G., and Buchanan, B. G. (1981) The role of critic in learning systems. Tech. Rep. STAN-CS-81-891, Stanford University, CA.
17. Ernst, G. W., and Goldstein, M. M. (1982) Mechanical discovery of classes of problem-solving strategies. *J. ACM 29*(1), 1–23.

18. Fitzpatrick, J. M., and Grefenstette, J. J. (1988) Genetic algorithms in noisy environments. *Machine Learn.* 3(2/3), 101–120.
19. Goldberg, D. E. (1989) *Genetic Algorithms in Search, Optimization, and Machine Learning.* Addison-Wesley, Reading, MA.
20. Goldberg, D. E., Deb, K., and Clark, J. H. (1982) Genetic algorithms, noise, and the sizing of populations. *Complex Syst.* 6, 333–362.
21. Goldberg, D. E., and Holland, J. H. (1988) Genetic algorithms and machine learning. *Machine Learn.* 3(2/3), 95–100.
22. Grefenstette, J. J. (1986) Optimization of control parameters for genetic algorithms. *Trans. Syst. Man Cybernet. SMC-16*(1), 122–128.
23. Grefenstette, J. J., Ramsey, C. L., and Schultz, A. C. (1990) Learning sequential decision rules using simulation models and competition. *Machine Learn.* 5, 355–381.
24. Heitkötter, J., and Beasley, D., Eds (1995) *The Hitch-Hiker's Guide to Evolutionary Computation: A List of Frequently Asked Questions (FAQ).* USENET: comp.ai.genetic. Anonymous FTP: rtfm.mit.edu:/pub/usenet/news.answers/ai-faq/genetic/.
25. Holland, J. H. (1975) *Adaptation in Natural and Artificial Systems.* University of Michigan Press, Ann Arbor, MI.
26. Ieumwananonthachai, A. (1996) *Automated Design of Knowledge-Lean Heuristics: Learning, Resource Scheduling, and Generalization.* Ph.D. Thesis, Dept. of Electrical and Computer Engineering, University of Illinois, Urbana, IL.
27. Ieumwananonthachai, A., Aizawa, A., Schwartz, S. R., Wah, B. W., and Yan, J. C. (1992) Intelligent process mapping through systematic improvement of heuristics. *J. Parallel Distrib. Comput.* 15, 118–142.
28. Ieumwananonthachai, A., and Wah, B. W. (1995) Statistical generalization of performance-related heuristics for knowledge-lean applications. In *Proc. Int. Conference on Tools for Artificial Intelligence*, Houston, TX, IEEE, 174–181.
29. Ieumwananonthachai, A., and Wah, B. W. (1995) TEACHER – an automated system for learning knowledge-lean heuristics. Tech. Rep. CRHC-95-08, Center for Reliable and High Performance Computing, Coordinated Science Laboratory, University of Illinois, Urbana, IL.
30. Ieumwananonthachai, A., and Wah, B. W. (1996) Statistical generalization of performance-related heuristics for knowledge-lean applications. *Int. J. Artif. Intell. Tools* 5(12), 61–79.
31. Janikow, C. Z. (1993) A knowledge-intensive genetic algorithm for supervised learning. *Machine Learn.* 13(2/3), 189–228.
32. Klopf, A. H. (1987) Drive-reinforcement learning: A real-time learning mechanism for unsupervised learning. In *Proc. Int. Conf. on Neural Networks*, vol. II, IEEE, 441–445.
33. Koza, J. R. (1992) *Genetic Programming.* MIT Press, Cambridge, MA.
34. Langley, P. (1985) Learning to search: From weak methods to domain-specific heuristics. *Cognitive Sci.* 9, 217–260.
35. Lenat, D. B. (1983) Theory formation by heuristic search: The nature of heuristics II: Background and examples. *Artif. Intell.* 21, 31–59.

36. Lowrie, M. B., and Wah, B. W. (1988) Learning heuristic functions for numeric optimization problems. In *Proc. Computer Software and Applications Conf.*, Chicago, IL, IEEE, 443–450.

37. Mehra, P., and Wah, B. W. (1995) *Load Balancing: An Automated Learning Approach*. World Scientific Publishing Co. Pte. Ltd.

38. Michalski, R. S. (1986) Understanding the nature of learning: Issues and research directions. In *Machine Learning: An Artificial Intelligence Approach*, R. S. Michalski, J. G. Carbonell, and T. M. Mitchell, Eds, vol. II. Morgan Kaufmann, Los Altos, CA, 3–25.

39. Minsky, M. (1963) Steps toward artificial intelligence. In *Computers and Thought*, E. A. Feigenbaum and J. Feldman, Eds. McGraw-Hill, New York, 406–450.

40. Minton, S., Carbonell, J. G., Knoblock, C. A., Kuokka, D. R., Etzioni, O., and Gil, Y. (1990) Explanation-based learning: A problem solving perspective. In *Machine Learning: Paradigms and Methods*, J. Carbonell, Ed. MIT Press, Cambridge, MA, 63–118.

41. Mitchell, T. M. (1983) Learning and problem solving. In *Proc. 8th Int. Joint Conf. on Artificial Intelligence*, Los Altos, CA, William Kaufmann, 1139–1151.

42. Mitchell, T. M., Utgoff, P. E., and Banerji, R. B. (1983) Learning by experimentation: Acquiring and refining problem-solving heuristics. In *Machine Learning*, R. S. Michalski, J. G. Carbonell, and T. M. Mitchell, Eds. Tioga.

43. Mitchell, T. M., Utgoff, P. E., Nudel, B., and Benerji, R. (1981) Learning problem-solving heuristics through practice. In *Proc. 7th Int. Joint Conf. on Artificial Intelligence*, Los Altos, CA, William Kaufman, 127–134.

44. Neave, H. R., and Worthington, P. L. (1988) *Distribution-Free Tests*. Unwin Hyman, London, UK.

45. Nguyen, D., and Widrow, B. (1989) The truck backer-upper: An example of self-learning in neural networks. In *Proc. Int. Joint Conf. on Neural Networks*, vol. II, IEEE, 357–363.

46. Niermann, T. M., and Patel, J. H. (1991) HITEC: A test generation package for sequential circuits. In *European Design Automation Conference*, 214–218.

47. Press, W. H., Teukolsky, S. A., Vetterling, W. T., and Flannery, B. P. (1992) *Numerical Recipes in C*, 2nd edn. Cambridge University Press, Cambridge, UK.

48. Ramsey, C. L., and Grefenstette, J. J. (1993) Case-based initialization of genetic algorithms. In *Proc. of the Fifth Int. Conf. on Genetic Algorithms*, Morgan Kaufmann, Int. Soc. for Genetic Algorithms, 84–91.

49. Rendell, L. A. (1983) A new basis for state-space learning systems and a successful implementation. *Artif. Intell. 20*, 369–392.

50. Robertson, G., and Riolo, R. (1988) A tale of two classifier systems. *Machine Learn. 3*(2/3), 139–160.

51. Rudnick, E. M., Patel, J. H., Greenstein, G. S., and Niermann, T. M. (1994) Sequential circuit test generation in a genetic algorithm framework. In *Proc. Design Automation Conf.*, ACM/IEEE.

52. Saab, D. G., Saab, Y. G., and Abraham, J. A. (1992) CRIS: A test cultivation program for sequential VLSI circuits. In *Proc. of Int. Conf. on Computer Aided Design*, Santa Clara, CA, IEEE, 216–219.

53. Samuel, A. L. (1959) Some studies in machine learning using the game of checkers. *IBM J. Res. Dev. 3*, 210–229.
54. Samuel, A. L. (1967) Some studies in machine learing using the game of checkers II: Recent progress. *J. Res. Dev. 11*(6), 601–617.
55. Schwartz, S. R., and Wah, B. W. (1992) Automated parameter tuning in stereo vision under time constraints. In *Proc. Int. Conf. on Tools for Artificial Intelligence*, IEEE, 162–169.
56. Sleeman, D., Langley, P., and Mitchell, T. M. (1982) Learning from solution paths: An approach to the credit assignment problem. *AI Magazine 3*, 48–52.
57. Smith, R. G., Mitchell, T. M., Chestek, R. A., and Buchanan, B. G. (1977) A model for learning systems. In *Proc. 5th Int. Joint Conf. on Artificial Intelligence*, Los Altos, CA, William Kaufmann, 338–343.
58. Smith, S. F. (1983) Flexible learning of problem solving heuristics through adaptive search. In *Proc. Int. Joint Conf. on Artificial Intelligence*, Morgan Kaufmann, 422–425.
59. Spears, W. M., DeJong, K. A., Bäck, T., Fogel, D., and de Garis, H. (1993) An overview of evolutionary computing. In *Proc. European Conf. on Machine Learning*, New York, Springer-Verlag, 442–459.
60. Sutton, R. S. (1994) *Temporal Credit Assignment in Reinforcement Learning.* Ph.D. thesis, University of Massachusetts, Amherst, MA.
61. Sutton, R. S., and Barto, A. G. (1984) Toward a modern theory of adaptive networks: Expectation and predicition. *Psychol. Rev. 88*(2), 135–170.
62. Teng, C.-C., and Wah, B. W. (1994) An automated design system for finding the minimal configuration of a feed-forward neural network. In *Proc. Int. Conf. on Neural Networks*, IEEE, III-1295–III-1300.
63. Teng, C.-C., and Wah, B. W. (1996) Automated learning of the minimal configuration of a feed forward neural network. *IEEE Trans. Neural Networks 7*(5), 1072–1085.
64. Tong, Y. L., and Wetzell, D. E. (1984) Allocation of observations for selecting the best normal population. In *Design of Experiments: Ranking and Selection*, T. J. Santner and A. C. Tamhane, Eds. Marcel Dekker, New York, 213–224.
65. Ullman, N. R. (1972) *Statistics: An Applied Approach.* Xerox College Publishing, Lexington, MA.
66. Wah, B. W. (1992) Population-based learning: A new method for learning from examples under resource constraints. *IEEE Trans. Knowl. Data Eng. 4*(5), 454–474.
67. Wah, B. W., Ieumwananonthachai, A., Chu, L. C., and Aizawa, A. (1995) Genetics-based learning of new heuristics: Rational scheduling of experiments and generalization. *IEEE Trans. Knowl. Data Eng. 7*(5), 763–785.
68. Wah, B. W., Ieumwananonthachai, A., Yao, S., and Yu, T. (1995) Statistical generalization: Theory and applications (plenary address). In *Proc. Int. Conf. on Computer Design*, Austin, TX, IEEE, 4–10.
69. Walsh, J. E. (1962) *Handbook of Nonparametric Statistics*, vol. 1. D. Van Nostrand, Princeton, NJ.
70. Widrow, B., Gupta, N. K., and Maitra, S. (1973) Punish/reward: Learning with a critic in adaptive threshold systems. *Trans. Syst. Man Cybernet. SMC-3*(5), 455–465.

71. Williams, R. J. (1988) On the use of backpropagation in associative reinforcement learning. In *Proc. Int. Conf. on Neural Networks*, vol. I, IEEE, 263–270.
72. Wilson, S. W., and Goldberg, D. E. (1989) A critical review of classifier systems. In *Proc. of the Third Int. Conf. Genetic Algorithms*, Int. Soc. for Genetic Algorithms, 244–255.
73. Yu, C. F., and Wah, B. W. (1988) Learning dominance relations in combinatorial search problems. *IEEE Trans. Software Eng. SE-14*(8), 1155–1175.

9. Fuzzy Logic Based Neural Network for Case Based Reasoning

Zhi-Qiang Liu

Abstract. This chapter provides a way of integrating the concepts of neuro-fuzzy computing and case based reasoning for designing an efficient decision support system. Multilayer networks with fuzzy AND-neurons as hidden nodes and fuzzy OR-neurons as output nodes are used for this purpose. Lingustic fuzzy sets are considered at the input level. Cases are described as fuzzy IF–THEN rules in order to handle imprecision and vagueness. Relations of the weighting factors antecedents of rules, the certainty factors and the network parameters are analyzed. The effectiveness of the system is demonstrated on various synthetic and real life problems including the area of telecommunication.

9.1 Introduction

In the realm of intelligent systems, case based reasoning (CBR) is an effective and efficient problem-solving paradigm. Quite simply, the basic CBR process is to find a solution in a stored *case* base that has solutions to problems similar to the problem at hand. CBR does not generalize cases beyond what has been learned and favors only similar cases. Usually, CBR finds solutions to problems that are in the same domain, which is different from analogical learning. However, in many applications, the solution to one problem may not be applicable *directly* to a new problem. As a consequence, case-solution adaptation is necessary.

Artificial neural networks (ANN) have found many successful applications. In supervised learning, we use samples to train neural networks by adjusting their connection weights, which is usually done by the backpropagation algorithm. For instance, for diagnostic applications, the training examples can be obtained from the previous diagnostic cases, with symptoms (problems) as inputs and diagnoses as outputs (solutions). As a result, the neural network can discover the underlying regularities in the problem domain by generalization. However, ANNs are not able to perform logic-like rules because the distribution of connection weights in the network is almost impossible to be interpreted in terms of IF–THEN rules. Recently, researchers [16,22,25] have proposed approaches to incorporate fuzzy logic elements into neural networks. The resulting network topology can perform fuzzy inference rules through analyzing the values of the connection weights. In this chapter, we develop a fuzzy logic based artificial neural network (FLNN) that use two types of fuzzy neurons: fuzzy AND-neuron and fuzzy OR-neuron. We use t-norms for AND operation and t-conorms for OR operation.

As an illustration, we develop a CBR system using the FLNN and apply it to decision support and diagnosis in telecommunication systems. The training data are obtained from call records collected from an Ericsson help-desk database. While these recorded data provide useful diagnostic information about the relationship between symptoms and diagnoses, they may also inevitably contain noise and inconsistent cases. With the noise rejection capability (as a result of generalization) of the ANN, the network's performance is insensitive to noise. In the presence of highly noisy and contradictory data, however, the network's performance will deteriorate gracefully. These properties make the fuzzy neural network ideally suitable for applications in decision support and diagnosis.

Section 9.2 discusses fuzzy IF–THEN rules in the inferencing process. In Section 9.3, we present the method to build the neural network using fuzzy logic based neurons, where we give a detailed discussion of the logic operations of the OR-neuron and the AND-neuron. Also presented in this section is the learning algorithm. In Section 9.4, we use a lookup table method for finding the possibility measures for fuzzy variables, which is especially useful in large systems. Section 9.5 describes the CBR system used in decision-support applications. In Section 9.6 we present four simple cases to test the performance of the system. Section 9.7 shows experimental results in a real telecommunications system.

9.2 Inference System Using Fuzzy Rules

CBR has found applications in many areas where episodic experiences can be represented as cases in (Problem, Solution) pairs. Typical CBR applications include diagnosis, decision support, classification, planning, configuration and design [18].

In a CBR system, we need a model or structure to represent rules or contexts. In order to find solutions from multiple case based rules, we also need a method for inference through the cases. In general, the building block in a rule based system, or an inference system, is a propositional statement of the form [29]

attribute of *object* is *value*

Formally, we can use 'V is A' to represent the propositional statement, where V is a variable standing for the attribute of an instance, and A is the current value of the variable in question. For example, a propositional statement about John's height can be expressed as

$$\underbrace{\text{John's height is}}_{V} \ \underbrace{\text{6.5 feet}}_{A} \text{(crisp description)},$$

$$\underbrace{\text{John's height is}}_{V} \ \underbrace{\text{tall}}_{A} \quad \text{(fuzzy description)}$$

Given the form of the propositional statement, an IF–THEN rule contains at least two propositional statements:

IF <u>V is A</u> THEN <u>U is B</u>

where 'V is A' is the antecedent in the IF–THEN rule; and 'U is B' represents the consequent of the rule. More generally for most real problems, the IF–THEN rule may contain multiple antecedents and multiple consequents:

IF V_1 is A_1 and V_2 is A_2 and $\cdots$ and V_n is A_n
THEN U_1 is B_1 and U_2 is B_2 and $\cdots$ and U_m is B_m .

In most decision-support and diagnostic systems, we may use multiple-antecedents–single-consequent rules for simplicity. However, this does not lose generality, because a multiple consequent situation can be broken down into multiple single-consequent rules with the same antecedents.

The following IF–THEN rule has a single fuzzy consequent:

IF V_1 is A_1 and V_2 is A_2 and $\cdots$ and V_n is A_n THEN U is B

1. If $V_1 \cdots V_n$ are crisp data and equal to $x_1 \cdots x_n$, respectively, as shown in [12,25], using the Min function for the t-norm, the possibility or certainty of 'U is B' is given by

$$\min[\mu_{A_1}(x_1), \mu_{A_2}(x_2), \cdots, \mu_{A_n}(x_n)] \tag{9.1}$$

where $\mu_{A_i}(x_i)$ is the membership grade of x_i in A_i, $i = 1, \cdots, n$.

2. If $V_1 \cdots V_n$ are fuzzy data and equal to $C_1 \cdots C_n$, respectively, the possibility of 'U is B' is given by

$$\min[P_{C_1|A_1}, P_{C_2|A_2}, \cdots, P_{C_n|A_n}] \tag{9.2}$$

where $P_{C_n|A_n}$ is the possibility of C_n given A_n, called a *possibility measure* which shows 'how true is $A_n = C_n$'.

It can be evaluated by

$$P_{C|A} = \sup_x \min[\mu_A(x), \mu_C(x)] \tag{9.3}$$

As in almost all reasoning processes, where case descriptions are imprecise and vague, fuzzy IF–THEN rules offer a powerful tool to capture imprecise case descriptions and to carry out effective reasoning in an environment of uncertainty and vagueness [2]. In an IF–THEN rule, some attributes (antecedents) might be less important than others in determining the consequent in the rule. To take care of this situation, we give weighting factors f to the antecedents. The relative importance of the attribute is characterized by f:

- If f = 0, the attribute plays no role in case description and can be deleted. In the AND operation of attributes, if f of 'V_1 is A_1' equals to 0, it implies that $P_{C_1|A_1}^{f=0} = 1$. Then $\min[1, P_{C_2|A_2}, \cdots, P_{C_n|A_n}] = \min[P_{C_2|A_2}, \cdots, P_{C_n|A_n}]$, which indicates that the possibility of 'V_1 is A_1' does not affect the certainty of 'U is B'.
- If f = 1, the attribute is not modified by the weight: $\mu_A(x)^{f=1} = \mu_A(x)$ and $P_{C|A}^{f=1} = P_{C|A}$.

In general, for a fuzzy proposition 'V is A', with weighting factor $f \in [0, 1]$,

$$\mu_A(x)^f = \max[(1 - f), \mu_A(x)], \ \forall x \in X \tag{9.4}$$

where max is selected for the t-conorm operation, and X is the attribute value set. If f is small, the $\mu_A(x)^f$ is closer to 1 and so is $P_{C|A}$; hence it has less influence on the operation of $\min[P_{C_i|A_i}], i = 1, n$.

Assigning the weighting factor assigned to each of the antecedents, we can replace $P_{C_i|A_i}$ in Equation 9.2 with $P_{C_i|A_i}^{f_i}$. The possibility of the consequent becomes

$$\min[P_{C_1|A_1}^{f_1}, P_{C_2|A_2}^{f_2}, \cdots, P_{C_n|A_n}^{f_n}] \tag{9.5}$$

9.3 Fuzzy Logic based Neural Networks

An intelligent system must possess two basic abilities:

- *Learning* with which the system can learn from experience, adapt to changes, update the knowledge base, and improve its performance.
- *Inference* with which the system can find solutions to a problem or a task based on qualitative, linguistic and symbolic descriptions which are usually vague and imprecise; and uncertain and incomplete information.

Therefore, it is natural and most effective that fuzzy logic be combined with neural networks in developing functional intelligent systems. Recently, fuzzy-neural systems and soft computing have gained considerable interest which has led to new theoretical developments and successful applications.

Specifically, in CBR, it is possible to use cases, i.e., (Problem, Solution) pairs, as training samples (e.g., antecedents as input and corresponding consequents as target output). A traditional neural network can learn the relationship between the problem and the solution in the task domain. However, in conventional neural networks, it is impossible to describe the distribution of connection weights in the network in terms of logical propositions like IF–THEN rules which are used in the reasoning process. In this section, we use two basic *logic* neurons, AND- and OR- neurons [22] to construct FLNNs.

FLNNs have three major advantages:

1. the domain knowledge can be incorporated into the network prior to training, and hence reduces the learning effort;
2. the resulting network after training can be interpreted by studying the connection weights, which may give rise to new domain knowledge;
3. as a consequence, the network size can be optimized by removing insignificant connections.

9.3.1 Fuzzy Logic based AND-Neuron

Let us consider a special type of artificial neuron that implements a standard fuzzy AND operation which is shown in Fig. 9.1. To make the AND-neuron perform a fuzzy IF–THEN rule in an inference system, inputs C_i are pre-processed by the fuzzy $P_{C|A}$ operation prior to being fed to the AND-neuron. The AND operation is basically a Min–Max cascade operation over its inputs and connection weights. This means that we can use simple Min and Max operations for the t-norm and t-conorm operations, respectively. For more details on other possible t-norm and t-conorm operations, please refer to [1,12,21].

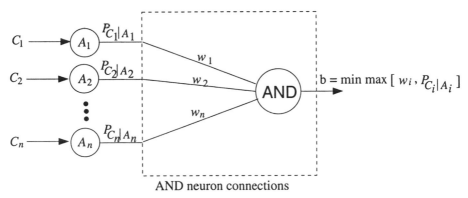

AND neuron connections

Fig. 9.1. An AND-neuron.

We define the *strength* of connections between the input neurons and the AND-neuron as weight w_i, which should not be confused with the weighting factor f for the antecedents of an IF–THEN rule discussed in the previous section, but later we will see that they have an interesting relationship. Nevertheless, w_i has the same purpose as that of the weighting factor f, namely, to reflect the relative importance of the inputs to the AND-neuron [11]. They can have values in [0,1], representing the strength of the corresponding connection. The stronger the connection, the closer the value of the weight is to 1. Let us look in more detail as to how the AND neuron network is actually implementing a fuzzy IF–THEN rule. As shown in Equation 9.4, for an antecedent with the weighting factor f,

$$\mu_A(x)^f = \max[(1-f), \mu_A(x)],$$
$$= \max_x[w, \mu_A(x)], \ \forall x \in X.$$

$$P_{C|A}^f = \sup_x \min[\mu_C(x), \mu_A(x)^f] = \sup_x \min\left[\mu_C(x), \ \max_x[w, \ \mu_A(x)]\right]$$
$$= \max_x\left[w, \ \sup_x \min[(C(x), (A(x))]\right] = \max_x[w, P_{C|A}] \qquad (9.6)$$

where $w = 1 - f$.

The AND-neuron performs a Min–Max cascaded operation and gives the following output:

$$b = \min_i \max[w_i, P_{C_i|A_i}], \ \forall i = 1, \cdots, n$$

From Equation 9.6, we have

$$b = \min_i[P_{C_i|A_i}^{f_i}], \ \forall i = 1, \cdots, n$$

which is the same as Equation 9.5 for a fuzzy IF–THEN rule with weighting factors for the antecedents. This implies that the AND-neuron connections (Fig. 9.1) are able to accomplish the inference function required for the fuzzy IF–THEN rule. Note, however, that the connection weights w_i are not the same as the weighting factors f_i discussed in Section 9.2.

9.3.2 Fuzzy Logic based OR-Neuron

In most real situations, several IF–THEN rules may have the same consequent at different confidence levels. Lets us consider a set of k rules that has the same consequent 'U is B':

Rule 1: IF V_{11} is A_{11} and V_{12} is A_{12} $\cdots$ and V_{1n} is A_{1n} THEN U is B
Rule 2: IF V_{21} is A_{21} and V_{22} is A_{22} $\cdots$ and V_{2m} is A_{2m} THEN U is B
:
:
Rule k: IF V_{k1} is A_{k1} and V_{k2} is A_{k2} $\cdots$ and V_{kp} is A_{kp} THEN U is B

When given k sets of input data: $C_{11}, \cdots, C_{1n}; C_{21}, \cdots, C_{2m}; \cdots; C_{k1}, \cdots, C_{kp}$, the set of k rules will generate k evident values for the consequent 'U is B'.

Using the OR operation on the k evident values, we can evaluate the certainty of 'U is B'. In expert systems, the attributes in each rule are collectively referred to as the *premises* of the rule. The k rules are then consolidated into a single propositional statement with all the k premises ORed together, resulting in a single rule:

IF premises_1 or premises_2 ... or premises_k THEN U is B

Using the Max function for the t-conorm operation of OR, we obtain the following possibility for 'U is B':

$$P_B = \max_j [P(\text{premises\_}j)], \quad j = 1, \cdots, k \tag{9.7}$$

Under different operating conditions, several rules may have the same consequent; however, the premises can have different confidence levels for the consequent. For instance, in diagnosis, different sets of symptoms can result in the same diagnosis. However, the confidence levels for different sets of symptoms that lead to the same diagnosis are different. In CBR, this amounts to choosing among the cases that have the highest confidence leading to the solution. This can be accomplished by the OR-neuron. The connection weights for the OR-neuron are called confidence levels (CL). Similar to that in Equation 9.6, we define

$$P(\text{premises})^{CL} = \min[CL, P(\text{premises})] \tag{9.8}$$

Again, in two extreme cases we have

1. CL $= 0$ indicates that $P(\text{premises})$ has no effect on P_B;
2. CL $= 1$ indicates that $P(\text{premises})$ is not modified in its effect on P_B.

Combining Equations 9.7 and 9.8, we obtain the following equation:

$$P_B = \max_j \min[\text{CL}, P(\text{premises}\_j)] \tag{9.9}$$

In this way, we can construct an OR-neuron to perform the Max–Min cascaded operations on CL and $P(\text{premises})$. The output of the OR-neuron is the value for P_B. (Note that $P(\text{premises}\_j)$ is the output of the AND-neuron for rule j.) The OR-neuron connections are shown in Fig. 9.2. It must be noted, however, that the Max and Min operations used in the equations are non-interactive. It is a single input that, combined with the corresponding connection weight of the neuron, exclusively determines the output.

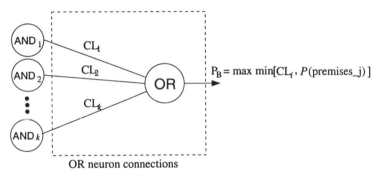

OR neuron connections

Fig. 9.2. An OR-neuron.

9.3.3 Learning

In our system supervised learning is implemented which is the process of estimating the connection weights from training samples. The result of training also determines the neural network topology by eliminating a connection if its weight is close to 1 for the AND node (or close to 0 for the OR node). Since an AND node represents the IF–THEN rule by adding attributes together and the OR node links more than one rule to the same consequent, the resulting network topology provides a logical construct which tells the logical relationship between the input attributes and the output consequent. Furthermore, it would also be useful to provide a rule reduction scheme in order to reduce an initial rule base built by human experts [28].

The backpropagation algorithm is used for the learning process. In each training epoch, the connection weights are adjusted to minimize the total least mean square (LMS) error in the output. This is achieved by following the direction of the steepest descent on the LMS error surface. For this purpose, the total output LMS error has to be defined, and its derivatives with respect to all the connection weights must be obtainable. To protect the learning from a lack of convergence or reaching a singular point where learning stops, certain mechanisms must be used to avoid discontinuous and zero derivatives [21]. We will illustrate this later while deriving the derivatives for the Max and Min functions.

9.3.4 Training the Fuzzy OR-Neuron

Referring to Fig. 9.3, we consider the OR node, with n input values $x_1, \cdots, x_n$. A set of N training data pairs (x_k, t_k) are available, where x_k is the k-th input training vector and t_k is the corresponding target output value. For notational simplicity we used w_i to denote connection weights.

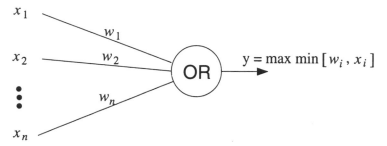

Fig. 9.3. Notations used for connections to one OR-neuron.

Define the performance index as

$$Q = \frac{1}{2} \sum_{k=1}^{N} (y_k - t_k)^2 \qquad (9.10)$$

where y_k is the actual output from the OR-neuron with input vector x_k, which referring to Equation 9.9 can be written as

$$y_k = \max_i \min(w_i, x_{ki}), i = 1, \cdots, n$$

By taking the partial derivative of $(y_k - t_k)^2$ with respective to one of the connection weight w_j, we have

$$\frac{\partial}{\partial w_j} (y_k - t_k)^2 = 2(y_k - t_k) \frac{\partial}{\partial w_j} (y_k - t_k) \qquad (9.11)$$

Since t_k is independent of all w_i, we obtain

$$\frac{\partial}{\partial w_j} (y_k - t_k) = \frac{\partial}{\partial w_j} y_k$$

$$= \frac{\partial}{\partial w_j} \{\max[\min(w_1, x_{k1}), \min(w_2, x_{k2}), \cdots, \min(w_n, x_{kn})]\}$$

Denoting $\min(w_i, x_{ki}) = M_{ki} \; \forall i \neq j$, and $f(w_j) = \min(w_j, x_{kj}) \; \forall i = j$, we have

$$\frac{\partial}{\partial w_j}(y_k - t_k) = \frac{\partial}{\partial w_j}\{\max[f(w_j), M_{k1}, M_{k2}, \cdots, M_{kj-1}, M_{kj+1}, \cdots, M_{kn}]\}$$

$$= \frac{\partial}{\partial f}\{\max[f(w_j), M_{k1}, M_{k2}, \cdots]\}\frac{\partial}{\partial w_j}[\min(w_j, x_{kj})]$$

$$= \begin{cases} 1, & \text{if } f(w_j) > M_{ki} \; \forall i \neq j \\ 0, & \text{if } f(w_j) < M_{ki} \; \forall i \neq j \end{cases} \times \begin{cases} 1, & \text{if } w_j < x_{ki} \\ 0, & \text{if } w_j > x_{ki} \end{cases}$$

$$(9.12)$$

where { } contains the possible values for the partial derivatives under different conditions, and $\times$ indicates that combination of values between the terms in the two { }'s is possible. This is due to the fact that all the $\min(w_i, x_{ki})$ terms are independent of each other, and that x_{ki} is independent of w_i. The result in Equation 9.12 can be broken down into three possible cases:

Case	Conditions	$\frac{\partial}{\partial w_j}(y_k - t_k) =$
1	$w_j < x_{kj}$ $f(w_j) > M_{ki} \; \forall i \neq j$	1
2	$w_j < x_{kj}$ $f(w_j) < M_{ki} \; \forall i \neq j$	0
3	$w_j > x_{kj}$	0

It should be pointed out, however, that the cases of $w_j = x_{kj}$ and $f(w_j) = M_{ki}, \; \forall i \neq j$ are not considered. Strictly speaking, the result is undefined for these cases since it is a transition from 1 to 0 or from 0 to 1. The potential, and quite pragmatic, aspect of the Boolean result is that the learning algorithm could eventually end up at a point where it is unable to learn any more. This can happen when all the derivatives are equal to zero. To avoid this problem, one approach would be to use Lukasiewicz's formula [12] to linearize the derivatives, such that

$$\frac{\partial}{\partial w_j}\min(w_j, x_{kj}) = \begin{cases} 1, & \text{if } w_j \leq x_{kj}, \\ 1 - w_j + x_{kj}, & \text{if } w_j > x_{kj} \end{cases} \qquad (9.13)$$

and

$$\frac{\partial}{\partial f}\max[f(w_j), M_{kj}^*] = \begin{cases} 1, & \text{if } f(w_j) \geq M_{kj}^*, \\ 1 + f(w_j) - M_{kj}^*, & \text{if } f(w_j) < M_{kj}^* \end{cases} \qquad (9.14)$$

where $M_{kj}^* = \max_i(M_{ki}) \; \forall i \neq j$.

In fact, this can be achieved by any parametrized family of the triangular norm. Although these methods are conceptually different, their effects on learning are similar. From Equations 9.11 and 9.10 we can obtain the following equation:

$$\frac{\partial Q}{\partial w_j} = \sum_{k=1}^{N}(y_k - t_k)\frac{\partial}{\partial w_j}\min(w_j, x_{kj})\frac{\partial}{\partial f}\max[f(w_j), M_{kj}^*] \qquad (9.15)$$

which can be evaluated using Equations 9.13 and 9.14. More generally, for a network with m output OR-neurons, we can define the performance factor Q as

$$Q = \frac{1}{2} \sum_{k=1}^{N} \sum_{j=1}^{m} (y_{kj} - t_{kj})^2$$

and

$$\frac{\partial Q}{\partial w_{j,p}} = \sum_{k=1}^{N} (y_k - t_k) \frac{\partial}{\partial w_{j,p}} \min(w_{j,p}, x_{kj,p}) \frac{\partial}{\partial f} \max \left[f(w_{j,p}), M_{kj,p}^* \right] \quad (9.16)$$

where j is the index for the output OR-neurons, and p is the index for the input AND-neurons.

9.3.5   Training the Fuzzy AND-Neuron

In order to train the connection weights for the AND-neuron, we have to backpropagate the output error (or performance factor) to the AND layer as shown in Fig. 9.4.

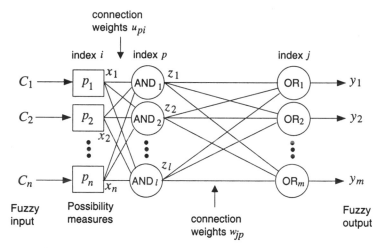

Fig. 9.4. Network topology for the fuzzy neural inference system.

The connection weight u_{pi} in the figure is referred to as the weighting factor discussed in Section 9.2, whereas the connection weight w_{jp} is the CL. The possibility measures given by the input layer are calculated according to Equation 9.3. Since the membership functions for the input fuzzy data C_i and the fuzzy attributes A_i in the rules are usually fixed, they are not subject to training. For a training pair (x_k, t_k), with m outputs, the total output error is reflected by the following performance factor:

$$Q = \frac{1}{2} \sum_{j=1}^{m} (y_j - t_j)^2 = \sum_{j=1}^{m} Q'$$

where $Q' = \frac{1}{2}(y_j - t_j)^2$. The partial derivative of Q' with respective to the weight u_{pi} is then

$$\frac{\partial Q'}{\partial u_{pi}} = \frac{\partial Q'}{\partial y_j} \frac{\partial y_j}{\partial z_p} \frac{\partial z_p}{\partial u_{pi}} \tag{9.17}$$

Since $\frac{\partial Q'}{\partial y_j} = (y_j - t_j)$ and according to the definition

$$\frac{\partial y_j}{\partial z_p} = \frac{\partial}{\partial z_p} \left[\max_p \min(w_j p, z_p) \right]$$

$$= \frac{\partial}{\partial f(z_p)} \left[\max[f(z_p), M_p^*] \frac{\partial}{\partial z_p} \min(w_{jp}, z_p) \right] \tag{9.18}$$

where $f(z_p) = \min(w_{jp}, z_p)$ and $M_p^* = \max[f(z_d)]$ $\forall d \neq p$. Finally, since $z_p = \min_i[g(u_{pi})]$ where $g(u_{pi}) = \max(u_{pi}, x_i)$, we have

$$\frac{\partial z_p}{\partial u_{pi}} = \frac{\partial}{\partial u_{pi}} \left\{ \min\left[g(u_{p1}), g(u_{p2}), \cdots, g(u_{pi}), \cdots, g(u_{pn}) \right] \right\},$$

$$\frac{\partial z_p}{\partial u_{pi}} = \frac{\partial}{\partial u_{pi}} \min\left[g(u_{pn}), M_i' \right] \frac{\partial}{\partial u_{pi}} \max\left[u_{pi}, x_i \right] \tag{9.19}$$

where $M_i' = \min[g(u_{ph})]$, $\forall h \neq i$.

From Equations 9.18 and 9.19, we rewrite Equation 9.17 as follows:

$$\frac{\partial Q}{\partial u_{pi}} = \left\{ \sum_{j=1}^m (y_j - t_j) \frac{\partial}{\partial f} \max[f(z_p, M_p^*] \frac{\partial}{\partial z_p} \min[z_p, w_{jp}] \right\} \cdot$$

$$\frac{\partial}{\partial g} \min[g(u_{pi}), M_i'] \cdot \frac{\partial}{\partial u_{pi}} \max(u_{pi}, x_i) \tag{9.20}$$

where $f(z_p) = \min(w_{jp}, z_p)$, $M_p^* = \max[f(z_d)]$ $\forall d \neq p$, $g(u_{pi}) = \max(u_{pi}, x_i)$, and $M_i' = \min[g(u_{ph})]$ $\forall h \neq i$.

We can evaluate the partial derivatives of Max and Min functions using Equations (9.13) and (9.14).

9.3.6 Updating Connection Weights

Initially, connection weights are randomly assigned with values in [0,1]. They are then updated using the backpropagation algorithm. After passing each epoch of the training data (i.e., all the training vector pairs), the weights are updated according to

$$\Delta w_i(t) = -\varepsilon \frac{\partial Q}{\partial w_j}(t) + \alpha \Delta w_j(t-1)$$

where ε is the learning rate and $\alpha \in [0,1]$ is the momentum, which improves the rate of convergence by taking into account the general trend of the error gradient. The derivative is evaluated by using Equation 9.20. The updating process stops when a pre-defined total output LMS error is reached, or the number of epochs has exceeded a certain defined maximum number, or there is no further improvement in the output error for a certain consecutive number of training epochs.

9.4   Lookup Table for the Possibility Measures

As shown in Fig. 9.4, the fuzzy input data C_i is not fed directly into the AND-neuron but via a possibility measure node which serves as the input node. The possibility measure is calculated according to Equation 9.3, which is given here for convenience:

$$P_{C|A} = \sup_x \min[\mu_A(x), \mu_C(x)]$$

where C is the fuzzy data for the proposition statement 'V is **A**' and $x \in X$, the universe of discourse for the attribute **V**.

Depending on the complexity of the membership functions $\mu_A(x)$ and $\mu_C(x)$, the evaluation of $P_{C|A}$ can be very computationally intensive and slow down the learning process. It is found, however, that expanding the fuzzy input vector and using lookup tables to find values of the possibility measures are computationally more efficient [20]. To apply this method, each fuzzy input is expressed in terms of membership values to each of its defined linguistic properties. Therefore, if each of the fuzzy inputs has three linguistic properties, an n-dimensional input vector may be expanded into a $3n$-dimensional vector as shown in Fig. 9.5.

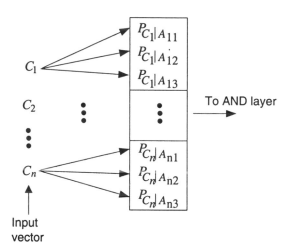

Fig. 9.5. Table lookup for the input layer to handle the possibility measures.

For example, if we define five linguistic properties for the attribute 'motor speed' according to the membership functions in Fig. 9.6, we can build a lookup table for looking up the values of $P_{C_i|A}$ for a given fuzzy data C_i as shown in Table 9.1. If the input is unknown, we set all the possibility measures for the linguistic properties to 0.5.

9.5   A Decision-Support System Using FLNN-CBR

Two of the typical applications of CBR are decision support and diagnosis [14,24]. Based on given (incomplete) information and often ambiguous terminology, a decision support system using known cases can provide the user with advice to the

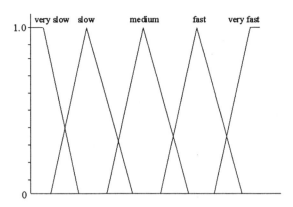

Fig. 9.6. Table lookup for the input layer to handle the possibility measures.

Table 9.1. Lookup table for the example in Fig. 9.6: possibility measure values $P_{C_i|A_j}$, with different A_j

Input C_i	very slow	slow	medium	fast	very fast
very slow	1.0	0.4	0.0	0.0	0.0
slow	0.4	1.0	0.4	0.0	0.0
medium	0.0	0.4	1.0	0.4	0.0
fast	0.0	0.0	0.4	1.0	0.4
very fast	0.0	0.0	0.0	0.4	1.0
UNKNOWN	0.5	0.5	0.5	0.5	0.5

problem. Similarly, diagnosis is the process of determining the cause of a problem based on some observable symptoms. Compared to decision-support systems, the diagnostic system works in a better defined domain usually with lower complexity. Over the last three decades, many expert systems have been built for decision support and diagnosis in medicine, engineering, geology, business and the military. As in most real-world applications, decision support and diagnosis intrinsically involve inexact intuition, heuristics and experimental knowledge, and expert systems must deal with situations where symptoms are poorly or vaguely described and where case descriptions are not simple (Problem, Solution) pairs. Furthermore, knowledge rules extracted from human experts generally have uncertain and ambiguous characteristics which expert systems have to be able to handle.

Several approaches are commonly used to manage uncertainty in expert systems [5,15,17], most notably, the Bayesian approach. There are two major problems with this approach:

1. it requires to obtain values for all the prior conditional and joint probabilities;
2. it assumes that all system relationships between evidence and hypotheses are independent, which may not be justified in many real-world applications; in particular, in diagnoses and decision support.

Due to the problems with the Bayesian assumptions, another approach using certainty factors was employed in developing the MYCIN system. The expert has to assign certainty factors to facts and rules and is restricted by the two assumptions required in the Bayesian statistics. However, the meaning of *certainty factors* is not rigorously defined as that in formal probability theory and hence the validity of the expert system's output may be questionable. On the other hand, in Dempster–Schafer theory, uncertainty is treated by creating *belief functions*: measurements of the degree of belief. Belief functions allow experts to use their knowledge to assign probabilities to events without having to specify the exact global probabilities. However, its high computational complexity makes it impractical in most real-world applications. Although researchers have proposed many new approaches to modeling the uncertainty, e.g., *certainty factors* in the MYCIN system and *belief functions* in the Dempster–Schafer theory [26], the difficulties still remain, which are largely due to the fact that most uncertainties encountered cannot be described by statistical means. Fuzzy set theory offers an alternative approach to handling uncertainty or ambiguous data encountered in real life [12]. Fuzzy set provides a natural means for handling vagueness and uncertainty in data; especially in decision support and diagnosis, for instance, in diagnosis people frequently use such fuzzy linguistic terms as 'possibly', 'less likely', 'large amount', and 'seriously' to describe symptoms. In this section, we present a decision support/diagnostic system using the CBR technique. In order to handle uncertainties in symptom descriptions and data, we use our FLNNs discussed in the previous sections. In the system, the case data are collected from call records of a help-desk set-up in a real telecommunications system support center.

9.5.1 CBR in Help-Desk Application

In customer service divisions of many companies, especially in the computer and telecommunications industries, there are various help-desks which collect information about callers and their problems. These records are usually used for monitoring the workload, billing customers, and keeping a log of problem cases that the customer support staff can refer to future call cases. However, they are not powerful enough in helping the technical support staff to quickly diagnose problems and to suggest viable solutions because of limited searching capability and unstructured knowledge. As pointed out in [13], most commercial help-desk software provides some sort of keyword or free-form text search; other products offer rule based expert systems technology by which users can create decision trees for systematically diagnosing problems. However, text and keyword search systems have some drawbacks. Their performance and accuracy rely largely on the user's consistency and diligence. As a consequence, if the user is not following the same criteria and rules for selecting keywords, which in practice is very difficult to enforce or to ensure, the keyword list can grow unmanageably long. Furthermore, if the user is too general in his/her search criteria, the amount of irrelevant information returned can be huge; on the other hand, if the user is too specific, the system may not be able to offer any useful solutions at all. In rule based systems, the relevant information from individual call records is organized into a structured set of questions which are used to ask the user for answers. Based on the answers, the system suggests the consequents through the built-in rules. However, it is time consuming, both for the system developer and the contributing expert, to extract and encode a collection of rules into a coherent knowledge base. Furthermore, it is difficult to update and maintain the knowledge base, especially when more different call cases arrive. In addition, the structured question-and-answer style can be too restrictive to the user. That is, it is user unfriendly. To avoid the disadvantages of text search system and rule based system, the CBR technique is proposed. CBR is based on the fact that human cognition and problem solving quite often involve recalling previous cases for reference, particularly in diagnosis and classification.

9.5.2 System Design

Fig. 9.7 shows the case based decision support system. At the front end, a user interface shell offers symptom selections. A symptom consists of an attribute (e.g., 'devices blocked') and a linguistic property which can be crisp (e.g., 'true', 'false') or fuzzy (e.g., 'a few', 'some', 'most', 'all'). The user selects the attribute first, and then finds the best linguistic property which goes with the attribute. The user can add new attributes and define new linguistic terms if needed. To make it more intelligent, a natural language parser can be developed to extract the attributes and description terms from the natural language input [13]. When a new linguistic property is defined, its associated characteristics (such as crisp or fuzzy) have to be defined as well. The symptoms are then used as input to the inference engine, which is realized by a FLNN. Based on its learned knowledge, the FLNN suggests a set of diagnoses (decisions) with different confidence values. Another user interface shell interprets these outputs and gives an ordered list of the most likely causes.

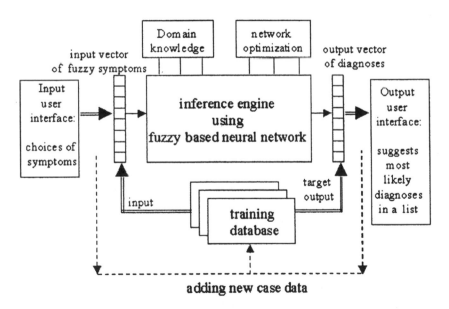

Fig. 9.7. Schematic diagram of the proposed diagnostic system (© IEEE 1997).

When a new case is encountered, the symptoms and respective diagnoses are put into the training database. The FLNN learns the new case data from the training database. To avoid possible interruption to the user, we independently train a separate off-line FLNN which updates the on-line feed-forward FLNN in a fixed time interval. Domain knowledge in the system is usually available from human experts and can be transformed into fuzzy IF–THEN rules. By mapping these rules directly into the structure of the FLNN, the knowledge can be represented in the FLNN without having to go through the training process. This reduces the amount of training required. This is also advantageous when there are insufficient case data available for some problems. As explained in Sections 9.3.1 and 9.3.2, the connection weights represent the weighting factors f in AND-neurons and the CL in OR-neurons. For the OR-neuron, those connections with weights close to zero (or below a certain threshold) can be eliminated, whereas for the AND-neuron those connections with weights close to one or above a certain threshold can be eliminated. This makes the interpretation process easier and simpler in the network structure in terms of fuzzy IF–THEN rules. Furthermore, with fewer network connections, the inference process can be performed faster.

9.6   Simulation Results on Simple Cases

In this section, we present the test results for four simple cases.

Test 1: Simple Boolean data
The input data are all binary in this test, which represent the simplest case. Our purpose is to see whether the network works for Boolean logic situation. Table 9.2 shows two training vector pairs consisting of three inputs and one output. The network has six inputs (to take care of the negated inputs as well), one hidden AND-neuron and one output OR-neuron.

Table 9.2. Test 1: training data

N	x_1	x_2	x_3	$\neg x_1$	$\neg x_2$	$\neg x_3$	target
1	1.0	1.0	0.0	0.0	0.0	1.0	1.0
2	1.0	0.0	1.0	0.0	1.0	0.0	1.0

Fig. 9.8 shows the learning curve which indicates that the total output LMS error is down to 0.005 after 14 passes (epochs) of the training data.

After training we obtained the following connection weights for the AND-neuron and the OR-neuron: $u = [0.007 \quad 1.000 \quad 0.989 \quad 1.000 \quad 1.000 \quad 1.000]$ and $w = 1.000$, respectively. This means that the output is determined only by x_1 since its weight value is close to zero whereas all the others in u are close to one. This is correct and expected, because the given training data show that the output can be solely determined by x_1. As a result, we can use only one antecedent for this problem.

Test 2: Contradicting Boolean data
In this test, we used the same Boolean data as those in Test 1. Here we examine the consistency of the system, for that we purposefully create undetermined situations by

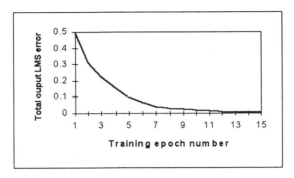

Fig. 9.8. Learning curve for Case 1 training data (© IEEE 1997).

setting some training data pairs to contradicting conditions: the same input in two separate data pairs have opposite target outputs as shown in Table 9.3.

Table 9.3. Case 2: training data, where * indicates those training data with opposite targets, e.g., Cases 5 and 6 have the same bit pattern in the attributes but *contradicting* target values

N	x_1	x_2	x_3	$\neg x_1$	$\neg x_2$	$\neg x_3$	target
1	1.0	1.0	0.0	0.0	0.0	1.0	1.0
2	1.0	1.0	1.0	0.0	0.0	0.0	1.0
3	1.0	0.0	1.0	0.0	1.0	0.0	1.0
4	1.0	0.0	0.0	0.0	1.0	1.0	1.0
5*	0.0	0.0	0.0	1.0	1.0	1.0	0.0
6*	0.0	0.0	0.0	1.0	1.0	1.0	1.0
7*	0.0	0.0	1.0	1.0	1.0	0.0	0.0
8*	0.0	0.0	1.0	1.0	1.0	0.0	1.0
9*	0.0	1.0	0.0	1.0	0.0	1.0	0.0
10*	0.0	1.0	0.0	1.0	0.0	1.0	1.0
11*	0.0	1.0	1.0	1.0	0.0	0.0	0.0
12*	0.0	1.0	1.0	1.0	0.0	0.0	1.0

The learning process cannot improve the performance after 35 epochs and stays with a total output LMS error of 0.083 as shown in Fig. 9.9. The reason is due to the contradicting training data for which the network output is 0.5, i.e., undetermined, which is what we expected. The weights for the AND-neuron are $u = [0.500 \quad 1.000 \quad 1.000 \quad 1.000 \quad 1.000 \quad 1.000]$ and the weight for the OR-neuron is $w = 1.000$. This indicates that the output is again determined by x_1 with a weight value of 0.5. The system outputs 0.5 for those contradicting input data, but generates 1.0 for the non-contradicting input data.

Test 3: Sinusoidal and noisy input data
In this test, we used two input data: a sinusoidal signal and a random signal. The target is the same sinusoidal data as the input. The purpose is to see whether the system can

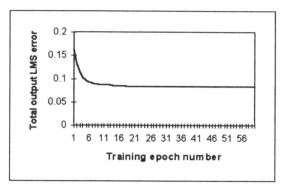

Fig. 9.9. Learning curve for Case 2 training data (© IEEE 1997).

track the sinusoidal input and disregard the noisy input data. For this test, we used a network with two hidden AND-neurons and one output OR-neuron. From Fig. 9.11 we can see that the network learns quickly and after 65 epochs the total output LMS error has been reduced to 0.0005.

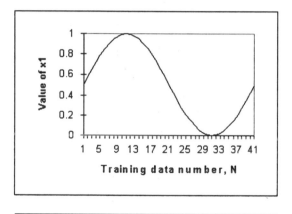

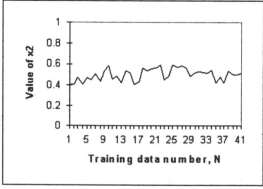

Fig. 9.10. Training data: the output defined as input x_1 (© IEEE 1997).

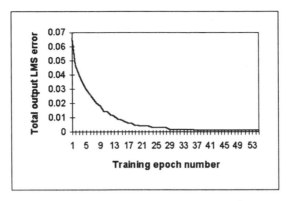

Fig. 9.11. The learning curve for Test 3 training data (© IEEE 1997).

After training, we obtain the following connection weights $u_1 = [0.002 \quad 0.795$ $1.000 \quad 1.000]$, $u_2 = [0.000 \quad 0.998 \quad 1.000 \quad 1.000]$ for the two AND-neurons and $w = [0.642 \quad 1.000]$ for the OR-neuron. Indeed, the network has learned to reject the noisy input effectively.

Test 4: Imprecise training data

In this test, two inputs are used. The first input is a two-part random function: the first part consists of 20 training samples with random values in a range of 0.7 and 1.0, which is followed by the second part consisting of four (abnormal) random samples between 0 and 0.3. The second input is the reversal of the first input. Fig. 9.12 shows the data for x_1 and x_2. The target output value t for each training data record is also a random variable ranging from 0.75 to 1.0 for all the 24 training data. This test is somewhat close to real-world situations in which we obtain imprecise information. Also, there can be some abnormal occasions which may give the opposite antecedents for a consequence, but usually the number of abnormal occurrences (in this case four) are outweighed by the number of normal ones (in this case twenty). It is therefore very important to test whether the network can learn the relationship when the input data are imprecise or fuzzy. For this dataset, one AND-neuron and one OR-neuron are used in the network.

As indicated in Fig. 9.13, the output error is down to 0.007 after 91 epochs. The connection weights for the AND-neuron and the OR-neuron are $u = [0.753 \quad 0.931]$ and $w = 0.827$, respectively. With these resulting connection weights, the output is able to follow the target t closely. This proves its ability to tolerate noise and partially incorrect data.

From these simple tests, we can see that the FLNN learns quite fast with good noise immunity. Furthermore, the FLNN are able to perform fuzzy IF–THEN rules. In other words, the FLNN can extract knowledge (or inference rules) from the input–output training sample pairs and generates simpler rule bases by performing rule induction and deduction. This also demonstrates that we can generate inference rules using the supervised learning process.

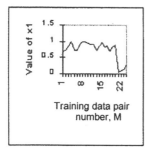
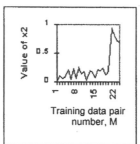
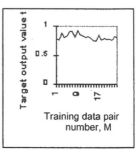

Fig. 9.12. Training data for Test 4 (© IEEE 1997).

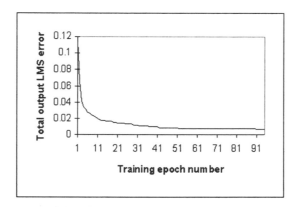

Fig. 9.13. The learning curve for Test 4 (© IEEE 1997).

9.7 Decision Support in a Telecommunications System

In this section, we apply our FLNN-CBR decision-support system to telecommunications systems manufactured by Ericsson, a Swedish multinational telecommunications equipment supplier. Its products cover many application areas. In Ericsson Australia, there is a customer service division providing system support to many of Ericsson's products, e.g., Public Switching Telephone Network (PSTN), Integrated Services Digital Network (ISDN), Analogue Mobile System (AMPS), Digital Mobile System (GSM), and Intelligence Network (IN). A help-desk is set up to serve as a central support dispatch station from which customer calls are logged, technical support engineers are contacted, progress on resolving each problem is monitored, and an escalation procedure is followed. When solving problems, the support engineer always has to perform a keyword search through the call logs to find any relevant, previous cases. This is a typical situation where the FLNN-CBR can help, which is especially useful in many on-line technical support applications over the Internet.

9.7.1 Case Collection

To fully represent the case space, it is ideal that the call logs represent every aspect of the problem domain by a number of cases proportional to the complexity of that aspect. If the domain is viewed as a problem space, the cases should be evenly distributed and as dense as possible. However, this is usually impossible and it is impractical to prepare every possible case before the system can be used. In reality, we must perform *case completion* to continuously collect cases while completing the task [3]. Case completion can be readily implemented in our system shown in Fig. 9.7. The system can be retrained on new cases and the case base can be updated from time to time. More cases are being processed and collected dynamically. This will ensure that the FLNN does not overgeneralize the rules which may neglect part of the problem space, resulting in an unsatisfactory performance for the data in the untrained problem space.

Table 9.4. Examples of symptoms, comprising attributes and respective linguistic properties (© IEEE 1997)

ATTRIBUTES	LINGUISTIC PROPERTIES
IO.[no heartbeat]	True, Seems to be, Not likely, False
IO.[link LED is blinking]	Very fast, Fast, Moderate, Slow, Very slow, Not
IO.[restarted]	True, Seems to be, Not likely, False
IO.[terminal locked up]	Many, A few, One only, None
IO.[ALHBE function busy]	True, False
IO.[ALHBI gives F/C 4]	True, False
IO.[file access failure]	All files, Many Files, A few files, False
IO.[running single side]	True, False
IO.[hanging alarm]	True, Most likely, Less likely, False
IO.[hanging dump]	True, Most likely, Less likely, False
EMG.[silent EM]	All EM, Many EM, A few EM, None
EMG.[traffic restriction]	True, Most likely, Less likely, False
EMG.[one way traffic]	True, Most likely, Less likely, False
EMG.[EMRP restart]	Cyclic, Frequently, Occasionally, Once, None
EMG.[RT devices locked up]	All, Many, A few, None
EMG.[EMTS falls down]	Quickly, Gradually, Slowly, False
EMG.[Control link falls down]	Quickly, Gradually, Slowly, False
EMG.[Control down after recovery]	Long time, Medium time, Short time, False
EMG.[noisy EM]	All EM, Many EM, A few EM, None
EMG.[TSB is ABL]	True, False

For illustration purposes, we have screened a total of 420 help-desk call logs that cover a large number of problem domains ranging from device locking up to total system failure. For initial testing, we selected two particular problem groups: (1) input/output (IO) subsystem problems and (2) EMG (one type of equipment)-related problems – with a total of 76 cases. Examples of symptoms, comprising attributes and respective linguistic properties, are shown in Table 9.4. Lookup tables for possibility measure values are also built accordingly.

Using the defined attributes and linguistic properties, we transformed each logged call case into a fuzzy IF–THEN rule. In the case completion process, for each new call case, extra attributes and linguistic properties were added if necessary.

Here are some examples of the fuzzy IF–THEN rules found from the call cases:

Case-(1) IF   IO.[no heartbeat] is 'True'
          AND   IO.[ALHBE function busy] is 'True'
          THEN   {procedure 4}
Case-(2) IF   IO.[no heartbeat] is 'Seems to be'
          AND   IO.[ALHBI gives F/C4] is 'True'
          THEN   {procedure 4}
Case-(3) IF   EMG.[traffic restriction] is 'True'
          AND   EMG.[RT devices locked up] is 'Many'
          THEN   {procedure 3}
Case-(4) IF   EMG.[Control link falls down] is 'Gradually'
          AND   EMG.[EMTS falls down] is 'Slowly'
          AND   EMG.[Control down after recovery] is 'False'
          THEN   {procedure 1}

9.7.2 Training by the Case Data

As shown before, using the input layer expansion model, we represent each attribute by a number of input nodes equal to that of the attribute's linguistic properties. All the attributes in every fuzzy IF–THEN rule are expanded in this manner to build the input layer. For each of the attributes, the linguistic feature is used to find the possibility measure values for all the other linguistic properties associated with the attribute. To simplify the computation, lookup tables are used to obtain all the possibility measure values. If an attribute is not in the symptoms of a case, the possibility measure is set to 0.5 to indicate unknown (neither true nor false) cases. These values are then used as input to the AND-neuron layer. Table 9.5 shows a complete list of the data used in cases (1) to (4),

In the call logs, we obtained a total of 18 cases: five cases for case (1), three for case (2), four for case (3), and six for case (4). The 18 training data pairs are used to train the FLNN, which consists of 28 input nodes (for all the linguistic properties) and five output OR-nodes (for all the output consequences). Eight AND-nodes are used in the hidden layer. The training behavior is shown in Fig. 9.14. The total output LMS error is trained down to 0.007 after 430 epochs. If the number of input attributes increases further, the training will become much slower and need many more epochs.

Table 9.5. Possibility measures for the case examples (1)–(4) (© IEEE 1997)

INPUT ATTRIBUTES	LINGUISTICS	Possibility measures for the case examples			
		(1)	(2)	(3)	(4)
IO.[no heartbeat]	True	1.0	0.6	0.5	0.5
	Seems to be	0.4	1.0	0.5	0.5
	Not likely	0.0	0.2	0.5	0.5
	False	0.0	0.0	0.5	0.5
IO.[ALHBE function busy]	True	1.0	0.5	0.5	0.5
	False	0.0	0.5	0.5	0.5
IO.[ALHBI gives F/C 4]	True	0.5	1.0	0.5	0.5
	False	0.5	0.0	0.5	0.5
EMG.[traffic restriction]	True	0.5	0.5	1.0	0.5
	Most likely	0.5	0.5	0.4	0.5
	Less likely	0.5	0.5	0.0	0.5
	False	0.5	0.5	0.0	0.5
EMG.[RT devices locked up]	All	0.5	0.5	0.6	0.5
	Many	0.5	0.5	1.0	0.5
	A few	0.5	0.5	0.2	0.5
	None	0.5	0.5	0.0	0.5
EMG.[Control link falls down]	Quickly	0.5	0.5	0.5	0.6
	Gradually	0.5	0.5	0.5	1.0
	Slowly	0.5	0.5	0.5	0.2
	False	0.5	0.5	0.5	0.0
EMG.[EMTS falls down]	Quickly	0.5	0.5	0.5	0.0
	Gradually	0.5	0.5	0.5	0.2
	Slowly	0.5	0.5	0.5	1.0
	False	0.5	0.5	0.5	0.2
EMG.[Control down after recovery]	Long time	0.5	0.5	0.5	0.0
	Medium time	0.5	0.5	0.5	0.0
	Short time	0.5	0.5	0.5	0.2
	False	0.5	0.5	0.5	1.0
OUTPUT SUBSEQUENT					
Procedure 1		0.5	0.5	0.5	1.0
Procedure 2		0.5	0.5	0.5	0.5
Procedure 3		0.5	0.5	1.0	0.5
Procedure 4		1.0	1.0	0.5	0.5
Procedure 5		0.5	0.5	0.5	0.5

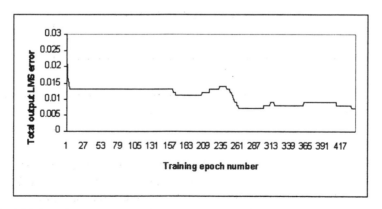

Fig. 9.14. The learning behavior for the mixed IO and EMG cases (© IEEE 1997).

To solve this problem, we used the divide-and-conquer approach by training *problem-specific* FLNNs. In our case based decision support system, we can classify cases

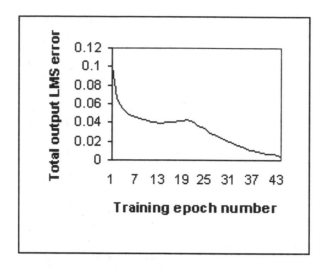

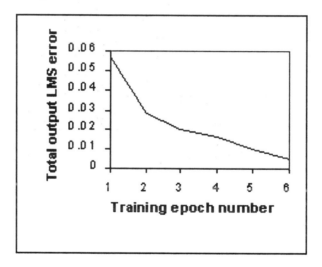

Fig. 9.15. The training results for two separate networks: the top figure shows the IO specific network, the bottom the EMG-specific network (© IEEE 1997).

into problem categories, e.g., IO and EMG. Most of the cases in the same problem category should have the same set of attributes and same set of diagnoses. By training an IO-specific FLNN and an EMG-specific FLNN separately, the size of individual network is much smaller, the training time is much shorter (even though they are not trained in parallel), and the resulting network performance is better. These can be seen in the training results shown in Fig. 9.15. The IO-specific network has eight input linguistic properties, four AND-nodes and three OR-nodes. The training took only six epochs to reach the error limit of 0.005. For the EMG-specific network, we used 20 inputs, four AND-nodes and four OR-nodes. The training was also very fast: it took 43 epochs to reach the 0.005 error limit.

9.7.3   Test on Real Cases

After the FLNN has been trained on the IO and the EMG problems, four call cases (not being used in the training data) which have the same attributes as those in the training cases are used to evaluate its performance. We used the symptom descriptions as input and fed forward through the FLNN to obtain advice. The advices were compared with that of the human expert. Table 9.6 shows the results.

Table 9.6. FLNN-CBR performance compared with that of human expert. Note: Only the advice with a CL greater than 65% was accepted, otherwise the result was entered as 'No suggestion'

Case	Symptoms	Expert advice	FLNN advice
(a)	IO.[no heartbeat] is 'False'; IO.[ALHBE function busy] is 'True'	Procedure 4	Procedure 4 (CL = 100%)
(b)	IO.[no heartbeat] is 'True'; IO.[ALHBI gives F/C 4] is 'True'; IO.[ALHBE function busy] is 'True'	Procedure 4	Procedure 4 (CL = 100%)
(c)	EMG.[traffic restriction] is 'False'; EMG.[RT locked up] is 'All'	Procedure 3	No suggestion
(d)	EMG.[EMTS falls down] is 'Gradually'; EMG.[control down after recovery] is 'False'	Procedure 1	Procedure 1 (CL = 77%)

© IEEE (1997)

In each case, the FLNN was able to give advice that was the same as the human expert's advice with a CL of over 77% . In the limited training data for IO problems, the attribute IO.[no heartbeat] appeared in two case examples with different linguistic properties. However, for both the cases the CBR suggested 'Procedure 4'. Through training, the FLNN then generalized the situation and indicated that whenever *IO.[ALHBE function busy] is 'True'* or *IO.[ALHBI gives F/C 4] is 'True'*, the diagnosis should be 'Procedure 4'. As a result, in test cases (a) and (b), it suggested 'Procedure 4'. This also implies that the attribute IO.[no heartbeat] is redundant and can be removed as far as the known cases are concerned. For case (c), as the symptoms did not match closely any of the trained cases, the system suggested nothing with a CL higher than 65%. For case (d), since the symptoms were close to the training case (4), the system suggested 'Procedure 1' with a confidence of 77%, which is the same as that given by the human expert.

9.8   Conclusions

An effective decision support system must be able to handle incomplete information, imprecision, ambiguity, and vagueness present in the descriptions of symptoms. In addition, noise and contradicting data will make the task even more difficult. CBR provides an effective framework for reusing knowledge and experience in solved cases. However, traditional CBR approaches lack the ability to adaptively update the case base and handle uncertainties in problem descriptions and measurements. Recently some researchers have investigated methods for dynamic case completion and uncertainty modeling in CBR, in particular, the use of fuzzy logic [4,30].

In this chapter, we presented a case based diagnostic system using fuzzy logic based neurons. Our experiments show that the FLNNs are capable of handling uncertainties and contradicting data, especially problems with vague liquistic descriptions. The results also demonstrate that the FLNN can learn from previous cases to generate the domain knowledge and reject noise present in the data. This has the advantage of eliminating the process of explicitly extracting knowledge by human experts which is time consuming and expensive.

Using the call logs from a help-desk, we carried out experiments on decision support for a real telecommunications system. The performance of our CBR system is comparable to that of the human expert. This shows that FLNN is useful in building CBR systems. However, we have to stress that FLNN is general enough to be applied to many other areas, for instance, e-commerce-related applications, web/data-mining, financial analysis and medical applications. By using fuzzy logic based neurons instead of the more traditional sigmoid neurons, we are able to interpret resulting network connections in terms of fuzzy IF–THEN rules.

Presently, we are investigating ways to incorporate domain knowledge and use competitive learning algorithms for training FLNN so that it can dynamically update the case base for new cases. In addition, we are studying some important theoretical aspects of FLNN, such as, optimization, self-organization (in competitive learning mode) and convergence properties.

References

1. P.P. Bonissone and N.C. Wood, T-norm Reasoning in Situation Assessment Applications, in *Uncertainty in Artificial Intelligence* 3, L.N. Kanal , T.S. Levitt, and J.F. Lemmer (Eds), North Holland, Amsterdam, 1989.

2. J.J. Buckley and W. Siler, Fuzzy Numbers for Expert Systems, in *Fuzzy Logic in Knowledge Based Systems, Decision and Control*, pp. 153-172, M.M. Gupta and T. Yamakawa (Eds) North Holland, Amsterdam, 1988.

3. H.-D. Burkhard, Extending Some Concepts of CBR: Foundations of Case Retrieval Nets, *Case-Based Reasoning Technology: From Foundations to Applications*, LNAI 1400, pp. 17–50, Springer-Verlag, Berlin, 1998.

4. D. Dubois, F. Esteva, P. Garcia, L. Godo, R.L. de Màntaras, and H. Prade, Fuzzy Modelling of Case-Based Reasoning and Decision, *Proc. 2nd International Conference on Case-Based Reasoning*, ICCBR-97, pp. 599–610, Providence, RI, July 25–27, 1997.

5. E. Castillo and E. Alvarez, *Expert Systems: Uncertainty and Learning*, Computational Mechanics Publications, Southampton and Boston, 1991.

6. K.J. Cios, I. Shin, and L.S. Goodenday, Using Fuzzy Sets to Diagnose Coronary Artery Stenosis, *IEEE Computer*, 24, 57–63, March 1991.

7. A. Hiramatsu, ATM Communication Network Control by Neural Networks, *IEEE Transactions on Neural Networks*, 1, 122–130, 1990.

8. R. Hoffman, The Problem of Extracting the Knowledge of Experts from the Perspective of Experimental Psychology, *AI Magazine*, 8(2), 53–67, 1988.

9. H. Ishibuchi, R. Fujioka, and H. Tanaka, Neural network that Learn from Fuzzy If-then Rules, *IEEE Transactions on Fuzzy Systems*, 1, 85–97, 1993.

10. J.R. Jang, Self-Learning Fuzzy Controllers Based on Temporal Back Propagation, *IEEE Transactions on Neural Networks*, 3, 714–723, 1992.

11. J.M. Keller, R. Krishnapuram, and F.C. Rhee, Evidence Aggregation Networks for Fuzzy Logic Inference, *IEEE Transactions on Neural Networks*, 3, 761–769, 1992.

12. G.J. Klir and T.A. Folger, *Fuzzy Sets, Uncertainty, and Information*, Prentice-Hall, New York, 1988.

13. M. Kriegsman and R. Barletta, Building a Case-Based Help Desk Application, *IEEE Expert: Intelligent Systems and their Applications*, 8, 18–26, 1993.

14. M. Lenz, E. Aurio, and M. Manago, Diagnosis and Decision Support, *Case-Based Reasoning Technology: From Foundations to Applications*, LNAI 1400, pp. 51–90, Springer-Verlag, Berlin, 1998.

15. K.S. Leung and W. Lam, Fuzzy Concepts in Expert Systems, *IEEE Computer*, 21, 43–55, 1988.

16. Z.Q. Liu and F. Yan, Fuzzy Neural Network in Case-Based Diagnostic System, *IEEE Transactions on Fuzzy Systems*, 5(2), 209–222, 1997.

17. G. Luger and W.A. Stubblefield, *Artificial Intelligence and the Design of Expert Systems*, Benjamin/Cummings Publishing Company, Inc., 1989.

18. T.M. Mitchell, *Machine Learning*, WCB/McGraw-Hill, New York, 1997.

19. H. Narazaki and A.L. Ralescu, An Improved Synthesis Method for Multilayered Neural Networks Using Qualitative Knowledge, *IEEE Transactions on Fuzzy Systems*, 1, 125–137, 1993.

20. S.K. Pal and S. Mitra, Multilayer Perception, Fuzzy Sets, and Classification, *IEEE Transactions on Neural Networks*, 3, 683–697, 1992.

21. W. Pedrycz, Fuzzy Neural Networks with Reference Neurons as Pattern Classifiers, *IEEE Transactions on Neural Networks*, 3, 770–775, 1992.

22. W. Pedrycz and A.F. Rocha, Fuzzy-Set Based Model of Neurons and Knowledge-Based Networks, *IEEE Transactions on Fuzzy Systems*, 1, 254–266, 1993.

23. R. Poli, S. Cagnoni, R. Livi, G. Coppini, and G. Valli, A Neural Network Expert System for Diagnosing and Treating Hypertension, *IEEE Computer*, 24, 64–70, 1991.

24. F. Puppe, *Systematic Introduction to Expert Systems*, Springer-Verlag, Berlin, 1993.

25. E. Sanchez, Fuzzy Logic Knowledge Systems and Artificial Neural Networks in Medicine and Biology, in *An Introduction to Fuzzy Logic Applications in Intelligent Systems*, Kluwer Academic Publishers, Dordrecht, 1989.

26. G.A. Shafer, *Mathematical Theory of Evidence*, Princeton University Press, Princeton, NJ, 1976.

27. H. Takagi, N. Suzuki, T. Koda, and Y. Kojima, Neural Networks Designed on Approximate Reasoning Architecture and their Applications, *IEEE Transactions on Neural Networks*, 5, 752–760, 1992.

28. I.B. Turksen and H. Zhao, An Equivalence between Inductive Learning and Pseudo-Boolean Logic Simplification: A Rule Generation and Reduction Scheme, *IEEE Transactions on Systems, Man and Cybernetics*, 23, 907–917, 1993.

29. R.R. Yager, Expert Systems Using Fuzzy Logic, in *An Introduction to Fuzzy Logic Applications in Intelligent Systems*, Kluwer Academic Publishers, Dordrecht, 1989.

30. R. Yager, Case-Based Reasoning, Fuzzy Systems Modeling and Solution Composition, *Proc. 2nd International Conference on Case-Based Reasoning*, ICCBR-97, pp. 633–642, Providence, RI, July 25–27, 1997.

10. Case Based Systems: A Neuro-Fuzzy Method for Selecting Cases

Rajat K. De and Sankar K. Pal

Abstract. Various case based systems designed in soft computing paradigms are, first of all, described in brief. This is followed by a detailed description of a fuzzy neural network for selection of cases. The notion of fuzzy similarity is used for selecting the same from both overlapping and non-overlapping regions. The architecture of the network is adaptively determined through *growing* and *pruning* of hidden nodes under supervised training. The effectiveness of the cases, thus selected by the network, is demonstrated for pattern classification problem using the 1-NN rule with the cases as the prototypes. Results are presented using real-life data.

10.1 Introduction

A case based system adapts old solutions to meet new demands, explains and critiques new situations using old instances (called cases), and performs reasoning from precedents to interpret new problems [1–3]. A case may be defined as a contextualized piece of knowledge representing an experience that teaches a lesson fundamental to achieving the goals of the system. The system learns as a byproduct of its reasoning activity. It becomes more efficient and more competent as a result of storing the experience of the system and referring to them in later reasoning. The case based system, in contrast to the traditional knowledge based system, operates through a process of remembering one or a small set of concrete instances or cases and basing decisions on comparisons between the new situation and the old one. The task of selection of cases constitutes an important and integral part of a case based system, particularly when the size of the data set is large.

Incorporation of fuzzy set theory enables one to deal with uncertainties in a system, arising from deficiency (e.g., vagueness, incompleteness) in information, in an efficient manner. Artificial neural networks (ANNs) having the capability of fault tolerance, adaptivity and generalization, and scope for massive parallelism, are widely used in dealing with learning and recognition tasks. Recently, attempts have been made to integrate the merits of fuzzy set theory and ANN under the heading 'neuro-fuzzy computing' for making the systems artificially more intelligent [4–7]. The theories of fuzzy sets, neural networks and neuro-fuzzy computing are tools of a new paradigm of research called 'soft computing' [8–11,4,12].

For the last few years, attempts have been made to develop methodologies integrating the theory of case based reasoning (CBR) and the aforesaid tools of soft computing. Outcomes of such investigations using the notion of fuzzy sets include an advanced case-knowledge architecture [13], fuzzy set modeling of CBR [14], case based fuzzy system in anesthesia [15], indexing and retrieval in case based systems [16], and a case based system for financial application [17]. Similarly, using neural networks resulted in hybrid case based connectionist systems [18–20], connectionist indexing approaches [21,22], connectionist methods for learning and retrieval of cases [23,24], case based system for oceanographic forecasting [25], and a case based legal expert system [26]. The literature on neuro-fuzzy case based systems is, on the other hand, comparatively scanty. A few attempts made under this framework are reported in [27–29] for diagnosing symptoms in electronic circuits, and for retrieval of cases and fuzzy inferencing.

In Section 10.2, we describe the basic features of some of these systems. As mentioned earlier, the issue of case selection is crucial for a case based system. In Sections 10.3–10.5, we describe a newly developed neuro-fuzzy system for selecting cases in pattern recognition problems. Here the cases are viewed as typically labeled patterns which represent different regions of the classes. A notion of fuzzy similarity is incorporated together with repeated *insertion* and *deletion* of cases in order to determine a stable case base. The architecture of the connectionist model is determined adaptively through *growing* and *pruning* of hidden nodes under a supervised mode of training. In order to demonstrate the effectiveness of the network (methodology) for pattern classification, we have considered the principle of k-NN classifier with $k = 1$ and the cases as the prototypes. Some results demonstrating its effectiveness, along with comparisons, are described using real-life speech [8] and medical data [30].

10.2   Different Soft Computing Case Based Systems

Here we describe a few case based systems which are designed in a soft computing framework for real-life applications. These include a fuzzy case based system for a financial application [17], connectionist case based system for oceanographic forecasting [25] and legal advice [26], and a neuro-fuzzy case based system for diagnosing symptoms in electronic circuits [27].

10.2.1   Fuzzy Case Based System for Financial Application

Bonissone and Cheetham [17] have developed a PROperty Financial Information Technology (PROFIT) system to estimate residential property values for real estate transactions. The system uses CBR techniques with fuzzy predicates expressing preferences in determining similarities between subject and cases. These similarities guide the selection and aggregation process, leading to the final property value estimate. The concept of fuzzy sets is used to generate a confidence value qualifying such estimate. The methodology involves:

(i) retrieving recent sales from a case base using a small number of features to select potential cases;

(ii) comparing the subject properties with those of the retrieved cases, and deriving a partial ordering (similarity measure) from the aggregation of fuzzy preference values;

(iii) adjusting the sales price of the retrieved cases to reflect their differences from the subject using a rule set;

(iv) aggregating the adjusted sales prices of the retrieved cases, selecting the best
     cases, deriving a single value estimate for the subject, and qualifying the estimate
     with a confidence value.

We now describe these steps briefly. The initial retrieval extracts a set of potential
cases using standard SQL queries for efficiency purpose. The selection is performed
by comparing specific attributes of the subject with the corresponding attribute of each
case. All the cases in the retrieved set have values within the allowable deviations.
Note that the initial retrieval stage uses the features – date of sale (within 12 months),
distance (within 1 mile), living area ($\pm$ 25%), lot size ($+100\%$ or -50%), number of
bedrooms (±3) and number of bathrooms (±3).

For each of the first four features, a preference criterion is defined using trapezoidal
membership function, which has a natural preference interpretation. The *support* of
the membership function represents the range of *tolerable* values and corresponds
to the interval value used in the initial retrieval query. The *core* represents the most
desirable range of values and establishes the top preference. A feature value falling
inside the core will receive a preference value of 1. As the feature value moves away
from the most desirable range, its associated preference will decrease from 1 to 0. At
the end of this evaluation, each case will have a preference vector, with each element
taking values in $(0, 1]$. These elements represent the partial degree of membership of
each feature value in the fuzzy sets and fuzzy relations representing the preference
criteria. The remaining two features, *number of bedrooms* and *number of bathrooms*,
are evaluated by two reflexive asymmetric fuzzy relations. Finally, these preference
values are aggregated using some weights.

All the properties found by the initial retrieval will undergo a series of adjustments
in their sales price to better reflect the subject property value. Any difference between
the subject and the case that would cause the case to be more (or less) valuable than
the subject produces an adjustment. If the case is inferior (superior) to the subject,
the adjustment will increase (decrease) the case price. After all the adjustments are
applied to the case sales price, the resulting value is called the case *adjusted price*.

When the best four to eight cases are found, their prices are combined to produce
the final estimate. Each case's contribution to this result is weighted by its similarity
score. In addition to producing the final estimate of the value of the subject, the system
provides a confidence in the estimate and the cases that justify the estimate.

10.2.2   Connectionist Case Based System for Oceanographic Forecasting

Corchado et al. [25] have presented a connectionist approach for oceanographic forecasting using the notion of CBR. This system combines the ability of a CBR system
for *selecting* previous similar situations and the *generalizing* ability of ANNs to guide
the adaptation stage of the CBR system. The system forecasts the thermal structure of
water up to 40 km ahead of an ongoing vessel. Here the CBR method has been used
to select a number of cases (from a large case base) and the neural network (radial
basis function network) produces a final forecast, in real time, based on these selected
cases.

In this system a case is created to represent the 'shape' of a set of temperature values. There are two different types of cases: *type A* and *type B*. A case of *type A* is composed of:

(i) a 40 km temperature input profile representing the structure of the water between the present position of the vessel and its position 40 km back;
(ii) a 10 km temperature output profile representing the structure of the water 10 km ahead of the present position of the vessel;
(iii) the latitude and longitude of the position of the vessel, time, day and year in which the data were recorded, and the tow orientation (north–south, south–east, etc.).

Similarly, a case of *type B* contains the same fields, with the difference that the input and output profiles are 160 km and 40 km respectively. Cases of *type A* are used to forecast up to 10 km ahead and those of *type B* up to 40 km ahead of the current position of the vessel.

The connectionist model acts as a function that obtains the most representative solution from a number of cases which are ones similar to the current situation. Thirty best matches are used to train a radial basis function neural network. The activation is fed forward from the input layer to the hidden layer where a *basis function*, which is the Euclidian distance between inputs and the centers of the basis function, is computed. The weighted sum of the hidden neurons' activations is calculated at the single output neuron. The complexity of the network depends on the difficulty of determining the centers and their locations. The network automates this process and guarantees a number of centers very close to the minimum number that gives optimum performance. An extended version of the system is described in a chapter of this book.

10.2.3   Case Based Legal Expert System in Connectionist Framework

The Hybrid Integrated Legal Decision Assistant (HILDA) of Egri and Underwood [26] incorporates some aspects of rule based reasoning (RBR) and CBR in the connectionist framework to assist the user in predicting legal outcomes and generating arguments and legal decisions. Knowledge extracted from a neural network is also used to iteratively refine the system's domain theory [31]. This refined domain theory is a way in which HILDA carries out RBR and CBR.

HILDA uses certain features of legislation and cases to implement some aspects of the *patchy domain theory* [31] present in the area of law. This allows HILDA to engage in RBR and CBR with (and without) refinement and modification of the patchy domain theory by a neural network. HILDA uses either some or all of the input features that are employed in a neural network where the weights of the links are selected by the user. The user employs the structure of the legislation and the cases to construct the initial domain theory. The system implements a knowledge based ANN for the insertion and refinement of domain rules using a connectionist model.

HILDA can also act as an 'advocacy' system by identifying whether the *case in question* (ciq) will ripple. If the ciq ripples, the nodes and links, node threshold values and link weights are set by the user or a neural network. On the other hand, if the ciq does not ripple, the system uses CBR in order to set nodes, links and node threshold values. Link weights are set by the user or a neural network as before. In the 'advocacy' mode, the user may not want the neural network to control HILDA's operation, but still uses the neural network's output to guide symbolic RBR and CBR. For instance, HILDA identifies those nodes which are not 'significant' to RBR and CBR. Again, the user can gain insights into the domain in which RBR and CBR are to take place by identifying the thresholds and weights given by HILDA whether any node/link is to be inserted/removed. Initially, the user conducts RBR and CBR with only the strong part of the domain theory and gradually use more and more of the weak part of the domain theory. In the 'adjudicatory' mode, HILDA helps the user to identify the best case for the Plaintiff and the best case for the Defendant at each level, using similar techniques employed in the 'advocacy' mode.

10.2.4 Neuro-Fuzzy Case Based System for Diagnosing Symptoms in Electronic Circuits

Liu and Yan [27] have designed a fuzzy logic based neural network (FNN) using the concept of CBR for diagnosing symptoms in electronic systems. The said network is able to perform fuzzy AND/OR logic rules and to learn from samples. The system achieves a performance similar to that of the human expert.

The system has a user interface shell at its front end, which provides the task of selecting symptoms. A symptom consists of an attribute (e.g., devices blocked) and linguistic property which can be crisp (e.g., true, false) or fuzzy (e.g., a few, some, most, all). The user selects the attribute first, and then finds the best linguistic property which goes with the attribute. The user can add a new attribute and define new linguistic terms if needed. When a new linguistic property is defined, its associated characteristics (such as crisp or fuzzy) have to be defined as well. The symptoms are then used as input to the inference engine which is realized by an FNN. Based on its learned knowledge, the FNN suggests a set of diagnoses with different confidence values. Another interface shell interprets these outputs and gives an ordered list of the most likely diagnoses.

When a new case is encountered, the symptoms and respective diagnoses are put into the training database. The FNN learns the new case data from the training database. In order to avoid possible interruption to the user, a separate off-line FNN is trained independently, which updates the on-line feed-forward-only FNN at regular time intervals.

Domain knowledge in the diagnostic system is usually available from human experts. This knowledge is transformed into fuzzy IF–THEN rules. By mapping these rules directly into the structure of the FNN, the knowledge is represented in the FNN without having gone through the training process. This reduces the amount of training required. This is also advantageous when there are insufficient case data for some possible problems to be diagnosed.

10.3 Neuro-Fuzzy Method for Selection of Cases

In this section, we develop a neuro-fuzzy method for the task of selection of few samples from each class as cases. (For the sake of convenience, the samples which are not selected as cases are referred to as patterns in the subsequent discussion.) For performing this task let us, first of all, define a similarity function for measuring the degree of similarity between a pattern and a case. The function is such that the higher its value, the higher is the degree of similarity between a pattern and a case.

Let $\mathbf{x} = [x_1, x_2, \ldots, x_i, \ldots, x_n]$ be a pattern vector of known classification in an n-dimensional feature space containing M classes. $\boldsymbol{\xi}_{l_k} = [\xi_{l_k 1}, \xi_{l_k 2}, \ldots, \xi_{l_k i}, \ldots, \xi_{l_k n}]$ denotes l_kth case from kth class C_k. $\mu_{l_k}(\mathbf{x})$ represents the degree of similarity of $\mathbf{x}$ to a case $\boldsymbol{\xi}_{l_k}$. $d_{l_k}(\mathbf{x})$ stands for the distance between $\mathbf{x}$ and $\boldsymbol{\xi}_{l_k}$.

10.3.1 Similarity Function and Selection of Cases

The degree of similarity between a pattern $\mathbf{x}$ and a case $\boldsymbol{\xi}_{l_k}$ is defined as

$$
\begin{aligned}
\mu_{l_k}(\mathbf{x}) &= 1 - 2(\tfrac{d_{l_k}(\mathbf{x})}{\lambda})^2 & 0 \le d_{l_k}(\mathbf{x}) < \tfrac{\lambda}{2}, \\
&= 2[1 - \tfrac{d_{l_k}(\mathbf{x})}{\lambda}]^2 & \tfrac{\lambda}{2} \le d_{l_k}(\mathbf{x}) < \lambda, \\
&= 0 & \text{otherwise}
\end{aligned}
\tag{10.1}
$$

where λ is the bandwidth of $\mu_{l_k}(\mathbf{x})$, i.e., the separation between its two (cross-over) points where $\mu_{l_k} = 0.5$. Note that $\mu_{l_k}(\mathbf{x})$ can be viewed as a π-type membership function characterizing a fuzzy set of points representing a region R_{l_k} with $\boldsymbol{\xi}_{l_k}$ as its center [32].

The distance $d_{l_k}(\mathbf{x})$ may be expressed in many ways. Considering Euclidian norm, we have

$$
d_{l_k}(\mathbf{x}) = [\sum_{i=1}^{n} (x_i - \xi_{l_k i})^2]^{\frac{1}{2}}
\tag{10.2}
$$

It is clear from Equation (10.1) that $\mu_{l_k}(\mathbf{x})$ decreases with the increase in $d_{l_k}(\mathbf{x})$ and vice versa. It is maximum ($= 1.0$), if $d_{l_k}(\mathbf{x})$ is zero (i.e., if a pattern $\mathbf{x}$ and the l_kth case are identical). The value of $\mu_{l_k}(\mathbf{x})$ is minimum ($= 0.0$), if $d_{l_k}(\mathbf{x}) \ge \lambda$. When $d_{l_k}(\mathbf{x}) = \tfrac{\lambda}{2}$, $\mu_{l_k}(\mathbf{x})$ is 0.5, i.e., an ambiguous situation arises. $\mu_{l_k}(\mathbf{x})$ implies that there is a crisp region R_{l_k} centered around a case $\boldsymbol{\xi}_{l_k}$, beyond which a pattern $\mathbf{x}$ is said to be dissimilar to $\boldsymbol{\xi}_{l_k}$. Note that one may define $\mu_{l_k}(\mathbf{x})$ in a different way satisfying the above mentioned characteristics.

A pattern $\mathbf{x}$ is selected randomly from any class C_k. $\mathbf{x}$ is considered as the first case if the case base B_k corresponding to class C_k is empty. Otherwise, $\mu_{l_k}(\mathbf{x})$ (Equation (10.1)) corresponding to the cases $\boldsymbol{\xi}_{l_k}$ in the case base B_k, are computed. $\mathbf{x}$ is selected as a new case, if

$$
\mu_{l_k}(\mathbf{x}) \le 0.5 \; \forall \, l_k
$$

When a case is selected, it is *inserted* into the case base. After repeating this process over all the training patterns, a set of cases constituting the case base for each class is obtained. The case base B for the entire training set is the union of all B_ks, i.e., $B = \cup_{k=1}^{M} B_k$.

After the formation of this case base B, a case $\boldsymbol{\xi}_{l_k}$ for which $\mu_{l_k}(\mathbf{x}) \le 0.5$ is minimum is *deleted* from B, if the number of patterns with $\mu_{l_k}(\mathbf{x}) > 0.5$ (or with $d_{l_k}(\mathbf{x}) < \tfrac{\lambda}{2}$). The processes of *insertion* and *deletion* are repeated until the case base becomes stable, i.e., the set of cases does not change further. This *deletion* process reduces the possibility of a spurious pattern being considered as a case.

Therefore, the class C_k can be viewed as a union of all the crisp regions R_{l_k} around its different cases, i.e.,

$$C_k = \cup_{l_k=1}^{s_k} R_{l_k}$$

where s_k is the number of cases in class C_k. Note that as the value of λ increases, the extent of R_{l_k}s representing different regions around ξ_{l_k}s increases, and therefore, the number of cases s_k decreases.

Effect of λ: As λ increases, the extent of the region around a case increases, and therefore the number of cases required for representing a class decreases. This implies that the generalization capability of an individual case increases with increase in λ. Initially, although the number of cases decreases with the increase in λ, the generalization capability of individual cases dominates. For further increase in λ, the number of cases becomes so low that the generalization capability of the individual cases may not cope with the proper representation of the class structures.

10.3.2 Formulation of the Network

Let us describe here the design of the network model, based on the methodology of case selection described in Section 10.3.1. Its architecture is determined adaptively through *growing* and *pruning* of hidden nodes. Note that these *growing* and *pruning* phenomena correspond to the tasks of *insertion* and *deletion* of cases.

10.3.2.1 Architecture
The connectionist model (Fig. 10.1) consists of three layers: input, hidden and class. The input layer represents the set of input features, i.e., for each feature there is a node (called input node) in the input layer. Similarly, for each case there is a node in the hidden layer. For each hidden node, there is an auxiliary node which makes the hidden node ON or OFF. An auxiliary node corresponding to a hidden node sends back a signal to the input layer only when it sends a signal to the hidden node for making it ON. The hidden nodes are made ON one at a time, keeping the remaining OFF. For the purpose of keeping class information of the cases, we have considered a class layer consisting of several nodes; each node (class node) representing a class.

The input nodes are connected to the hidden and auxiliary nodes by feedforward and feedback links respectively. The weight of a feedforward link connecting ith input node and l_kth hidden node is

$$w_{l_k i}^{(0)} = 1, \ \forall l_k, i \tag{10.3}$$

The weight $w_{l_k i}^{(fb)}$ of a feedback link connecting the auxiliary node corresponding to l_kth hidden node and ith input node is the same as the ith feature value of the l_kth case ($\xi_{l_k i}$). That is,

$$w_{l_k i}^{(fb)} = \xi_{l_k i} \tag{10.4}$$

The hidden layer is connected to the class layer via feedforward links. The weight $(w_{k l_k}^{(1)})$ of the link connecting l_kth hidden node and kth class node is 1, iff the case

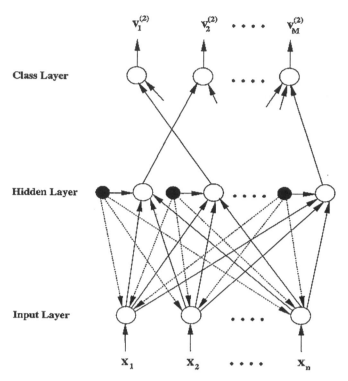

Fig. 10.1. A schematic diagram of the neural network model. Black circles represent the auxiliary nodes, and white circles represent input, hidden and class nodes.

corresponding to the hidden node belongs to class C_k. Otherwise, there is no such link between hidden nodes and class nodes. That is,

$$w_{kl_k}^{(1)} = 1, \, if \, \xi_{l_k} \in C_k,$$
$$= 0, \text{ otherwise} \tag{10.5}$$

At the begining, since the case base is empty, there is no hidden node. Hence, the connectivity between the layers is not established. When there is at least one hidden node, a pattern **x** is presented to the input layer of the network. The activation of ith input node when the l_kth hidden node is ON is given by

$$v_{l_k i}^{(0)} = (u_{l_k i}^{(0)})^2 \tag{10.6}$$

$u_{l_k i}^{(0)}$ is the total input received by the ith input node when the l_kth hidden node is ON, and is given by

$$u_{l_k i}^{(0)} = x_{pi} - u_{l_k i}^{(fb)} \tag{10.7}$$

where $u_{l_k i}^{(fb)} = (-1) * w_{l_k i}^{(fb)}$ (-1 being the feedback activation value of the auxiliary node corresponding to the l_kth hidden node) is the feedback input received by the input node. The total input received by the l_kth hidden node when it is made ON is

$$u_{l_k}^{(1)} = \sum_i v_{l_k i}^{(0)} * w_{l_k i}^{(0)} \tag{10.8}$$

The activation function of an l_kth hidden node is the same as $\mu_{l_k}(\mathbf{x})$ (Equation (10.1)). Thus, the activation $(v_{l_k}^{(1)})$ of the l_kth hidden node is given by

$$\begin{aligned}
v_{l_k}^{(1)} &= 1 - 2\left(\frac{(u_{l_k}^{(1)})^{\frac{1}{2}}}{\lambda^2}\right), \quad 0 \le (u_{l_k}^{(1)})^{\frac{1}{2}} < \frac{\lambda}{2}, \\
&= 2[1 - \frac{(u_{l_k}^{(1)})^{\frac{1}{2}}}{\lambda}]^2, \quad \frac{\lambda}{2} \le (u_{l_k}^{(1)})^{\frac{1}{2}} < \lambda, \\
&= 0, \qquad\qquad\qquad \text{otherwise}
\end{aligned} \tag{10.9}$$

Here the value of λ is stored in all the hidden nodes.

10.3.2.2   Training and Formation of the Network

The network described in Section 10.3.2.1 is formed through *growing* and *pruning* of the hidden nodes during the training phase under supervised mode. Initially there is only input and class layers. The patterns are presented in a random sequence to the input layer of the network. The first pattern presented to the network is considered as a case. A hidden node along with its auxiliary node representing this case is added to the network. The connections of these auxiliary and hidden nodes with the input and class layers are established as described by Equations (10.3)–(10.5).

For the remaining patterns, their degrees of similarity with the cases represented by existing hidden nodes are computed, and if they are decided to be new cases (Section 10.3.1) hidden nodes are added through a *growing* operation. After the process of addition is over, it is checked if there is any redundant hidden node. This is done through a *pruning* operation depending on the criterion mentioned in Section 10.3.1. In this connection, one may note the as λ increases the number of cases and hence the number of hidden nodes decreases. These two operations, which together constitute a single iteration, are continued until the structure of the network becomes stable, i.e., until

$$\sum_k \sum_{l_k i} |w_{l_k i}^{(fb)}(t)| = \sum_k \sum_{l_k i} |w_{l_k i}^{(fb)}(t-1)| \tag{10.10}$$

where t is the number of iterations. The aforesaid *growing* and *pruning* operations are described below.

Growing of hidden nodes: For a pattern $\mathbf{x} \in C_k$, if $v_{l_k}^{(1)} \le 0.5$ and $\mathbf{w}_{l_k}^{(fb)} = \boldsymbol{\xi}_{l_k} \in C_k$ for all the hidden nodes, $\mathbf{x}$ is selected as a case. A hidden node along with its auxiliary node is added to the network for representing this case and the links are established accordingly, using Equations (10.3)–(10.5). This process is called *growing of hidden nodes*. Note that the task 'insertion' of cases described in Section 10.3.1 is performed through this process.

Pruning of hidden nodes: An l_kth hidden node is deleted, if

$$v_{l_k}^{(1)} = \min_{\boldsymbol{\xi}_{l_k} = \mathbf{w}_{l_k}^{(fb)} \in C_k} v_{l_k}^{(1)} \le 0.5$$

and the number of training samples for which $v_{l_k}^{(1)} > 0.5$ is less than a pre-defined value. In this way, the network is pruned. Note that the task 'deletion' of cases described in Section 10.3.1 is performed through this process.

10.4   1-NN Classification Using the Cases

In order to demonstrate the effectiveness of the network model (i.e., the capability of the cases in representing respective classes) for pattern classification, we have considered the principle of 1-NN rule with the cases as the prototypes. According to this rule, an unknown sample x is said to be in class C_j if for an L_jth case

$$v_{L_j}^{(1)} = \max_{k,l_k}\{v_{l_k}^{(1)}\}, \ j, k = 1, 2, \ldots, M$$

For performing this task, each node in the class layer (Fig. 10.1) is considered to function as a winner-take-all network. A kth class node receives activations only from the hidden nodes corresponding to the cases in C_k. That is, the activation received by the kth class node from the l_kth hidden node is

$$u_{kl_k}^{(2)} = v_{l_k}^{(1)} * w_{kl_k}^{(1)} \tag{10.11}$$

The output of kth class node is

$$v_k^{(2)} = \max_{l_k}\{u_{kl_k}^{(2)}\} \tag{10.12}$$

$v_k^{(2)}$ represents the degree of belongingness of x to class C_k. Therefore, decide $\mathbf{x} \in C_j$ if

$$v_j^{(2)} > v_k^{(2)}, \ j, k = 1, 2, \ldots, M, \ j \neq k$$

10.5   Experimental Results

In this section, the effectiveness of the network (methodology) for automatic selection of cases is demonstrated by making the cases function as prototypes for a 1-NN classifier. We have considered real-life speech (vowel) [8] and medical data [30] as input. In both cases, the data set has been divided into two subsets: *training* and *testing*. While *perc*% samples are considered during training, the remaining $(100 - perc)\%$ is used for testing.

The vowel data [8] consists of a set of 871 Indian Telugu vowel sounds. These were uttered in a consonant–vowel–consonant context by three male speakers in the age group of 30–35 years. The dataset has three features, F_1, F_2 and F_3, corresponding to the first, second and third vowel formant frequencies obtained through spectrum analysis of the speech data. Fig. 10.2 shows the overlapping nature of the six vowel classes (viz., ∂, a, i, u, e, o) in the F_1–F_2 plane (for ease of depiction). The details of the data and its extraction procedure are available in [8]. This vowel data is being extensively used for more than two decades in the area of pattern recognition.

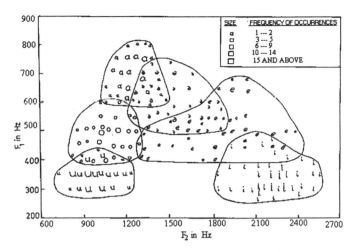

Fig. 10.2. Scatter plot of the vowel data in F_1–F_2 plane.

The medical data consisting of nine input features and four pattern classes, deals with various *hepatobiliary disorders* [30] of 536 patient cases. The input features are the results of different biochemical tests, viz., glutamic oxaloacetic transaminase (GOT, Karmen unit), glutamic pyruvic transaminaze (GPT, Karmen Unit), lactate dehydrogenase (LDH, iu/l), gamma-glutamyl transpeptidase (GGT, mu/ml), blood urea nitrogen (BUN, mg/dl), mean corpuscular volume of red blood cells (MCV, fl), mean corpuscular hemoglobin (MCH, pg), total bilirubin (TBil, mg/dl) and creatinine (CRTNN, mg/dl). The hepatobiliary disorders alcoholic liver damage (ALD), primary hepatoma (PH), liver cirrhosis (LC) and cholelithiasis (C) constitute the four classes.

Tables 10.1 and 10.2 depict some of the results obtained with the above datasets for different values of λ when $perc = 30$ is considered. The first column of these tables indicates the number of iteration(s) required by the network until it stabilizes during training. It is found from these tables that the recognition scores on the training set, as expected, are higher than those on the test set. The recognition score during training decreases with the increase in the value of λ. On the other hand, for the test data, the recognition score increases with λ up to a certain value, beyond which it decreases. This can be explained as follows.

During training, the recognition score increases with decrease in λ due to better abstraction capability; while for the test data, as λ decreases, the modeling of class structures improves because of the increase in the number of cases, and therefore, the recognition score increases up to a certain value of λ. Beyond that, as mentioned in Section 10.3.1, the number of cases with poor generalization capability (i.e., similarity functions with very small bandwidth) increases. As a result, the recognition score decreases due to *overlearning*.

As mentioned in Section 10.3.2.2, the number of hidden nodes of the network decreases with the increase in λ, for all the cases (Tables 10.1–10.2). Since class 'e' of vowel data is most sparse, it needs maximum number of cases (and hence maximum number of hidden nodes) for its representation. This is reflected in Table 10.1. Similar

Table 10.1. Classification performance for different λ using vowel data for $perc = 30$

Number of iterations	λ	Class	Number of hidden nodes	Recognition score (%) Training set	Testing set
3	100.0	∂	21	95.24	41.18
		a	22	100.0	84.13
		i	42	98.04	72.73
		u	31	97.78	81.13
		e	53	98.39	67.59
		o	38	94.44	89.68
		Overall	207	97.30	75.0
3	150.0	∂	18	95.24	64.71
		a	13	96.15	93.65
		i	23	96.08	86.78
		u	20	88.89	86.79
		e	37	96.77	80.0
		o	26	92.59	85.71
		Overall	137	94.21	83.82
3	200.0	∂	16	80.95	64.71
		a	13	92.31	90.48
		i	21	98.04	87.60
		u	19	91.11	85.85
		e	36	93.55	81.38
		o	25	90.74	86.51
		Overall	130	92.28	83.99
1	250.0	∂	12	71.43	58.82
		a	9	88.46	80.95
		i	11	92.16	85.95
		u	9	84.44	72.64
		e	20	91.94	80.69
		o	14	81.48	74.60
		Overall	75	86.49	77.29
1	300.0	∂	10	57.14	52.94
		a	8	92.31	80.95
		i	10	92.16	86.78
		u	8	97.78	83.96
		e	20	88.71	80.69
		o	11	64.81	59.52
		Overall	67	83.78	75.82

Table 10.2. Classification performance for different λ using the medical data for $perc = 30$

Number of iterations	λ	Class	Number of hidden nodes	Recognition score (%) Training set	Recognition score (%) Testing set
1	150.0	ALD	17	61.76	32.93
		PH	30	81.13	48.80
		LC	19	91.89	73.56
		C	13	42.86	27.71
		Overall	79	71.07	46.42
1	160.0	ALD	20	71.43	56.79
		PH	35	70.37	29.84
		LC	17	78.95	66.28
		C	8	58.33	57.32
		Overall	80	69.94	50.13
1	170.0	ALD	20	71.43	58.02
		PH	34	68.52	29.03
		LC	17	78.95	66.28
		C	8	55.56	54.88
		Overall	79	68.71	49.60
1	180.0	ALD	20	68.57	56.79
		PH	34	72.22	31.45
		LC	16	71.05	61.63
		C	8	55.56	54.88
		Overall	78	67.48	49.06
1	190.0	ALD	19	80.00	61.73
		PH	33	77.78	36.29
		LC	14	76.32	68.60
		C	6	8.33	12.20
		Overall	72	62.58	43.97
7	200.0	ALD	15	76.47	58.54
		PH	25	71.70	45.60
		LC	14	72.97	68.97
		C	11	25.71	9.64
		Overall	137	62.89	45.89

Table 10.3. Classification performance for different λ and $perc$ on vowel data

λ	Recognition score (%)						
	$perc = 10$	$perc = 20$	$perc = 30$	$perc = 40$	$perc = 50$	$perc = 60$	$perc = 70$
150.0	70.99	81.55	83.82	80.42	84.67	86.29	87.01
200.0	75.70	82.12	83.99	83.27	84.67	85.71	86.20
250.0	75.06	80.11	77.29	80.23	82.38	83.43	84.03

observations hold good for medical data where class PH, being most sparse, has the maximum number of hidden nodes. Note from Tables 10.1 and 10.2 that, for both the datasets, the stability of the architecture of the networks is achieved with a very few iterations.

In order to demonstrate the effect of the size of a training set on the performance of the network, we have considered only the vowel data. Different values of $perc$ considered are 10, 20, 30, 40, 50, 60 and 70 with $\lambda = 150.0$, 200.0 and 250.0. (Note that the network achieves the best generalization capability for $\lambda = 200.0$ (Table 10.1).) Table 10.3 shows that the recognition score on the test set, as expected, increases in general with the size of the training set.

Table 10.4. Comparative recognition score of various classifiers on the datasets

Data set	Class	Recognition score (%)					
		CBNN		Bayes		k-NN	
		Training	Testing	Training	Testing	Training	Testing
vowel	∂	80.95	64.71	38.10	43.14	23.81	33.33
	a	92.31	90.48	88.46	85.71	80.77	85.71
	i	98.04	87.60	90.20	85.12	88.24	85.12
	u	91.11	85.85	91.11	90.57	86.67	76.42
	e	93.55	81.38	75.81	80.69	75.81	77.93
	o	90.74	86.51	92.59	85.71	92.59	88.89
	Overall	92.28	83.99	83.01	81.70	79.92	78.43
medical	ALD	71.43	56.79	61.76	50.00	52.94	46.34
	PH	70.37	29.84	54.72	64.80	69.81	77.60
	LC	78.95	66.28	51.35	36.78	21.62	29.89
	C	58.33	57.32	91.43	75.90	54.29	61.45
	Overall	69.94	50.13	63.52	57.56	51.57	56.23

10.5.1 Comparison

In a part of the experiment, we have compared the performance of the said classifier (where the cases are considered as prototypes) with that of the following ones:

(i) A standard k-NN classifier with $k = \sqrt{s}$ (s being the number of training samples) where all the $perc\%$ samples, selected randomly, are considered as prototypes. (It is known that as s goes to infinity, if the values of k and k/s can be made to approach infinity and zero respectively, then the performance of the k-NN classifier approaches that of the (optimal) Bayes classifier [33]. One such value of k for which the limiting conditions are satisfied is $\sqrt{s}$.)

(ii) Bayes maximum likelihood classifier where a multivariate normal distribution of samples with different class dispersion matrices and *a priori* probabilities ($= \frac{s_j}{s}$, for s_j patterns from class C_j) are assumed, and all the $perc\%$ samples are used to compute the mean vectors and the covariance matrix.

Table 10.4 depicts that the network (CBNN) performs better than k-NN ($k = \sqrt{s}$) and Bayes maximum likelihood classifiers for vowel data. In the case of medical data, while the performance of CBNN on the training set is better than those obtained by the others, the reverse is true on the test samples.

10.6   Conclusions

In this article we have, first of all, described a few case based systems designed in a soft computing paradigm (e.g., fuzzy, connectionist and a neuro-fuzzy framework) for real life applications. This is followed by a new method of case selection in a neuro-fuzzy framework. A notion of fuzzy similarity, using π-type membership function, is incorporated together with the process of repeated *insertion* and *deletion* of cases in order to determine a stable case base. Cases are stored as network parameters during their supervised training for pattern recognition problems. The architecture of the network is determined adaptively through *growing* and *pruning* of hidden nodes. The effectiveness of the cases, thus selected by the network, has been demonstrated for pattern classification problems by considering them as prototypes of a 1-NN classifier.

Experimental results demonstrate that the number of hidden nodes increases with the decrease in extent λ of the π-function (Equation 10.1). As λ decreases, the performance during training increases because of the higher number of representative cases. On the other hand, during testing, it increases with the decrease in λ up to a certain value, beyond which the performance deteriorates because of *overlearning* (poor generalization capability of the cases).

It has been found that CBNN performs better than k-NN, with $k = \sqrt{s}$, and Bayes maximum likelihood classifiers for vowel data. In other words, the class representation capability of the fewer cases selected by the CBNN is seen to be superior to those of the entire *perc%* samples selected randomly for k-NN, with $k = \sqrt{s}$, and Bayes classifiers. However, for medical data, the generalization capability of CBNN is seen to be poorer.

One may further note a drawback of the k-NN classifier, that it needs to store all the prototypes (and hence to compute the distances from all of them). In this respect, the merit of the CBNN in selecting cases from all the training samples is evident from the point of space and time complexity.

References

1. J. L. Kolodner, *Case Based Reasoning*. San Mateo: Morgan Kaufmann, 1993.
2. I. Watson, *Applying Case based Reasoning: Techniques for Enterprise Systems*. Boston: Morgan Kaufmann, 1997.
3. A. Aamodt and E. Plaza, Case based reasoning: Foundational issues, methodological variations, and system approaches, *Artificial Intelligence Communications*, vol. 7, pp. 39–59, 1994.
4. S. K. Pal and S. Mitra, *Neuro-Fuzzy Pattern Recognition: Methods in Soft Computing*. New York: John Wiley, 1999.

5. S. Mitra, R. K. De, and S. K. Pal, Knowledge-based fuzzy MLP for classification and rule generation, *IEEE Transactions on Neural Networks*, vol. 8, pp. 1338–1350, 1997.

6. R. K. De, J. Basak, and S. K. Pal, Neuro-fuzzy feature evaluation with theoretical analysis, *Neural Networks*, vol. 12, pp. 1429–1455, 1999.

7. S. K. Pal, R. K. De, and J. Basak, Unsupervised feature evaluation : A neuro-fuzzy approach, *IEEE Transactions on Neural Networks*, vol. 11, pp. 366–376, 2000.

8. S. K. Pal and D. Dutta Majumder, *Fuzzy Mathematical Approach to Pattern Recognition*. New York: John Wiley (Halsted Press), 1986.

9. J. C. Bezdek and S. K. Pal, eds, *Fuzzy Models for Pattern Recognition: Methods that Search for Structures in Data*. New York: IEEE Press, 1992.

10. S. K. Pal and P. P. Wang, eds, *Genetic Algorithms for Pattern Recognition*. Boca Raton, FL: CRC Press, 1996.

11. S. K. Pal and A. Skowron, eds, *Rough Fuzzy Hybridization: A New Trend in Decision-Making*. Singapore: Springer-Verlag, 1999.

12. S. K. Pal, A. Ghosh, and M. K. Kundu, eds, *Soft Computing for Image Processing*. Heidelberg: Physica-Verlag, 2000.

13. W. Dubitzky, A. Schuster, J. Hughes, and D. Bell, An advanced case-knowledge architecture based on fuzzy objects, *Applied Intelligence*, vol. 7, pp. 187–204, 1997.

14. D. Dubois and H. Prade, Fuzzy set modeling in case based reasoning, *International Journal of Intelligent Systems*, vol. 13, pp. 345–373, 1998.

15. J. Petersen, Similarity of fuzzy data in a case based fuzzy system in anaesthesia, *Fuzzy Sets and Systems*, vol. 85, pp. 247–262, 1997.

16. B. C. Jeng and T. Liang, Fuzzy indexing and retrieval in case based systems, *Expert Systems with Applications*, vol. 8, pp. 135–142, 1995.

17. P. P. Bonissone and W. Cheetham, Financial applications of fuzzy case based reasoning to residential property valuation, in *Proceedings of the 6th IEEE International Conference on Fuzzy Systems*, (Barcelona, Spain), pp. 37–44, 1997.

18. P. Thrift, A neural network model for case based reasoning, in *Proceedings of the DARPA Case Based Reasoning Workshop* (K. J. Hammond, ed.), (California), Morgan Kaufmann, 1989.

19. B. Yao and Y. He, A hybrid system for case based reasoning, in *Proceedings of the World Congress on Neural Networks*, (San Diego, CA), pp. 442–446, 1994.

20. P. B. Musgrove, J. Davis, and D. Izzard, A comparison of nearest neighbour, rule induction and neural networks for the recommendation of treatment at anticoagulant out-patient clinics, in *Proceedings of the 2nd UK Workshop on Case Based Reasoning* (I. Watson, ed.), (Salford, UK), 1996.

21. E. Domeshek, A case study of case indexing: Designing index feature sets to suit task demands and support parallelism, in *Advances in Connectionist and Neural Computation Theory* (J. Barnden and K. Holyoak, eds), vol. 2: Analogical Connections, Norwood, NJ, Ablex, 1993.

22. M. Malek, A connectionist indexing approach for CBR systems, in *Case Based Reasoning Research and Development* (M. Veloso and A. Aamodt, eds), Berlin: Springer-Verlag, 1995.

23. C. Milare and A. d. Carvalho, Using a neural network in a CBR system, in *Proceedings of the International Conference on Computational Intelligence and*

Multimedia Applications, ICCIMA'98, (Victoria, Australia), pp. 43–48, February 1998.

24. E. Reategui, J. A. Campbell, and S. Borghetti, Using a neural network to learn general knowledge in a case based system, in *Case Based Reasoning Research and Development* (M. Veloso and A. Aamodt, eds), Berlin: Springer-Verlag, 1995.

25. J. M. Corchado, B. Lees, C. Fyfe, N. Rees, and J. Aiken, Neuro-adaptation method for a case based reasoning system, in *Proceedings 1998 IEEE International Joint Conference on Neural Networks (IJCNN'98)*, (Anchorage, USA), pp. 713–718, 1998.

26. P. A. Egri and P. F. Underwood, HILDA: Knowledge extraction from neural networks in legal rule based and case based reasoning, in *Proceedings of the IEEE International Conference on Neural Networks*, pp. 1800–1805, 1995.

27. Z.-Q. Liu and F. Yan, Fuzzy neural network in case based diagnostic system, *IEEE Transactions on Fuzzy Systems*, vol. 5, pp. 209–222, 1997.

28. J. Main, T. S. Dillon, and R. Khosla, Use of fuzzy feature vectors and neural vectors for case retrieval in case based systems, in *Proceedings of the NAFIPS 1996 Biennial Conference of the North American Fuzzy Information Processing Society*, (New York, USA), pp. 438–443, 1996.

29. L. Ding and Z. Shen, Neural network implementation of fuzzy inference for approximate case based reasoning, in *Neural and Fuzzy Systems* (S. Mitra, M. M. Gupta, and W. F. Kraske, eds), pp. 28–56, Washington: SPIE Optical Engineering Press, 1994.

30. Y. Hayashi, A neural expert system with automated extraction of fuzzy if–then rules and its application to medical diagnosis, in *Advances in Neural Information Processing Systems* (R. P. Lippmann, J. E. Moody, and D. S. Touretzky, eds), pp. 578–584, Los Altos, CA: Morgan Kaufmann, 1991.

31. B. W. Porter, E. R. Bareiss, and R. C. Holte, Concept learning and heuristic classification in weak theory domains, *Artificial Intelligence*, vol. 45, pp. 229–263, 1990.

32. S. K. Pal and P. K. Pramanik, Fuzzy measures in determining seed points in clustering, *Pattern Recognition Letters*, vol. 4, pp. 159–164, 1986.

33. K. Fukunaga, *Introduction to Statistical Pattern Recognition*. New York: Academic, 1972.

11. Neuro-Fuzzy Approach for Maintaining Case Bases

Simon C. K. Shiu, X. Z. Wang and Daniel S. Yeung

Abstract. In practical use of case based systems, there are always changes in the reasoning environment. Over time, the case library may need to be updated in order to maintain or improve the performance in response to these changes. The larger the case library, the more the problem space covered. However, it would also downgrade the system performance if the number of cases grows to an unacceptably high level. In order to maintain the size of a case based system as well as preserving its competence, we propose an approach of selecting representative cases using soft computing techniques. The approach consists of three phases. In the first phase, we determine the degree of membership of each case record to different classes using a neural network. This phase will generate a fuzzy set defined on the cluster space for each record. The second phase is to refine these fuzzy sets by a transformation, where the transformed coefficients are determined by gradient-descent technique, such that the degrees of membership can be as crisp as possible. The last phase uses the fuzzy class membership value of each record to formulate the deletion policy. The case density of each record is computed to determine the percentage of record to be deleted. Using this approach, we could maintain a reasonable size of the case base without losing a significant amount of information.

11.1 Introduction

The expert system is one of the branches of artificial intelligence that has successfully moved from laboratories to real-life applications. Among the various expert system paradigms, case based reasoning (CBR) is a relatively recent technique that is attracting increasing attention. The main reasons of the CBR success are [1–3]:

- It is closer to actual human decision processes (i.e., solving the problem by comparing similar situations in the past).
- Automation of the process of incorporating new knowledge in the knowledge base.
- Better explanation and justification of the decisions by showing previous examples.
- It does not require an explicit domain model and so knowledge elicitation becomes a task of gathering case histories.

A CBR system typically consists of four processes:

- Retrieve the most similar case.
- Reuse the case to attempt to solve the problem.
- Revise the proposed solution if necessary.
- Retain the new solution as a part of a new case.

When the number of cases increases over time, inductive learning methods could be used to induce general rules from the cases. These rules may be in the form of a decision tree, where each leaf carries a class name, and each inner node specifies an attribute with a branch corresponding to each possible value. In analyzing the similarities among cases that involve uncertainty, fuzzy production rules are used to calculate the membership degrees for each case, or to find similar cases in the case library [4–7]. When similar cases have accumulated to warrant maintenance, anomalies may exist in the case library, such as redundant cases, conflicting cases, ambiguous cases, subsumed cases and unreachable cases [8,9].

In addition, performance problems such as degradations of retrieval efficiency will become a real issue if uncontrolled case base growth is allowed. Techniques that can automatically maintain the size of the case base as well as detecting problem cases in the case library are therefore crucial to the future success of CBR technologies [10–13].

Currently, the CBR community has largely ignored the issue of maintenance although CBR is becoming a more mature knowledge based technology. This chapter proposes a neuro-fuzzy approach for maintaining CBR systems. The approach consists of three phases. In the first phase, we determine the degree of belonging of each case record to different classes using a neural network. This phase will generate a fuzzy set defined on the cluster space for each record. The second phase is to refine these fuzzy sets by a transformation, where the transformed coefficients are determined by gradient-descent technique, such that the degrees of membership can be as crisp as possible. This phase may be skipped according to the degree of fuzziness of training results with respect to classification, i.e., according to the number of cases in ODD class (ODD class consists of those cases where their degree of belonging to a class is ambiguous, e.g. 0.65 for class A, and 0.7 for class B etc). The last phase uses the fuzzy class membership value of each record to formulate their deletion policy. The case density of each record is computed to determine the percentage of record to be deleted. Using this approach, we could maintain the size of the case base without losing a significant amount of information.

A glass classification problem consisting of 214 records is used as an illustration of our approach; the neural network software NEURALWORKS PROFESSIONAL II/PLUS© is used to develop the network. It was shown that it could reduce the size of the case library by 28% if we select those records that have an overall class membership of at least 0.8 and case density over 0.95. Future work will include integrating adaptation rules for building deletion policy. By using this approach, uncontrolled case base growth can be avoided, hence the performance and retrieval efficiency could be maintained.

This chapter is organized into five sections. The first section gives the introduction. Section 11.2 reviews some of the current investigations on applying neural networks in case based expert systems. Section 11.3 describes our methodology in detail, and Section 11.4 uses a public domain database, i.e. glass database donated by Diagnostic Products Corporation, to illustrate our approach; the experimental results are also described and analyzed in this section. Finally, Section 11.5 provides the conclusions and scope of future work.

11.2 Literature Review

In traditional CBR systems, case retrieval relies mainly on algorithms such as the nearest neighbor search. It looks for cases stored in memory that consist of the greatest number of characteristics that are the same as or similar to the current case. There are many limitations to such an approach:

- Determining which characteristics are more important in retrieval of cases is a difficult task.
- Matching of selected feature is an all-or-nothing affair.
- It requires a very large case base to cover the entire problem space.
- Features that define a case can be of different types, which must be indexed or represented in different ways.

Recently, fuzzy neural networks are being used for indexing and retrieval of cases. The following is a brief and incomplete review. Vasudevan et al. [15] proposed briefly to use fuzzy logic in CBR. Main et al. [16] used fuzzy feature vectors and neural networks to improve the indexing and retrieval steps in case based systems. They used a supervised neural networks to accept inputs of various formats, such as Boolean, continuous, multi-valued and fuzzy. They have shown that the use of fuzzy representation for some features enhanced the accuracy of retrieval because the cases retrieved tended to match most closely on the fuzzy attributes. Egri and Underwood [17] established a knowledge extraction system, called HILDA, which incorporates some aspects of rule based reasoning and CBR to assist users in predicting case outcome and generating arguments and making case decisions. The system could use neural networks to guide rule based reasoning and CBR in a number of ways. Jeng and Liang [18] proposed a technique of fuzzy indexing and retrieval in CBR. Liu and Yan [19] proposed a fuzzy logic-based neural network to develop a case based system for diagnosing symptoms in electronic systems. They demonstrated through data obtained from a call-log database that the neural network is able to perform fuzzy AND/OR logic rules and to learn from examples. De and Pal [20] suggested a kind of case based classification using fuzziness and neural networks.

In addition to the applications of fuzzy neural networks to indexing and retrieval of cases, case base maintenance is considered to be another important issue for cased based expert systems. In [14], Leak and Wilson defined case base maintenance as the process of refining a CBR system's case base to improve the system's performance, i.e. case base maintenance implements policies for revising the organization or contents (representation, domain content, accounting information, or implementation) of the case base in order to facilitate future reasoning for a particular set of performance objectives. They presented a first attempt at identifying the dimensions of case base maintenance. In [11], Smyth and McKenna introduced the concept of competence of case base. They considered that some cases could be critical to competence while others may be largely redundant. Based on this idea, they proposed the use of case based density and the concept of case coverage to determine maintenance policy.

In this chapter, we integrate Smyth's idea [11] with the use of neural networks to obtain a new approach to determine the deletion policy. The main idea is using the fuzzy class membership value of each record, determined by a trained neural network, to guide the record deletion. Each class is considered to contain some representatives and some redundant cases. To reduce the fuzziness of classification, this chapter also incorporates the information feature weight. Learning feature weight can be via a gradient-descent technique, which has been used by Pal and his colleagues [20]. It aims to acquire features' importance and eliminate irrelevant features in a given database. One important thing in the CBR community is to distinguish the salient features from all the features in the database; feature selection methods can reduce the task's dimensionality when they eliminate irrelevant features [21]. The unsupervised approach in [20] is very useful in dealing with those databases in a knowledge-poor domain and in helping to reduce the dimension size of the case bases.

11.3 Methodology

Our case maintenance methodology is divided into three main phases as illustrated in Fig. 11.1. In the first phase, we determine the degree of belonging of each case record to different classes using a neural network. This phase will generate a fuzzy set defined on the cluster space for each record. The second phase is to refine these fuzzy sets by a transformation, where the transformed coefficients are determined by gradient-descent technique, such that the degrees of membership can be as crisp as possible. This phase may be skipped according to the degree of fuzziness of training results with respect to classification, i.e., according to the number of cases in ODD class. The last phase uses the fuzzy class membership value of each record to formulate their deletion policy. A similarity measure is used to calculate the case density of each record, and a deletion policy is then used to determine the percentage of record to be deleted. In detail, we formulate these three phases in the following three subsections.

Throughout this section, we consider a case library in which all features are supposed to take values of real numbers. It should be noted that the real-valued features discussed here could, without difficulty, be extended to the features that take values in a normed vector space.

Let $CL = \{e_1, e_2, \dots, e_N\}$ denote our discussed case library. Each case in the library can be identified by an index of corresponding features. In addition each case has an associated action. More formally we use a collection of features $\{F_j (j = 1, \dots, n)\}$ to index the cases and a variable V to denote the action. The i-th case e_i in the library can be represented as an $n + 1$-dimensional vector, $i.e.$ $e_i = (x_{i1}, x_{i2}, \dots, x_{in}, \nu_i)$ where x_{ij} corresponds to the value of feature $F_j (1 \le j \le n)$ and ν_i corresponds to the action $(i = 1, ..., N)$. $\nu_i (i = 1, ..., N)$ are considered to be class symbols and the total number of classes is supposed to be M. The M classes are denoted by $CM = \{C_1, C_2, ..., C_M\}$.

11.3.1 Case Classification Using Neural Network

This section aims to model the classification using a neural network with three layers. The classification result will be a fuzzy set on cluster space CM. The key structure of the constructed neural network is described as follows.

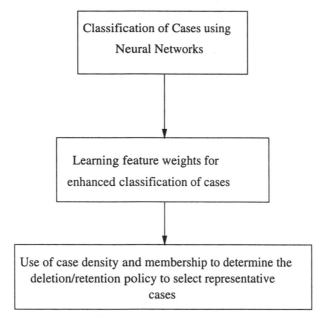

Fig. 11.1. Case base maintenance steps.

Input layer: The number of nodes in this layer is equal to the number of features of the case base. Each node represents a feature.

Hidden layer: The number of nodes in this layer is determined according to real applications. Experimentally, the number is bigger than n but less than $2n$, where n is the number of nodes in input layer.

Output layer: This is the classification layer which contains M nodes, where M is the number of clusters. Each node represents a fuzzy cluster. The training result will be the form of fuzzy vector (discrete fuzzy set defined on the cluster space CM). The meaning of each output value is the membership value, which indicates to what degree the training case belongs to the cluster corresponding to the node.

The popular sigmoid function is selected as the activation function. According to assumptions, there are n, L, M nodes in the input, hidden and output layers respectively. For a given input case (the m-th case, $1 \le m \le N$), the forth-propagation process of the input vector is described as follows:

The input layer: $\{x_{mi} | i = 1, 2, ..., n\}$ (the given input vector);

The hidden layer: $y_{mj} = f\left(\displaystyle\sum_{i=1}^{n} u_{ij} x_{mi}\right) \quad j = 1, 2, ..., L \qquad (11.1)$

$$\text{The output layer: } \mu_{mk} = f\left(\sum_{j=1}^{L} \nu_{jk} y_{mj}\right) \quad k = 1, 2, ..., M \qquad (11.2)$$

Where u_{ij} and ν_{jk} are the connection weights of the neural network, and the notation f represents the sigmoid function, defined as $f(x) = \frac{1}{1+e^{-x}}$.

This is a traditional full connection network with three layers. The standard BP algorithm can be used to train this network. In other words, the popular gradient descent technique can be used to find the values of weights u_{ij} and ν_{jk} such that the error function

$$E = \sum_{m=1}^{N}\left(\frac{1}{2}\sum_{k=1}^{M}(\mu_{mk} - c_{mk})^2\right) = \sum_{m=1}^{N} E_m \qquad (11.3)$$

achieves a local minimum, where c_{mk} taking either 0 or 1 corresponds to the action of the m-th case, e.g., $(c_{m1}, c_{m2}, ..., c_{mM})=(1, 0, ..., 0)$ if the m-th case belongs to the first cluster.

After finishing this training, a fuzzy set on the cluster space $\{C_1, C_2, ..., C_M\}$ can be given for each case according to Equations 11.1 and 11.2. Denoting the fuzzy set by $(\mu_{m1}, \mu_{m2}, ..., \mu_{mM})$, in which each component μ_{mj} represents the degree of the m-th case belonging to the j-th cluster, we can reclassify the case base according to the following criterion (A) or (B).

Consider a case, e_m, to be reclassified. The training result of this case is supposed to be $(\mu_{m1}, \mu_{m2}, ..., \mu_{mM})$. α and β are two given thresholds.

Criterion (A): If Entropy$(e_m) < \beta$ and $\mu_{mk}=\text{Max}_{1\leq j\leq M}\mu_{mj} \geq \alpha$, then case e_m is classified to the k-th cluster where

$$\text{Entropy}(e_m) = -\sum_{j=1}^{M} \mu_{mj}.lin\mu_{mj} \qquad (11.4)$$

Criterion (B): If Nonspec$(e_m) < \beta$ and $\mu_{mk}= \text{Max}_{1\leq j\leq M}\mu_{mj} \geq \alpha$, then the case e_m is classified to the k-th cluster where

$$\text{Nonspec}(e_m) = \sum_{j=1}^{M}(\mu_{mj}^* - \mu_{m(j+1)}^*)lnj \qquad (11.5)$$

in which $(\mu_{m1}^*, \mu_{m2}^*, ..., \mu_{mM}^*)$ is the permutation of $(\mu_{m1}, \mu_{m2}, ..., \mu_{mM})$, sorted so that $\mu_{mj}^* \geq \mu_{m(j+1)}^*$ for $j = 1, 2, ..., M$ and $\mu_{m(M+1)}^* = 0$.

Criterion (A) is based on the fuzzy entropy (Equation 11.4) [22], which will tend to zero when all μ_{mj} tend to either 0 or 1. Criterion (B) is based on the non-specificity (Equation 11.5) [13], which will tend to zero when only one μ_{mj} tends to 1 and the others tend to 0. The fuzzy entropy and the non-specificity provide two different kinds of uncertainty. The former is the suitable probability distribution while the latter is the possibility distribution.

According to criterion (A) or (B), the case base can be classified to $M+1$ clusters. The $(M + 1)$-th cluster, called ODD class, is the remaining cases which cannot be explicitly classified into certain one of the M classes. The cases in the ODD class have poor training results. Obviously we expect that the number of cases in the ODD class is as small as possible. However, this number depends strongly on the training of the neural network. When the training result (or the number of cases in the ODD class) is not desirable, we attempt to improve it by the following feature weight learning.

11.3.2 Learning Feature Weight Information

Let the training results be $\{(\mu_{m1}, \mu_{m2}, \dots, \mu_{mM}), m = 1, 2, \dots, N\}$ for N cases $\{e_m, m = 1, 2, \dots, N\}$, where $\mu_{mk}(\in [0, 1])$ represents the degree of the m-th case belonging to the k-th cluster. An index evaluation function which is similar to one given in [20,24] is defined as

$$E(w_1, w_2, \dots, w_n) = \sum_{m=1}^{N} \sum_{k=1}^{M} \left(\mu_{mk}^{(w)}(1 - \mu_{mk}) + \mu_{mk}(1 - \mu_{mk}^{(w)}) \right) \quad (11.6)$$

in which μ_{mj} is computed according to Equations 11.1 and 11.2, and $\mu_{mj}^{(w)}$ according to the following Equations 11.7 and 11.8:

$$\mu_{mk}^{(w)} = f\left(\sum_{j=1}^{L} \nu_{jk} y_{mj}^{(w)} \right) \quad k = 1, 2, ..., M \quad (11.7)$$

$$y_{mj}^{(w)} = f\left(\sum_{i=1}^{n} w_i u_{ij} x_{mi} \right) \quad j = 1, 2, ..., L \quad (11.8)$$

where u_{ij} and ν_{jk} are the weights trained already in the previous phase, and $f(x) = \frac{1}{1+e^{-x}}$ represents the sigmoid function.

In Equation 11.6, $\{w_i : w_i \in [0, 1], i = 1, 2, ...n\}$ are called feature weights, which remain to be determined. They indicate that, for the trained neural network in the previous phase, different features have different degrees of importance to the training classification.

The evaluation function Equation 11.6, which has been appllied by Pal [24] and his group to feature exttraction in [20], is designed according to a simple function $g(x, y) = x(1 - y) + y(1 - x)$ $(1 \le x, y \le 1)$. Noting that $\frac{\partial g}{\partial x} = 1 - 2y$, $\frac{\partial g}{\partial x} > 0$ if $y < 0.5$, $\frac{\partial g}{\partial x} < 0$ if $y > 0.5$, one can easily find that Equation 11.6 has the following characteristics:

(a) If $\mu_{mk} < 0.5$ and $\mu_{mk}^{(w)} \to 0$, then $E \to 0$ (minimum);
(b) If $\mu_{mk} > 0.5$ and $\mu_{mk}^{(w)} \to 1$, then $E \to 0$ (minimum);
(c) If $\mu_{mk} = 0.5$ and $\mu_{mk}^{(w)} = 0.5$, then E attains maximum.

The main task of this phase is to minimize the index function $E(w_1, w_2, ..., w_n)$ with respect to the weights $w_1, w_2, ..., w_n$. More formally, we attempt to find $(w_1^*, w_2^*$

$, ..., w_n^*)$ such that

$$E(w_1^*, w_2^*, ..., w_n^*) = \text{Min}\{E(w_1, w_2, ..., w_n)|w_i \in [0, 1], i = 1, 2, ..., n\} \quad (11.9)$$

Minimizing the index function E is regarded as a process of refinement of membership values to crispness. If we consider μ_{mk} and $\mu_{mk}^{(w)}$ as the membership degrees of the m-th case belonging to the k-th cluster before refinement and after refinement respectively, the minimization of Equation 11.6 attempts to make the membership degree after refinement being more crisp than the membership degree before refinement. That is, we expect that the minimization of Equation 11.6 can make the membership degree after refinement close to 0 if the membership degree before refinement is less than 0.5; and the membership degree after refinement close to 1 if the membership degree before refinement is bigger than 0.5. It is also expected that the number of cases in the ODD class determined in the previous phase can be reduced by using the new membership degrees.

To solve Equation 11.9, a neuro-fuzzy method which is similar to that in [20] can be used. However, for simplicity, we do not design a fuzzy neural network but directly use a gradient-descent technique to minimize Equation 11.6. The change in w_i (i.e. Δw_i) is computed as

$$\Delta w_i = -\eta \frac{\partial E}{\partial w_i} \quad (11.10)$$

for $j = 1, ..., n$, where η is the learning rate. For the computation of $\frac{\partial E}{\partial w_i}$, the following expressions are used:

$$\frac{\partial E}{\partial w_i} = \sum_{m=1}^{N} \sum_{k=1}^{M} \left((1 - 2\mu_{mk}) \frac{\partial \mu_{mk}^{(w)}}{\partial w_i} \right) \quad (11.11)$$

$$\frac{\partial \mu_{mk}^{(w)}}{\partial w_i} = f\left(\sum_{j=1}^{L} v_{jk} y_{mj}^{(w)} \right) \left(1 - f\left(\sum_{j=1}^{L} v_{jk} y_{mj}^{(w)} \right) \right) \frac{\partial y_{mj}^{(w)}}{\partial w_i} \quad (11.12)$$

$$\frac{\partial y_{mj}^{(w)}}{\partial w_i} = f\left(\sum_{p=1}^{n} w_p u_{pi} x_{mp} \right) \left(1 - f\left(\sum_{p=1}^{n} w_p u_{pj} x_{mp} \right) \right) . u_{ij} x_{mi} \quad (11.13)$$

where $f(x) = \frac{1}{1+e^{-x}}$ represents the sigmoid function and other notations have the same meaning as Equations 11.6–11.8.

The training algorithm is described as follows.

Step 1. Select the learning rate η.
Step 2. Initialize w_i with random values in $[0, 1]$.
Step 3. Compute Δw_i for each i using Equation 11.10.
Step 4. Update w_i with $w_i + \Delta w_i$ for each i if $w_i + \Delta w_i \in [0, 1]$.
Step 5. Repeat steps 3 and 4 until convergence, i.e., until the value of E becomes less than or equal to a given threshold, or until the number of iterations exceeds a certain pre-defined number.

After training, the function $E(w_1, w_2, ..., w_n)$ attains a local minimum. We expect that, on average, the membership degrees $\{\mu_{mk}^{(w)} : m = 1, ..., N; k = 1, ..., M\}$ with trained weights are closer to 0 or 1 than $\{\mu_{mk} : m = 1, ..., N; k = 1, ..., M\}$ without trained weights.

11.3.3 Determine the Deletion Policy

According to the membership degrees obtained by training a neural network in phase 1 or after refining them in phase 2, the case base can be classified to $M + 1$ clusters by using criterion (A) or (B) mentioned previously. The $(M + 1)$-th cluster is the ODD class in which the cases cannot be explicitly classified into certain M classes. This phase is based on such an idea that there exist several representatives in each class of cases. Therefore, the aim of this phase is to select these representatives. Our selection strategy is mainly based on the case density and membership degree. Before introducing our selection strategy, we briefly and incompletely review some related work for case deletion.

In [11], Smyth and Keane described a technique for measuring the local coverage of individual cases with respect to a system's retrieval and adaptation characteristics. They also suggested deleting cases based on their coverage and reachability. The coverage of a case is defined as the set of target cases that can be adapted to solve, while the reachability of a case is the set of cases in the case base that can be adapted to solve that case. Based on these measures, Smyth et al. classified cases within the case base into four groups: Pivotal (if its reachability is a singleton consisting of itself), Auxiliary (if its coverage is subsumed by the coverage of a case to which it is reachable), Spanning (if its coverage space links regions covered by other cases) and Support (groups of cases having the same coverage). The deletion policy (footprint policy) suggested by Smyth et al. [11] was to delete auxiliary cases first, then support cases, then spanning cases and finally pivotal cases. If more than one case is a candidate for deletion, sub-strategy is formulated when deciding on which case to delete. Two problems of the footprint deletion policy are that the coverage and reachability of a case are dependent on the adaptation knowledge available, and secondly, it is unclear why a pivotal case would ever need to be deleted [23].

Rather than using a deletion strategy, we prepare to select several representatives in each class of cases. This selection makes use of the membership degree and the concept of case density [11], defined as follows:

$$\text{Case Density}(c, G) = \frac{\sum_{c \in G - \{c\}} \text{Sim}(c, c')}{|G| - 1} \qquad (11.14)$$

$$\text{Sim}(c, c') = 1 - \frac{\left[\sum_i w_i (c_i - c_i')^2\right]^{\frac{1}{2}}}{n} \qquad (11.15)$$

in which G denotes a class of cases, $|G|$ is the number of cases in class G, c and c' are two cases, c_i and c_i' are the i-th component of cases c and c' respectively, n is the number of features, w_i is the feature weight learned in phase 2 (all w_i will be equal to

1 if phase 2 is skipped), and $Sim(c, c')$ represents the similarity between cases c and c'.

Our selection algorithm is described as follows:

Step 1. Select two thresholds α and β for membership value and case density.
Step 2. Compute case density for every case in each class except for ODD class.
Step 3. Select all cases in ODD class.
Step 4. Select representative cases from every other class if their membership degrees (of belonging this class) are greater than or equal to α and their case densities are greater than or equal to β.

11.4   Glass Identification Database

In order to illustrate the effectiveness of our approach, we apply it to a glass identification problem. The glass identification database downloaded from UML [25], as shown in Table 11.1, consists of 214 records, and each record has 11 attributes as follows:

1. Id number: 1 to 214
2. RI: refractive index
3. Na: Sodium (unit measurement is weight percent in corresponding oxide, as are attributes 4–10)
4. Mg: Magnesium
5. Al: Aluminum
6. Si: Silicon
7. K: Potassium
8. Ca: Calcium
9. Ba: Barium
10. Fe: Iron
11. Type of glass: window glass / non-window glass

Table 11.1. Sample cases

RI	Na	Mg	Al	Si	K	Ca	Ba	Fe	Type
1.51215	12.99	3.47	1.12	72.98	0.62	8.35	0	0.31	W
1.51768	12.56	3.52	1.43	73.15	0.57	8.54	0	0	W
1.51652	13.56	3.57	1.47	72.45	0.64	7.96	0	0	W
1.51969	12.64	0	1.65	73.75	0.38	11.53	0	0	N
1.51754	13.39	3.66	1.19	72.79	0.57	8.27	0	0.11	W
1.51911	13.9	3.73	1.18	72.12	0.06	8.89	0	0	W

We used the neural network package NEURALWORKS PROFESSIONAL II/PLUS © version 5.3 for testing various types of neural networks performance on fuzzy classification of data. We have tried the following network models: backpropagation model, probabilistic model and SOM model. All of them are suitable for our purpose, and we have finally chosen the backpropagation network to perform detail analysis of the case base. The learning rule algorithm is delta-rule, and the transfer function is a sigmoid function. After about 50,000 cycles of training, the network converged and the RMS error was 0.1322, which was considered to be successfully trained.

Furthermore, the confusion matrix graph shown in Fig. 11.2 represents the following results, the x-axis representing the desired output and the y-axis representing the actual output. The confusion matrix breaks the diagram into a grid. If the probe point produces an output of 0.7 and the desired output was 0.5, then the bin around the intersection of 0.7 from the y-axis and 0.5 from the x-axis receives a count. A bar within the bin displays counts, and the bar grows as counts accumulated. The bin that received the most counts is shown at full height, while all of the other bins are scaled in relation to it. The confusion matrix is also equipped with a pair of histograms.

The histogram that runs across the top of the instrument shows the distribution of the desired outputs. The histogram along the right shows the distribution of the actual outputs. Any actual outputs that lay outside the range of the graph will be added to the top or bottom bins along the right (depending on their value). By looking at the two confusion matrices, the desired outputs and actual outputs intercept quite well and this also indicates that the network was trained satisfactorily.

We then tested the network by the original set of data, and only accept correct classification if the fuzzy membership value is higher than 0.8; even with such a high membership degree, the overall accuracy of correct classification is 94%. We expected that it would go up to as high as 99% if more tolerance of fuzziness were allowed. The typical output after training is shown in Table 11.2 and the network architecture is shown in Fig. 11.2.

Table 11.2. Sample output from training

Expected value 1 = window glass 0 = non-window glass		Fuzzy membership for window glass	Fuzzy membership for non-window glass
1	0	0.999998	0.000002
1	0	0.997225	0.002775
1	0	0.998020	0.001980
0	1	0.007992	0.992008
1	0	0.999834	0.000166
1	0	0.999047	0.000954
0	1	0.457469	0.542531
1	0	0.999737	0.000263

We select those records having WINDOW-GLASS membership value higher than 0.8 and label them as WINDOW-GLASS class and those records having a NON-WINDOW-GLASS membership value higher than 0.8 and label them as NON-WINDOW-GLASS class. The remaining records are labeled as ODD class; i.e. they belong neither to WINDOW-GLASS nor NON-WINDOW-GLASS to a satisfactory degree. The results are as shown in Table 11.3:

Table 11.3. Classification of the records

Class name	No. of cases in this class
WINDOW-GLASS	158
NON-WINDOW-GLASS	43
ODD (the remaining)	13

Noting that the number of cases in the ODD class is 13, we consider that the feature weight learning is unnecessary (i.e., phase 2 can be skipped). For each class, we could use the similarity measurement and case density calculation to compute every case's case density according to Equations 11.14 and 11.15 where the feature weights are considered to be 1, as shown in Table 11.4.

Table 11.4. Sample result of case density

Fuzzy membership for window glass	Fuzzy membership for non-window glass	Class we defined according to fuzzy membership value	Case density
0.999834	0.000166	Window glass	0.963236
0.999047	0.000954	Window glass	0.959489
0.999737	0.000263	Window glass	0.964335
0.412578	0.587422	Not sure	0.940094
0.999975	0.000025	Window glass	0.939792
0.999985	0.000015	Window glass	0.939759
0.995205	0.004795	Window glass	0.9396
0.000004	0.999996	Non-window glass	0.938816
0.999962	0.000038	Window glass	0.93853
0.000023	0.999977	Non-window glass	0.938372

From the result, in WINDOW-CLASS class, we select those cases whose case density is greater than 0.95 and has a WINDOW-CLASS membership value greater than 0.95 as the representative cases, and delete the others in this class. Similarly, in NON- WINDOW-GLASS class, we select those cases whose case density is greater than 0.95 and has a NON-WINDOW-GLASS membership value greater than 0.95 as the representative cases, and delete the others in this class. In addition, we retain all the cases in the ODD class. We could also use the case density to select some cases as representative cases in the ODD class as well. (In this experiment, we choose to retain all the cases in the ODD class.) The final case maintenance result is shown in Table 11.5.

Using the above approach, we could delete 60 cases, giving a 28% decrease in the size of the case base.

Table 11.5. Case maintenance result

Class name	No. of cases originally	No. of cases remain
WINDOW-GLASS	158	112
NON-WINDOW-GLASS	43	29
ODD class	13	13
TOTAL	214	154

11.5 Conclusions

There is always a trade-off between the number of cases to be stored in the case library of a case based expert system and the retrieval efficiency encountered. In this chapter, we have developed an approach for maintaining the size of a case based expert system. This involves computation of the fuzzy class membership values of each record determined by a trained neural network. The case base is classified into several clusters according to the membership values and each cluster is considered to contain some representative cases and several redundant cases. A similarity measure is used to calculate the case density of each record. A deletion strategy is then used to determine the percentage of records to be deleted. A testing glass/non-glass case base consisting of 214 records is used as an illustration, and NEURALWORKS PROFESSIONAL II/PLUS © is used for implementation. It was shown that we could reduce the size of the case library by 28% by selecting representative cases that have an overall class membership of over 0.8 and case density of over 0.95. Future work includes extension of the fuzzy feature selection concepts for identifying important case features for ranking, development of a neural network with unsupervised learning to determine the class membership, integration of data mining techniques, such as discovering of adaptation rules, for guiding the deletion policy, and use of a classifier to validate the results.

Acknowledgement

This project is supported by Hong Kong Polytechnic University grant PA25.

References

1. Ketler, K., Case-Based Reasoning: An Introduction, *Expert Systems with Applications*, 6, 3–8, 1993.
2. Marir, F. and Watson, I., Case-Based Reasoning: A Categorised Bibliography, *Knowledge Engineering Review*, 9(4), 355–381, 1994.
3. Watson, I. and Marir, F., Case-Based Reasoning: A Review, *Knowledge Engineering Review*, 9(4), 327–354, 1994.
4. Dubitzky W. et al., An Advanced Case-Knowledge Architecture Based on Fuzzy Objects, *Applied Intelligence*, 7(3), 187–204, 1997.
5. Petersen, J., Similarity of fuzzy data in a case based fuzzy system in anaesthesia, *Fuzzy Sets and Systems*, 85, 247–262, 1997.

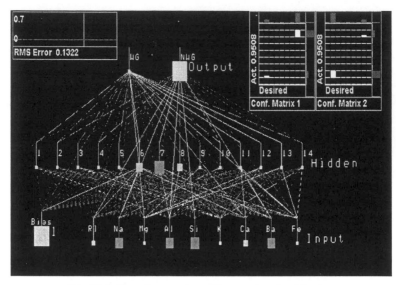

Fig. 11.2. Neural network architecture for classification

6. Yeung, D.S. and Tsang, E.C.C., Improved Fuzzy Knowledge Representation and Rule Evaluation Using Fuzzy Petri Nets and Degree of Subsethood, *International Journal of Intelligent Systems*, 9, 1083–1100, 1994.
7. Yeung, D.S. and Tsang, E.C.C., A Comparative Study on Similarity-Based Fuzzy Reasoning Methods, *IEEE Transactions on SMC*, 27(2), 216–227, 1997.
8. O'Leary, D.E., Verification and validation of case-based systems, *Expert Systems with Applications*, 6, 57–66, 1993.
9. Shiu, S.C.K., Formal Description Techniques for the Verification of Expert Systems, PhD Thesis, Department of Computing, Hong Kong Polytechnic University, 1997.
10. Shiu, S.C.K., Tsang, E.C.C., and Yeung, D.S., Maintaining Case-Based Expert Systems Using Fuzzy Neural Network, in *Proceedings of 1999 IEEE SMC*, Vol. III, pp. 424–428.
11. Smyth, B. and McKenna E., Modelling the Competence of Case-Bases, in *Proceedings of Fourth European Workshop, EXCBR-98*, pp. 207–220, 1998.
12. Heister F. and Wilke W., An Architecture for Maintaining Case-Based Reasoning Systems, in *Proceedings of EWCBR-98*, pp. 221–232, 1998.
13. Higashi, M. and Klir, G.J., Measures on Uncertainty and Information Based on Possibility Distribution, *International Journal of General Systems*, 9, 43–58, 1983.
14. Leake, D.B. and Wilson, D.C., Categorizing Case-Base Maintenance: Dimensions and Directions, in *Proceedings of 4th European Workshop, EXCBR-98*, pp. 196–207, 1998.
15. Vasudevan, C., Smith, S.M. and Ganesan, K., Fuzzy Logic in Case-Based Reasoning, *NASA Joint Technology Workshop on Neural Network and Fuzzy Logic, NAFIPS/IFIS/NASA'94*, pp. 301–302, 1994.
16. Main, J., Dillon T.S. and Khosla R. Use of Neural Networks for Case-Retrieval in a System for Fashion Shoe Design, in *Proceedings of Eighth International Con-*

ference on Industrial and Engineering Applications of Artificial Intelligence and Expert Systems, Melbourne, Australia, June 1995, pp. 151–158.

17. Egri, P.A. and Underwood, P.F., HILDA: Knowledge Extraction from Neural Networks in Legal Rule Based and Case Based Reasoning, in *IEEE International Conference on Neural Networks*, 1995, Vol. 4. pp. 1800–1805.

18. Jeng, B.C. and Liang, T.P., Fuzzy Indexing and Retrieval in Case-Based Systems, *Expert Systems with Applications*, 8(1), 135–142, 1995.

19. Liu, Z.Q. and Yan, F., Case-Based Diagnostic System Using Fuzzy Neural Networks, *IEEE Transactions on Fuzzy Systems*, 5(2), 209–222, 1997.

20. De, R.K. and Pal, S.K., Case-Based Classification using Fuzziness and Neural Networks, *Knowledge Discovery and Data Mining* (Digest No. 1998/310), IEE Colloquium, 1998, pp. 6/1–6/3.

21. Basak, J., De, R.K. and.Pal, S.K., Unsupervised Feature Selection Using a Neuro-Fuzzy Approach, *Pattern Recognition Letters*, 19, 998–1006, 1998.

22. Wettscherck, D. and Aha, D.W., Weighting Features, Case-Based Reasoning Research and Development, in *First International Conference, ICCBR-95*, Sesimbra, Portugal, pp. 347–358, 1995.

23. De Luca, A. and Termin, S., A Definition of a Nonprobabilistic Entropy in the Setting of Fuzzy Set Theory, *Information and Control*, 20, 301–312, 1972.

24. Anand, S.S., Patterson, D., Hughes, J.G., and Bell, D.A., Discovering Case Knowledge Using Data Mining, in *Second Pacific Asia Conference, PAKDD-98*, Australia, pp. 25–35, 1998.

25. Pal S.K. and Mitra S., *Neuro-Fuzzy Pattern Recognition: Methods in Soft Computing*, Wiley, New York, 1999.

26. Glass Identification Database, donated by Diagnostic Products Corporation. UML machine learning repository database.

12. A Neuro-Fuzzy Methodology for Case Retrieval and an Object-Oriented Case Schema for Structuring Case Bases and their Application to Fashion Footwear Design

Julie Main and Tharam S. Dillon

Abstract. Case based reasoning is a powerful mechanism for developing systems that can learn from and adapt past experiences to solve current problems. One of the main tasks involved in the design of case based systems is determining the features that make up a case and finding a way to index these cases in a case base for efficient and correct retrieval. The focus of this chapter is to look at how the use of fuzzy feature vectors and neural networks can improve the indexing and retrieval steps in case-based systems. The practicality of such a system is illustrated by application to the problem of fashion footwear.

12.1   A Brief Resumé of Case Based Reasoning

Case based reasoning (CBR) is a subset of the field of artificial intelligence that deals with storing past experiences or cases and retrieving relevant ones to aid in solving a current problem. CBR consists of: storing and indexing cases so that the appropriate ones are retrieved; retrieval of the appropriate case; and then adapting the retrieved case to help solve the current problem case. Problems remain with the case based approach both in deriving efficient characteristics for indexing and with the retrieval methods used for recovering the past case(s). There are several main types of retrieval that have been traditionally used in case based systems (see Chapter 1 and references [1,4,5,6,8]). The simplest way of retrieving cases is using a nearest neighbor search. A nearest neighbor search looks for those cases stored in memory that have the greatest number of characteristics that are the same as the current problem. The weighting of characteristics used has to be determined by the implementer. It is frequently difficult to decide which characteristics of a case are more important than the others, in that they contribute more to the successful outcome of a particular case.

Inductive approaches to case retrieval use learning algorithms to determine which characteristics of cases are most important in the retrieval of those cases. Inductive approaches are often better at achieving correct weightings than the weightings used in nearest neighbour search, but inductive indexing methods have their own drawbacks. One problem is that a large number of cases are required for deriving satisfactory weightings for the attributes of the cases. Another is that not all cases are determined by the same order of importance of their characteristics. For example, one case may be primarily determined by three particular characteristics and those characteristics may have little or no importance in determining the outcome of another case. Knowledge based approaches to the retrieval of cases use domain knowledge to determine the characteristics that are important for the retrieval of a particular case, for each individual case. In other words, a case is indexed in this type of approach by the features that are important in determining that case's success or failure. This is a good method for case indexation because it is efficient in retrieving the correct case as the cases can be stored in a hierarchical fashion, thus limiting the cases to be searched. Unfortunately, to implement this type of indexing system, a large amount of domain knowledge must be available, acquired and applied to the cases.

There is obviously room for improvement as all of these retrieval methods have their limitations. The authors believe that the use of neural networks for indexing and retrieval and, further, the use of fuzzy feature vectors for the representation of inputs to the network is an important alternative to the other, more traditional, methods.

12.2   Representation of Features

The features that define a case and index that case in a case base can be of a number of different types which all must be represented in different ways. What follows is a brief summary of each input type, how it may be represented and an example of each type.

Boolean: Boolean data, or the type of variables that can be true or false, are needed to represent factors of a case that can be present or absent, true or false. For example, a person could have a car or not have a car. This could be represented by a Boolean variable has-car.

Continuous: An example of continuous data is an interest rate. Such a value could be 7%, 8% or 9%. It can be 8.5%, 7.11% or 6.976%. Hence, the representation of this type of data will be a decimal number with any number of decimal places.

Multi-valued: Multi-valued data can have several different yet deterministic values. An example of a multi-valued variable could be car-colour. Car-colour, for example could be white, red, blue or green. There are a number of different types of multi-valued variables that can be distinguished. The first of these types is interval data. Interval data can take a number of different values, for instance w, x, y, z and these values have two conditions upon them; that $w < x < y < z$ and that the intervals between the values are the same, i.e. that $x - w = y - x = z - y$. Ordinal data is similar but has only one of the above conditions. The data must still be ordered: $w < x < y < z$; however $x - w$ does not necessarily equal $z - y$. Finally nominal data values have no relationships between them. Car-colour above is an example of a nominal data type as we do not say for example that $white < red < blue$. This creates a further problem for the use of nearest neighbor search as it uses a distance vector to determine the closeness of match as that implies that it uses interval data.

Fuzzy: Perhaps the most interesting type of data encountered is fuzzy data. It is best explained by an example. The height of a person can be very short, short, average, tall or very tall. If we have to classify actual data into these five ranges of values we have to determine which values fit into each category and this is a problem as values can be considered to be between groups or in more than one group. A person of 7 foot we could easily say was very tall and likewise a person of 4 foot, very short. When it comes to a value of 5 foot, is that short or very short? what about 5 foot 1 inch?, 5 foot 2 inches?. What is the boundary between short and very short? A large number of the features that characterize cases frequently consist of linguistic variables which are best represented using fuzzy feature vectors. A common definition of a fuzzy feature is given below.

Definition. Let T be a complete linguistic set, which provides a fuzzy partitioning of the domain of the measured attribute. Then $\forall t \in T$, a membership function μ_t is defined as scalar values, $\mu_t(Null) = 0$ and the range of μ_t is the interval $[0, 1]$. Then the fuzzy attribute is given by the two tuple $\langle t, \mu_t(v) \rangle$ where v is defined over a measurement space $\{v\}$.

We believe that the previous case based indexing methodologies, in not allowing the use of fuzzy features, suffer from a major deficiency.

12.3 Case Retrieval

Let F be the feature space with n dimensions $F_1, .., F_n$ i.e. $F = F_1 \times .... \times F_n$, where F_i could be taken from binary, real, discrete or fuzzy. Furthermore the discrete values could be interval, ordinal or nominal.

A case c belonging to a finite case base C (i.e., $c \in C$) is represented by a vector $[f_1, ...f_n]$ in which f_i belongs to F_i and is given by some measurement process.

The general problem of case retrieval can be stated as a general query where given a query case q with feature vector $[f_1^q, ...f_n^q]$ find the subset C_s of similar cases $c^1, ..., c^m$ from the case base C where $C_s \subseteq C$.

This statement of the case retrieval problem presupposes a clarification of the idea of similar cases, based upon a notion of similarity. There are a number of possible approaches to defining similarity including the use of a binary relation between objects from the case base C, a measurement of the degree of similarity and a distance measure. The distance measure is widely used in nearest neighbor techniques for case retrieval, but is considered inappropriate in our problem statement because we allow for ordinal and nominal data in addition to interval data. If we think of binary relations as a special case of similarity measures with only binary values, then we can concentrate on the notion of similarity measures.

The similarity measure $S1M(a, b)$ characteristics the degree of similarity between two cases $a = [f_1^a, ..., f_n^c]$ and $b = [f_1^b, ..., f_n^b]$ ranges over some interval I; such that

$$S1M : F \times F \to I$$

An additional aspect in defining the notion of similarity in CBR is the importance given to particular feature when carrying out a retrieval. This can be expressed in terms of a weight associated with the different dimensions of the weight vector. However, it is quite likely that when carrying out different queries a different importance may be assigned to the different dimensions of the weight vector.

One could think of the subset of similar cases C_s as belonging to different similarity classes that are defined as fuzzy sets drawn from the set C. The cardinality, number and kind of similarity class would of course vary depending on the level, desired closeness and context of the retrieval.

If one had only one type of feature as dimensions of the feature vector, i.e., all the features were real or all the features were fuzzy, it is more possible to develop an explicit expression for the notion of similarity. However, in our problem statement, the different feature vector dimensions should be allowed to be drawn from different types of features, and therefore it is difficult to define an explicit mapping.

One could, therefore, characterize the retrieval process as defining a relationship R between the feature space and the similarity classes C_s.

An implicit similarity measure which is able to deal with such diverse types of feature dimensions is a multilayer feedforward neural network with backpropagation learning.

Now if we designated each dimension of our feature vector f by one or more input nodes, and treated the outputs as the similarity classes C_s, we can train the network using the previously available cases in the case base C. Then on presenting the feature vector $[f_1^q, ..., f_2^q]$ to the neural network it would provide the required mapping to the output similarity classes $C_{s1}, ..., C_{sm}$.

Note that the neural network would automatically learn the importance given to each dimension, of the feature vector and develop the required weightings accordingly.

12.4 Neural Networks for Case Retrieval

After considering numerous retrieval methods from the nearest neighbor, inductive and knowledge-guided approaches to case retrieval, and comparing them to the retrieval capabilities of neural networks, we decided that neural networks would best satisfy the retrieval problem in our system.

The benefits of neural networks for retrieval include the following: essentially case retrieval is the matching of patterns, a current input pattern (case) with one or more stored patterns or cases. Neural networks are very good at matching patterns. They cope very well with incomplete data and the imprecision of inputs, which is of benefit in the many domains, as sometimes some portion is important for a new case while some other part is of little relevance.

To use neural networks for case retrieval presents some problems of its own. In the system described shortly, over 400 cases are contained in the case base. It is impractical that a single neural network be expected to retrieve a single case from hundreds of possible cases. The size of the network would be too big and retrieval would be slow. Therefore we suggest that such a large number of cases should be grouped into like types, firstly at a high-level and then each of those high level groups into further and more detailed sub-groups. This means that one neural network can be used to classify all the cases into the highest-level classes. For each of those high-level classes, a further neural network will be used to divide the cases in that class into its sub-classes. This is repeated for each sub-class until the lowest level sub-classes are reached.

Domains that use the CBR technique are usually complex. This means that the classification of cases at each level is normally non-linear and hence that for each classification a single-layer network is not sufficient and a multi-layered network is required [2]. Therefore, for the system described later in the chapter, three-layered networks, i.e. with one hidden layer, are used at each level to determine the classification [7,10]. The use of a three-layered network allows the networks to build their own internal representation of the inputs and determine the best weightings.

As it is known how each particular case is classified into its classes and subclasses, supervised learning is taking place. In other words because the input features and the output goal are provided, a teacher can be said to be training the network, hence 'supervised' as opposed to 'unsupervised' learning is taking place with the neural network.

The next step from here is to define the learning algorithm that is used to determine changes in weights during training. Taking into account the use of multilayer networks and supervised learning, the use of the backpropagation algorithm for learning is an obvious choice.

12.5 Neural Network Issues

12.5.1 Structuring the Features of Classes

The determination of the features that are important in the classification of cases into each class is a major knowledge engineering task. For example, to determine the features that should be used as inputs into the highest-level neural network we had to look at the classes into which the super-class is to be divided, and how the cases in each of those sub-classes differ from each other.

Distinguishing these features is not easy. If it were, we could easily construct rules to do the classification. Determining the correct features involves looking at the cases, seeing the major differences between them, and using these features to attempt to successfully train a network. When a network learns the input patterns to give a low sum of errors, then the features we have determined are correct. If there are patterns that this network could not classify, we need to add new features that would distinguish between these cases. For example, sometimes the input values to a neural network are the same for cases in more than one output class. When this occurs, obviously there is a difference between these cases that the attributes defined have not captured.

It is still helpful when the networks do not train successfully as the cases that were not learned lead us to distinguishing important features that were previously undetected. Once the additional features have been determined, the input patterns for the neural network need to be modified to include the additional attributes and the networks retrained. This training and testing cycle continues until all the networks have low error rates.

12.5.2 Hierarchy of Classes

Creating the hierarchy of classes is another significant task. Each class (except the lowest level) has to be divided into sub-classes, and at the lowest level instances (particular designs) may have to be attached to the appropriate sub-classes.

In each layer of classification, the division is not clear cut. For each class there is more than one way of subdividing the class. The desired classification is the one in which the cases that are retrieved most closely match the problem specification and these cases in the class will be useful in the design problem. Therefore design of the class structure for the system has to be carried out in a way that divides cases into groups that are similar conceptually and from a design perspective. It is never possible in most domains to arrive at a definitive solution. However, it is possible that in the majority of cases the class hierarchy will group the cases usefully.

12.6   Meta-Control Strategy

To control the reasoning process a meta-control strategy needs to be decided upon. Rules were a possibility as were methods, but it was believed that the most appropriate strategy for this system was to use daemons attached to slots within the objects. Thus, not classical objects but objects as described by Dillon and Tan [3] were used. Rules combined with calls to the neural networks would be able to control the reasoning process; however, they are deficient in their lack of a structuring facility. They make modification and addition to the system difficult as it involves comprehensive restructuring of the rules. Using methods associated with the objects was also a possibility and this overcomes the rule's modularity problem. Methods ensure encapsulation and aid in the ease in which the system may be adapted and maintained.

Daemons were chosen, however, as not only are they encapsulated within the objects, but the meta-control strategy is more flexible, and control is passed down the hierarchy as the system narrows down the possible classification through the class–sub–class hierarchy. To actually use these slots and daemons for the retrieval process, the following occurs: firstly, a slot in the highest-level class ('shoe') is changed, and this sets off the daemon attached to the if-changed part of the slot. The daemon that is set off calls the highest-level neural network (external to the object). This network returns a value that determines which sub-class the current specification is best classified in. On receipt of this information, the daemon changes a slot in the appropriate sub-class and the process repeats again. The slot that is changed in the sub-class likewise sets off a daemon which calls a lower-level network. This continues until the lowest-level sub-classes are reached.

Once the cases have been classified as members of particular low-level sub-classes, simple rules are used to display the relevant cases attached to that sub-class. If the low-level category still contains a reasonably large number of cases, but not enough for a further classification, simple rules could be used to retrieve only the best cases. In such a situation where there are a number of cases that cannot be divided into smaller groups, the cases tend to be very similar, with very little variation between them.

12.7   An Object Memory Model to Represent Cases and Case Schema for Description of the Logical Structure of a Case Base

The next question that arose is how the cases would be represented for storage. As instances of cases can frequently be divided into classes and sub-classes and each case is an instance of a class, an object-oriented representation is a good solution. Particular cases can be represented as objects, being instances of particular classes.

Groupings can be represented as sub-classes and every sub-class or individual object is a division of a super-class of cases. Conceptual modelling of this domain as outlined in Dillon and Tan [3] can be carried out. This leads to the important ideas of a *class case* and *instance case*, where a class case consists of a collection of instance cases which share some characteristics. In more complex domains, we may have cases that consist of components of other cases. Again such composite cases can be represented using the aggregation or composition facilities in object-oriented systems.

In addition there may be association relationships between one class case and another. The object-oriented representation allows a structuring facility within the case base, through the use of the different relationships, namely

(a) ISA relationship;
(b) composition relationship; and
(c) association relationship.

This structuring facility allows one to organize the case base into a logical structure which will help with search through the case base. This structuring facility will lead to a case schema description which is an object-oriented conceptual model that describes the logical organization of the case base.

This case schema description is the analog of a schema for a database. It is important that we move towards a structured case base with a case schema description. This move would be analogous in moving from a purely record-oriented database consisting of a single file (or table) to one that is organized according to a better logical structure such as a relational database with several tables representing entities and relationships or an object-oriented database with several classes and relationships. This structuring facility will be critical for large case bases.

12.8 Application to Fashion Footwear Design

12.8.1 Background

As early as 3700 BC the ancient Egyptians wore sandals made of plant fibers or leather. Most civilizations since then have made and worn some type of foot covering either as protection or decoration. Although people have made footwear for thousands of years, it was only in the mid-1800s with the invention of Howe's sewing machine and more specialist footwear manufacturing equipment that the mass production of shoes in factories started. From this time on there has been a growing desire to reduce the cost of manufacture by using components across various styles and streamlining production. Starting with the move away from bespoke footwear (the individual making of a pair of shoes where a person would order a pair of shoes for themselves and an individual last[1] would be made on which to create this shoe) to the use of standardized lasts (to make multiple pairs of the same style for the general public), component and tool reuse has now become essential for today's mass production.

---

[1] A last is a form, shaped like a foot, on which shoes are made.

It is not hard to understand why. Looking at some of the development costs of shoes it becomes obvious why there is a need to minimize pre-production and tooling-up costs. In creating a ladies' fashion shoe in the late 20th century there are many costs involved in creating a new design, even before reaching the stage of volume production (see Appendix).

To give an estimate of how much these pre-production or tooling-up costs contribute to the cost of an item we can specify the minimum number of pairs needed, using each tool, to make it worthwhile producing it. To make it cost effective the tooling-up costs need to be no more than 10% of the wholesale cost of the shoe. The minimum pairing to be sold before creating the following tools is shown in Table 12.1.

Table 12.1. Pairings to justify volume production

Sole molds:	
Injection molded PVC-nitrile rubber	200,000 pairs over 2–3 years
Thermoplastic rubber	20,000 pairs over 1 season
Polyurethane	10,000 pairs over 1 season
lasts:	
Minimum run of 30 pair of lasts 2,000 pairs over 1 season	
knives:	
Minimum set of metal clicking knives 1,000 pairs over 1 season	

These figures are hard to achieve, especially in an isolated country such as Australia where the consumer base is small. As soon as large runs of any item occur it becomes cheaper to source the goods in a country with a lower labor rate. Therefore, if large pairings are needed but cannot be obtained on individual items, tool and mold reuse becomes vital.

12.8.2 Component and Tool Sharing

There are many different ways that components and tools can be shared between styles in the footwear manufacturing area (Fig. 12.1 shows some of these).

Increasing the drive for component reuse in the ladies' fashion footwear domain is the way fashions change from season to season, and even mid-season. Fashion trends tend to have a cyclic behavior, in that a fashion 'look' will often go 'out' and a number of years later make another appearance. Another factor in women's fashion is its diversity. Even within a single trend there are a multitude of variations. Customers usually want something that is up to date, but a little different, or a little better than the other shoes on the market.

In a company that produces women's fashion shoes there are hundreds of designs produced each year and a designer forgets all but a few of the key designs in a rela-

Lasts

Sole Molds

Clicking Knives

Materials

Fig. 12.1. Some types of component and tool reuse in footwear designs.

tively short span of time. Thus, when a fashion trend makes a second (or third) appearance, or when a designer wants to reuse parts of existing designs, the previous designs have been forgotten and the new shoes are redesigned from scratch. This forgetting and starting over procedure is a problem that, if overcome, could not only increase the number of parts reused, but could lead to a faster design stage and also to the input of a wider variety of ideas than the designer has access to at that time.

To address this problem we designed a CBR system that stores the past shoe designs and retrieves a number of designs that are close to a design specification that the designer inputs. The output from this system is a set of previous designs that most closely approximate the desired design. From these designs most importantly we can determine as many components for reuse as possible and through adaptation adapt the design to use components from other designs to make up for any discrepancies between the retrieved designs and the desired designs.

It is of course impossible always to adapt and reuse. Fashion styling is such that new parts frequently have to be made but there are also often parts that are able to be reused. The more components and tools that can be shared between styles, the lower the tooling-up costs. While it was indicated above that the maximum that tooling-up costs should contribute to the cost of a shoe was 10% of the wholesale cost, sharing parts can push down the tooling-up costs to a more desirable 0.5%.

12.9   A CBR to Maximize Reuse

The type of system we set out to create was an intelligent knowledge based system that would retrieve design specifications and provide lists of the components that could be reused and adaptation suggestions. It is primarily for standardizing components across styles and reducing pre-production costs [10]. What we were not trying to achieve was a CAD/CAM design package. There are other excellent footwear-specific systems for doing that. We are not providing a tool for designing at the lower level of patterns, lasts and molds, such as these, but rather a complementary pre-manufacturing system for the higher-level design including the identification of possible common or standard parts.

12.9.1   Case Base Creation

There were two very distinct components of knowledge available to create a case based reasoner, both of which had to be used together to determine the required solution. These were:

- The large collection of previously existing designs. To create a case base for Main Jenkin Pty Ltd, a Melbourne-based footwear manufacturer, we needed their previous designs with descriptive attributes as well as the lists of components composing each design.
- The expertise of footwear designers to classify, analyze and provide adaptation rules.

Cases include two components:

- Their design feature description by which they are indexed and retrieved.
- Their technical description including the components and manufacturing techniques needed for production.

12.9.2   The Object-Oriented Memory Model for Shoe Design

The initial structuring of the domain was carried out manually. Some designs were so similar that we felt it was best to group these designs together. Further combining of similar groups created a hierarchical structure incorporating all designs. Although the hand grouping of cases is not really desirable for large case bases it was an initial solution that has worked well. To apply this system to other manufacturers or other types of goods, it would be better to apply an automated solution. The best way of determining the structure of the domain is still being refined.

When it came to determining how cases would be represented for storage and organized in memory, a number of factors had to be taken into account. As the shoes are divided into larger and smaller groups in a hierarchy and the lowest-level groups consist of individual designs, it emerged that an object-oriented representation was the best solution. Particular shoe designs could be represented as objects, being instances of particular classes. Groupings such as 'sandals' could be represented as sub-classes with every sub-class or individual object as a division of the super-class of shoes.

Individual shoes could then be attached statically to the lowest-level classes in the hierarchy to be easily retrieved when the lowest sub-class to which the current input can be associated has been determined. The possible number of objects that can be attached to a sub-class is large, but it needs to be limited to a small number so that only the most relevant cases are retrieved. Each sub-class can have varying numbers of instance objects associated with it depending on how many cases are associated with it. This may range from as little as one to as many as 20 depending on the popularity of the type of design.

The actual creation of the hierarchy of classes was a significant task. Each class (except the lowest level) had to be divided into component sub-classes, and at the lowest level instances (particular designs) had to be attached to the appropriate sub-classes.

In each layer of classification, the division is not clear cut. For each class there is more than one way of subdividing that class. The super-class can be said to consist of the union of the instances contained in its sub-classes. This corresponds to the union type of inheritance [9].

The desired classification was the one in which the cases that are retrieved most closely match the problem specification and in which those retrieved cases in the class will be useful in the new shoe design. Therefore, design of the class structure for the system was carried out in a way that divided cases into groups that are similar from a design and conceptual perspective.

It is not possible in a domain such as footwear to arrive at a definitive solution. However, it is possible that in the majority of cases the class hierarchy will group the cases in a useful way.

12.10   Neural Networks in Retrieval for Shoe Design

For each classification a single-layer network is insufficient and a multi-layered network is required. Therefore, for the footwear design system, three-layered networks (i.e. with one hidden layer) were used at each level to determine the classification. The use of a three-layered network allowed the networks to build their own internal representation of the inputs and determine the best weightings.

As it is was known how each particular case was classified into its classes and sub-classes, supervised learning was to take place. In other words because of the use of multilayered networks and supervised learning, we chose to use the backpropagation algorithm for training the neural networks.

12.10.1 Features as Inputs to the Neural Networks

The determination of the features that are important in the classification of cases into each class was a major knowledge-engineering task, as explained earlier. For example, to determine the features that should be used as inputs into the highest-level neural network we had to look at the classes into which the super-class was divided, and how the cases in each of those sub-classes differed from each other.

Distinguishing these features is not easy in the case of the shoe design problem. If it were, we could easily construct rules to do the classification. Determining the correct features involved looking at the cases of previous designs, seeing the major differences between them, and using these features to attempt to successfully train a network. We then utilize the method described in Section 12.4, i.e. (i) when a network learned the input patterns to give a low sum of squared error, then the features we had determined were correct; (ii) if there were patterns that this network could not classify, we needed to add new features that would distinguish between these cases. Once the additional features had been determined, the input patterns for the neural network needed to be modified to include the additional attributes and the networks retrained. This training and testing cycle continued until all the networks had negligible error rates. While it would be possible to input all features into each network and let the neural network dismiss some features by giving them a low rating, we agreed it was better to eliminate those features of little importance. This was to minimize the number of case descriptors that had to be input by the user, and reduce the number of input nodes and therefore the size of the network.

12.11 Representation of Features for Shoe Design

The features that define a case and index that case in a case base can be of a number of different types which all must be represented in different ways. What follows is a number of actual features that had to be represented and what types they were.

Does the shoe have an open toe?
This can only be true or false so it was represented as a Boolean type. Boolean data values are needed to represent factors of a case that can be present or absent, true or false.

How much is the shoe open or cut out?
As this is best defined as a percentage it is represented as a continuous type. Such a value could be 7%, 8% or 9%. It can be 8.5%, 7.11% or 6.976%. Hence, the representation of this type of data will be a decimal number with any number of decimal places.

What is the toe shape? What degree of toe shape does this shoe have?
This has multiple values. As explained earlier, multi-valued data can have several different yet deterministic values. There are a number of different types of multi-valued variables that can be distinguished, namely interval, ordinal and nominal.

For ordinal data, the data must still be ordered: $w < x < y < z$; however, $x - w$ does not necessarily equal $z - y$. Degree of toe shape is an example of ordinal data as it can take the values *minimal, average, large and extreme*.

Finally nominal data values have no relationships between them. Toe shape above is an example of a nominal data type as we do not say, for example, that *round < chiselled < square.*

How high is the shoe? Is the footwear item a sandal, shoe, short boot or long boot?
This was represented as a fuzzy data type: perhaps the most interesting type of data encountered in the footwear domain. It is best explained by our example. The height of a shoe can be small (sandal), medium (shoe), high (short boot) or very high (long boot). If we have to classify actual data into these four ranges of values, we have to determine which values fit into each category. This is a problem as values can be considered to be between groups or in more than one group (Fig. 12.2) . A pair with an inside back height of 30 cm would be considered very high (a long boot) and likewise a pair with an inside back height of 5 cm would be considered medium (a shoe), and 10 cm high (a short boot). When it comes to a value of 7 cm, is that average or high? What about 8 cm or 9 cm? What is the boundary between a shoe and a short boot? A large number of the features that characterize shoe design cases frequently consist of linguistic variables which are best represented using fuzzy feature vectors.

When determining the features and the type of features of the cases we had the following criteria. Firstly, as far as the user is concerned, the number of properties that had to be defined should not be large, and the values of the properties were relevant to the shoe domain, not requiring any conversion for the computer to accept them. For example, values for toe shape are 'pointed', and 'chiseled'. These are both the terms used by the designers and also what is input into the system making the system accessible for designers. Most importantly the features and their characterization had to be accurate and produce the desired outcomes of retrieving cases that were similar to the desired case.

12.11.1 Fuzzy Representation

As was detailed above the inside back height of a shoe can be classified as very high (a long boot), high (a short boot), medium (a shoe) or low (a type of sandal), but some shoes will not fit into the crisp separations of categories. If a shoe has a height of 7 cm we want to represent that it is partly a shoe and partly a boot.

This can be represented for input to the neural network by using four attributes: 'low', 'medium', 'high' and 'very high'. Each shoe would have a value for each of these four variables. A low shoe (e.g. a mule) would have attributes with these values:

low: 1   medium: 0   high: 0   very high: 0

A long boot with a large inside back height would have the following:

low: 0   medium: 0   high: 0   very high: 1

A traditional shoe (of 5 cm) would have the following values:

low: 0   medium: 1   high: 0   very high: 0

This is straightforward for the instances that fall exactly into one of the main categories. However, for those cases that do not fit so nicely (e.g. the 7 cm case), we needed to define a function that determines the value for in-between cases.

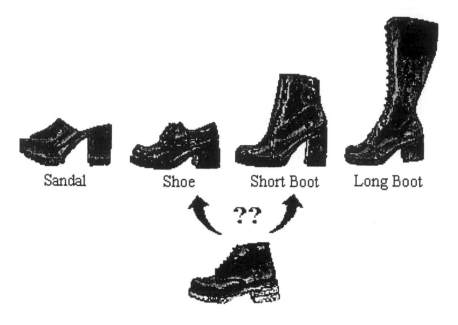

Fig. 12.2. A footwear item between height categories.

This function can take many forms, but as an initial function we used piecewise linear functions. The actual function to determine the values associated with the height of the shoe is shown in Fig. 12.3. In this case the values for the shoe with height 7 cm can be seen to be:

low: 0   medium: 0.6   high: 0.4   very high: 0

Fuzzy data can be represented using two or more functions. They do not have to be straight or continuous functions.

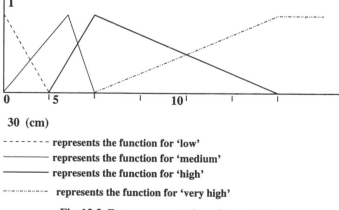

- - - - - - - represents the function for 'low'
————— represents the function for 'medium'
————— represents the function for 'high'
- - - - - - - represents the function for 'very high'

Fig. 12.3. Fuzzy representation of shoe height.

12.12   Case Adaptation

After retrieval of the best case we can modify the design (or do case adaptation) by searching individually for components to see if we can make up the parts where the retrieved design does not meet the required design from components from other designs.

12.12.1   Learning

Every time a new design was created, whether through the CBR system or completely independently by a footwear designer, the new design (assuming it is successful) had to be added to the case base, as every design that can be made increases the likelihood of finding components to reuse. Every time a case is added, the system 'learns' a little. By adding a case the CBR system may now be able to retrieve a design with more components to reuse than it could before the case was added.

To add a new case to the footwear design system, the case must first be classified or grouped as best possible with similar designs. This may involve some change to the hierarchical structure of the case base. Once the case has been classified, the neural networks used in its classification must be retrained. This is a simple matter assuming the normal case where new features are not needed for the classification. If the addition of a new case requires the addition of some new input to a neural network then a new neural network has to be created and trained.

12.13   Application to Other Industries

The problems encountered in the manufacture of footwear, as outlined in Section 12.8.1, are found in many other industries. Other fashion industries, such as clothing, would have similar tooling-up costs, similar problems and similar numbers of styles in a season. We believe the techniques we applied to obtain our solution for Main Jenkin could easily be applied to these other industries with comparable results.

12.14   Conclusion

This chapter describes the development of a CBR system for shoe design that maximizes reuse. The special features of the system include an object memory model, use of several genres of features including binary, continuous, discrete ordinal, discrete categoric, discrete interval and fuzzy linguistic. To carry out case retrieval, multi-level supervised neural nets were used. An important additional contribution is the introduction of an object- oriented case schema as the basis for structuring case bases.

The use of neural networks and fuzzy logic was found to be a useful means of retrieval. In testing, the retrieved cases were the closest match of the cases in the case base in 95% of tests carried out. In the other 5% the retrieved case was still useful for adaptation, though not the closest possible match.

Acknowledgement

The management and staff of Main Jenkin Pty Ltd provided essential domain expertise for which we would like to thank them.

Appendix: Tooling up and Other Pre-production Costs

Costs from the conception of design to creation of pullovers (trials)

Consultation	Stylist's time and labor
Styling costs	Pattern design and cutting
Manufacture of pullovers	Making of initial trials

Costs from the pullover to sample stage (for sales department)

Designer	Time and labor for the development of specifications
Sample lasts	Single sample size last creation
Sample patterns	Usually a metal pattern for hand-cutting samples
Sample materials	Samples are tried in various materials
Sample soles or heels	May include creation of sole or heel molds
Costings	For establishing wholesale and retail pricing

Selling in of the range

Mass samples	Creation of mass samples for sales representatives
Presentation of range	Sales representative's time and labor
Taking orders	Reception and entry of orders
Order compilation	Collation of orders and determination of sufficient sales volume of styles to justify their production

Costs for tooling-up for volume production

Production lasts	Right and left foot lasts for each size and half size and width fitting(s) required
Grading for knives and soles	Professional scaling up and down from sample to all sizes required
Production knives	Metal knives for each pattern piece in every size
Production sole or heel molds	Left and right foot sole/heel molds for each size required
Production dies and punches	Metal punches and cut-out knives if required
Sourcing of materials	Materials must be sourced at required costs and be available to meet delivery requirements

---

References

1. Ashley, K.D. *Modeling Legal Argument: Reasoning with Cases and Hypotheticals*. MIT Press, Cambridge, MA, 1990.
2. Beale, R. and Jackson, T. *Neural Computing: An Introduction*. Hilger, Bristol, 1990.
3. Dillon, T.S. and Tan, P.L. *Object-Oriented Conceptual Modeling*. Prentice-Hall, Australia, 1993.
4. Hammond, K.J CHEF: A Model of Case-Based Planning. In *Proceedings of the Fifth National Conference on Artificial Intelligence, AAAI-86*, Philadelphia, PA, 1986, Morgan Kaufmann, pp. 267–271.
5. Hennessey, D. and Hinkle, D. Applying Case Based Reasoning to Autoclave Loading. *IEEE Expert*. 7(5):21–26, 1992.
6. Kolodner, J. *Case Based Reasoning*. Morgan Kaufmann, San Mateo, CA, 1993.
7. Main, J., Dillon T.S. and Khosla R. Use of Neural Networks for Case-Retrieval in a System For Fashion Shoe Design. In *Proc. Eighth International Conference on Industrial and Engineering Applications of Artificial Intelligence and Expert Systems* (IEA/AIE 95), Melbourne, Australia, 1995, Gordon & Breach, pp. 151–158.
8. Riesbeck, C K. and Schank, R.C. *Inside Case based Reasoning*. Lawrence Erlbaum, Hillsdale, NJ, 1989.
9. Rahayu, W. and Chang E. A Methodology for Transforming an Object-Oriented Data Model into a Relational Database Design. In *Proceedings of the 12th International Conference on Technology Object-Oriented Languages and Systems*, Melbourne, pp. 99–115, 1993.
10. Main J., Dillon T.S. and Khosla R. Use of Fuzzy Feature Vector and Neural Nets for Case Retrieval in Case Based Systems. In *Proc. NAFIPS*, New York, pp. 438–443, 1996.
11. Main J. and Dillion T.S. Hybrid Case Based Reasons for Footwear Design. In *Proc. Int. Conf. on Case Based Reasoning*, Berlin, pp. 499–509, 1999.

13. Adaptation of Cases for Case Based Forecasting with Neural Network Support

Juan M. Corchado and B. Lees

Abstract. A novel approach to the combination of a case based reasoning system and an artificial neural network is presented in which the neural network is integrated within the case based reasoning cycle so that its generalizing ability may be harnessed to provide improved case adaptation performance. The ensuing hybrid system has been applied to the task of oceanographic forecasting in a real-time environment and has produced very promising results. After presenting classifications of hybrid artificial intelligence problem-solving methods, the particular combination of case based reasoning and neural networks, as a problem-solving strategy, is discussed in greater depth. The hybrid artificial intelligence forecasting model is then explained and the experimental results obtained from trials at sea are outlined.

13.1 Introduction

This chapter describes the application of a hybrid artificial intelligence (AI) approach to prediction in the domain of oceanography. A hybrid AI strategy for forecasting the thermal structure of the water ahead of a moving vessel is presented. This approach combines the ability of a case based reasoning (CBR) system for identifying previously encountered similar situations and the generalizing ability of an artificial neural network (ANN) to guide the adaptation stage of the CBR mechanism. The system has been successfully tested in real time in the Atlantic Ocean; the results obtained are presented and compared with those derived from other forecasting methods.

Research into AI has produced various hybrid problem-solving methods, which may be applied to give more powerful computer based problem-solving capabilities than may be obtained using purely algorithmic methods. The reason for the application of an AI approach is very often precisely because the nature of the problem to be addressed is such that no appropriate algorithm is either known or is applicable. For example, if the knowledge about a problem is incomplete or fuzzy, it may be difficult to select or to develop an algorithm or even an AI approach to solve it. It is in such situations where hybrid AI systems may be effective.

CBR systems have proved to be successful in situations where prior experience of solving similar problems is available. But the nature of a complex problem solving situation may be such that there are different aspects of the problem that may best be addressed through the application of several distinct problem-solving methodologies. This chapter focuses on the combination of CBR and ANNs as complementary methods to solve a forecasting problem.

The application of AI methods to the problem of describing the ocean environment offers potential advantages over conventional algorithmic data-processing methods. An AI approach is, in general, better able to deal with uncertain, incomplete and even inconsistent data. Neural network, case based and statistical forecasting techniques could be used separately in situations where the characteristics of the system are relatively stable [1]. However, time series forecasting, based on neural network or statistical analysis, may not provide sufficiently accurate forecasting capability in chaotic areas such as are found near a *front* (i.e. an area where two or more large water masses with different characteristics converge). This chapter presents a *universal* forecasting strategy, in which the term universal is taken to mean a forecasting tool which is able to operate effectively in any location, of any ocean.

This chapter shows how a hybrid system can solve the problem of forecasting the surface temperature of the ocean at certain distances ahead of a moving vessel. The CBR system is used to select a number of stored cases relevant to the current forecasting situation. The neural network retrains itself in real time, using a number of closely matching cases selected by the CBR retrieval mechanism, in order to produce the required forecasted values.

The structure of the chapter is as follows. First the integration of CBR and ANN problem-solving methods is introduced. Then a brief outline of work elsewhere on the integration of CBR and neural network methods is given. The application of a hybrid neural network case based approach for real-time oceanographic forecasting is presented. Finally, a summary of the experimental results obtained to date are presented, which indicates that the approach performs favorably in comparison with the use of statistical and neural network forecasting methods in isolation.

13.2 Hybrid Systems

The term *hybrid* refers to systems that consist of one or more integrated subsystems, each of which can have a different representation language and inference technique. The subsystems are assumed to be tied together semantically and influence each other in some way. The goal of hybrid system research includes the development of techniques to increase the efficiency and reasoning power of intelligent systems. For example, some of the work developed with the aim of increasing efficiency makes use of specialized reasoners strategically called by control or supervisor modules that decide which reasoning method to use at different times [2]. Hybrid systems are capable of addressing some practical problems that have been addressed with traditional AI approaches. From a fundamental perspective, hybrid systems may also give further insight into cognitive mechanisms and models [2].

Many researchers are investigating the integration of different AI approaches [3,4]. The issues under study range from fundamental questions about the nature of cognition and theories of computation to practical problems related to implementation techniques. There are many different directions in this research and several models for integration have been identified.

The three main models of integration of AI techniques that characterize the trends in the research in this area are the computational intelligent classification [5], the IRIS [6]and the classification of Medsker and Bailey [7].

13.2.1   The Computational Intelligent Classification

Bezdek [5] proposes a framework for thinking about the real goals of research and development in intelligent systems. This model focuses on different levels of integrated activities, systems, and AI technologies. Bezdek defines three levels of increasing complexity, from computational to artificial tasks and then to biological activities. In this model the artificial intelligent components are built on symbolic modules that add relatively small pieces of knowledge to computational processes and data, in order to get closer to biological intelligence. This model does not consider computational and AI systems '*intelligent*' by themselves and for Bezdek words such as learning must be very carefully used when applied to low levels of complexity. This is a general classification in which hybrid systems are seen as ways to extend the low-level computational intelligence techniques through the AI level toward the goal of modeling biological intelligence.

13.2.2   IRIS Classification

Soucek [6] developed the Integration of Reasoning, Informing and Serving (IRIS) model. This is an architecture that facilitates the combination of software, hardware and system levels present in any intelligent system. The aim of this methodology is to facilitate the design of systems using more efficient technologies, products and services to meet business needs. For Soucek, the development of a hybrid system requires the integration of different scientific disciplines including biology, cognitive psychology, linguistics, epistemology, and computer science.

The IRIS model identifies the need for 10 ingredients of integration:

- mixing of technologies (ANN, CBR, knowledge based systems, etc.);
- paradigms for integration;
- standard software modules;
- special languages;
- software development tools and environments;
- automated discovery such as interactive intelligent databases and interfaces;
- standard control and automation modules;
- case studies of working applications;
- concurrency-tools for developing and monitoring;
- signal-to-symbol transformations and pattern-to-category mappings.

This is not just a classification that describes mechanisms of interaction between AI models. It shows how AI models can be integrated within other computer technologies to create successful knowledge based systems.

13.2.3   The Classification of Medsker and Bailey

Medsker and Bailey [7] have defined five models of integration from a practical point of view: stand-alone models, transformational, loose coupling, tight coupling and full integration. This classification presents several ways of combining connectionist and symbolic models. The integration between models can be done depending on the problem to be solved and the data and knowledge available.

Stand-Alone model: This model combines intelligent system applications consisting of independent software components. Since the components do not interact in any way, the stand-alone model cannot be considered a real form of integration; it is only used to compare different AI models in order to learn more about them and about the problems to be solved.

Transformational model: This model is similar to the previous one. The difference is that in the transformational model, the system begins as one type and ends up as the other. For example an ANN can be used to identify trends and relationships among datasets and the results obtained with it could be used to develop a knowledge based system.

Loose coupling model: This is the first true form of integrating artificial intelligent systems. The application is composed of separate intelligent systems that communicate via data files. This model allows the interaction between systems with very different characteristics. Typical cases of this type are:

- *Pre-processors:* In this case an ANN could serve as a front-end that processes data prior to passing it on to a knowledge based system. Following the principles of this model an ANN can be used to perform data fusion, to remove errors, to identify objects and to recognize patterns. Then the knowledge based system can play the main role.
- *Post-processors:* In this case, for example, a knowledge based system can produce an output that is passed via a data file to an ANN. The knowledge based system can perform data preparation and manipulation, classify inputs, etc. and the ANN can then perform functions such as forecasting, data analysis, monitoring, etc.
- *Co-processors:* This type of integration involves data passing in both directions, allowing interacting and cooperative behavior between the ANN and the knowledge based system. Although not very often used, this approach has the potential for solving difficult problems such as incremental data refinement, iterative problem solving and dual decision making.
- *User interfaces:* An ANN can be used, for example, for pattern recognition to increase the flexibility of user interactions with knowledge based systems.

Tight coupling model: This model is similar to the previous one; however, here the information is passed via memory-resident data structures rather than external data files. This improves the interactive capabilities of tightly coupled models in addition to enhancing their performance. The sub-models of this approach are the four mentioned in the previous subsection: pre-processors, post-processors, co-processors and user interfaces. In this type of situation the implementation is more complex and the operation time is smaller than in the previous case.

Fully integrated models: Fully integrated models share data structures and knowledge representations. Communication between different components is accomplished via the dual nature of structures (symbolic and connectionist). Reasoning is accomplished either cooperatively or through a component designated as a controller. Several variations of fully integrated systems exist; for example, connectionist knowledge based systems are one of the most common varieties of this model. They rely on local knowledge representation, as opposed to the distributed representation of most ANNs, and reason through spreading activation. Connectionist knowledge based systems represent relationships between pieces of knowledge, with weighted links between symbolic nodes.

Each of the three classifications here presented considers the hybridization process from different points of view. The computational intelligence classification considers the hybridization of AI models as a way to obtain AI systems that are capable of simulating aspects of biological intelligence. The IRIS classification shows how AI systems should be integrated with other computational systems and with the environment and finally the classification proposed by Medsker and Bailey defines five different ways of combining connectionist and symbolic AI systems from a practical point of view.

13.3   Combining CBR Systems and Neural Networks

CBR systems have been successfully used in several domains: diagnosis, prediction, control and planning [8]. Although there are many successful applications based on just CBR technology, from an analysis of this type of system it appears that CBR systems can be successfully improved, combined or augmented [9] by other technologies. A hybrid CBR system may have a clearly identifiable reasoning process. This added reasoning process could be embedded in any of the stages that compose the CBR cycle. For example, the most common approaches to construct hybrid based CBR systems are as follows:

- The CBR may work in parallel with a co-reasoner and a control module activates one or the other, i.e.: ROUTER [9].
- A co-reasoner may be used as a pre-processor for the CBR system as happens in the PANDA system [9].
- A CBR may use the co-reasoner to augment one of its own reasoning processes [10].

The last approach is used in the majority of CBR hybrid systems. Hunt and Miles [9] have investigated areas where AI approaches (used as co-reasoners by this type of hybrid CBR based systems) are applied. Most early work in this area combined CBR systems with rule based reasoning systems, but the number of applications in which other AI techniques are combined with CBR systems is increasing continually and quickly, as has been reported by Medsker [2], Sun and Alexandre [11], and Lees [4].

CBR systems are flexible systems capable of using the beneficial properties of other technologies to their advantage; in particular, the interest here is in the advantages of combining CBR and ANN. During the last decade an increasing number of scientists have been researching into the hybridization of CBR systems and ANNs. Before reviewing this area it is necessary to clearly define when and where ANN can be used in this context.

ANNs are not especially appropriate for stepwise expert reasoning and their explanation abilities are extremely weak. Nevertheless their learning and generalization capabilities can be useful in many problems. Therefore they can only be used as part of CBR systems in those areas that do not involve knowledge explanation and reasoning. In particular, they can be used in areas involving knowledge generalization. Learning is a powerful feature of most ANNs, and learning forms an intrinsic part of many stages of the CBR cycle, so ANNs can be used to learn to retrieve the closest case to a particular situation, or in other words to learn to identify the closest matching case. For an ANN it is reasonably easy in most situations to learn new cases and to learn how to generalize (adapt) a case from a pool of cases.

CBR systems and ANNs are complementary techniques: ANNs deal easily (and normally) with numeric datasets whereas CBR systems deal normally with symbolic knowledge. Even when symbolic knowledge can be transformed into numeric knowledge and numeric into symbolic, by doing this there is always the risk of losing accuracy and resolution in the data and hence obtaining misleading results. Therefore a combination of CBR systems and ANNs may avoid transforming data and therefore gain precision. As mentioned before, generalization is a useful ability of most ANNs, but in many cases it is necessary to hold information about special cases, and this is a natural ability of CBR systems.

When CBR systems and ANN [3] are used together, the most common approach [12] is to hold the cases as an integral part of the ANN because CBR systems can successfully use them in the indexing and retrieval stages. For example, in the hybrid system created by Myllymaki and Tirri [12], cases are identified as neurons of an ANN. The CBR system uses Bayesian probabilistic reasoning and is implemented as a connectionist network (also called a belief network), which uses probability propagation to provide the theoretical explanation for the case-matching process. Cases are represented as neurons in the middle layer of the ANN in this particular model.

Becker and Jazayeri [13] have developed a hybrid system focused on design problems, in which cases are represented as neurons in the middle layer of an ANN and case retrieval is done with a hybrid structure. Thrift [14] uses an ANN with a backpropagation learning algorithm for case filtering; the ANN selects the most relevant cases from the case base depending on some constraints (input to the ANN). GAL [15] is based on a similar architecture, the difference being that GAL uses the prototype-based incremental principle, in which every class of objects is represented by the accumulation of relevant samples of the class and the modification of other class representations. Similar to a nearest neighbor algorithm, this ANN grows when it learns and shrinks when it forgets because only representative cases are kept.

INSIDE [16] and ARN2 [17] are very similar to GAL. In these systems, the neurons of the input layer of the ANN represent attributes, the nodes or neurons of the second layer correspond to prototypes (which are represented by n-dimensional vectors) and the neurons or nodes of the output layer represent classes. Each n-dimensional vector has an area of influence of a determined dimension. During learning the dimension of the areas of influence of the activated vector (prototype) is reduced if the ANN answer is wrong. Although INSIDE and ARN2 are very similar they differ in the methods that they use for learning the prototypes and adjusting their areas of influence.

The Prototype Based Indexing System (PBIS) [18] was developed with the aim of improving the performance of the ARN2 model by keeping both prototypical and non-prototypical cases. PBIS has the memory divided into two levels. The first level is the middle layer of the ARN2 ANN and contains prototypical cases. The second level is a flat memory in which similar cases are grouped together in regions. Each region with similar cases is connected to the closest prototype of the same class.

PBIS also contains a region to store boundary cases that fall into uncertain areas. When a new case is presented to the ANN the prototype with the highest output is selected, if only one class is activated. When several classes are activated, the memory zones associated with the activated prototypes are selected and the most similar case is retrieved from these memory zones. If none of the prototypes are activated the system searches for similar cases in the atypical memory area.

Quan et al. have developed an algorithm for neural network based analogical case retrieval [19]. This algorithm has been applied to industrial steam turbine design. Main et al. have investigated the use of fuzzy feature vectors and neural networks as a means of improving the indexing and retrieval steps in CBR systems [20].

PATDEX/2 is a CBR-ANN hybrid system in which the relationship between the CBR and the ANN is different from the previous models [21]. PATDEX/2 is a fault diagnosis system based on CBR technology. Cases are symptom vectors together with their associated diagnoses. In PATDEX/2, an ANN using a competitive learning algorithm is the core of the retrieval algorithm. The similarity measure is based on a matrix that associates the relevance of every symptom to every possible diagnosis. The weights of this matrix are learned and modified by the ANN: after each diagnosis, the weights of the matrix are updated depending on the success of the diagnosis.

Garcia Lorenzo and Bello Pérez use an ANN as a basis for calculating a measure of similarity between a new problem case and each stored candidate case [22]. The ANN provides a mechanism to retrieve cases using information that in other models would require a parallel architecture. The connection between both CBR and rule based reasoning mechanisms and high-level connectionist models has been investigated by Sun in the process of exploring the use of such models for approximate common-sense reasoning [3].

Agre and Koprinska propose a different type of relationship between the CBR and the ANN in their hybrid model, which combines a CBR system and a knowledge based ANN [23]. The CBR is applied only for the correction of the knowledge based ANN solutions that seems to be wrong. Potential corrections are carried out by matching the current situation against the cases that constitute the knowledge based ANN training dataset. Agre and Koprinska have shown that the performance of knowledge based ANNs (which are concerned with the use of domain knowledge to determine the initial structure of an ANN) can be considerably improved with the use of CBR systems.

Reategui et al. have been working on several hybrid ANN-CBR models and on general classifications of this type of system [12,24]. Basically their hybrids are composed of two separate modules: a CBR system and an ANN. Both modules work independently; the reasoning process is interleaved between them and both cooperate via a central control unit. In one of Reategui's experiments, while the ANN learns general patterns of use and misuse of credit cards, the CBR system keeps track of credit card transactions carried out for a particular card (thus different sets of cases are used by the neural network and the CBR system). The central control mediates answers given by the two separate mechanisms.

In the domain of medical diagnosis, Reategui et al. have used an integrated CBR-ANN approach [12]. The task of the neural network is to generate hypotheses and to guide the CBR mechanism in the search for a similar previous case that supports one of the hypotheses. The model has been used in developing a system for the diagnosis of congenital heart diseases. The hybrid system is capable of solving problems that cannot be solved by the ANN alone with a sufficient level of accuracy.

Liu and Yan have explored the use of a fuzzy logic based ANN in a case based system for diagnosing symptoms in electronic systems [25]. The aim of the hybrid system is to overcome the problems related to the descriptions of uncertain and ambiguous symptoms.

Corchado et al. have also investigated the combination of CBR systems and supervised ANN [10]. They have proposed an agent architecture for oceanographic forecasting in which the CBR agents and the ANN agents complement each other at different stages of the forecast. They have also developed a CBR model in which an ANN automates the adaptation of cases, to solve a forecasting problem with high syntactical (numerical) connotations.

Recently, several hybrid systems that combine CBR systems with Bayesian or belief networks have been presented. These systems integrate general knowledge with concrete knowledge from past situations. Aamòdt and Langseth present a knowledge -intensive CBR, where explanations are generated from a domain model consisting partly of a semantic network and partly of a Bayesian network [26]. Dingsoyr has also used Bayesian networks during the retrieval stage of CBR systems [27]. He uses the network to compute similarity metrics among cases. Shinmori shows that probabilistic models or Bayesian networks are suitable for modeling software-troubleshooting processes in today's computing environment [28]. He also uses such networks for case retrieval. Friese shows how Bayesian belief networks can be used to improve the Greek system, which is a well-developed knowledge-intensive CBR designed for problem solving and sustained learning [29]. In this case the Bayesian network is used to support the CBR problem solver by calculating the explanational arc weights.

Following the work of Medsker and Bailey and inspecting the type of hybridization used by the previously introduced authors [7], it may be appreciated that the two dominant models are *full integration*, in the form of a symbolic ANN, and a model in which both components of the hybrid system are *totally or partially coupled*. In the latter case, most of the hybrid systems use an ANN in the retrieval stage of the CBR cycle. In some systems both co-processors are controlled by a meta-system and in other cases both co-processors simply work in parallel doing independent tasks. The developers of the previously mentioned systems critically analyze the advantages and disadvantages of their models; in all cases the beneficial properties of the hybrids overcome their disadvantages. Studying this classification it is clear that there is a huge scope for investigating the combination of ANN and CBR systems. For example, different types of ANN can be used at different stages of the CBR life cycle to solve different problems.

ANNs have been used in the retrieval stage of a CBR system in situations in which there was no prior knowledge from constructing a k-NN (k-nearest neighbor) algorithm or a rule based system (RBS). Although the use of ANN for retrieving cases has been shown to be successful [20,30], it is not considered good practice if there is knowledge sufficient to build a k-NN or an RBS. Also the real time constraints imposed by the nature of some problems must be taken into consideration to define whether or not it is possible to afford the time overhead for the training of the ANN.

Although the creation of neuro-symbolic models requires the existence of prototypical cases and a certain amount of knowledge, almost any CBR system can be represented as a neuro-symbolic system in which the neurons are prototypical cases or RBS. The connections between neurons could be defined also by rules. The following sections show how a neuro-symbolic approach has been used to solve a complex oceanographic forecasting problem.

13.4 The Forecasting Problem

Oceans are dynamic habitats in which circulation is mainly driven by three external influences: (i) wind stress, (ii) heating and cooling, and (iii) evaporation and precipitation – all of which are, in turn, driven by radiation from the sun [31]. The ocean circulation is what determines the mixture of water masses with different properties (such as temperature) and the variation of these properties with time in a particular geographical location. A water mass (or province) can be defined as a body of water with a common formation history. Oceans are in a continual state of flux [32]. Taken together, this biophysical partitioning provides the descriptors of regional ecosystems or biogeochemical provinces, each with discrete boundaries and each having distinct flora and fauna. In each of these provinces, the water properties are moderately homogeneous and its variability can be described relatively easily. Our present knowledge of the ocean structure is still too weak to create a full model of its behavior. Oceans are dynamic systems, in which the water masses are influenced by so many factors that it is extremely difficult to create even a partial model of the ocean. Therefore to develop a universal system for forecasting the temperature of the water ahead of an ongoing vessel is complicated.

Forecasting the structure of the water in such conditions is a difficult task due to the nature and behavior of the ocean waters, the movement of which causes the water temperature to change in a complex manner [32].

The forecasting task in such a complex environment requires the use of both historical data and the most recent real-time data available, thus enabling the forecasting mechanism to learn from past experience in order to be able to predict, with sufficient confidence and accuracy, the values of desired parameters at some future point or points in time or distance.

Over the last few years researchers at the Plymouth Marine Laboratory (PML) and the University of Paisley have applied AI methods to the problem of oceanographic forecasting. Several approaches have been investigated; both supervised ANN [33] and unsupervised ANN [10] techniques have been investigated, as well as CBR and statistical techniques [10] with the aim of determining the most effective forecasting method. The results of these investigations suggest that, to obtain accurate forecasts in an environment in which the parameters are continually changing both temporally and spatially, an approach is required which is able to incorporate the strengths and abilities of several AI methods.

The problem of forecasting, which is currently being addressed, may be simply stated as follows:

- **Given:** a sequence of data values (which may be obtained either in real time or from stored records) relating to some physical parameter;
- **Predict:** the value of that parameter at some future point(s) or time(s).

The raw data (on sea temperature, salinity, density and other physical characteristics of the ocean) which are measured in real time by sensors located on the vessel consist of a number of discrete sampled values of a parameter in a time series. These data values are supplemented by additional data derived from satellite images, which are received weekly. In the present work the parameter used is the temperature of the water mass at a fixed depth. Values are sampled along a single horizontal dimension, thus forming a set of data points.

13.5   Hybrid CBR–Neural Network System

This section presents the hybrid system developed in this investigation. The hybrid system is composed of a CBR system and a *radial basis function* ANN. It is a universal forecasting model. *Universal* in this context means the ability to produce accurate results anywhere in any ocean at any time. The system is capable of adapting itself in real time to different oceanographic water masses.

To facilitate the understanding of the model this section focuses on the forecasting of the temperature of the water up to 5 km ahead. The concepts here presented are valid for longer distances; the metrics, dimensions of the vectors and some algorithms have been adapted for such longer distances as will be shown in the following sections.

Fig. 13.1 shows the top-level relationships between the processes comprising the hybrid CBR system. The cycle of operation is a derivation from the CBR cycle of Aamodt and Plaza [34], and of Watson and Marir [35]. In Fig. 13.1, shadowed boxes (together with the dotted arrows) represent the four steps of a typical CBR cycle; the arrows represent data coming in or out of the case base (situated in the center of the diagram) and the text boxes represent the result obtained after each of the four stages of the cycle. Solid lines indicate data flow and dotted lines show the order in which the processes that take part in the life cycle are executed.

In the operational environment, oceanographic data (e.g. sea-surface temperature) is recorded in real time by sensors in the vessels; also, satellite pictures are received on a weekly basis. The satellite pictures are stored in a centralized database. A problem case is generated every 2 km using the temperatures recorded by the vessel during the last 40 km and consists of a vector of 40 temperature values, recorded at 1 km intervals. The problem case is used to retrieve the k most closely matching cases from the case base. Experiments carried out with datasets recorded in the Atlantic Ocean (cruise AMT 4) have shown that having 40 data values at 1 km intervals was appropriate for the problem case [36].

Each of the cases stored in the case base is defined by an input vector $(I_1, I_2, ..., I_{40})$ of water temperature values, a forecast value F (representing the value of the temperature of the water 5 km ahead of the point at which I_{40} was recorded) and several parameters defining its importance (how many times it has been retrieved, etc.) (refer to Section 13.6.3). Both F and I_k must be recorded by a vessel following a straight line.

The k retrieved cases are adapted by a neural network during the reuse phase to obtain an initial (proposed) forecast. Through the revision process, the proposed solution is adjusted to generate the final forecast using error limits, which are calculated taking into account the accuracy of previous predictions. Learning (retaining) is achieved by storing the proposed forecast, modifying some parameters of the cases (as will be shown in the following sections) and storing knowledge (ANN weights and centers) acquired by the ANN after the training and case adaptation.

While Fig. 13.1 presents the basic concepts of CBR as a cycle of operations, Fig. 13.2 shows the detailed information flow throughout the CBR cycle and in particular how the ANN has been integrated with the CBR operation to form a hybrid forecasting system. Data acquisition (top of Fig. 13.2) is through sensors on board the vessel (in real time) and from satellite pictures (which are received weekly). The data is indexed so it can be transformed into cases and stored in the case base as required.

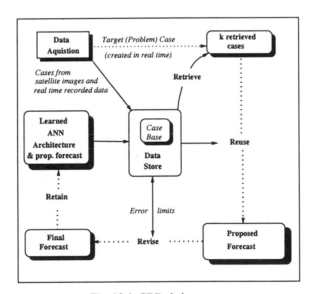

Fig. 13.1. CBR skeleton.

To obtain an accurate forecast in the vast and complex ocean it is imperative to use up- to-date satellite data. Fortunately, current technology now enables detailed satellite images of the oceans to be obtained on a weekly basis. The relevant data from these images is appropriately indexed for fast retrieval in a centralized database. Data is also acquired in real time as a vessel moves across the ocean; average sea surface temperatures are recorded every kilometer. Satellite images are used in this particular

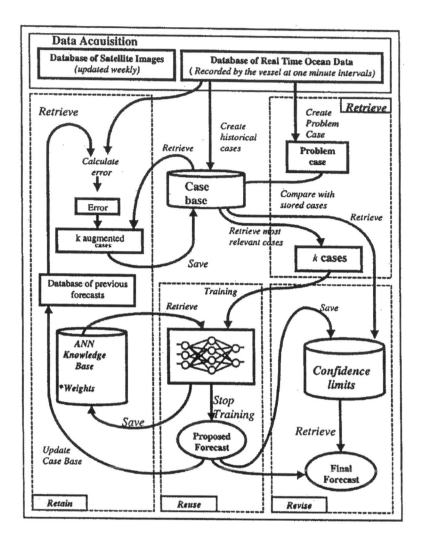

Fig. 13.2. Hybrid system control flow.

context because from them can be obtained the temperature of the water of the ocean in the form of thermal vectors. These thermal data vectors can be transformed into cases and stored in the case base (refer to Sections 13.5.1 and 13.5.3).

During the retrieval phase, the k cases that most closely match the problem case are selected from the case base using k-NN matching algorithms. These k cases are then used to compute the forecast value of the temperature of the ocean a constant distance ahead of the vessel. The set of k retrieved cases is used in the reuse phase of the CBR life cycle to train an ANN, the output of which is the proposed forecast (see Fig. 13.2). The radial basis function ANN is retrained in real time to produce the forecast; during this step the weights and the centers of the ANN, used in the previous prediction, are retrieved from the knowledge base and adapted, based on the new training set. The goal of the ANN is to extract a generalized solution from the k cases (refer to Section 13.5.5).

In the revised phase the final forecast is obtained by modifying the proposed forecast taking into account the accuracy of the previous predictions. Each case has an associated average error which is a measure of the average error in the previous predictions for which this case was used to train the ANN. The error limits are calculated by averaging the average error of each of the k cases used to train the ANN to produce the current forecast. Learning is achieved in two different ways:

1. after *retraining the ANN*, by saving the internal structure of the ANN, i.e. the weights and centers. The ANN is continuously retrained and its internal structure is saved after each forecast is made;
2. by modifying some of the constituent parameters of the cases (as will be shown later).

A database records all the forecasts done during the last 5 km and all the cases used to train the ANN to obtain these forecasts. These forecasts are eventually compared with their corresponding real values of the temperature of the water (there is a 5 km lag between the point at which the forecast is made and the point for which the forecast is made). The forecasting errors are then used to modify relevant features of the cases, to prune the case base and to determine error limits, etc.

13.5.1 Case Representation

A case represents specific knowledge about a particular situation. A case is created to represent the 'shape' of a set of temperature values (a vector of values) and the most representative characteristics of this vector. Each case is composed of the fields listed in Table 13.1.

A 40 km profile has been empirically found to give sufficient resolution (using representative datasets) to characterize the problem case (and the input vector I_k). The parametric features of the different water masses that comprise the various oceans vary substantially, not only geographically, but also seasonally. Because of these variations it is therefore inappropriate to attempt to maintain a case base with cases from all the water masses of the ocean. Furthermore:

- There is also no need to refer to cases representative of all the possible orientations that a vessel can take in a given water mass. Vessels normally proceed in a given pre-defined direction. So only cases corresponding to that particular orientation are normally required at any one time.
- Recall also that the aim is to create a forecasting system which is able to adapt to the changes in the ocean environment, in time and space.

With the above considerations, the strategy adopted was to maintain a centralized database in which all the thermal data tracks and satellite pictures, available for all the water masses in the world, could be stored, in a condensed form; and then only retrieve from it (transformed into cases and stored in the case base) the data relevant to a particular geographical location.

Table 13.1. Case attributes

IDENTIFICATION	DESCRIPTION
Identification	Unique identification: positive integer number (between 0 and 64,000)
Input vector I_k	A 40 km temperature input profile $(I_1, I_2, \ldots, I_k$, where $k = 40)$ representing the temperature of the water between the present position of the vessel and its position 40 km back
Output value: F	a temperature value representing the water temperature 5 km ahead of the present position of the vessel
Source	Data source from which the case was obtained (satellite image or data track). Its acquisition date, time and geographical coordinates identify each source e.g.: SAT1501981030500-4910 i.e. a satellite picture taken on 15 January 1998, at 10:30, the top left corner having latitude 50.00° and longitude −49.10°
Time	Time when recorded. Although giving some redundancy of information, this field helps to ensure fast retrieval
Date	Date when the data was recorded (incorporated for the same reasons as for the previous field)
Geographical position	The geographical coordinates of the location where the value I_{40} (of the input vector) was recorded
Retrieval	The number of times the case has been retrieved to train the ANN (a non-negative integer)
Orientation	An integer $x(1 \leq x \leq 12)$ corresponding to the approximate direction of the data track, as indicated in Fig. 13.3
Retrieval time	Time when the case was last retrieved
Retrieval date	Date when the case was last retrieved
Retrieval location	Geographical coordinates of the location in which the case was last retrieved
Average error	The average error in all forecasts for which the case has been used to train the ANN

PML maintains a database composed of thousands of data profiles recorded during the last decade, together with satellite images. The database is updated weekly. For the purpose of the current research a new database has been constructed for a region of the Atlantic Ocean between the UK and the Falkland Islands (between latitude 50 to -52 and longitude 0 to -60). This database is a subset of the main PML database.

13.5.2   Case Indexing Mechanism

Time is a very important factor in real-time forecasting. Therefore the indexing mechanism used to retrieve both the data stored in the database and the cases in the case base must be fast and reliable. Also the selection mechanism for the creation of cases from data stored in the database must be accurate. Research has also shown in the IN-RECA project that very large case bases have poor performance results [37]. Therefore only representative cases must be created and stored. This fact, together with the need for creating them within a small period of time, makes a good indexing algorithm essential.

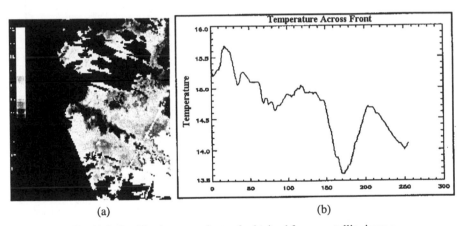

(a)   (b)

Fig. 13.3. Satellite image and a track obtained from a satellite image.

There are several approaches for organizing the information held by a case base. Commonly used approaches are:

- *flat memory system*, which requires a large memory when the case base become large;
- *shared-features network*, which has a hierarchical case organization and requires a rigid network structure; hard to modify once the case base is in use and cases are added into the case base.

The complexity and the quantity of the data with which this system is dealing require a simple but rigid indexing mechanism in order to minimize the retrieval time of the cases.

The relevant cases to be retrieved are those geographically close to the position of the vessel. The cases stored in the case base at any one time are always geographically close to the position of the vessel. This is enforced by the algorithms in charge of retrieving data from the database and storing it in the case base. These algorithms also give priority to the retrieval of the most recent cases.

Because more refined spatial and temporal selection is required a simple indexing structure has been implemented which groups cases, taking into account their geographical proximity and secondly their temporal proximity. Cases within the same geographical region defined by a square of side $0.1°$ (10 km) are stored together. This group is divided again into smaller units, each of which has been recorded in the same week.

Table 13.2. Rules for case construction

Classif.	Description
1	Cases within an area delimited by a circle of radius P km centered on the present position of the vessel i.e. $P = X + (X * 0.25)$ where • X is the distance between the present position of the vessel and the *geographical position* of the case with a *retrieval* field equal to 4 and in which the *averaged error* is smaller than 0.05 and which has been retrieved within the last 20 km or 24 hours. If there is no case with a retrieval field equal to 4, the one having a value closest to 4 will be chosen. These threshold values have been empirically obtained in experiments carried out with datasets obtained in AMT (Atlantic Meridional Transect) cruises. • $25 \leq P \leq 200$
2	Cases with the same orientation as the present cruise track
3	Cases from data recorded during the same month as the cases that are stored in the case base in which the forecasting error is less than 0.05 and which have been used during the last 24 hours or 50 km. Cases are also constructed from data recorded in the previous month under the same conditions
4	Cases are constructed from data recorded in the last two weeks

13.5.3   Transformation of Data into Cases

Cases are constructed from the data held in the database and stored in the case base, according to the rules defined in Table 13.2.

The classification of cases presented in Table 13.2 have been empirically obtained as a result of much experimentation [40]. The following section shows how cases are selected during the CBR operation to create the final output, how they are deleted from the case base and how they can be reused.

13.5.4   Case Retrieval

From the data recorded in real time, the input profile, I, of the problem case is created. A search is made in the case base to retrieve all cases having similar profiles. Five metrics are used to determine the similarity between the problem case and each of the retrieved cases.

At this stage the aim is to retrieve all the cases that are similar to the problem case. The cases stored in the case base have been extracted from satellite images or data tracks. Therefore it is required to recover as many cases similar to the problem case as possible so that in the following stage a forecasting model based on all the recovered cases may be created.

The metrics used in the retrieval process give priority to cases based on complementary criteria. They enable cases to be retrieved whose input profiles are similar to the problem case with respect to their temperature profiles ($Metric1$ and $Metric2$), general trend in temperature ($Metric3$), similarity in terms of the frequency of oscillation of the Sobel filter of the profile ($Metric4$), and similarity with respect to the average sea temperature over the distance represented by the case ($Average Temperature Metric$).

13.5.4.1   Metric 1
This metric calculates the difference between I_{40} and eight other values of the *input profile (of the problem case)*, spread along the input profile at 5 km intervals (starting with I_1). This is repeated for all the cases stored in the case base. The value of the gradients are weighted, giving a higher value to the ones closer to I_{40}. The weighted gradient of each case (retrieved from the case case) is compared with the value of the weighted gradients of the *input profile of the problem case*, and the absolute value of the differences are added up. The value of Gradient 1 used to retrieve the cases is given by

$$\text{Metric } 1 = \sum_{i=0}^{7} \left(|(I_{40} - I_{i*5+1}) - (IA_{40} - IA_{i*5+1})| * (84 + i * 2)/100 \right)$$

where the vector $I_j (j = 1, 2, ..., 40)$ represents the input profile of the problem case and $IA_j (j = 1, 2, ..., 40)$ represents the input profile of the case being considered from the case base. The closer that the profiles being compared match, the smaller will be the value of Metric 1. This metric provides a general idea of the degree of similarity between the problem case and all the cases of the memory of the CBR.

13.5.4.2   Metric 2
This metric is similar to the previous one; the difference is that the input profile is first smoothed using a window of four values. This metric uses the difference between I_{40} and each of 13 other values of the input profile of the problem case relating to points at 3 km intervals (starting at I_1). The values obtained are weighted and summed as in the calculation of Metric 1. This is repeated for all the cases stored in the case base. This metric gives a more general indication of the similarity between the present case and the retrieved cases than Metric 1. This metric provides a stronger degree of similarity than the previous one owing to its higher level of granularity and the fact that

by smoothing the case vector irrelevant features (such as noise) are eliminated. The smaller the value of the metric, the more similar is the retrieved case to the *present input profile*.

13.5.4.3   Metric 3

The output of this metric is the absolute value of the difference between the gradient of the *problem input profile* and each of the cases of the case base. The gradient is calculated using the average value from the first and last 20% of each *input profile*. A percentage of 20 has been empirically found to be an adequate value to calculate a gradient that defines, in general terms, whether the temperature is increasing or decreasing.

$$\text{Metric 3} = \left| \left(\left(\sum_{i=1}^{5} I_{i+35} - \sum_{i=1}^{5} I_i \right) /5 \right) - \left(\left(\sum_{i=1}^{5} IA_{i+35} - \sum_{i=1}^{5} IA_i \right) /5 \right) \right|$$

This metric compares the general trend of the problem case with the general trend of the retrieved cases so, for example, it can be identified in cases which show a similar general increment or decrement in the temperature.

13.5.4.4   Metric 4

The *Sobel filter* value is calculated for the present case and all the *input profiles* of the retrieved cases [38]. The output of *Metric 4* is the absolute value of the difference between the number of oscillations of the Sobel filter of the input profile of the retrieved cases and the problem case.

The value of the Sobel filter for a case is calculated as follows:

$$(\forall x_i : 3 < i < 38) : Sobel\_x_i = \left(\left(\sum_{j=i-2}^{i+2} x_j \right) - x_i \right) /4$$

This metric gives priority to the cases, in which the Sobel filter is similar to the Sobel filter of the input vector of the problem case. This metric helps to identify cases from water masses of similar characteristics because case vectors extracted from similar water masses have similar Sobel filters [38].

13.5.4.5   Average Temperature Metric

The average temperature metric compares the average temperature, over the distance represented by each retrieved case, with that of the problem case. This case is used to identify cases that have been extracted from the sea in similar seasons of the year and similar water masses because cases extracted from the same areas of the ocean and extracted during the same season have similar average temperatures.

After applying the above metrics to all the cases in the case base, the best matches to the problem case are used to obtain the final forecast. The best matches of each metric will be used to train a radial basis function ANN in the adaptation stage of the reuse phase. The number of best matches selected from the outcome of each metric is determined as follows:

1. For each metric, the value of the outcome is expressed on an absolute scale between 0 and 1. Thus cases which are more similar to the problem case will have a value closer to 0 and the more distant cases will have a value closer to 1.

2. For each metric, the 200 best matches are used in the adaptation phase of the CBR cycle to train the ANN. If the value of the metric associated with any of these 200 cases is bigger than three times the value of the best match, this case is not used in the training of the ANN.

A reasonable number k of cases is required to train the ANN; empirically it has been observed that a value of between 500 and 1000 produces satisfactory results. If k is greater than 1000 it becomes impossible to train the ANN in the time available, while a value smaller than 500 may restrict the ANN's generalization ability. The same cases may be selected using different metrics, and will have a higher influence during the adaptation step of the reuse phase.

The metrics presented above are only applied to the cases which have a *date* field equal to or within two weeks of the date field of any of the cases used to train the ANN in the most recent forecast, or for which the geographical position differs by less than 10 km to the geographical position of any of the cases used to train the ANN in the most recent forecast.

13.5.5   Case Reuse (Adaptation)

Several hybrid systems have been developed in which CBR components cooperate with one or more reasoning elements [9]. In particular, there are a number of CBR systems that use constraint satisfaction, numeric constraint satisfaction, model based reasoning, etc., for case adaptation.

Case adaptation is one of the most problematic aspects of the CBR cycle. Most adaptation techniques are based on generalization and refinement heuristics. This section proposes a novel approach based on ANNs and their ability to generalize. The ANN acts as a function that obtains the most representative solution from a number of cases. This ANN does not require any type of human intervention and has only a small number of rules that supervise the training of the ANN.

In the context of the present problem, instance based reasoning is required to compensate for the lack of guidance from specific and accurate background knowledge about the propagation of the temperature of the water of the oceans, with a relatively large number of instances [39]. This is a highly syntactic CBR approach, in the sense that a simple feature vector (refer to Section 13.5.1) is only needed to represent each instance and no user is required in the CBR life cycle.

Each of the cases or instances retrieved from the CBR represents a particular problem and its solution (feature vector). The aim of the CBR operation is to determine which of the cases stored in the CBR case base characterizes better the present situation so that it may be reused. The determination of an algorithm to automate this process and retrieve the best case at any point is difficult because of the complexity of the environment, its dynamism and its heterogeneity.

The method adopted is to use a mechanism able to absorb the knowledge of all the cases that are representative of one particular problem and extrapolate from them a solution. To this end, experiments were carried out with nearest neighbor algorithms (which find the case among the retrieved cases that is most similar to the present problem), averaging techniques and ANNs. A radial basis function ANN has been found to be able to absorb the underlying model represented by the retrieved cases, and generalize a solution from them, better than any other technique [33]. This ANN is retrained before any forecast is made using the retrieved cases and the internal knowledge (weights and centers) of the radial basis function ANN. Every time that the ANN is retrained, its internal architecture is adapted to the new problem and the cases are adapted to produce the solution, which is a generalization of those cases.

Radial basis function ANNs are adequate in this problem because they can be trained fast, they have very good generalizing abilities (though being better at interpolating than at extrapolating) [40], and they learn without forgetting by adapting their internal structure (adding new centers) [41]. This last property is particularly interesting in the present situation because since the ANN is continuously being retrained, it can learn new features within one particular water mass without forgetting a number of the others previously learned (for a variable number of training iterations).

Although this increases the training time, it improves the generalization since at any time the forecast is not only based on the last k cases used to retrain the ANN, but also on those cases used in the more recent past which also influence the forecast; this contributes to the generation of a continuous, coherent and accurate forecast.

In the RBF network that has been built, cases are coded in order to create the input and output vectors used to train the ANN. The ANN uses nine input neurons, between 20 and 35 neurons in the hidden layer and one neuron in the output layer. The input data is the difference between the last temperature (of the input profile) and the temperature values of the input profile taken every 4 km. Only one neuron is used in the output layer to forecast up to 5 km. The output is the difference between the temperature at the present point and the temperature 5 km ahead.

13.5.5.1   Center and Weight Adaptation

Initially, 20 vectors are randomly chosen from the first training dataset (composed of the retrieved cases), and are used as centers in the middle layer of the ANN. This number changes with training and the training dataset determines it. The topology of the ANN (i.e., number of neurons in each layer) has been empirically chosen after many tests with datasets extracted in the AMT cruises [38]. The number of initial centers has been chosen taking into consideration the number of neurons in the input and the output layer.

All the centers are associated with a Gaussian function the width of which, for all the functions, is set to the mean value of the Euclidean distance between the two centers that are separated the most from each other.

The closest center to each particular input vector is moved toward the input vector by a percentage α of the present distance between them. By using this technique the centers are positioned close to the highest densities of the input vector dataset. The aim of this adaptation is to force the centers to be as close as possible to as many vectors from the input space as possible. An adaptation of this type is particularly important because of the high dimensionality of the input layer. α is initialized to 20 every time that the ANN is retrained, and its value is linearly decreased with the number of iterations until α becomes 0; then the ANN is trained for a number of iterations (between 10 and 30 iterations for the whole training dataset, depending on the time left for the training) in order to obtain the best possible weights for the final value of the centers. The thresholds that determine the centers and weights adaptation have been empirically determined).

The delta rule is used to adapt the weighted connections from the centers to the output neurons [42]. In particular, for each presented pair of input and desired output vectors, one adaptation step, according to the delta rule, is made.

13.5.5.2 Insertion of New Units

A new center is inserted into the network when the average error in the training dataset does not fall more than 10determine the most distant center C, the Euclidean distance between each center and each input vector is calculated and the center whose distance from the input data vectors is largest is chosen. A new center is inserted between C and the center closest to it. Centers are also eliminated when they do not contribute much to the output of the ANN. Thus, a neuron is eliminated if the absolute value of the weight associated with a neuron is smaller than 20% of the average value of the absolute value, of the five smallest weights. The number of neurons in the middle layer is maintained above 20. This is a simple and efficient way of reducing the size of the ANN without dramatically decreasing its memory.

13.5.5.3 Termination of Training

The ANN is trained for a maximum time of 2 minutes. In the real-time operation the ANNs must produce a forecast every 2 km (6 minutes for a speed of 12 knots, which is the maximum speed that the vessel can attain). After that time the new set of training cases is retrieved and the ANNs are retrained. Therefore, even if the error is high the ANNs should produce a forecast. It has been found empirically that these training times are sufficient to train the network and obtain a forecast with small errors [40]. At any point, if the average error in the training dataset is smaller or equal to 0.05 the training is stopped to prevent the ANN from memorizing the training vectors. This threshold has been chosen empirically. It has been shown that the ANN around this point stops the generalization process and starts to learn and to memorize the training vectors.

13.5.6 Case Revision

After case adaptation a crisp value is obtained for the forecast temperature 5 km ahead of the vessel. This value is rarely 100% accurate; therefore revision is required to obtain a more realistic output.

Since this is a real-time problem it is not possible to evaluate the outcome of the system before it is used. The solution to this problem is to define error limits, which will substitute the crisp output with a band or error interval around the output of the ANN. If the error limits are too wide the forecast will be meaningless; therefore a trade-off is made between a broad error limit (that will guarantee that the real solution is always within its bands) and the crisp solution.

The expected accuracy of a prediction depends on two elements: the water mass in which the forecast is required and the relevance of the cases stored in the case base for that particular prediction.

Each water mass has been assigned a default error limit CL_0, which has been empirically obtained. Every time a cruise crosses a water mass, a new error limit CL_z (where $0 < z < 6$) is calculated by averaging the error in all the predictions made. If, for a certain water mass, z is equal to 5, and a vessel crosses it again, the older CL is substituted by a new one. Therefore there are at most five error limits associated to a water mass. This number is not critical; a smaller value can also guarantee stability in such error limits, and a larger number does not provide a better result. The CL_z error limits are used in collaboration with the *average error* of the cases used to train the ANN for a given forecast. The error limit determines the interval centerd in the crisp temperature value, obtained by the ANN, for which there is a high probability that the forecast is within this interval. The value of the probability varies deepening on the distance of the forecast, but must be higher than 90%. Then, if the output of the ANN is F, the average value of the accumulated errors of the cases taking part in a given forecast is AE and ACL is the average value of the CL_z error limits, the error interval is defined by

$$[F - ((AE * 0.65) + (ACL * 0.35)), F + ((AE * 0.65) + (ACL * 0.35))]$$

The values used in this formula have been empirically obtained using a sufficient amount of data from all the water masses of the Atlantic Ocean. However, these values may not be appropriate for water masses from different oceans.

13.5.7 Case Retention and Learning

Incorporating into the case base what has been learned from the new prediction is the last stage of the CBR life cycle. Learning is achieved in different ways in the system. When the ship has traveled a distance of 5 km (on a straight course) after making a forecast, it is possible to determine the accuracy of that forecast, since the actual value of the parameter for which the forecast was made is then known. This forecasting error is used to update the average error attribute of the cases used in that particular forecast. The cumulative error field of the cases used to train the neural network is continuously being updated and contributes to the learning strategy of the system. Accurate error limits are obtained only if the average error attribute of the cases is modified in this way.

Pruning the case base also contributes to the learning; cases in which average error attribute is very high are removed. The maximum permissible average error needs to be defined. Empirically it has been found that for cases in which the average error attains a value of 0.12, the average error never subsequently reduces to a value smaller than 0.05. Therefore a threshold of 0.1 in the *average error* was chosen to determine which cases must be deleted. If the average error of a case is equal to or higher than 0.1, the case is removed from the case base. Furthermore, cases which have not been used during the previous 48 hours are deleted; so also are cases which have not been used in the previous 100 km.

It is necessary to determine when the case base must be updated with additional cases from the database. This is done when the database receives new satellite images (once per week). If the forecasting error is higher than 0.2 for more than 20 predictions, additional cases are created from data stored in the database. This is a measure used to include fresh cases in the case base; this helps to reduce the forecasting error.

If, over a period of operation in a particular water mass, it is found that most of the cases selected from the case base are clustered around some point a distance x, say, either ahead or behind the vessel, this suggests that the whole water mass has moved this distance x since the data, from which the cases were created, were obtained. In such a situation, the operational strategy is then to utilize cases relating to this indicated area, which is centered on a position a distance x from the current position.

The modification and storage of the internal structure of the ANN contribute substantially to the learning of the system. The weights and centers of the network, and also the width of the Gaussian functions associated with the centers, are modified during the adaptation process and stored in the network knowledge base.

Learning is a continuous process in which the neural network acts as a mechanism that generalizes from the input data profiles and learns to identify new patterns without forgetting previously learned ones. The case base may be considered as a *long-term memory* since it is able to maintain a huge number of cases that characterize previously encountered situations.

In contrast, the network knowledge base may be considered to behave as a *short-term memory* that has the ability to recognize recently learned patterns (i.e. the knowledge stored in the internal architecture of the neural network) that enable it to adapt the system to cope with localized situations.

13.6 Results and Discussion

This chapter has described the hybrid system developed to forecast in real time the temperature of the water ahead of an ongoing vessel. The hybrid system is composed of a CBR system and an ANN. The ANN assists the CBR system during the adaptation of cases and also contributes to the learning of the system.

The hybrid system holds in its memory a huge amount of data relating to forecasting events and selects from it those that are the most similar to the new forecasting situation. The ANN uses the retrieved cases to create a model, in real time, for a particular water mass. This reasoning model makes use of the most up-to-date data to generate a solution in real time in order to overcome the difficulties of predicting the evolution of a dynamic system in real time. Although the present chapter has focused on the prediction of the temperature 5 km ahead, the same strategy has been used to forecast up to 20 km. A complete analysis of the results obtained with this system may be found in Corchado [40].

The approach presented here combines the advantages of both connectionist and symbolic AI. The hybrid system was tested in the Atlantic Ocean in September 1997 on a research cruise from the UK to the Falkland Islands [40]. The results obtained were very encouraging and indicate that the hybrid system is able to produce a more accurate forecast than any of the other techniques used in this experiment.

Although the experiment has been carried out with a limited dataset (over a distance of 11,000 km between the latitudes 50° North and 50° South), 11 water masses with different characteristics were traversed, six of them containing fronts; the Falkland Front, in particular, is one of the most chaotic oceanographic areas in the world. It is believed that these results are sufficiently significant to be extrapolated to the whole Atlantic Ocean.

Table 13.3. Average error and percentage of inadmissible predictions with the hybrid system

Prediction distance (km)	Hybrid system average error (deg. C)	Hybrid system: % of inadmissible predictions
5	0.020	2.6
10	0.048	6.2
15	0.132	8.1
20	0.260	7.5

Table 13.3 shows the results obtained with the hybrid system when forecasting the water temperature at different distances. The table also shows that the percentage of inadmissible predictions (those that show that the temperature of the water is rising when it is decreasing and vice versa) is always smaller than 10%. This percentage is above this limit when forecasting further ahead than 20 km.

The forecasting ability of the system is highest in areas with small instabilities and where there are many data profiles from which to choose in the retrieval stage of the CBR cycle. The forecast is less accurate in areas with large changes and many instabilities. The system is not able to forecast if there are no data profiles in the region where the forecast is made.

Experiments have also been carried out to evaluate the performance of the hybrid forecasting approach in comparison with several separate neural networks and statistical forecasting methods [10]: a finite impulse response (FIR) model, an RBF network alone (trained with the data recorded during the 160 km previous to the forecast point), a linear regression model, an auto-regressive integrated moving average (ARIMA) model and a CBR system alone (using the cases generated during the 160 km preceding the forecast point). Table 13.4 shows the average error in the forecast using these methods.

Table 13.4. Average forecasting error with different methods.

	Forecasting method					
Prediction distance (km)	FIR4*4 (deg. C)	FIR8*5 (deg. C)	RBF (deg. C)	Linear regression (deg. C)	ARIMA (deg. C)	CBR (deg. C)
5	0.099	0.096	0.114	0.174	0.129	0.12
10	0.206	0.192	0.226	0.275	0.231	–
15	0.343	0.324	0.351	0.429	0.372	–
20	0.468	0.435	0.469	0.529	0.471	–

The success of the system in generating effective forecasts may be attributed to the combination of an extensive database of past cases, supported by the neural adaptation mechanism which, each time around the forecasting cycle, enables the forecasting process to learn from all the selected closely matching cases.

The experimental results obtained to date indicate that the neural network supported CBR approach is effective in the task of predicting the future oceanographic parameter values. Extrapolating beyond these results, it is believed that the approach may be applicable to the problem of parametric forecasting in other complex domains using sampled time series data.

Acknowledgements

The contributions of N. Rees and Prof. J. Aiken at the Plymouth Marine Laboratory in the collaborative research presented in this chapter are gratefully acknowledged.

References

1. Lees B., Rees, N. and Aiken, J. (1992). Knowledge-based oceanographic data analysis, *Proc. Expersys-92*, Attia F., Flory A., Hashemi S., Gouarderes G. and Marciano J. (eds), IITT International Paris, October 1992, pp. 561–565.
2. Medsker L. R. (1995). *Hybrid Intelligent Systems*. Kluwer Academic Publishers, Boston, MA.
3. Sun R. (1996). Commonsense reasoning with rules, cases, and connectionist models: a paradigmatic comparison. *Fuzzy Sets and Systems*, 82(2), 187–200.
4. Lees B. (1999). Hybrid case based reasoning: an overview. *Int. Workshop on Hybrid CBR Systems, ICCBR 99*, Munich, July, 1999.
5. Bezdek J. C. (1994). What is Computational Intelligence?, in *Computational Intelligence: Imitating Life*, Zurada J. M., Marks II R. J. and Robinson C. J. (eds). IEEE Press, New York, pp. 1–12.
6. Soucek B. and IRIS group (1991). *Neural and Intelligent Systems Integration*. Wiley, New York.
7. Medsker L. R. and Bailey D. L. (1992). Models and guidelines for integrating expert systems and neural networks, in *Hybrid Architectures for Intelligent Systems*, Kandel A. and Langholz G. (eds). CRC Press, Boca Raton, FL, pp 131–164.
8. López de Mántaras R. and Plaza E. (1997). Case-based reasoning: an overview. *AI Communications*, 10, 21–29.
9. Hunt J. and Miles R. (1994). Hybrid case based reasoning. *Knowledge Engineering Review*, 9(4), 383–397.
10. Corchado J. M., Lees B., Fyfe C., Rees N. and Aiken J. (1998). Neuro-adaptation method for a case based reasoning system. *International Joint Conference on Neural Networks*. Anchorage, AK, May 4–9, pp. 713–718.
11. Sun R. and Alexandre F. (1997). Connnectionist-Symbolic Integration: From Unified to Hybrid Approaches. Lawrence Erlbaum Associates, Mahwah, NJ.
12. Reategui E. B., Campbell J. A. and Leao B. F. (1996). Combining a neural network with case based reasoning in a diagnostic system. *Artificial Intelligence in Medicine*, 9(1), 5–27.

13. Bezdek J. C. and Jazayeri K. (1989). A connectionist approach to case based reasoning, in K. J. Hammond (ed.), *Proceedings of the Case Based Reasoning Workshop*, Pensacola Beach, FL, Morgan Kaufmann, San Mateo, CA, pp. 213–217.

14. Thrift P. (1989). A neural network model for case based reasoning, in Hammond K. J., (ed.), *Proceedings of the Case Based Reasoning Workshop*, Pensacola Beach, FL. Morgan Kaufmann, San Mateo, CA, pp. 334–337.

15. Alpaydin G. (1991). Networks that grow when they learn and shrink when they forget. *Technical Report TR 91-032*. International Computer Science Institute, May 1991.

16. Lim H. C., Lui A., Tan H. and Teh H. H.(1991). A connectionist case based diagnostic expert system that learns incrementally. *Proceedings of the International Joint Conference on Neural Networks*, pp. 1693–1698.

17. Azcarraga A. and Giacometti A. (1991). A prototype-based incremental network model for classification tasks. *Fourth International Conference on Neural Networks and their Applications*, Nimes, France, pp. 78–86.

18. Malek M. (1995). A connectionist indexing approach for CBR systems, in Veloso M. and Aamodt A., (eds), *Case-Based Reasoning: Research and Development. First International Conference, ICCBR-95*. Sesimbra, Portugal. Springer Verlag, London, pp. 520–527.

19. Quan Mao, Jing Qin, Xinfang Zhang and Ji Zhou. (1994). Case prototype based design: philosophy and implementation, in Ishii K. (ed.), *Proc. Computers in Engineering* Vol.1, 11–14 September, Minneapolis, MN. ASME, New York, pp. 369–374.

20. Main J., Dillon T. S. and Khosla R. (1996). Use of fuzzy feature vectors and neural networks for case retrieval in case based systems. *Proc. Biennial Conference of the North American Fuzzy Information Processing Society – NAFIPS*. IEEE, Piscataway, NJ, pp. 438–443.

21. Richter A. M. and Weiss S. (1991). Similarity, uncertainty and case based reasoning in PATDEX, in Boyer R. S. (ed.), *Automated Reasoning*. Kluwer, Boston, MA, pp. 249– 265.

22. Garcia Lorenzo M. M. and Bello Pérez R. E. (1996). Model and its different applications to case based reasoning. *Knowledge-Based Systems*. 9(7), 465–473.

23. Agre G. and Koprinska, I. (1996). Case based refinement of knowledge-based neural networks. In Albus J., Meystel A. and Quintero R. (eds), *Proceedings of the International Conference on Intelligent Systems: A Semiotic Perspective*, Vol.II, pp. 37–45.

24. Reategui E. B. and Campbell J. A. (1995). A classification system for credit card transactions, in Haton J. P., Keane M. and Manago M. (eds), *Advances in Case Based Reasoning: Second European Workshop. EWCBR-94*, Chantilly, France. Springer-Verlag, London, pp. 280–291.

25. Liu Z. Q. and Yan F. (1997). Fuzzy neural network in case based diagnostic system *IEEE Transactions on Fuzzy Systems*, 5(2), 209–222.

26. Aamodt A. and Langseth H. (1998). Integrating Bayesian networks into knowledge-intensive CBR. *AAAI'98, Workshop Technical Report WS-98-15, Case Base Reasoning Integrations*, 27 July 1998, Wisconsin, pp. 1–6.

27. Dingsoyr T. (1998). Retrieval of cases by using a Bayesian network. *AAAI'98, Workshop Technical Report WS-98-15, Case Base Reasoning Integrations*, 27 July 1998, Wisconsin, pp. 50–54.
28. Shinmori A. (1998). A proposal to combine probabilistic reasoning with case-based retrieval for software troubleshooting. *AAAI'98, Workshop Technical Report WS- 98-15, Case Base Reasoning Integrations*, 27 July 1998, Wisconsin, pp. 149–154.
29. Friese T. (1999). Utilization of Bayesian belief networks for explanation-driven case based reasoning. *IJCAI '99. Workshop ML-5: Automating the Construction of Case Based Reasoners*, Stockholm, Sweden, pp. 73–76.
30. Mao Q., Qin J., Zhang X. and Zhou J. (1994). Case prototype based design: philosophy and implementation, in Ishii K. (ed.), *Proc. Computers in Engineering*, Vol. 1, 11-14 September, Minneapolis, MN, pp. 369–374.
31. Palmen E. and Newton C. W. (1969). *Atmospheric Circulations Systems*. Academic Press, London, p. 602.
32. Tomczak M. and Godfrey J. S. (1994). *Regional Oceanography: An Introduction*. Pergamon, New York.
33. Corchado J. M., Lees, B., Fyfe, C. and Rees, N. (1997). Adaptive agents: learning from the past and forecasting the future, *Proc. PADD97–First International Conference on the Practical Application of Knowledge Discovery and Data Mining*, London, 23–25 April, Practical Application Co., pp. 109–123.
34. Aamodt A. and Plaza E. (1994). Case-based reasoning: foundational issues, methodological variations, and system approaches. AI Communications, 7(1), 39–59.
35. Watson I. and Marir F. (1994). *Case-Based Reasoning: A Review. The Knowledge Engineering Review*, Vol. 9, No. 3. Cambridge University Press, Cambridge, UK.
36. Rees N., Aiken J. and Corchado J. M. (1997). *Internal Report: STEB Implementation*. PML, Plymouth, UK, 30 September.
37. Wess S., Althoff K-D. and Derwand, G. (1994). Using K-D trees to improve the retrieval step in case-based reasoning, in Wess S., Althoff K-D. and Richter M. M. (eds), *Topics in Case Based Reasoning*, Springer-Verlag, Berlin, pp. 167–181.
38. Corchado J. M., Rees N. and Aiken J. (1996). *Internal Report on Supervised ANNs and Oceanographic Forecasting*. PML, Plymouth, UK, 30 December.
39. Aha D. W. (1990). A study of instance-based learning algorithms for supervised learning tasks: mathematical, empirical, and psychological evaluations. *Technical Report 90-42*. University of California, Department of Information and Computer Science, Irvine, CA.
40. Corchado J. M. (2000) Neuro-symbolic model for real-time forecasting problems. Ph.D. dissertation, University of Paisley, UK.
41. Fritzke B. (1994). Fast learning with incremental RBF networks. *Neural Processing Letters*. 1(1), 2–5.
42. Bishop C. R. (1995). *Neural Networks for Pattern Recognition*. Clarendon Press, Oxford.

14. Armchair Mission to Mars: Using Case Based Reasoning and Fuzzy Logic to Simulate a Time Series Model of Astronaut Crews

Gerry Stahl

Abstract. Computer simulation of long missions in space can provide experience and predictions without the expense and risk of actual flights. Simulations are most helpful if they can model the behavior of key psychological factors of the crew over time, rather than simply predicting overall mission success. Because of the lack of experience with interplanetary trips and the problems of generalizing and adapting data on analog missions, it is not possible to formulate a set of formal rules adequate for building an expert system. Rather, a case based reasoning approach to constructing a time series model is pursued. Even for this approach, however, the case base must be supplemented by adaptation rules. These rules of thumb are gleaned from the social science literature on small group interactions under extreme conditions of isolation and confinement. The non-quantitative nature of these rules lends itself to formulation and computation using fuzzy logic. The application domain presents several technical issues for traditional case based reasoning: there is no natural hierarchy of parameters to use in optimizing installation and retrieval of cases, and there are large variations in behavior among similar missions. These problems are addressed by custom algorithms to keep the computations tractable and plausible. Thus, the harnessing of case based reasoning for this practical application requires the crafting of a custom, hybrid system.

14.1 Preface

14.1.1 Background of the Research

During the period of space exploration around 1993, planners at NASA (the US space agency) were concerned about interpersonal issues in astronaut crew composition. The nature of astronaut crews was undergoing significant change. In the past, astronauts were primarily young American males with rigorous military training; missions were short; crews were small. Prior to a mission, a crew trained together for about a year, so that any interpersonal conflicts could be worked out in advance. The future, however, promised crews that would be far less homogeneous and regimented: international crews speaking different languages, mixed gender, inter-generational, larger crews, longer missions. This was the start of Soviet–American cooperation and planning for a space station. While there was talk of a manned expedition to Mars, the more likely scenario of an international space station with six-month crew rotations was a realistic concern.

There was not much experience with the psychological effects on crews confined in isolated and extreme conditions for months at a time. The data from submarines and Antarctic winter-overs provided some indications, but it was limited, inappropriately documented and inconsistent. NASA was beginning to conduct some experiments where they could collect the kinds of data they needed. But they required a way of analyzing such data, generalizing it and applying it to projected scenarios.

14.1.2 The Soft Computing Algorithms

NASA wanted a way of predicting how a given crew – with a certain mix of astronauts - might respond to mission stress under different scenarios. This would require a complex model with many parameters. There would never be enough relevant data to derive the parameter values statistically. Given a modest set of past cases, the method of case based reasoning (CBR) suggested itself. A case based system requires (1) a mechanism for retrieving past cases similar to a proposed new case and (2) a mechanism for adapting the data of a retrieved case to the new case base on the differences between the two.

For the retrieval mechanism, we defined a number of characteristics of astronauts and missions. The nature of our data and these characteristics raised a number of issues for retrieval and we had to develop innovative modifications of the standard CBR algorithms, as described in detail below.

For the adaptation mechanism, we developed a model of the mission based on a statistical approach known as interrupted time series analysis. In addition, we derived a set of adaptation rules based on the social science literature about confined and isolated crews. We formulated these rules in English and represented them in the software using fuzzy logic.

14.1.3 The Software System

We developed a CBR software system named CREW. To make the retrieval of cases tractable, scalable and efficient, we developed the system in a database programming environment. We selected FoxPro because it was highly optimized, included a general purpose programming language and was compatible with both Windows and the Macintosh.

Most of the software code consisted of the algorithms described in this chapter. Because CREW was intended to be a proof-of-concept system, its data entry routines and user interface were minimal. The user interface consisted of a set of pull-down menus for selecting a variety of testing options and a display of the results in a graph format (see Fig. 14.1). Some of the steps in the reasoning were printed out so that one could study the reasoning process.

By the end of the project, we successfully demonstrated that the time series model, the CBR and the fuzzy logic could all work together to perform as designed. The system could be set up for specific crews and projected missions and it would produce sensible predictions quickly. The next step was to enter real data that NASA was just beginning to collect. Because of confidentiality concerns, this had to be done within NASA, so we turned over the software to them for further use and development.

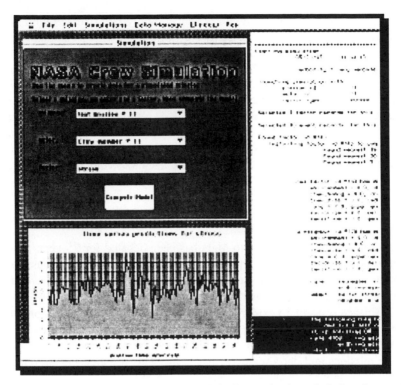

Fig. 14.1. A view of the CREW interface. Upper left allows selection of mission characteristics. Menu allows input of data. Lower left shows magnitude of a psychological factor during 100 points in the simulated mission. To the right is a listing of some of the rules taken into account.

14.1.4 The People Involved

The research was sponsored by the Behavioral and Performance Laboratory at Johnson Space Center in Houston, Texas, part of NASA's Astronaut Support Division. We worked closely with NASA researchers Dr Joanna Wood and Dr Albert Holland on the design of the software and the data. At the end of the project, we delivered the software to them to continue the work.

The research was conducted at Owen Research, Inc. (ORI) in Boulder, Colorado. ORI is a small research lab founded and run by Dr Robert Owen. Owen is a physicist specializing in laser optics. He also has a Ph.D. in anthropology, and his dissertation in that field led to this research in modeling small group behavior using AI (artificial intelligence) techniques. I developed the technical approach and programmed the system. Dr Brent Reeves assisted with the fuzzy logic algorithms. To help collect and analyze social science literature related to small groups in isolated conditions, we worked with Professor Russell McGoodwin of the Anthropology Department at the University of Colorado (CU) and his student, Nick Colmenares. In addition, I conducted several interviews of an experienced astronaut, Mike Lounge, and discussed our project with him.

I began this project immediately after completing my Ph.D. dissertation in computer science at CU, where I had specialized in AI. Since my undergraduate years at MIT in the mid-1960s and a Ph.D. in philosophy in the mid-1970s, I have worked as a systems programmer, software developer and computer consultant. Following this project, I continued to work with ORI on software for an optical bench to stabilize interferometry equipment during space flight and on an Internet- based system for teachers to share curriculum ideas. After working at ORI, I returned to CU, where I am now a Research Professor in cognitive science and computer science. My current research involves Web-based environments for collaborative learning and knowledge-building - for further information or to contact me, see http://www.cs.colorado.edu/~gerry.

14.2   Introduction

The prospect of a manned mission to Mars has been debated for 25 years since the first manned landing on the moon [1]. It is routinely argued that this obvious next step in human exploration is too costly and risky to undertake, particularly given our lack of experience with lengthy missions in space [7].

Social science research to explore issues of the effects of such a mission on crew members has focused on experience in *analog* missions under extreme conditions of isolation and confinement, such as Antarctic winter-overs, submarine missions, orbital space missions and deep sea experiments [4]. This research has produced few generalizable guidelines for planning a mission to Mars [2].

We have undertaken to simulate the effects of interplanetary missions in a computer program named CREW. This program is for use by NASA to assist in astronaut crew selection and mission planning [8]. Given descriptions of tentatively selected crew members and of scheduled activities, CREW simulates the mission and reports on the probable course of particular factors during the duration of the mission.

We are working with staff at the psychology labs of NASA's astronaut support division, so we have focused on psychological factors of the crew members, such as stress, morale and teamwork. NASA has begun to collect time series psychological data on these factors by having crew members in space and analog missions fill out a survey on an almost daily basis. As of the conclusion of our project (June 1995), NASA had analyzed data from an underwater mission designed to test their data collection instrument, the IFRS (Individualized Field Recording System) survey, and was collecting data from several Antarctic traverses. The IFRS survey was scheduled to be employed on a joint Soviet–American shuttle mission. Its most likely initial use would be as a tool for helping to select crews for the international space station.

Our task was to design a system for incorporating eventual IFRS survey results in a model of participant behavior on long-term missions. Our goal was to implement a proof-of-concept software system to demonstrate algorithms for combining AI techniques like CBR and fuzzy logic with a statistical model of IFRS survey results and a rule base derived from the existing literature on extreme missions.

This chapter reports on our system design and its rationale. The CREW system predicts how crew members in a simulated mission would fill out their IFRS survey forms on each day of the mission, that is, how they would self-report indicators of stress, motivation, etc. As NASA collects and analyzes survey data, the CREW program can serve as a vehicle for assembling and building upon the data – entering empirical cases and tuning the rule base. Clearly, the predictive power of CREW will depend upon the eventual quantity and quality of the survey data.

14.3   Modeling the Mission Process

NASA is interested in how psychological factors such as those tracked in the IFRS surveys evolve over time during a projected mission's duration. For instance, it is not enough to know what the average stress level will be of crew members at the end of a nine-month mission; we need to know if any crew member will be likely to be particularly stressed at a critical point in the middle of the mission when certain actions must be taken. To obtain this level of detail of prediction, we created a *time series* model of the mission.

The model is based on standard statistical time series analysis. McDowall et al. [6] argue for a stochastic ARIMA (Auto Regressive Integrated Moving Average) model of interrupted time series for a broad range of phenomena in the social sciences. The most general model takes into account three types of considerations: (1) trends, (2) seasonality effects and (3) interventions. An observed time series is treated as a realization of a stochastic process; the ideal model of such a process is statistically adequate (its residuals are white noise) and parsimonious (it has the fewest parameters and the greatest number of degrees of freedom among all statistically equivalent models).

14.3.1   Trends

The basic model takes into account a stochastic component and three structural components. The stochastic component conveniently summarizes the multitude of factors producing the variation observed in a series which cannot be accounted for by the model. At each time t there is a stochastic component α_t which cannot be accounted for any more specifically. McDowall et al. claim that most social science phenomena are properly modeled by first-order ARIMA models. That is, the value Y_t of the time series at time t may be dependent on the value of the time series or of its stochastic component at time $t - 1$, but not (directly) on the values at any earlier times. The first-order expressions for the three structural components are:

$$\text{autoregressive}: \quad Y_t = \alpha_t + \phi Y_{t-1}$$
$$\text{differenced}: \quad Y_t = \alpha_t + Y_{t-1}$$
$$\text{moving average}: \quad Y_t = \alpha_t + \theta a_{t-1}$$

We have combined these formulae to produce a general expression for all first- order ARIMA models:

$$Y_t = \alpha_t + \phi Y_{t-1} + \theta \alpha_{t-1}$$

This general expression makes clear that the model can take into account trends and random walks caused by the inertia (or momentum) of the previous moment's stochastic component or by the inertia of the previous moment's actual value.

14.3.2 Seasonality

Many phenomena (e.g., in economics or nature) have a cyclical character, often based on the 12-month year. It seems unlikely that such seasonality effects would be significant for NASA missions; the relevant cycles (daily and annual) would be too small or too large to be measured by IFRS time series data.

14.3.3 Interventions

External events are likely to impact upon modeled time series. Their duration can be modeled as exponential decay, where the nth time period after an event at time e will have a continuing impact of $Y_{e+n} = \delta^n \omega$ where $0 \leq \delta \leq 1$. Note that if $\delta = 0$ then there is no impact and if $\delta = 1$ then there is a permanent impact. Thus, δ is a measure of the rate of decay and ω is a measure of the intensity of the impact.

We have made some refinements to the standard time series equations, to tune them to our domain and to make them more general. First, the stochastic component, $\alpha_i(t)$, consists of a mean value, $\mu_i(t)$, and a normal distribution component governed by a standard deviation, $\sigma_i(t)$. Second, mission events often have significant effects of anticipation. In general, an event j of intensity ω_{ij} at time t_j will have a gradual onset at a rate ε_{ij} during times $t < t_j$ as well as a gradual decay at a rate δ_{ij} during times $t > t_j$. The following equation incorporates these considerations:

$$Y_i(t) = \alpha_i(t) + \phi_i Y_i(t-1) + \theta_i \alpha_i(t-1) + \sum_{\substack{j=1 \\ (\text{for } t < t_j)}}^{n} \left[\varepsilon_{ij}^{(t_j - 1)} \omega_{ij} \right]$$

$$+ \sum_{\substack{j=1 \\ (\text{for } t \geq t_j)}}^{n} \left[\delta_{ij}^{(t - t_j)} \omega_{ij} \right]$$

where:

$Y_i(t)$ = value of factor i for a given actor in a given mission at mission time t
t_j = time of occurrence of the jth of n intervening events in the mission
α = noise: a value is generated randomly with mean μ and standard deviation σ
μ = mean of noise value $0 \leq \mu \leq 10$
σ = standard deviation of noise $0 \leq \sigma \leq 10$
ϕ = momentum of value $-1 \leq \phi \leq 1$
θ = momentum of noise $-1 \leq \theta \leq 1$
ε = rise rate of interruption $0 \leq \varepsilon \leq 1$
δ = decay rate of interruption $0 \leq \delta \leq 1$
ω = intensity of interruption $-10 \leq \omega \leq 10$

The model works as follows. Using IFRS survey data for a given question answered by a given crew member throughout a given mission and knowing when significant events occurred, one can use standard statistical procedures to derive the parameters of the preceding equation: μ, σ, ϕ and θ as well as ε, δ and ω for each event in the mission. Then, conversely, one can use these parameters to predict the results of a new proposed mission. Once one has obtained the parameters for a particular psychological factor, a crew member and each event, one can predict the values that crew members would enter for that survey question i at each time period t of the mission by calculating the equation with those parameter values.

This model allows us to enter empirical cases into a case base by storing the parameters for each *factor* (i.e., a psychological factor for a given crew member during a given mission) or *event* (i.e., an intervention event in the given factor time series) with a description of that factor or event. To make a time series prediction of a proposed factor with its events, we retrieve a similar case, adapt it for differences from the proposed case and compute its time series values from the model equation.

14.4 Using Case Based Reasoning

The time series model is quite complex in terms of the number of variables and factors. It must produce different results for each time period, each kind of mission, each crew member personality, each question on the IFRS survey and each type of intervention event. To build a rule based expert system, we would need to acquire thousands of formal rules capable of computing predictive results for all these combinations. But there are no experts on interplanetary missions who could provide such a set of rules. Nor is there data that could be analyzed to produce these rules. So we took a CBR approach. We take actual missions – including analog missions – and compute the parameters for their time series.

Each survey variable requires its own model (values for parameters μ, σ, ϕ and θ), as does each kind of event (values for parameters ε, δ and ω). Presumably, the 107 IFRS survey questions can be grouped into several factors – although this is itself an empirical question. We chose six psychological factors that we thought underlay the IFRS questionnaire: crew teamwork, physical health, mental alertness, psychological stress, psychological morale and mission effectiveness. In addition, we selected a particular question from the survey that represented each of these factors. The CREW system currently models these 12 factors.

There is no natural taxonomy of events. Our approach assumes that there are categories of events that can be modeled consistently as interventions with exponential onsets and decays at certain impact levels and decay rates. Based on the available data, we decided to model eight event types: start of mission, end of mission, emergency, conflict, contact, illness, discovery, failure.

The case base consists of instances of the 12 factors and the eight event types. Each instance is characterized by its associated mission and crew member, and is annotated with its parameter values. Missions are described by 10 characteristics (variables), each rated from 0 to 10. The mission characteristics are: harshness of environment, duration of mission, risk level, complexity of activities, homogeneity of crew, time of crew together, volume of habitat, crew size, commander leadership and commander competence. Crew member characteristics are: role in crew, experience, professional status, commitment, social skills, self-reliance, intensity, organization, sensitivity, gender, culture and voluntary status. In addition, events have characteristics: event type, intensity and point in mission.

Because there is only a small handful of cases of actual IFRS data available at present, additional cases are needed to test and to demonstrate the system. Approximate models of time series and interventions can be estimated based on space and analog missions reported in the literature, even if raw time series data is not available to derive the model statistically. Using these, we generate and install supplemental demo cases by perturbating the variables in these cases and adjusting the model parameters in accordance with rules of thumb gleaned from the literature on analog missions. This database is not rigorously empirical, but it should produce plausible results during testing and demos. Of course, the database can be recreated at a later time when sufficient real data is available. At that point, NASA might change the list of factor and event types to track in the database or the set of variables to describe them. Then the actual case data would be analyzed using interrupted time series analysis to derive empirical values for μ, σ, ϕ and θ for the factors.

Users of CREW enter a scenario of a proposed mission, including crew composition and mission characteristics. They also enter a series of n anticipated events at specific points in the mission period. From the scenario, the system computes values for μ, σ, ϕ and θ for each behavioral factor. For events $j = 1$ through n, it computes values for δ_j, ε_j and ω_j. The computation of parameters is accomplished with CBR, rather than statistically. The missions or events in the case base that most closely match the hypothesized scenario are retrieved. The parameters associated with the retrieved cases are then adjusted for differences between the proposed and retrieved cases, using rules of thumb formulated in a rule base for this purpose. Then, using the model equation, CREW computes values of Y_t for each behavioral factor at each time slice t in the mission. These values can be graphed to present a visual image of the model's expectations for the proposed mission. Users can then modify their descriptions of the mission scenario and/or the sequence of events and re-run the analysis to test alternative mission scenarios.

CREW is basically a database system, with a system of relational files storing variable values and parameter values for historical cases and rules for case adaptation. For this reason it was developed in the FoxPro database management system, rather than in Lisp, as originally planned. FoxPro is extremely efficient at retrieving items from indexed database files, so that CREW can be scaled up to arbitrarily large case bases with virtually no degradation in processing speed. CREW runs on Macintosh and Windows computers.

14.5   The Case Retrieval Mechanism

A key aspect of CBR is its case retrieval mechanism. The first step in computing predictions for a proposed new case is to retrieve one or more similar cases from the case base. According to Schank [11], CBR adopts the dynamic memory approach of human recall.

As demonstrated in exemplary CBR systems [10], this involves a hierarchical storage and retrieval arrangement. Thus, to retrieve the case most similar to a new case, one might, for instance, follow a tree of links that begins with the mission characteristic, harshness of environment. Once one followed the link corresponding to the new case's environment, one would select the link for the next characteristic and so on until one arrived at a leaf of the tree with a particular case. The problem with this method is that not all domains can be organized in such a hierarchy meaningfully. Kolodner [5] notes that some CBR systems need to define non-hierarchical retrieval systems. In the domain of space missions, there is no clear priority of characteristics for establishing similarity of cases.

A standard non-hierarchical measure of similarity is the n-dimensional Euclidean distance, which compares two cases by adding the squares of the differences between each of the n corresponding variable values. The problem with this method is that it is intractable for large case bases because you must compare a new case with every case in the database.

CREW adopts an approach that avoids the need to define a strict hierarchy of variables as well as the ultimately intractable inefficiency of comparing a new case to each historic case. It prioritizes which variables to compare initially in order to narrow down to the most likely neighbors using highly efficient indices on the database files. But it avoids strict requirements even at this stage.

The retrieval algorithm also responds to another problem of the space mission domain that is discussed in the section on adaptation below: the fact that there are large random variations among similar cases. This problem suggests finding several similar cases instead of just one to adapt to a new case. The case retrieval algorithm in CREW returns n nearest neighbors, where n is a small number specified by the user. Thus, parameters for new cases can be computed using adjusted values from several near neighbors, rather than just from the one nearest neighbor as is traditional in CBR. This introduces a statistical flavor to the computation in order to soften the variability likely to be present in the empirical case data.

The case retrieval mechanism consists of a procedure for finding the n most similar factors and a procedure for finding the n most similar events, given a proposed factor or event, a number n and the case base file. These procedures in turn call various subprocedures. Each of the procedures is of computational order n, where n is the number of neighbors sought, so it will scale up with no problem for case bases of arbitrary size. Here are outlines of typical procedures:

nearest_factor(new_factor, n, file)

1. find all factor records with the same factor type, using a database index
2. of these, find the $4n$ with the **nearest_mission**
3. of these, find the n with the **nearest_actor**

nearest_mission(new_mission, n, file)

1. find all mission records with environment = new mission's environment ± 1 using an index
2. if less than $20n$ results, then find all mission records with environment = new mission's environment ± 2 using an index
3. if less than $20n$ results, then find all mission records with environment = new mission's environment ± 3 using an index
4. of these, find the $3n$ records with minimal |mission's duration $-$ new mission's duration| using an index

5. of these, find the n records with minimal $\sum \text{dif}_i^2$

nearest_actor(new_actor, n, file)

1. find up to n actor records with minimal $\sum \text{dif}_i^2$

Note that in these procedures there is a weak sense of hierarchical ordering. It is weak in that it includes only a couple of levels and usually allows values that are not exactly identical, depending on how many cases exist with identical matches. Note, too, that the n-dimensional distance approach is used (indicated by 'minimal $\sum \text{dif}_i^2$'), but only with $3n$ cases, where n is the number of similar cases sought. The only operations that perform searches on significant portions of the database are those that can be accomplished using file indexes. These operations are followed by procedures that progressively narrow down the number of cases. Thereby, a balance is maintained that avoids both rigid prioritizing and intractable computations.

CBR often imposes a hierarchical priority to processing that is hidden behind the scenes. It makes case retrieval efficient without exposing the priorities to scrutiny. The preceding algorithms employ a minimum of prioritizing. In each instance, priorities are selected that make sense in the domain of extreme missions based on our understanding of the relevant literature and discussions with domain experts at NASA. Of course, as understanding of the domain evolves with increased data and experience, these priorities will have to be reviewed and adjusted.

14.6   Rules and Fuzzy Logic

Once n similar cases have been found, they must be adapted to the new case. That is, we know the time series parameters for the similar old cases and we now need to adjust them to define parameters for the new case, taking into account the differences between the old and the new cases. Because the database is relatively sparse, it is unlikely that we will retrieve cases that closely match a proposed new case. Adaptation rules play a critical role in spanning the gap between the new and the retrieved cases.

The rules have been generated by our social science team, which has reviewed much of the literature on analog missions and small group interactions under extreme conditions of isolation and confinement, e.g., (Radloff and Helmreich [9]). They have determined what variables have positive, negligible or negative correlations with which factors. They have rated these correlations as either *strong* or *weak*. The CREW system translates the ratings into percentage correlation values. For instance, the rule, 'teamwork is strongly negatively correlated with commander competence' would be encoded as a -80% correlation between the variable *commander competence* and the factor teamwork.

The rules function roughly as follows in CREW: one rule, for instance, is used to adjust predicted stress for a hypothetical mission of length *new-duration* from the stress measured in a similar mission of length *old-duration*. Suppose that the rule states that the correlation of psychological stress to mission *duration* is $+55\%$. All mission factors, such as stress, are coded on a scale of 0 to 10. Suppose that the historic mission had its duration variable coded as 5 and a stress factor rating of 6, and that the hypothetical mission has a duration of 8. We use the rule to adapt the historic mission's stress rating to the hypothetical mission given the difference in mission durations (assuming all other mission characteristics to be identical). Now, the maximum that stress could be increased and still be on the scale is 4 (from 6 to 10); the *new-duration* is greater than the old by 60% ($8 - 5 = 3$ of a possible $10 - 5 = 5$); and the rule states that the correlation is 55%. So the predicted stress for the new case is greater than the stress for the old case by: $4 \times 60\% \times 55\% = 1.32$ – for a predicted stress of $6 + 1.32 = 7.32$. Using this method of adapting outcome values, the values are proportional to the correlation value, to the difference between the new and old variable values and to the old outcome value, without ever exceeding the 0 to 10 range.

There are many rules needed for the system. Rules for adapting the four parameters (μ, σ, ϕ and θ) of the 12 factors are needed for each of the 22 variables of the mission and actor descriptions, requiring 1056 rules. Rules for adapting the three parameters (ε, δ and ω) of the eight event types for each of the 12 factors are needed for each of the 24 variables of the mission, actor and intervention descriptions, requiring 6912 rules. Many of these 7968 required rules have correlations of 0, indicating that a difference in the given variable has no effect on the particular parameter.

The rules gleaned from the literature are rough descriptions of relationships, rather than precise functions. Because so many rules are applied in a typical simulation, it was essential to streamline the computations. We therefore made the simplifying assumption that all correlations were linear from zero difference between the old and new variable values to a difference of the full 10 range, with only the strength of the correlation varying from rule to rule.

However, it is sometimes the case that such rules apply more or less depending on values of other variables. For instance, the rule 'teamwork is strongly negatively correlated with commander competence' might be valid only 'if commander leadership is very low and the crew member's self-reliance is low'. This might capture the circumstance where a commander is weak at leading others to work on something, while the crew is reliant on him and where the commander can do everything himself. It might generally be good for a commander to be competent, but problematic under the special condition that he is a poor leader and that the crew lacks self-reliance.

Note that the original rule has to do with the difference of a given variable (*commander competence*) in the old and the new cases, while the condition on the rule has to do with the absolute value of variables (*commander leadership, crew member's self-reliance*) in the new case. CREW uses fuzzy logic [3] to encode the conditions. This allows the conditions to be stated in English language terms, using values like *low, medium,* or *high*, modifiers like *very* or *not*, and the connectives and or or. The values like *low* are defined by fuzzy set membership functions, so that if the variable is 0 it is considered completely low, but if it is 2 it is only partially low. Arbitrarily complex conditions can be defined. They compute to a numeric value between 0 and 1. This value of the condition is then multiplied by the value of the rule so that the rule is only applied to the extent that the condition exists.

The combination of many simple linear rules and occasional arbitrarily complex conditions on the rules provides a flexible yet computationally efficient system for implementing the rules found in the social science literature. The English language statements by the researchers are translated reasonably into numeric computations by streamlined versions of the fuzzy logic formalism, preserving sufficient precision considering the small effect that any given rule or condition has on the overall simulation.

14.7   The Adaptation Algorithm

Space and analog missions exhibit large variations in survey results due to the complexity and subjectivity of the crew members' perceptions as recorded in survey forms. Even among surveys by different crew members on relatively simple missions with highly homogeneous crews, the recorded survey ratings varied remarkably. To average out these effects, CREW retrieves n nearest neighbors for any new case, rather than the unique nearest one as is traditional in CBR. The value of n is set by the user.

The parameters that model the new case are computed by taking a weighted average of the parameters of the n retrieved neighbors. The weight used in this computation is based on a similarity distance of each neighbor from the new case. The similarity distance is the sum of the squares of the differences between the new and the old values of each variable. So, if the new case and a neighbor differed only in that the new case had a mission complexity rating of 3 while the retrieved neighbor had a mission complexity rating of 6, then the neighbor's distance would be $(6 - 3)^2 = 9$.

The weighting actually uses a term called *importance* that is defined as (sum − distance)/(sum × $(n-1)$), where distance is the distance of the current neighbor as just defined and sum is the sum of the distances of the n neighbors. This weighting gives a strong preference to neighbors that are very near to the new case, while allowing all n neighbors to contribute to the adaptation process.

14.8   Conclusions and Future Work

The domain of space missions poses a number of difficulties for the creation of an expert system:

- Too little is known to generalize formal rules for a rule based system.
- A model of the temporal mission process is needed more than just a prediction of final outcomes.
- The descriptive variables cannot be put into a rigid hierarchy to facilitate case based retrieval.
- The case base is too sparse and too variable for reliable adaptation from one nearest neighbor case.
- The rules that can be gleaned from available data or relevant literature are imprecise.

Therefore, we have constructed a hybrid system that departs in several ways from traditional rule based as well as classic case based systems. CREW creates a time series model of a mission, retrieving and adapting the parameters of the model from a case base. The retrieval uses a multi-stage algorithm to maintain both flexibility and computational tractability. An extensive set of adaptation rules overcomes the sparseness of the case base, with the results of several nearest neighbors averaged together to avoid the unreliability of individual cases.

Our proof-of-concept system demonstrates the tractability of our approach. For testing purposes, CREW was loaded with descriptions of 50 hypothetical missions involving 62 actors. This involved 198 intervention parameters, 425 factor parameters and 4047 event parameters. Based on our reading of the relevant literature, 7968 case adaptation rule correlation figures were entered. A number of fuzzy logic conditions were also included for the test cases. Given a description of a crew member and a mission, the CREW system predicts a series of one hundred values of a selected psychological factor in a minute or two on a standard Macintosh or Windows desktop computer.

Future work includes expanding the fuzzy logic language syntax to handle more subtle rules. Our impression from conflicting conclusions within the literature is that it is unlikely that many correlation rules hold uniformly across entire ranges of their factors.

We would also like to enhance the explanatory narrative provided by CREW in order to increase its value as a research assistant. We envision our system serving as a tool to help domain experts select astronaut crews, rather than as an automated decision maker. People will want to be able to see and evaluate the program's rationale for its predictions. This would minimally involve displaying the original sources of cases and rules used by the algorithms. The most important factors should be highlighted. In situations strongly influenced by case adaptation rules or fuzzy logic conditions derived from the literature, it would be helpful to display references to the sources of the rules if not the relevant excerpted text itself.

Currently, each crew member is modeled independently; it is undoubtedly important to take into account interactions among them as well. While crew interactions indirectly affect survey results of individual members (especially to questions like: How well do you think the crew is working together today?), additional data would be needed to model interactions directly. Two possible approaches suggest themselves: treating crew interaction as a special category of event or subjecting data from crew members on a mission together to statistical analyses to see how their moods, etc. affect one another. Taking interactions into account would significantly complicate the system and would require data that is not currently systematically collected.

Use of the system by NASA personnel will suggest changes in the variables tracked and their relative priority in the processing algorithms; this will make end-user modifiability facilities desirable. In order to quickly develop a proof-of-concept system, we hard-coded many of the algorithms described in this chapter. However, some of these algorithms make assumptions about, for instance, what are the most important factors to sort on first. As the eventual system users gain deeper understanding of mission dynamics, they will want to be able to modify these algorithms. Future system development should make that process easier and less fragile.

Data about individual astronauts, about group interactions and about mission progress at a detailed level is not public information. For a number of personal and institutional reasons, such information is closely guarded. Combined with the fact that NASA was just starting to collect the kind of time series data that CREW is based on, that made it impossible for us to use empirical data in our case base. Instead, we incorporated the format of the IFRS surveys and generated plausible data based on the statistical results of completed IFRS surveys and the public literature on space and analog missions. When NASA has collected enough empirical cases to substitute for our test data, they will have to enter the new parameters, review the rule base, and reconsider some of the priorities embedded in our algorithms based on their new understanding of mission dynamics. However, they should be able to do this within the computational framework we have developed, confident that such a system is feasible. As NASA collects more time series data, the CREW database will grow and become increasingly plausible as a predictive tool that can assist in the planning of expensive and risky interplanetary missions.

Acknowledgement

'Armchair missions to Mars' describes research conducted during a two-year SBIR (Small Business Innovative Research) grant (Project 91-1-II-1201-9027) from NASA in 1993–1995. This chapter (except for the Preface) is reprinted from *Knowledge-Based Systems*, Volume 9, Stahl et al, Armchair missions to Mars using case-based reasoning and fuzzy logic to simulate a time series model of astronaut crews, pp. 409–415, 1996, with permission from Elsevier Science.

References

1. American Astronomical Society (1966) *Stepping Stones to Mars Meeting*. American Institute of Aeronautics and Astronautics, New York.
2. Collins, D (1985) *Psychological Issues Relevant to Astronaut Selection for Long Duration Spaceflight: A Review of the Literature*. USAF Systems Command, Brooks Air Force Base, Texas.
3. Cox, E (1994) *The Fuzzy Systems Handbook*. Academic Press, Boston, MA.
4. Harrison, A, Clearwater, Y, McKay C (1991) From Antarctica to Outer Space: Life in Isolation and Confinement. *Behavioral Science*. 34, 253–271.
5. Kolodner, J (1993) *Case Based Reasoning*. Morgan Kaufmann. San Mateo, CA.
6. McDowall, D, McLeary, R, Meidinger, E, Hay, R Jr (1980) *Interrupted Time Series Analysis*. Sage, Beverly Hills, CA.
7. McKay, C (ed.) (1985) *The Case for Mars II*. American Astronautic Society, San Diego, CA.
8. Owen, R, Holland, A, Wood, J (1993) A Prototype Case Based Reasoning Human Assistant for Space Crew Assessment and Mission Management. In Fayyad, U, Uthurusamy, F (eds), *Applications of Artificial Intelligence 1993: Knowledge - Based Systems in Aerospace and Industry*. SPIE, Vol. 1963, pp. 262–273, Bellingham, WA.
9. Radloff, R, Helmreich, R (1968) *Groups Under Stress: Psychological Research in Sealab II*. Appleton Century Crofts, New York.
10. Riesbeck, C, Schank, R (1989) *Inside Case Based Reasoning*. Lawrence Earlbaum, Hillsdale, NJ.
11. Schank, R (1982) *Dynamic Memory*. Cambridge University Press, Cambridge, UK.

15. Applications of Soft CBR at General Electric

Bill Cheetham, Paul Cuddihy and Kai Goebel

Abstract. General Electric has used soft computing techniques in a variety of fielded case based reasoning systems. In doing so we were able to leverage the tolerance for imprecision and uncertainty which is intrinsic to soft computing techniques. The pay-off of this conjunctive use of soft computing and case based reasoning techniques is a more accurate and robust solution than a solution derived from the use of any single technique alone. The fielded systems for medical equipment diagnostics and residential property valuation used fuzzy membership functions for greater selection accuracy through their noise tolerance and for the ability to determine a confidence in a result. A plastic color-matching system used fuzzy logic to combine several selection criteria which allowed its users to detect potential problems during the case selection phase while previously these problems were not detected until the color match was complete. Finally, adaptive fuzzy clusters were used for fault classification of aircraft engine sensor data. The advantages of this system were its ability to deal with extremely noisy sensors and to adjust to unpredictable slow drift.

15.1 Introduction

General Electric (GE) has fielded a set of case based reasoning (CBR) [1,2,9,23] applications that use techniques from soft computing (SC) [22,28]. The SC techniques allow reasoning with uncertainty and imprecision that is beneficial to the CBR process. This chapter will show those benefits for each of the applications from the field of medical equipment diagnosis, plastics color matching, residential property valuation, and aircraft engine monitoring. We will show improvement of case selection accuracy, handling of multiple selection criteria, producing a confidence value for a specific result, and dealing with non-stationary cases. In particular, the use of membership functions allows a greater accuracy and smoothness in the selection phase. Handling multiple selection criteria enables the systems to detect potential problems during the selection phase. The ability to determine confidence in a result makes the systems more useful to the end users.

Finally, cases of non-stationary systems are tracked and updated atomically. Each application has been under development for multiple years, used in the field for over a year, and most are still in use. Fig. 15.1 shows the duration of time when each application was developed with a solid line and the time the application has been in use with a dotted line. The following sections will briefly describe an application, then go into detail on how soft computing techniques were integrated with the traditional CBR process.

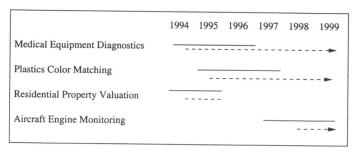

Fig. 15.1. Tool development and usage.

15.2 Medical Equipment Diagnosis

This section examines the use of SC techniques to boost the performance and quantify the confidence of answers generated by a case based diagnostic system built for GE Medical Systems (GEMS).

15.2.1 Introduction

ELSI (Error Log Similarity Index) [1,12–14] was first conceived in the early 1990s to solve a diagnostic challenge with computed tomography (CT) scanners. GEMS had built an infrastructure to allow service technicians to dial in to imaging equipment and diagnose failures while still on the phone with the customer. Once the service engineer had taken a look at the equipment remotely, the customers' issues could often be resolved over the phone. If parts and repairs were needed, the service engineer could send out a field engineer with the correct parts already in hand.

Some of the most promising diagnostic information on the machines was in error logs generated by the computer processes controlling the machines. The error logs, however, had been primarily designed as debugging tools for developers, not as diagnostic tools for service technicians. The logs were not well formatted, and contained a mix of normal status messages and error messages. The messages were documented one by one, yet equipment failures were found to generate more complex cascades of errors.

Recognizing these combinations of error messages was purely an art form practiced by the more experienced service engineers. An automated system was needed to find these patterns and catalog them, thus creating a common experience base across service engineers. ELSI set out to meet this challenge.

ELSI's primarily case based approach also provided platform independence (the system could be used on different models and types of equipment), little need for knowledge collection from the equipment designers, and the ability to keep up with design changes as new cases arrived.

Fig. 15.2 describes the ELSI process. After error logs have been obtained in step 1, they are pre-processed in step 2. Here, diagnostically extraneous information such as dates and scan numbers is removed. In rare cases useful numeric values are rounded to make exact matches with other logs more likely. In step 3 the logs are compared to other logs with the same fix, and the largest possible blocks of completely matching

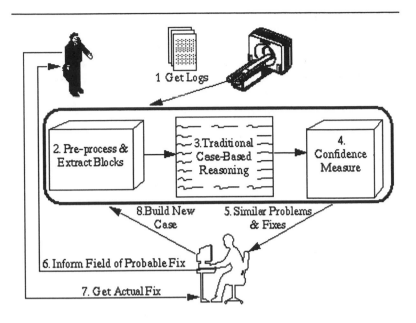

Fig. 15.2. High-Level ELSI architecture.

lines are extracted. When a new case comes in to be diagnosed, its logs are searched for all known blocks, and its similarity to known cases is determined through the formula:

$$\text{similarity}(\text{new},N) = \sqrt{\frac{\sum \text{weights(matching)}}{\sum \text{weights(new)}} \times \frac{\sum \text{weights(matching)}}{\sum \text{weights}(N)}}$$

This translates to simply reporting which past cases share the most symptoms (after weighting) with the new case. The cases with the highest similarity were shown to the service engineers, who could look at the matching blocks and the notes from matching cases to make the final determination of how to fix the machine.

In step 4, the blocks of error log are then given weights inversely proportional to the number of different kinds of problems that have generated the block. Blocks that appear only for one fix are given the highest weight. Those that appear for many different fixes are thrown out altogether. Steps 5–8 are concerned with updating and reporting tasks.

15.2.2   Noise Handling

Although this system was successful when first fielded, it did not effectively handle the high level of noise in the case base. Fig. 15.3 shows a simplified view of the types of noise encountered in the case bases. Each letter represents a different fix. The numbers 1–4 represent new cases.

Notice these types of noise:

1. Fixes like 'x' are tightly clustered, while others like 'y' are not.
2. Fixes like 'z' have multiple clusters; they have different failure modes.
3. Some groups of failures like 'w' 'x' 'y' 'z' generate nearly identical logs.

Given this noise, cases like (1) match fine. The other cases do not. Case (2) is equally close to 'x' and 'y' cases, but the 'y' cluster is much looser. Therefore the case is probably a better match to 'y'. Case (3) is most similar to a 'z', but that 'z' is stranded among 'y' cases. Again 'y' seems like the answer we should be most confident in.

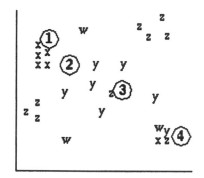

Fig. 15.3. Types of noise in the case base.

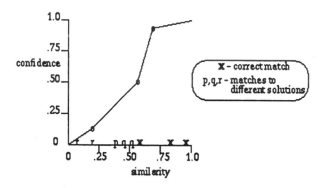

Fig. 15.4. Confidence membership function

It was case (4) that raised the red flags first. In some examples, ELSI would report perfect matches to many different cases, all with different fixes. This is because they all happened to have the same routine status messages or minimally helpful error messages and no really useful blocks. The total symptoms matched perfectly, however.

Initial attempts at setting a high threshold for weights of blocks (throwing out all but the best ones) had a very bad impact on the system. Trying to find a good k for k-

nearest neighbors was frustrated by the widely varying frequencies at which different problems occurred. Early efforts to represent case base noise in a formal statistical way indicated that the calculations needed would be too complex to implement in a practical manner.

As a result, the 'confidence measure' was devised as a way to use soft computing methods to automatically determine how confident the system should be in each match. It is a method of building membership functions which are modeled after the procedure the ELSI system developers had used to diagnose problems with the system.

15.2.2.1 Representing Confidence
Before we can proceed, we will introduce a graphical notation for confidence membership functions. An example is shown in Fig. 15.4.

This graph represents similarity versus confidence for one case stored in the case base. Note the symbols along the x-axis. These represent the case's neighbors. An 'x' represents the similarity of a case with the same fix as our target case. Other symbols 'p', 'q', 'r', etc. represent cases with other fixes (i.e., wrong answers).

15.2.2.2 Confidence Based on Fraction of Better Matches
An initial attempt at a confidence measure was based on counting all the matches higher than a certain point, and determining what fraction of them are 'right'. Fig. 15.5 shows two examples of such a confidence measure.

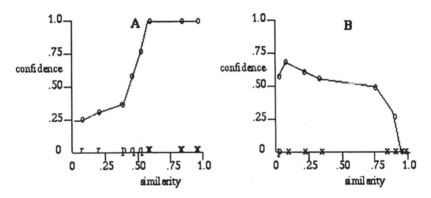

Fig. 15.5. Using fraction of closer cases with correct fix.

In these examples, confidence was calculated at each similarity where a match occurred. The confidence was calculated as the fraction of cases with similarity greater than or equal to the current level which matched the same solution. The points were then connected to form a membership function.

Example A turned out as one might expect. The confidence rises as the match becomes stronger. Example B, however, has obvious problems. The confidence drops as similarity rises. Clearly, this approach needs to be revised.

15.2.2.3 Number of Solutions with Better Matches
An alternative confidence measure is based on counting all the matches higher than

a certain point, and determining how many different solutions are represented. Confidence would be $1/$ < number of solutions > as long as one of the solutions is correct. Otherwise, confidence remains level. Again, confidence is calculated at each similarity where a match exists, and the points are connected into a line. Fig. 15.6 shows two examples of such a confidence measure.

With this technique, example A changed very little. Example B has been transformed into a straightforward and sensible function. Namely, since there are two solutions ('x' and 'r') which occur above 0.05 similarity, the confidence is around 50% for this entire range.

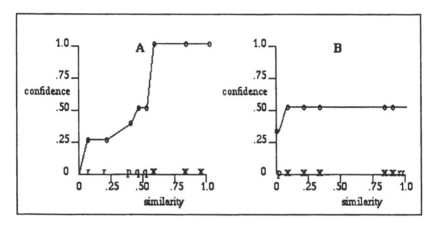

Fig. 15.6. Using number of fixes in closer cases.

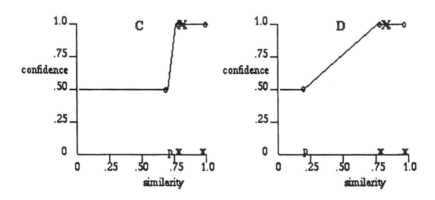

Fig. 15.7. Problem remaining in this approach.

Fig. 15.7 shows one area in which this approach remains to be improved. A 0.75 match to each of the cases C and D yields a confidence of 1.0. However, case C has an incorrect match at 0.74, while case D has no incorrect matches anywhere near 0.75.

Clearly, we should be less confident in our 0.75 match to case C than we are in a 0.75 match to case D. Another weakness in this approach is the propensity toward large plateaus at 1.0, 1/2, 1/3, 1/4, etc. This produces more confidence value ties than is necessary.

15.2.2.4 Final Confidence Measure
The final solution we implemented was based on the same formula as above, but we calculate a confidence at fewer points. The formula, again, is 1 / <number of solutions with better matches>. Moving from best match to worst match (right to left) we start at the first correct match, and continue by calculating a value only at the best match for each solution. Fill in the rest of the function with a distance- weighted average between points (connecting the dots), connecting to the origin at the left, and maintaining a constant value (horizontal line) on the right. Fig. 15.8 shows the resulting functions.

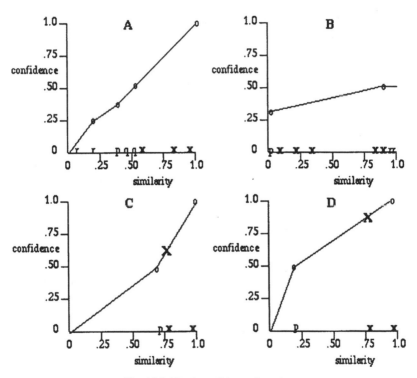

Fig. 15.8. Final confidence functions.

This final algorithm gives satisfactory membership functions in all the cases examined so far. In case A, confidence starts at 0 and passes 0.5 when it passes the best matching incorrect answer. From that point it rises steadily to confidence of 1 at similarity of 1. For cases like B where the best matches are to cases with a different solution, confidence never rises above 0.5. This accurately reflects the fact that no case can ever be so similar to case B that there are not at least two likely solutions.

This approach smoothes out the plateaus in all four cases, and improves the distinction between the 0.75 matches to cases C and D properly. That is, the confidence is lower at 0.75 in case C since there is an incorrect match at 0.74, while it is higher in case D.

15.2.3   Results

Using soft computing techniques to build a 'confidence' member function for ELSI increased the accuracy and lowered the maintenance requirements of the system.

Applying this confidence measure to two noisy case bases on top of three different traditional similarity measures yielded fairly standard improvements of 13% in first-guess accuracy. That means that, using leave-one-out testing, 13cases had best confidence matches with the same fix than had best similarity matches with the same fix.

Equally notable is the fact that while similarities above 0.9 were only correct 59% of the time (averaged across all techniques), confidences above 0.9 were correct 92% of the time. All similarity measures tested showed marked improvements in this area. This increased end-user's satisfaction with the system.

Although the designers of diagnostic systems love to dwell on the accuracy of the system, the real measure of the quality of a system may be in the users' ability to maintain it. This is where the confidence function played its most important role.

The confidence function is a formal way of handling noise in the case base. This translates directly into tolerating the addition of cases which do not have enough information in the logs to narrow down the fix to one part, or cases where the fix is entered incorrectly.

This tolerance of noise allowed for a much simpler case base maintenance procedure. Without it, cases would have to go through a very complicated verification procedure to determine not only that the fix was correct, but also that there was enough information in the error log to diagnose it. With the confidence measure, all available cases could be added. Only periodically would a maintainer need to look through the case base for a build-up of cases which did not diagnose correctly, and remove them.

The confidence measure played a key role in enabling ELSI to be handed off to users with limited computing skills, where they added hundreds of new cases and ran diagnostics on thousands of problems over several years without requiring major help from the system developers.

15.3   Property Valuation

A division of GE Mortgage purchases mortgage packages on the secondary market as investments. These packages can contain up to 1000 mortgages. Property valuations are needed to evaluate the current value of mortgage packages that may be purchased. However, it is not cost effective to have humans appraise these mortgage packages. To automate the valuation process we have developed the Property Financial Information Technology (PROFIT) system [5,8,19], which uses fuzzy logic to enhance CBR.

15.3.1 Introduction

Residential property valuation [3] is the process of determining a dollar estimate of the property value for given market conditions. Residential property is restricted to a single family residence designed or intended for owner-occupancy. The value of a property changes with market conditions, so any estimate of its value must be periodically updated to reflect those market changes. Any valuation must also be supported by current evidence of market conditions, e.g. recent real estate transactions.

The current manual process for valuing properties usually requires an on-site visit by a human appraiser, takes several days, and costs about $500 per subject property. This process is too slow and expensive for batch applications such as those used by banks for updating their loan and insurance portfolios, verifying risk profiles of servicing rights, or evaluating default risks for securitized packages of mortgages. The appraisal process for these batch applications is currently estimated, to a lesser degree of accuracy, by sampling techniques. Verification of property value on individual transactions may also be required by secondary buyers. Thus, this work is motivated by a broad spectrum of application areas.

In most cases, the most credible method used by appraisers is the sales comparison approach. This method consists of finding comparables (i.e., recent sales that are comparable to the subject property using sales records); contrasting the subject property with the comparables; adjusting the comparables' sales price to reflect their differences from the subject property (using heuristics and personal experience); and reconciling the comparables' adjusted sales prices to derive an estimate for the subject property (using any reasonable averaging method). This process assumes that the item's market value can be derived by the prices demanded by similar items in the same market.

The PROFIT CBR process also consists of selecting relevant cases, adapting them, and aggregating those adapted cases into a single estimate of the property value. This process is shown in Fig. 15.9.

Upon entering the subject property attributes, PROFIT retrieves potentially similar comparables from the case base. This initial selection uses six attributes: address, date of sale, living area, lot area, number of bathrooms, and bedrooms. The comparables are rated and ranked on a similarity scale to identify the most similar ones to the subject property. This rating is obtained from a weighted aggregation of the decision-making preferences, expressed as fuzzy membership distributions and relations. Each property's sales price is adjusted to better reflect the subject's value. These adjustments are performed by a rule set that uses additional property attributes, such as construction quality, conditions, pools, fireplaces, etc. The best four to eight comparables are then selected. Finally, the adjusted sales price and similarity of the selected properties are combined to produce an estimate of the value of the subject, a reliability in that estimate, and a justification for the estimate.

15.3.2 Fuzzy Case Retrieval

The initial retrieval extracts a set of potential comparables using standard SQL queries for efficiency purpose. The selection is performed by comparing specific attributes of

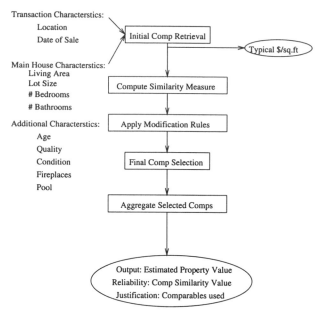

Fig. 15.9. Property valuation process.

the subject with the corresponding attribute of each comparable. All the comparables in the retrieved set have values within the allowable deviations. If the size of the retrieved set is too small, e.g., less than 10, the allowable deviations could be relaxed to increase its size at the expense of retrieval quality.

This initial retrieval stage uses the following attributes and their corresponding maximum allowable deviations (written after each attribute):

- date of sale (within 12 months);
- distance (within 1 mile);
- living area ($\pm 25\%$);
- lot size ($+100\%$ or -50%);
- number of bedrooms (± 3);
- number of bathrooms (± 3).

Fig. 15.10 describes our preference criteria for the first four features. The trapezoidal membership distributions representing these criteria have a natural preference interpretation. For each feature, the support of the distribution represents the range of tolerable values and corresponds to the interval value used in the initial retrieval query. The core represents the most desirable range of values and establishes our top preference. By definition, a feature value falling inside the core will receive a preference value of 1. As the feature value moves away from the most desirable range, its associated preference value will decrease from 1 to 0. At the end of this evaluation, each comparable will have a preference vector, with each element taking values in the (0,1] interval. These values represent the partial degree of membership of each feature value in the fuzzy sets and fuzzy relations representing our preference criteria.

For example, by using the preference distributions shown in Fig. 15.10 we can see that the preference value for the attribute date-of-sale of a comparable that was sold within three months of today's date is 1. If the date was six months ago, its preference value would be 2/3. Any comparable with a date of sale of more than 12 months would be given a preference value of zero.

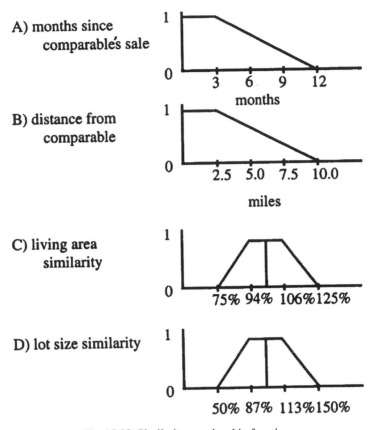

Fig. 15.10. Similarity membership functions.

The remaining two features, 'Number of bedrooms' and 'Number of bathrooms', are evaluated in a similar fashion. Their preference functions are represented by two reflexive asymmetric fuzzy relations, illustrated in Fig. 15.11 and Fig. 15.12, respectively.

For instance, using Table 15.1, we can observe that for a subject with five bedrooms the preferred comparable would also have five bedrooms (preference = 1), while a six-bedroom comparable would meet that preference criterion to a degree of 0.8. Similarly, using Table 15.2, we can observe that, for a subject with two bathrooms, the preferred comparable would also have two bathrooms (preference value = 1), while a 2.5-bathroom comparable would meet that preference criterion to a degree of 0.7.

Table 15.1. Fuzzy relation for bedrooms

Comparable's # bedrooms		1	2	3	4	5	6+
	1	1.00	0.50	0.05	0.00	0.00	0.00
Subject's	2	0.20	1.00	0.50	0.05	0.00	0.00
# bedrooms	3	0.05	0.30	1.00	0.60	0.05	0.00
	4	0.00	0.05	0.50	1.00	0.60	0.20
	5	0.00	0.00	0.05	0.60	1.00	0.80
	6	0.00	0.00	0.00	0.20	0.80	1.00

Table 15.2. Fuzzy relation for bathrooms

Subject's	Comparable								
	1	1.5	2	2.5	3	3.5	4	4.5	5+
1	1.00	0.75	0.20	0.05	0.01	0.00	0.00	0.00	0.00
1.5	0.60	1.00	0.60	0.25	0.10	0.05	0.00	0.00	0.00
2	0.10	0.70	1.00	0.70	0.25	0.05	0.00	0.00	0.00
2.5	0.05	0.20	0.75	1.00	0.75	0.20	0.05	0.00	0.00
3	0.01	0.10	0.40	0.80	1.00	0.80	0.40	0.10	0.05
3.5	0.00	0.05	0.15	0.45	0.85	1.00	0.85	0.45	0.30
4	0.00	0.00	0.05	0.20	0.50	0.90	1.00	0.90	0.70
4.5	0.00	0.00	0.00	0.10	0.30	0.70	0.95	1.00	0.95
5+	0.00	0.00	0.00	0.05	0.15	0.35	0.75	0.95	1.00

15.3.3 Fuzzy Confidence

The users will make critical decisions based on the estimates generated. Therefore, we need to tell them when the system produces an accurate, reliable solution. We achieve this goal by attaching a reliability measure to each estimate. Ideally we would like to have subjects with the highest reliability exhibiting the lowest errors. At the same time we would like to assign high reliability values to as many subjects as possible.

The reliability value is calculated from the following five quantitative characteristics of the CBR process:

- number of cases found in the initial retrieval;
- average of the similarity values for the best four cases;
- typicality of problem with respect to the case base (i.e., if the attributes of the subjects' fall within typical ranges for the subjects' five-digit zip code region);
- span of adjusted sales prices of highest reliability solutions (i.e., the highest adjusted sale price minus the lowest adjusted sale price among the selected comparables);

- distribution of adjusted sales prices of highest reliability solutions (i.e., average percentage deviation of the adjusted sales price of the comparables from the estimated value of the subject).

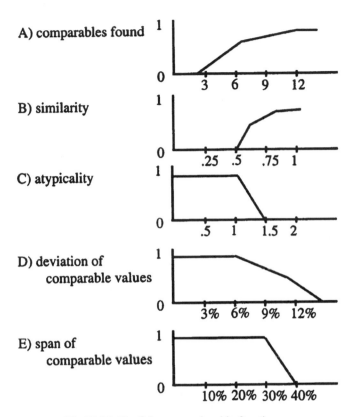

Fig. 15.11. Confidence membership functions.

These characteristics are evaluated using the fuzzy membership functions illustrated in Fig. 15.11. These functions map the numerical value of each parameter into a standard numerical reliability, which ranges from 0 to 1. These standardized reliability values are then aggregated into a final reliability value. Given the conjunctive nature of this aggregation, we decided to use the *minimum* of the standardized reliability values.

Fig. 15.11A shows that if two or fewer comparables are found then the standardized reliability for comparables found is 0. If between two and seven comparables are found, the reliability is $((n-2)*0.15))$, i.e., the reliability increases 0.15 for each comparable over two to reach 0.75 when there are seven comparables. Between seven and 12 comparables, the reliability is $(((n-7)*0.05)+0.75)$, i.e., the reliability increases 0.05 for each comparable over seven and reaches 1.0 with 12 comparables. Since the aggregation method is minimum operator, a low reliability in any of the characteristics will cause a low reliability in the result regardless of other excellent reliability values for the other characteristics. The other figures show similar membership functions for the other reliability measures.

Fig. 15.11B shows that we have no reliability in an estimate whose similarity is lower than 0.5. Otherwise the reliability rises to 1 at a similarity of 0.8, and is 1 for anything over 0.8. Fig. 15.11C is used to determine our reliability based on the subject's atypicality. Atypicality is computed as a normalized deviation in the region's average lot size, living area, number of bedroom, bathrooms, etc. We have no reliability in subjects with atypicality greater than 1.5. Our reliability rises linearly as the atypicality decreases from 1.5 to 1.0 and is one when atypicality is less than 1.0. Fig. 15.11D shows our reliability for the average deviations in the values of the comparables. We have zero reliability in an estimate if the average comparable deviates from the estimated price by more than 15%. Finally, Fig. 15.11E is used to determine our reliability based on the size of the span of the adjusted values of the comparables. If the span is greater than 40% of the value of the subject then we considered it too scattered and have no reliability in the estimate.

To create the membership functions for the five characteristics, which are illustrated in Fig. 15.11, we ran our system on 7293 properties from Contra Costa County in California. The predicted sales price of each property was calculated and compared with its actual sales price to derive the estimate's error. The percentage error and its five reliability characteristics were calculated each subject. Table 15.3 shows the values calculated for a random sample of ten of the 7293 subjects. Each row is a different subject. The columns show the estimate error, the five characteristics calculated along with the estimate, and the reliability value obtained by taking the minimum of the evaluation of the membership functions of Fig. 15.11 using the estimate's five characteristics.

Table 15.3. Confidence calculation

Error	Comps found	Simil.	Atyp.	Comps dev.	Comps span	Conf. value
-9.8	3	0.63	1.42	2.02	6.32	0.15
-2	35	0.94	0.38	2.24	8.57	1.00
17.3	11	0.71	0.94	5.67	19.0	0.70
0.5	24	0.85	0.66	2.05	7.24	1.00
-1.6	14	0.95	0.29	2.89	9.33	1.00
5.2	15	0.90	0.73	3.24	12.0	1.00
5.2	12	0.74	0.17	4.50	18.0	0.80
3.1	19	0.74	0.81	2.83	8.11	0.80
-13.9	12	0.82	1.97	3.85	15.0	0.00
7.8	11	0.77	1.34	4.24	13.0	0.32

Then we analyzed the conditional distributions of the estimate error, given each of its five reliability characteristics, and tried to predict the error. We used C4.5 [16], a decision tree tool, to create rules predicting the error from the system's characteristics. Then we validated these rules via data visualization. Finally, the rules were manually transformed into the membership functions illustrated in Fig. 15.11. The estimate's reliability value is the conjunctive evaluation of all the rules.

15.3.4   Results

At our customer's request, the reliability value generated by the rules was subdivided into three groupings (*good, fair*, and *poor*). The reliability measure should then produce the largest good set with the lowest error. Of the 7293 subjects, we could classify our reliability in 63% as *good*. The *good* set has a medium absolute error of 5.4%, an error which is satisfactory for the intended application. Of the remaining subjects, 24% were classified as *fair*, and 13% as *poor*. The fair set has a medium error of 7.7%, and the *poor* set has a median error of 11.8%. The PROFIT system was technical success, but shortly after it was completed GE got out of the business of appraising residential property.

15.4   Plastics Color Matching

GE Plastics (GEP) currently provides a color-matching service to customers. Customers give GEP a physical sample of the color plastic they want and GEP either finds a close match from their color library or formulates a new color to meet the customer's needs. GEP currently has over 30,000 previously matched colors on file and performs approximately 4000 color matches per year. When GEP does do a custom color match and formula development, there is a significant cost to GEP and the turnaround for the customer averaged two weeks. The goal was to reduce this cost and shorten the turnaround time.

15.4.1   Introduction

Selecting the colorants and loading levels for a color formula was previously accomplished using a combination of human working experience and computationally expensive computer programs. The color-matching process that was in place starts with a color matcher inspecting the color request for the type of plastic, physical color standard supplied by customer, and special properties requested. The matcher would then compare the customer's color standard with previous color chips that were stored in a filing cabinet. The filing cabinet held about 2000 plastic chips that were about $2 \times 3 \times 1/8$ inches. These chips were sorted by color. The matcher would select the most similar color from the filing cabinet. Each chip was labeled and another filing cabinet held a formula card for each chip. The matcher would then inspect the physical chip selected from the filing cabinet to determine if it matched the color and special properties requested by the customer. If it did match, then the formula that was associated with the selected chip would be used for the customer and the match was finished.

If the best chip from the filing cabinet was not a satisfactory match, then the matchers used experience along with commercially available computer programs to adapt the colorant loadings. The new loadings would be used to create a small chip containing the adapted loadings. This chip would be compared with the standard. If it was acceptable the adapted formula would be used for the customer and the chip would be placed in the filing cabinet for future reference. If the color was unacceptable then the formula would be adapted repeatedly until an acceptable formula was obtained.

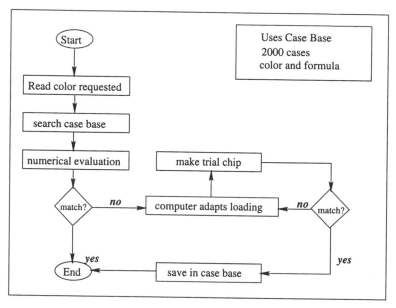

Fig. 15.12. Color matching process.

15.4.2 Automated CBR Process

The current process was already a case based approach, where the filing cabinets acted as the case base and the color matcher searching through the filing cabinet was the case selection. Creating a tool to automate this involved creating a machine-readable version of the information in the filing cabinets and then creating the CBR software that performed the search. A numerical representation of the color of the plastic chips and their formulas was stored in a database that acted as the case base. The automated color-matching process developed is shown in Fig. 15.12. Fig. 15.12 shows that the color matcher places the physical color standard in a spectrophotometer and reads the spectrum of the color standard into the color-matching system. Next, the color matcher enters key information such as the resin and grade of material in which to generate the match. FormTool then searches its case base of previous matches for the 'best' previous match and adjusts those previous matches to produce a match for the new standard. There are multiple criteria which the color match must satisfy: the color of the plastic must match the standard under multiple lighting conditions, there must be enough pigments to hide the color of the plastic, the cost of colorant formula should be as low as possible, only a limited amount of light can be transmitted through the plastic (optical density), and the color should not change when the plastic is molded at different temperatures.

15.4.3   Fuzzy Case Retrieval

This section describes a method to evaluate the quality of a specific color formula [4]. A selection process that uses this method to evaluate a formula can be used to find the formula that will reproduce a specified color and meet all desired attributes for the application of the specified color. A nearest neighbor retrieval is used. However, the nearest neighbor must be determined by evaluating the degree of match in all of the attributes described above. This evaluation needs to provide a consistent meaning of an attribute similarity throughout all attributes. The consistency is achieved through the use of fuzzy linguistic terms, such as Excellent, Good, Fair, and Poor, which are associated with measured differences in an attribute. Any number of linguistic terms can be used. A fuzzy preference function is used to calculate the similarity of a single attribute of a case with the corresponding attribute of the subject (see Fig. 15.13). In this figure, a difference of 1 unit in the values of that attribute for the subject and comparable would be considered excellent, a difference of 2 would be good, 3 would be fair, and 4 would be poor. This rating is then transformed into the fuzzy preference function in Fig. 15.13.

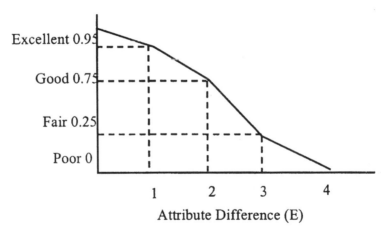

Fig. 15.13. Example membership function.

The result of using fuzzy preference functions is a vector, called the fuzzy preference vector. The vector contains a fuzzy preference value for each attribute. The values in this vector can be combined, through weighted aggregation, to produce a robust similarity value. The use of fuzzy preference functions allows for smooth changes in the result when an attribute is changed, unlike the large changes that are possible when step functions are used.

A fuzzy preference function is used to transform a quantifiable value for each attribute into a qualitative description of the attribute that can be compared with the qualitative description of other attributes. A fuzzy preference function allows a comparison of properties that are based on entirely different scales such as cost measured in cents per pound and spectral curve match measured in reflection units. Based on discussions with experts and work to classify previous matches into various sets of linguistic terms, we found that there was enough precision in our evaluation of the similarity of the attributes to have four linguistic terms. Table 15.4 shows the linguistic terms and the numeric similarity score that corresponds to each term.

Table 15.4. Linguistic terms and similarity

Fuzzy rating	Maximum score	Minimum score
Excellent	1	0.95
Good	0.94	0.75
Average	0.74	0.25
Poor	0.24	0

Fuzzy preference functions were created for each of the following attributes of the color match:

- color similarity;
- total colorant load;
- cost of colorant formula;
- optical density of color; and
- color shift when molded under normal and abusive conditions.

The remainder of this section describes how the fuzzy preference functions were constructed for each attribute.

15.4.3.1 Color Similarity

Two different ways of rating the quality of a color match are the spectral color curve match and metamerism of the color. Matching the spectral curve is the best way to match a color for all possible lighting conditions. Minimizing metamerism reduces the color difference under the most common lighting conditions. Minimizing metamerism is the traditional way a color match was done before there was a spectrophotometer that could read the reflectance of a color. Both of these methods are useful in matching a color.

The spectral color curve match is a rating of how closely the color of the formula created matches the color of the standard. A spectral curve is a representation of the amount of light that is reflected from an object at each wavelength of the visible spectrum. Comparing spectral curves of objects is the best way to compare their color, because if the two objects have the same spectral curve, then their colors will match under all lighting conditions. Other color matching techniques only match colors under one lighting condition, so the colors can look quite different under other lighting conditions.

The spectral curve match is characterized by the sums of the squared differences in the reflection values at 31 wavelengths from 400 to 700 nm at a 10 nm interval. Table 15.5 shows the value of that sum of squares that is needed for an Excellent, Good, Fair, or Poor match. These values are determined by having an expert rate the curve matches in the case base and then finding the minimum value for each of the ratings, excluding a few outliers.

Table 15.5. Fuzzy curve match

Fuzzy rating	Maximum sum of squares difference
Excellent	0.000124
Good	0.000496
Fair	0.001984
Poor	0.007936

For example, a sum of square difference of 0.000124 is the maximum difference for an excellent rating, from Table 15.5. The score corresponding to this would be 0.95, the minimum score for excellent from Table 15.5. Sum of square values between the minimum and maximum values have scores that are linearly interpolated from the minimum and maximum values for that rating. Fig. 15.14 shows the fuzzy preference function for curve match.

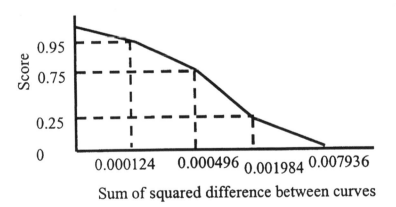

Fig. 15.14. Color match membership function.

A second measure of the curve match is the metamerism index. Metamerism takes place when two objects are the same color under one lighting condition, but different under another lighting condition. Two color chips can look the same under one lighting condition (sunlight) and different under another (indoor light). This is the effect of metamerism. There are specific lighting conditions that are more common than others.

If the spectral curve match is good, there can still be metamerism among the primary lighting conditions. This metamerism should be as small as possible.

The metamerism index is measured in dE* units using the International Commission on Illuminations L*a*b* color scale [81]. In order to calculate dE*, the stimulus color is determined from the multiple of the spectral power curve of a light source and the reflectance of the object in question. The L*a*b* scale is a three- dimensional space for representing color with L (lightness) on the up–down axis, a (red–greenness) on the left to right axis, and b (yellow–blueness) on the front-to-back axis. This color space represents color under one lighting condition (spectral power curve), unlike the spectral curve that represents color under all lighting conditions. The difference in L*a*b* values is computed by determining the difference in the L*, a*, and b* values of the two colors. These differences are called dL*, da*, and db* respectively. Then, dE* is calculated using the formula $E = \sqrt{((L_1 - L_2)^2 + (a_1 - a_2)^2 + (b_1 - b_2)^2)}$.

In order to use the L*a*b* color scale an illuminant needs to be selected. The standard illuminants that we selected are C (overcast–sky daylight), D65 (normal daylight), and F7 (fluorescent light). These represent the most common lighting conditions and give visual emphasis on the high, middle, and low wavelengths of the spectral curve respectively. dE* is the sum of the squared differences in the L*, a*, b* values of two colors.

The metamerism index is the sum of the three dE* using each of the three illuminants. The mapping of the metamerism to the fuzzy preference scale is presented in Table 15.6. This table and all other similar ones are generated from an analysis of the case base. The fuzzy preference function generated from Table 15.6 is created easily from the table. These two properties (i.e., curve match and metamerism) specify how closely the color produced by a formula matches the color of a standard.

Table 15.6. Linguistic terms for metamerism

Fuzzy rating	Maximum dE*
Excellent	0.05
Good	0.15
Fair	0.40
Poor	1.0

15.4.3.2 Total Loading

The total colorant load is total volume of all colorants used for a set volume of plastic. It is best to use the least volume of colorants that makes an acceptable match, for reasons relating to the manufacturing of the plastic.

The quality of the remaining properties depends on the color that is being matched. For example, a cost that is good for a red color might be poor for a white because reds are much more expensive. In order to use fuzzy preference functions for these attributes the case base must be subdivided into portions that have consistent values for the properties. We have divided the case base into 11 classes. For each attribute, the fuzzy ratings needed to be calculated separately for each subclass.

An attribute that uses these subclasses is the total loading of colorant in the formula. The total colorant loading of the formula can be characterized in parts per hundred (pph) parts of base material such as plastic. The total colorant loading is dependent upon the color to be made. Table 15.7 shows the fuzzy ratings for total colorant loading for the white and green color subclasses. The rest of the subclasses are similar to the ones presented. Historically, whites tend to require much more colorant than a green color. This is because it takes more of the white colorant to hide the color of the plastic. The difference in typical loadings is accounted for by using separate tables for separate colors. A fuzzy preference function can be easily constructed for each subclass.

Table 15.7. Linguistic terms for total loading

Fuzzy rating	White pph	Green pph
Excellent	3	0.4
Good	5	0.7
Fair	7	1.1
Poor	11	3.2

15.4.3.3   Cost

The cost of the colorants in the formula should be kept to a minimum to maximize the profitability of the manufacturing process. The attribute cost is measured in units of cents per pound. The fuzzy ratings for this attribute are specific for particular color subclasses, as illustrated for the red and blue subclasses in Table 15.8. There is a difference in the mapping for the red and blue color families because the cost to make a red tends to be more than the colorants used to make a blue.

Table 15.8. Linguistic terms for cost

Fuzzy rating	Red cost (cents/lb)	Blue cost (cents/lb)
Excellent	4.5	2
Good	9.0	3.5
Fair	25	10
Poor	72	28

15.4.3.4   Optical Density

The optical density of plastic is the thickness of plastic that is required to stop all light from radiating through the plastic. A specific optical density is required for many applications. For the majority of color formulas, it is desired to make the material opaque to prevent light from transmitting though the material. Optical density can be used to characterize how much light is transmitted through a sample. The type of colorants used in a formula and the loading level of the colorants determine the optical density of the material. The qualitative values of optical density are color dependent. For example, it is easier to obtain the needed optical density in an opaque gray color formula than in a red color.

Table 15.9 shows fuzzy rating of optical density for a gray and a red color.

Table 15.9. Terms for optical density

Fuzzy rating	Gray dE*	Red dE*
Excellent	5.9	5.9
Good	5.8	5
Fair	5.5	2
Poor	4	1

15.4.3.5   Hide Color Shift

The color shift when molding under normal and abusive conditions comes from the fact that the plastic can be molded at low and high temperatures. The same plastic is a slightly different color when molded at different temperatures, because plastic tends to yellow at higher temperatures. In order to minimize the color shift, extra colorant loadings need to be used. A formula must also be robust enough to hide these color changes in the base plastic. One way to characterize this attribute of hiding variations due to process conditions is to measure the color of the material under normal processing conditions and under abusive processing conditions. The difference in color between these two processing conditions is then measured in dE* units using the CIE L*a*b* color scale. Table 15.10 shows the process color change in dE* units mapped between the gray and yellow color subclasses. Visually, a larger change in color due to processing conditions can be tolerated in a light yellow color than a gray color as shown by this mapping based on historical data.

Table 15.10. Linguistic terms for color shift

Fuzzy rating	Gray dE*	Yellow dE*
Excellent	0.05	0.05
Good	0.10	0.15
Fair	0.20	0.40
Poor	0.50	1.00

15.4.4   Aggregate Fuzzy Preference Values

Each of the above properties including spectral color match, metameric index, loading level, cost, optical density, and color shift due to processing conditions is based on different scales of units. By mapping each of these properties to a global scale through the use of fuzzy preferences and linguistic terms such as Excellent, Good, Fair, and Poor, it becomes possible to compare one attribute with another.

The next step is to create a summation of the preference value of each attribute. This can be done with a weight of unity for each attribute, or the end user can supply weights of their own if they desire to emphasize one attribute over another. Dividing this summation term by the summation of the weights gives the global preference value for the system.

15.4.5 Results

GEP has obtained significant savings in both time and money by using the CBR software for color matching since the beginning of 1995. The hard savings that have been documented come from the optimization of pigment and dye concentrations and the reduction in the number of trial batches required for a color match. When the tool was first rolled out at the end of 1994, the optimization algorithms for pigment and dye concentrations were run against the historical database of formulas, resulting in the identification of formulas that could have their colorant concentrations reduced while still maintaining the quality of the color match. These changes led to a reduction in the raw material cost of the final product, generating significant cost reductions to the company. The reduction in the number of trial batches required to obtain a color match has led GEP to cut its lead time for a custom color match down from an average of two weeks to a 48-hour turn-around time. This lead time reduction has been a great help to our customers. Many of our customers have been trying to shorten the development time for their new products. If we can shorten the color selection time by two weeks then it can shorten their development cycle time by two weeks at no cost to them.

15.5 Adaptive Fuzzy Classification in Aircraft Engines

The CBR application shown here diagnoses aircraft engine based on sensor readings taken at the engines. This is a difficult diagnostic problem because the baseline for the sensor values changes unpredictably within bounds over time. To cope with that situation, the implemented system continuously adapts cases to match criteria set up for baseline cases. This can conceptually be done by either adapting the baseline cases or by adapting the complement set. To allow the process to be applied to a multitude of different engines, we chose to adapt the baseline case and to keep the complement set fixed. The adaptation was performed marrying statistical process control techniques with fuzzy k-nearest neighbor [7]. In a further step, the incoming cases are not actually stored. Rather, a prototype case is updated with the new information. This allows a substantial reduction of storage requirements because only a few parameters are needed to be carried forward through time. In addition, it eliminates the need to delete older samples because that information is already integrated into the parameters. The remaining system is comprised of a fixed set of cases evenly spaced through the problem domain. Incoming cases are pre-processed to fit that scheme and then are used to update the pre-processing scheme. The operation is shown for abnormal condition detection on a continuous data stream from engine measurements of an aircraft engine from GE Aircraft Engines (GEAE).

15.5.1 Introduction

It is desirable to be able to detect incipient failures before they cause costly secondary damage or result in equally undesired engine shutdowns. To that end, service providers have long tracked the behavior of engines by measuring and analyzing a multitude of system parameters to become aware of changes that might be indicative of developing failures [15]. However, often times faults may not be recognized distinctively because the 'normal' operation condition varies unpredictably. This is owing in part to large amounts of noise, poor corrections of first-principle models or regression models, changes of schedules, maintenance, poorly calibrated and deteriorating sensors, faulty data acquisition, etc.

When the sensor readings are analyzed in trend analysis tools, the data and parameter settings are evaluated for deviations from normal operating conditions. An alarm is raised when threshold settings are exceeded, assuming the reading is not an outlier. To create awareness of potential problems before they turn into events that result in revenue loss (such as grounding of an airplane, damage to the engine, departure delays, etc.) the settings used in trend analysis are typically below the limit that would cause an immediate shutdown. Once made aware, the analyst examines trend charts to determine whether something real has happened. If he/she can corroborate the initial finding, remedial actions (boroscoping, engine washing, overhauls, etc.) are suggested. A fully automated notification is hard to come by because of the need to detect all abnormal conditions. This implies that thresholds have to be set to a level that can insure zero false negatives. However, in the presence of very noisy and drifting systems, this means that alarms are generated excessively. That in turn means the user must look at trends more often than desired to weed out the faulty alarms from the true ones.

Prior work in this area was done, among others, by Karamouzis and Feyock, who proposed system integrating model based and CBR techniques [20]. This system contained a self-organizing memory structured as a frame-based abstraction hierarchy for storing previously encountered problems. The cases were aircraft accident reports. Sensor inputs were gas temperature, engine pressure ratio, and human input such as sound of explosion and smell of smoke in passenger cabin. The time sequence was also of importance in establishing a causal relation such as an aberrant reading of the fan speed before an abnormal observation of the compressor speed. The system incorporated a functional dependency implemented via a digraph and a causality submodel describing transitions between various states of the system. The system searched its case library for the most similar case by a weighted count of corresponding symptoms and gave a higher degree of similarity for symptoms occurring early in the fault occurrence.

Reibling and Bublin proposed a system that integrates pattern-matching techniques with causal networks for OMS to model normal and abnormal behavior [26]. Fernandez-Montesinos used Kohonen's feature maps and expert systems to support the interpretation of in-flight monitoring data and to ensure more consistent engine condition monitoring (ECM) [16]. ECM was supported by performance trend analysis software (ADEPT), which captured deterioration and failure of engine parts. Shift patterns allowed the localization of problems within the engine modules. The two main tasks tackled were recognition of a pattern indicating a possible problem, and interpretation and further analysis. Kohonen's feature maps were chosen because of their self-organizing properties and the incremental extension of the domain of the patterns. Output of the Kohonen's feature map was an error code that indicated whether the module recognized a problem. As starting points for the network, fingerprints provided by the engine manufacturer (GE) were used. An expert system controlled the proposed neural net and interpreted the output.

Records and Choi [25] investigated strategies to filter spurious symptoms in aircraft engine fault-monitoring systems (resulting from the monitoring system's inability to accurately assess the expected value from an engine model). They used a back-end knowledge based approach and a front-end neural network that generated expectation values for the monitored sensor.

Gomm [18] and Patel [24] both suggested the use of a self-adaptive neural network with on-line learning capabilities. Gomm used radial basis function networks to which new output nodes were automatically added when a new process fault is encountered. Adaptation was achieved using recursive linear algorithms that train the localized network parameters.

15.5.2 Fuzzy Adaptive Clusters

The approach for adaptive CBR combines multivariate data evaluation using fuzzy clusters with an exponential filter, which lets the clusters adapt to changing environments. The adaptive properties of the clusters allow the centroids to move and their shape to vary [6,7].

15.5.2.1 Fuzzy Clusters

In contrast to traditional trend analysis tools, we evaluated fault conditions in multivariate feature space. Small changes in one variable may result in small changes of other system variables and this behavior can be detected more easily in multivariate space. For example, engine variables exhaust gas temperature (EGT), fuel flow (w_f), and turbine speed (n_2) are correlated for some faults. If air leaks from the compressor, a 'bleed' problem, the engine will run less efficiently. To maintain a demanded thrust level the controller will cause more fuel to be injected into the combustors. This in turn will raise the turbine speed as well as the exhaust gas temperature. Depending on the amount of bleed, the change in any of the engine parameters may be too small to be recognized alone. However, the change is more pronounced in a higher-dimensional space, and should therefore be detected more easily. Yet, depending on the amount of noise, there may still be overlap between the clusters, i.e., variables cannot be partitioned clearly, and the potential for misclassification remains high. Adding more features to the classification scheme does not necessarily improve the result because the decreasing information gain in Euclidean space is blurred additionally by decreasing feature quality, assuming one starts out using the highest-quality feature and adding others in decreasing order of value. Beyond a certain threshold, adding more features may actually decrease the classification ability.

Within the EGT-w_f-n_2 space, data have different meaning depending on where they are located. Data behaving normally will be found mostly in a cluster labeled 'normal'. Data representing an alarm condition, such as EGT, w_f, and n_2 data that are larger than data in the normal cluster are located in the 'leak fault' cluster. We avoid using rate of change as a feature based on the assumption that the abnormal condition will show up at least an order of magnitude faster than a slow normal drift (for example due to expected wear). The clusters are of non-uniform size with typically non-linearly decreasing boundaries. That is, the evaluation of the cluster membership is carried out such that the degree of membership is largest at the cluster center, non-linear slope outward. This allows training data to be separated more easily. We use the fuzzy c-means clustering algorithm [27] for this purpose which seeks to minimize an objective function defined by

$$\min J(U,V) = \sum_{j=1}^{n} \sum_{i=1}^{k} u_{ij}^m d^2(x_j, v_i)$$

where:
U is a set of a fuzzy k-partition of the data set
V is a set of k prototypes
x is the feature vector of the normalized data $\cdot$
v is the centroid of a cluster
u is the degree of membership of x_j on cluster i
m is a weighing component which control the fuzziness of the cluster
$d^2(x_j, v_i)$ is an inner product metric (e.g., distance) between x_j and v_i
n is the number of data points
k is the number of clusters

After choosing the initial number of clusters and their position, the membership is determined by

$$u_{ij} = \frac{\left(\frac{1}{d^2(x_i, v_j)}\right)^{\frac{1}{m-1}}}{\sum_{k=1}^{n} \left(\frac{1}{d^2(x_i, v_j)}\right)^{\frac{1}{m-1}}} .$$

Next, a new centroid v_i is determined using

$$v_i = \frac{\sum_{j=1}^{n} (u_{ij})^m x_j}{\sum_{j=1}^{n} (u_{ij})^m} .$$

At this point the u_{ij} are updated again and the cycle is repeated until a stopping criterion such as

$$\sum_{j=1}^{k} \sum_{i=1}^{n} (u_{ij} - u_{ij_{new}})^2 < \varepsilon$$

is reached.

15.5.2.2   Cluster Adaptation

Since thermal, chemical, and mechanical wear degrade the performance of the engine, normal behavior is constantly redefined. Although these changes are expected, they are hard to predict with necessary accuracy because they are driven to a large degree by a whole host of external factors. For example, the effect of maintenance such as replacement of parts, cleaning, etc. is very hard to capture. To retain desirable classification properties these changes must also be echoed in changes of the clusters. Therefore we guided the centroids with slow exponential weighted moving average filters. Only data belonging to a cluster were used for updating the centroid of that particular cluster. For example, data of type 'normal' were used to update the cluster 'normal' but not the cluster 'leak fault' and vice versa. After choosing the initial number of clusters, their position and membership, the adaptation of a fuzzy cluster is performed with an exponential weighted moving average filter, which we express as [7]:

$$^{new}\breve{v} = {}^{old}\breve{v} + \breve{\alpha} \left(\frac{\sum_{i=1}^{n} \breve{u}_i^m y_i}{\sum_{i=1}^{n} \breve{u}_i^m} - {}^{old}\breve{v} \right)$$

where:

superscript '˘' denotes the winner
superscript '^' denotes the loser
$^{new}\breve{v}$ is the new cluster position
$^{old}\breve{v}$ is the old cluster position

$\breve{\alpha}$ is the adaptive learning coefficient calculated (for two clusters) by

$$\breve{\alpha} = \alpha(1 - |\breve{u} - \hat{u}|)$$

where:

α is a constant term, e.g., $\alpha = 0.05$
u is the membership value
y_i is the data point under consideration

The adaptation rate, given by $\breve{\alpha}$, tries to minimize ambiguity. When the degree of membership in a winning cluster is medium (ambiguous), $\breve{u}$ and $\hat{u}$ are almost the same. In that case, $\breve{\alpha}$ is large, thus trying to untangle the indeterminate situation, and moving the winning cluster farther toward the new data point. Moreover, it causes a higher rate of change near the true fault cluster boundaries and less change where the fault classification is already working well. Thus, it has the effect of focusing its learning where it is needed most, as dictated by recent data. As a result, the centroids move with changing normal conditions. The scheme will dampen the effects of noise as well, since it gives some weight to past data and acts as an averaging scheme. It will also, like all filters, lag behind true changes in the system.

15.5.2.3   Alertness Filter

Another approach to increase robustness is to judiciously track the cumulative occurrence of 'suspect' readings, rather than triggering the alarm after just one 'fault' classification. We used an *alertness filter* [7] for doing this, which forces the recurrence of several suspicious readings before an alarm is issued. If only one suspicious reading is encountered, the value of an 'alertness counter' – which would be zero under normal conditions – is incremented. If a second suspicious reading is encountered immediately afterwards, the counter value is increased. Otherwise, it is decreased. In the latter case, the first suspicious reading is treated just as an outlier and no maintenance is recommended. If it is not an outlier, i.e., the condition persists, the level of the alertness will go up until a full alarm is issued. At that point the user will be alerted. Further fault readings will not increase the alertness level once the alarm threshold is reached. The alertness level threshold is limited to a user- specified number. This saturation avoids lengthy recovery from alarm conditions when the system recovers either spontaneously or through maintenance. The purpose of the alertness filter is to further improve the classification rate of the system.

15.5.3 Results

The adaptive CBR scheme was tested with historical gas turbine data. Different events of similar fault conditions were examined and divided into training and test cases. For training, the use of both deliberate placement and random seed points (for the cluster centroids) were investigated. Placing the starting points into the general expected neighborhood resulted in faster learning and convergence. Convergence was on average accomplished after about 20 iterations, depending on the start conditions and final acceptable convergence error. Typically, there is a much larger amount of data for normal conditions and only few data for fault conditions. To prevent a fitting bias for normal conditions, that data was undersampled so that 'normal' and 'faulty' operations were equally represented. Fig. 15.15 shows the distribution of clusters after training in EGT-n_2 space.

After training, the system was used for classification of on-line test data. The false negative rate is as low as with traditional trending tools (none observed with the test data available) and the false positive rate improved from 95% to less than 1%. Fig. 15.16 shows the adaptation of a cluster during operation.

The 'x' denotes the location of the centroid of cluster 'normal' and the squares denote the location of a fault cluster. The normal region changes initially slowly with normal wear and then undergoes a considerably change in one dimension as seen by the vertical jump of the operating point upward in the graph. Because there were no changes in the other two dimensions, the algorithm adapts correctly to the new location while retaining the ability to detect faults. The adaptation also exhibits the lag introduced by the exponential filter.

15.6 Summary and Conclusion

We demonstrated how SC techniques were used in a variety of fielded CBR systems. In doing so we were able to leverage the tolerance for imprecision and uncertainty which is intrinsic to SC techniques. The pay-off of this conjunctive use of SC and CBR techniques is a more accurate and robust solution than a solution derived from the use of any single technique alone. This synergy comes at comparatively little expense

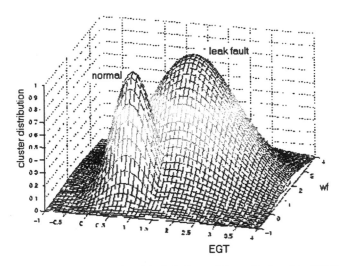

Fig. 15.15. Fuzzy cluster for normal and leak fault conditions displayed in $EGT - w_f$ space.

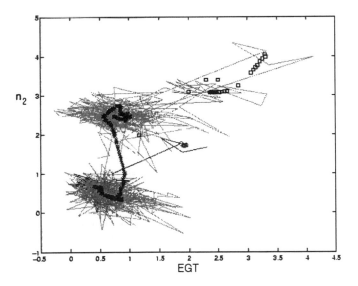

Fig. 15.16. Adaptation of clustering during operation [7].

because typically the methods do not try to solve the same problem in parallel but they do it in a mutually complementary fashion.

In the examples of medical equipment diagnostics and residential property valuation, we showed how simple membership functions can be used to implement the case selection and confidence evaluation. The membership functions allowed a greater selection accuracy through their noise tolerance. The ability to determine a confidence in a result made the systems much more useful to the end users. In addition, confidence membership functions also facilitated maintainability.

The third example, a plastic color-matching system, combined several selection criteria. Handling multiple selection criteria allowed the color matchers to detect potential problems during the case selection phase while previously these problems were not detected until the color match was complete. This avoided a considerable amount of rework and frustration by the color matchers.

Finally, we have presented the use of adaptive fuzzy clusters for fault classification of aircraft engine sensor data. The advantages of this system were its ability to deal with extremely noisy sensors and to adjust to unpredictable slow drift. Dramatic performance improvement was demonstrated during testing. This application also featured hybrid use of soft computing techniques by employing both statistical process control techniques as well as fuzzy techniques within the same system.

A step in further improving system performance is the use of more hybrid systems, such as evolutionary computing for parameter learning or the exploitation of parallel systems. The latter may be designed to rely to the maximum amount on non-overlapping data and use different techniques to arrive at their conclusions in an information fusion [17] scheme where the outputs of these heterogeneous models will be compared, contrasted, and aggregated.

References

1. Aamodt A (1994) Case Based Reasoning: Foundational Issues, Methodological Variations, and System Approaches. *AICOM* 7(1), 39–59.
2. Althoff K-D (1995) *A Review of Industrial Case Based Reasoning Tools*. AI Intelligence, Oxford, UK.
3. Appraisal Institute (1994) *Appraising Residential Properties*. Part VI Chicago, IL.
4. Billmeyer F (1981) *Principles of Color Technology*, (2nd edn). Wiley, New York.
5. Bonissone P, Cheetham W (1998) Fuzzy Case Based Reasoning for Residential Property Valuation. In *Handbook of Fuzzy Computation*. Institute of Physics Publishing, Section G14.1, Bristol, UK.
6. Bonissone P, Goebel K (1999) Soft Computing Techniques for Diagnostics and Prognostics. *AI in Equipment Maintenance Service and Support, 1999 AAAI Spring Symposium, Technical Report SS–99–04*. AAAI Press, Menlo Park, CA
7. Bonissone P, Chen Y, Goebel K, Khedkar P (1999) Hybrid Soft Computing Systems: Industrial and Commercial Applications. *Proceedings of the IEEE*. 87(9), 1641–1667.
8. Case K, Shiler R (1987) Prices of Single-Family Homes Since 1970: New Indexes for Four Cities. *New England Economic Review*, Sept./Oct.
9. Cheetham W (1996) Case Based Reasoning with Confidence. Ph.D. thesis, Rensselaer Polytechnic Institute.
10. Cheetham W, Graf J (1997) *Method and System for Formulating a Color Match*. US Patent No. 5,668,633.
11. Cheetham W, Graf J (1997) *Method and System for Selecting a Previous Color Match from a Set of Previous Matches*. U.S. Patent No. 5,841,421.

12. Cuddihy P, Shah R (1995) *Method and System for Analyzing Error Logs for Diagnostics*. US Patent No. 5,463,768.

13. Cuddihy P, Cheetham W (1998) *System and Method for Estimating a Measure of Confidence in a Match Generated from a Case-based Reasoning System*. US Patent No. 5,799,148.

14. Cuddihy P, Cheetham W (1999) ELSI: A Medical Equipment Diagnostic System. *Third International Conference on Case-Based Reasoning*, Munich, Germany.

15. Doel D (1990) The Role for Expert Systems in Commercial Gas Turbine Engine Monitoring, *Proceedings of the Gas Turbine and Aeroengine Congress and Exposition*, Brussels, Belgium.

16. Fernandez-Montesinos M, Janssens P, Vingerhoeds R (1994) *Enhancing Aircraft Engine Condition Monitoring. Safety, Reliability and Applications of Emerging Intelligent Control Technologies*. A postprint volume from the IFAC Workshop on Emerging Intelligent Control Technologies, pp. 161–166. Hong Kong.

17. Goebel K (1999) Diagnostic Information Fusion for Manufacturing Processes. *Proceedings of the Second International Conference on Information Fusion*, Vol. 1, Sunnyvale, CA, pp. 331–336.

18. Gomm J-B (1995) Process-Fault Diagnosis Using a Self-Adaptive Neural Network with On-Line Learning Capabilities. *Proceedings of IFAC On-Line Fault Detection and Supervision in the Chemical Process Industry*. Newcastle upon Tyne, UK, pp. 69–74.

19. Gonzalez A (1992) A Case Based Reasoning Approach to Real Estate Property Appraisal. *Expert Systems with Applications*, 4, 229–246.

20. Karamouzis S, Feyock S (1993) A Performance Assessment of a Case-Based Diagnostic System for Aircraft Malfunctions. *Proceedings of the Sixth International Conference on Industrial and Engineering Applications of Artificial Intelligence and Expert Systems*, Edinburgh, Scotland. pp. 71–78.

21. Keller J, Gray M, Givens, J (1985) A Fuzzy K-Nearest Neighbor Algorithm, *IEEE Transactions on Systems Man & Cybernetics*, SMC-15(4), 580–585

22. Klir G, Folger, T (1988) *Fuzzy Sets, Uncertainty, and Information*. Prentice-Hall, Englewoods Cliffs, NJ.

23. Kolodner J (1993) *Case-based Reasoning*. Morgan Kaufmann, San Mateo, CA.

24. Patel V-C, Kadirkamanathan, Thompson H-A (1996) A Novel Self-Learning Fault Detection System for Gas Turbine Engines. *Proceedings of the UKACC International Conference on Control '96*, Exeter, UK, pp. 867–872.

25. Records R, Choi J (1994) Spurious Symptom Reduction in Fault Monitoring Using a Neural Network and Knowledge as Hybrid System. *Proceedings of the Twelfth National Conf. on Artificial Intelligence*, Vol. 2, Seattle, WA. pp. 865–870.

26. Reibling R, Bublin S (1993) Diagnostic Reasoning Technology for the On-Board Maintenance System. *Proceedings of the IEEE 1993 National Aerospace and Electronics Conference, NAECON 1993*. Vol. 2. Dayton, OH. pp. 930–936.

27. Ruspini E (1963) A New Approach to Clustering, *Information and Control*, 15(1), 22–32.

28. Zadeh L (1965) Fuzzy Sets. *Information and Control*, 8, 338–353.

Index

About the Editors

Sankar K. Pal is a Professor and Distinguished Scientist at the Indian Statistical Institute, Calcutta. He is also the Founding Head of the Machine Intelligence Unit at the Institute. He received the M.Tech. and Ph.D. degrees in Radio physics and Electronics in 1974 and 1979 respectively, from the University of Calcutta. In 1982 he received another Ph.D. in Electrical Engineering along with a DIC from Imperial College, University of London. He worked at the University of California, Berkeley and the University of Maryland, College Park during 1986–87 as a Fulbright Post-doctoral Visiting Fellow; at the NASA Johnson Space Center, Houston, Texas during 1990–92 and 1994 as a Guest Investigator under the NRC-NASA Senior Research Associateship program; and at the Hong Kong Polytechnic University, Hong Kong in 1999 as a Visiting Professor. He served as a Distinguished Visitor of the IEEE Computer Society (USA) for the Asia–Pacific Region during 1997–99.

Prof. Pal is a Fellow of the IEEE, USA, Third World Academy of Sciences, Italy, and all the four National Academies for Science/Engineering in India. His research interests include Pattern Recognition, Image Processing, Soft Computing, Neural Nets, Genetic Algorithms, and Fuzzy Systems. He is a co-author of seven books including *Fuzzy Mathematical Approach to Pattern Recognition*, John Wiley (Halsted), New York, 1986, and *Neuro-Fuzzy Pattern Recognition: Methods in Soft Computing*, John Wiley, New York, 1999, and about 300 research papers.

He has received the 1990 S. S. Bhatnagar Prize (which is the most coveted award for a scientist in India), 1993 Jawaharlal Nehru Fellowship, 1993 Vikram Sarabhai Research Award, 1993 NASA Tech Brief Award, 1994 *IEEE Transactions on Neural Networks* Outstanding Paper Award, 1995 NASA Patent Application Award, 1997 IETE – Ram Lal Wadhwa Gold Medal, 1998 Om Bhasin Foundation Award, and the 1999 G. D. Birla Award for Scientific Research.

Prof. Pal is an Associate Editor, *IEEE Transactions on Neural Networks* (1994–98), *Pattern Recognition Letters, Neurocomputing, Applied Intelligence, Information Sciences, Fuzzy Sets and Systems*, and *Fundamenta Informaticae*; a Member, Executive Advisory Editorial Board, *IEEE Transactions on Fuzzy Systems* and *International Journal of Approximate Reasoning*, and a Guest Editor of many journals including the *IEEE Computer*.

Tharam S. Dillon is a Professor of Computer Science at La Trobe University, Melbourne, Australia. He obtained his B.E. (Hons) and Ph.D. in 1968 and 1974 respectively from Monash University, Melbourne, Australia. He worked as a Guest Professor at the Institute für Electrische Anlagen Rhein Westfalliche Technische Hochschule, Germany in 1977, Consulting Engineer at the Swedish State Power Board, Stockholm in 1977 and 1984, Visiting Academic at the Centre of Information Technology, Queen Mary College, London in 1984, and Visiting Professor, Department of Computer Science, University of California, Los Angles in 1984.

At present he is working as a Professor in the Department of Computing, Hong Kong Polytechnic University, Hong Kong. He is a Fellow of the IEEE, Institute of Engineers (Australia), Safety and Reliability Society (UK) and the Australian Computer Society. His research interests include database systems, production planning methods, telecommunication network management and maintenence scheduling. He has about 350 research papers and seven books to his credit.

Prof. Dillon is the Editor-in-Chief of three international journals and an Advisory Editor of *IEEE Transactions on Neural Networks*.

Daniel S. Yeung received the Ph.D. degree in Applied Mathematics from Case Western Reserve University, Cleveland, OH, in 1974.

He is currently a Chair Professor in the Department of Computing, Hong Kong Polytechnic University, Hong Kong. He was an Assistant Professor of Mathematics and Computer Science at Rochester Institute of Technology, Rochester, NY, and has worked as a Research Scientist in the General Electronic Corporate Research Centre, and a System Integration Engineer at TRW, Inc. His current research interests include knowledge based systems, case based reasoning, Chinese computing and fuzzy expert systems.

Prof. Yeung is a senior member of the IEEE and he was the President of the IEEE Computer Chapter of Hong Kong in 1991 and 1992.